THE MOTORCYCLE INDUSTRY IN NEW YORK STATE

Second Edition

THE UNIVERSITY OF THE STATE OF NEW YORK

Regents of The University

Lester W. Young, Jr., *Chancellor*, B.S., M.S., Ed.D.	Beechhurst
Josephine Victoria Finn, Vice Chancellor, B.A., J.D.	Monticello
Roger Tilles, B.A., J.D.	Manhasset
Christine D. Cea, B.A., M.A., Ph.D.	Staten Island
Wade S. Norwood, B.A.	Rochester
Kathleen M. Cashin, B.S., M.S., Ed.D.	Brooklyn
James E. Cottrell, B.S., M.D.	New York
Judith Chin, B.S., M.S.Ed.	Little Neck
Catherine Collins, R.N., N.P., B.S., M.S.Ed., Ed.D.	Buffalo
Elizabeth S. Hakanson, A.S., B.A., M.A., C.A.S.	Syracuse
Luis O. Reyes, B.A., M.A., Ph.D.	New York
Susan W. Mittler, B.S., M.S.	Ithaca
Frances G. Wills, B.A., M.A., M.Ed., C.A.S., Ph.D.	Ossining
Ruth B. Turner, B.S.W., L.C.S.W., M.Ed.	Rochester
Aramina Vega Ferrer, B.A., M.S.Ed., Ph.D.	Bronx
Shino Tanikawa, B.A., M.S.	Manhattan
Roger P. Catania, B.A., M.A., M.S., C.A.S., Ph.D.	Saranac Lake

Commissioner of Education and President of The University
Betty A. Rosa, B.A., M.S.Ed., M.Ed., Ed.D.

Deputy Commissioner of Cultural Education and New York State Museum Director
Mark Schaming, B.F.A., M.F.A.

The State Education Department does not discriminate on the basis of race, creed, color, national origin, religion, age, sex, military status, marital status, familial status, domestic violence victim status, carrier status, disability, genetic predisposition, sexual orientation, or criminal record in its recruitment, educational programs, services, and activities. NYSED has adopted a web accessibility policy, and publications designed for distribution can be made available in an accessible format upon request. Inquiries regarding this policy of nondiscrimination should be directed to the Office of Human Resources Management, Room 528, Education Building, Albany, NY 12234.

THE MOTORCYCLE INDUSTRY IN NEW YORK STATE

Second Edition

A Concise Encyclopedia of
Inventors, Builders, and Manufacturers

GEOFFREY N. STEIN

Revised and with a Foreword by
BRAD L. UTTER

EXCELSIOR
EDITIONS

Published by State University of New York Press, Albany

© 2023 New York State Education Department

All rights reserved

Printed in the United States of America

No part of this book may be used or reproduced in any manner whatsoever without written permission. No part of this book may be stored in a retrieval system or transmitted in any form or by any means including electronic, electrostatic, magnetic tape, mechanical, photocopying, recording, or otherwise without the prior permission in writing of the publisher.

Excelsior Editions is an imprint of State University of New York Press

For information, contact State University of New York Press, Albany, NY
www.sunypress.edu

Library of Congress Cataloging-in-Publication Data

Names: Stein, Geoffrey N., author. | Utter, Brad L., writer of foreword. | University
   of the State of New York.
Title: The motorcycle industry in New York State : a concise encyclopedia of inventors,
   builders, and manufacturers / Geoffrey N. Stein ; foreword by Brad L. Utter.
Description: Second edition. | Albany, NY : State University of New York Press, [2023] |
   Series: Excelsior editions | Includes bibliographical references and index.
Identifiers: LCCN 2022037692 | ISBN 9781438493022 (hardcover : alk. paper) |
   ISBN 9781438493046 (ebook) | ISBN 9781438493039 (pbk. : alk. paper)
Subjects: LCSH: Motorcycle industry—New York (State)—History—Encyclopedias.
Classification: LCC HD9710.5.U53 N77 2023 | DDC 338.4/7629227509747—dc23/eng/20230201
LC record available at https://lccn.loc.gov/2022037692

10 9 8 7 6 5 4 3 2 1

Contents

Foreword to the Second Edition — vii

Foreword to the First Edition — ix

Acknowledgments — xi

New York's Role in the American Motorcycle Industry: An Introduction to This Encyclopedia — 1

Resources and Documentation — 3

Organization of This Encyclopedia — 5

Inventors, Builders, and Manufacturers — 7

Index — 231

Foreword to the Second Edition

Identifying all of New York's motorcycle inventors and builders continues to be "an ambitious but impractical goal," as stated in the foreword to the first edition, which was published by the New York State Museum in 2001. Even with the vast resources provided by the internet, it is still an unattainable goal. However, building on the first attempt of such a list is a worthy endeavor. What started as a project to reprint the first edition with a small introduction has turned into much more.

While reading through the first edition, I found myself turning to my computer . . . often. Sometimes just to learn more about a particular topic or person, but other times I found myself trying to answer what could not be answered in 2000. After a few of these types of searches, I realized the book needed to be more than a reprint. I needed to use the resources, literally at my fingertips, to provide some updates. Thanks to the vast archives now available via the internet, I was able to search through newspapers, periodicals, census records, directories, and more—at my desk. Instead of going to the Library of Congress to read through as many motorcycle periodicals from the early 1900s as possible, I can now find many of those periodicals online, and they are searchable. These resources and more enabled me to answer some of the questions raised but not answered in the first edition. Answers to some of the questions still proved elusive and will remain unknown unless original company records turn up. I was able to update many of the entries in this book, especially in relation to the people involved with the endeavors discussed.

The project continued to expand: in addition to updating original entries when possible, we decided to add any missed entries brought to light since the publication of the first edition and to cover the last twenty years. Again, a worthy goal, but not without its challenges, and in the end the book includes a sampling of New York State–based builders from the past twenty years.

The 2000s brought custom choppers and custom motorcycles to the mainstream. With television series like *Motorcycle Mania*, *Biker Build-Off*, and *American Chopper*, people outside of the motorcycle world started to take an interest in custom-made motorcycles. One of the results was a proliferation of custom-chopper shops. Inspired by the likes of Indian Larry (q.v.; New York City), Jesse James (Los Angeles), Paul Teutul Sr. and Paul Teutul Jr. (Orange County, NY; s.v. "Orange County Choppers"), and others, the custom-chopper industry not only found a growing market but also inspired many to join the ranks of custom builders. The resulting motorcycles were functioning, one-of-a-kind works of art—some were meant to be looked at, but any long ride on them would be difficult, while others were meant to be as rideable as a production bike. There are more than a few builders in this book who were inspired to build one-of-a-kind motorcycles because of these shows.

Similar to the first motorcycle boom in the early 1900s, the custom-chopper boom of the early twenty-first century has seen many businesses come and go. Production of one-of-a-kind motorcycles requires not only skill and business savvy but also the time to dedicate to the labor-intensive process resulting in a limited, high-cost output. This is a hard business model to follow, and many upstarts did not survive very long. This leads to one of the challenges of this second edition: how to document the large number of small shops that have come and gone in the last twenty-plus years. Many builders were unable to sustain a storefront, while others have thrived—or at least survived—by expanding their offerings to repairs and maintenance. Another way to make it work is to forego the storefront, keep your day job, and build at night. This method has worked for a few of the new entries in the book.

There are numerous active shops in the state of New York that produce unique custom motorcycles—bobbers, café racers, choppers, touring, and so on. Most of those shops use parts already on the market to build or customize motorcycles, minus a few custom parts. In order to make the number of entries manageable for this publication, we have decided to include a sampling of those custom builders who fabricate or modify a majority of the parts on their builds (based on available information). When a builder claims a custom, ground-up build, it could be that they make their own parts, buy parts from suppliers and make a unique combination, or a mix of the two. With that in mind, even though my goal was to only include builders from the twenty-first century who fabricate most of the parts they use, I had to make some judgment calls based on the available information.

There is an interesting difference in motivations for building or inventing a motorcycle when you compare the 1890s–1910s and the 2000s–2020. In the early days, some of the technologies we may take for granted today were just being invented; the kinks were being worked out. Some people we discuss in this book had numerous patents, inventions that may or not have been related to motor development. It must have been an exciting time for those who were mechanically inclined. What were the motivations for the early builders? Were they tinkering to make transportation for themselves? Were they hoping to invent the next big thing and mass-produce their products? For most, the latter was the end goal. A good number of the inventors and builders moved on to produce marine, automobile, and even airplane engines. The number of possible applications of the new combustion engine technology was growing, and for many, two wheels was just the beginning.

Most builders of the last twenty years based in New York State are not looking to compete with the mass-produced Harley-Davidsons of the world. Instead, they are making limited runs; building ground-up, one-of-a-kind custom rides; or customizing manufactured motorcycles. Likewise, new patents relating to motorcycles are rare among New York builders today (see entry for Terence Musto for an exception). While some of the builders today have adopted modern equipment like CNC (computer numerical control) machines to practice their craft, others stick to older techniques that use hand tools or a combination of both old and new. Either way, they are artists, working to put their individual or team vision into the products they create. The combination of unique mobile art, making a living, and creating an enjoyable ride is more in line with the builders of the last twenty years than those of the early 1900s.

An exception to the trends is the arrival of the electric motorcycle (e-motorcycle) and electric bicycle (e-bike). The two companies we cover in this book are only a few years old, and they are on the cutting edge of this technology. From the early 1900s through the early 2000s, the electric power plants were not practical for motorcycle use. But as of 2022 this has changed; e-motorcycles are being developed in New York, and production is promised soon. If this is successful, it is possible that one of the next big American motorcycle companies will be based in New York State.

Also worthy of note but outside the scope of this work are the few businesses who make custom parts for motorcycles in New York but do not build motorcycles. One example is GigaCycle Garage in Rochester.

This publication largely remains the work of Geoffrey N. Stein. It is a true encyclopedia and the result of years of work on the part of Stein. Although retired, he still comes into the New York State Museum to volunteer. I am honored to learn from him and to have the opportunity to add to this book. He has been a tremendous help in putting together this second edition.

The original foreword, acknowledgments, introduction, and resources and documentation sections have not been altered except for minor edits. Second-edition updates to those sections, excepting the foreword, have been added at the end of each section. Any updates or changes to entries within the book were incorporated into the existing text and not separated in any way.

Brad L. Utter

Foreword to the First Edition

Identifying all New York's motorcycle inventors and builders is an ambitious but impractical goal. Even with unlimited time and funding, there would be no way to uncover evidence of every motorcycle enterprise. Many makers likely came and went with no record other than the memory of the principals involved. With nearly a century passed since the heyday of motorcycle experimentation and manufacture, the dreamers and builders are beyond contact by any terrestrial researcher.

On the other hand, a decade's research at the New York State Museum has resulted in three file drawers of data and several extensive essays about individual motorcycle enterprises. Some of the material already has found its way into print,[1] while other lengthy stories await future publication. Combined, the histories of the leading New York manufacturers, such as the Emblem Manufacturing Company, Ner-A-Car Corporation, G. H. Curtiss Manufacturing Company, E. R. Thomas Motor Company, and Pierce Cycle Company, would fill a volume hundreds of pages longer than this one.

For now, the New York State Museum presents a guide to the builders of New York's motorcycles. In some cases, the information here contained in no more than a sentence or two is all that the author has learned about individual enterprises. In other cases, such as the builders of the Emblem, Neracar, Curtiss, Thomas, and Pierce motorcycles, the several pages devoted to each are distillations of complex histories that deserve more expansive treatment elsewhere. When available, pictures of motorcycles, motorcycle builders, and motorcycle factories supplement the text in this encyclopedia. In some cases, these views are the sole images discovered for individual enterprises. In other cases, the pictures here are only a fraction of the graphics on file.

It is the author's wish that whatever their length or comprehensiveness, the individual entries prove informative and interesting to their readers, and that in its entirety, the volume might serve to indicate the breadth of motorcycle development and manufacture in New York State.

Geoffrey N. Stein

---

1. See, for example, Geoffrey N. Stein, "Motorcycle Production at the Pierce Cycle Company, 1909–1914," *The Arrow* 98, no. 2 (1998): 1–40.

Acknowledgments

Acknowledgments to the First Edition

Researched and written during the course of the writer's work as a curator at the New York State Museum, this volume in part owes its existence to the patience and encouragement of his supervisors and colleagues. They made it possible for the extended effort consuming portions of nine years, 1991–2000.

Production work at the museum involved the efforts of Publications Program Manager John B. Skiba, image scanner John Yost, and outside reader coordinator Craig Williams. Ed Landing, Bob Daniels, and Penny Drooker acted as in-house reviewers. Mort Wood and Mark Mederski served as outside readers, offering helpful comments and encouragement. Laurel Carroll served as consulting editor. Pat Mulligan designed the book except for the cover, which was produced by Pat McFarland.

Generously assisting in the research from outside the Museum were Herbert Gale, Frank Westfall, Patrick Cullen, Damon Dardaris, Jim Dennie, Robert Fornwalt, Ken Philp, Bruce Linsday, Frederick D. Hirsch, Whitney Point village historian Juanita Aleba, the Buffalo and Erie County Historical Society, Cortland County Historical Society, and the Glenn H. Curtiss Museum; all shared libraries or scholarship or both. David Dingley, in the Division of Corporations of the New York State Department of State, over the course of several years provided copies of the corporate records of many motorcycle manufacturers. David D'Alfonso, a history student at Siena College, spent a considerable portion of a three-month internship checking census, city directory, and patent records for evidence of motorcycle inventors and builders. Thory Monsen, a University at Albany intern, worked at coordinating illustrations and tying up loose research ends in the weeks before the editorial deadline. The author is grateful for having had access to the New York State Library as well as to the Library of Congress. The latter institution houses perhaps the country's most comprehensive collection of trade journals, which have provided the bulk of the data for this encyclopedia.

The author apologizes for unwittingly having overlooked anyone in this list of acknowledgments.

Acknowledgments to the Second Edition

The second edition would not have been possible without the help and support of Geoffrey N. Stein, who wrote the first edition. Bridget Enderle was a tremendous help with locating all of the images that appeared in the first edition, organizing them, and helping sort all of the new images for this edition. New York State Museum chief curator Dr. Jennifer Lemak was the driving force to make this edition happen, and her support has been invaluable. Other New York State Museum staff members helped in various ways to make the book possible, including photographers Andrew Meier, Jacqui Monkell, and Allison Munsell; web specialist Nicholas Lue; graphic designer Ben Karis; and museum volunteer Bill Schollenberger, who scanned images for the project.

Thank you to Betty and Susan Bogardus, who each donated a separate set of images from their ancestors' adventures on Emblem motorcycles.

A special thank-you to Ted Doering and Catherine Stack from the Motorcyclepedia Museum in Newburgh, NY, for their time and expertise.

New York's Role in the American Motorcycle Industry

An Introduction to This Encyclopedia

The promise of motor vehicles aroused wide interest in the 1890s. It was a time when inventors, engineers, and mechanics experimented with engines fitted to two-, three-, and four-wheeled creations, all known as "automobiles." To veterans of the bicycle industry, motor bicycles appeared the logical and practical means to economical, universal, self-propelled transportation.

By the beginning of the twentieth century, the ill-handling motor tricycle had disappeared. *Automobile* had come to denote four-wheeled vehicles only. And *motorcycle* began to displace *moto cycle* and *motor cycle* for designating single-track, two-wheeled machines, almost all of which were based on the lines of the diamond-frame safety bicycle. Capitalizing on innovation and development work, manufacturers began to offer motorcycles to the buying public.

Aside from a few experiments with steam engines and battery-powered electric motors, almost all early motorcycles utilized one-cylinder, four-stroke, air-cooled, gasoline-fueled engines. At first, however, these motors were mounted in a variety of locations on the motorcycle—above the front wheel, above the rear wheel, in the seat tube, and in the down tube, as well as various sites within the frame—before the bottom of the larger frame triangle became standardized.

While many builders settled on belt drive for its elasticity and limited isolation of the pulsing engine from the rear driving wheel, a few makers used roller chain drive. Other shops experimented with belt drive to the front wheel from a fork-mounted engine or with a movable roller drive on top of either tire to provide for partial or complete disengagement. Sometimes an idler in a belt transmission served as a clutch. But often there was no way to disconnect the engine from the driven wheel; when the engine ran, the wheel turned. To stop the motorcycle, the engine had to be turned off.

Given only the recent history of the motorcycle industry, one might conclude that the Harley-Davidson Motor Company of Milwaukee, Wisconsin, has thrived from the beginning of manufacture as the sole significant producer of American machines. Yet, looking back to the pioneer period of the industry, one finds the records of hundreds of production initiatives, many predating the Harley-Davidson organization in 1903. With a broad industrial base stretching from east of New York City to west of Buffalo, New York State was home to a significant portion of the nation's motorcycle inventors and manufacturers. Among the first firms turning out motorcycles in numbers, for example, was the E. R. Thomas Motor Company of Buffalo in 1901.

From the mid-1890s to the mid-1920s, New York hosted an interesting variety of motorcycle enterprises. To readers of this encyclopedia, some of the earliest proposals described here may seem outlandish. Projects such as an engine fueled by gunpowder likely remained only ideas on paper, while electric motorcycles, even after one hundred years of development, remain impractical [as of the year 2001]. But many early designs were both innovative and useful, resulting in the production of hundreds or thousands of New York–built motorcycles from individual makers.

In the 1900s and early 1910s, the motorcycle achieved a higher level of performance. Two-cylinder machines, such as those offered early on by Glenn H. Curtiss in Hammondsport, delivered more power. The Pierce Cycle Company in Buffalo built the first American four-cylinder, shaft-driven machines. On many different motorcycles, clutches and two-speed transmissions made operation easier. Chain drive better handled increased engine power. Other components, still often based on bicycle antecedents, were made more robust for greater reliability and safety.

Yet the motorcycle never took hold the way its proponents envisioned. In part, the motorcycle required an athleticism of its rider not needed in driving an automobile, catching a train, taking a streetcar, or even walking. Riders of early machines needed to assist their engines by pedaling up grades. Motorcycling on the unimproved roads of the day was risky, with the omnipresent prospect of falling. And motorcyclists, wittingly or not, often discouraged potential recruits to their ranks by appearing as an unsavory group, covered with mud or oil and operating their machines sans mufflers and in a reckless manner.

More importantly, the automobiles many predicted would be much more expensive than motorcycles became more easily attainable. The Ford Model T, especially, in the 1910s offered seats for five riders as well as a roof, doors, and windshield for not much more than the cost of a motorcycle. By the early 1920s, the Ford was selling for less than three hundred dollars, and used cars were even cheaper.

For the 1915 model year, the Ford Motor Company alone turned out over 300,000 cars, while the entire United States motorcycle industry produced about 100,000 machines. And of the motorcycles built, New York's share by then had fallen far behind major competitors in Massachusetts (Hendee Manufacturing Company, among other builders), Illinois (Excelsior Motor Manufacturing & Supply Company and the Aurora Automatic Machinery Company, among others), and Wisconsin (Harley-Davidson, among others). Now sometimes fitted with sidecars, motorcycles largely became the province of a few police officers and commercial delivery services as well as a larger group of recreational riders.

Many New York factories closed by the mid-1910s (as did plants elsewhere). Other producers turned to lightweight motorcycles and bicycle motors, some powered by two-stroke engines, thought to appeal to riders who were too young to buy or who could not afford to buy automobiles. Some manufacturers developed unconventional and innovative designs, such as the seatless Autoped scooter from New York City or the Neracar (i.e., nearly a car), with automotive-influenced components, from Syracuse. But by the end of the 1920s, the American motorcycle industry numbered only a few builders, none of them in New York.

At the beginning of the twenty-first century, the motorcycle remains largely a seasonal, recreational vehicle. Happily, the exhilaration of piloting a motorcycle, on or off road, now motivates an increasing number of enthusiastic riders. While most machines come from factories in other states and other countries, some original New York–built motorcycles still appear. These latest bikes might be viewed as homemade, as riders build their own machines, or part of a cottage industry, as small shops turn out a handful of motorcycles for sale each year. These new New York–made motorcycles often are created with singularly focused use rather than general road riding in mind. For example, on Grand Island, two entrepreneurs deliver drag-racing motorcycles. In Himrod, a company builds road bikes resembling dirt-track racing machines. And in several places throughout the state, builders deliver custom motorcycles for road riding utilizing modified Harley-Davidson or similar components. Often, these machines are styled as choppers, the customized motorcycles (usually Harley-Davidsons) popular since the late 1960s. Although this encyclopedia identifies several active custom builders, others remain to be documented.

Resources and Documentation

Resources for the First Edition

Several entries in this encyclopedia have been excerpted from the author's essays about New York's motorcycle enterprises. Some of those individual histories extend forty or fifty pages in addition to extensive endnotes. In the interest of saving space in this volume, foot- and endnotes have been omitted in the entries, although most essays incorporate references to important sources. Readers interested in the specific documentation are encouraged to contact the author.

Trade journals provided the greater portion of the material consulted in the preparation of this encyclopedia. Among the more important periodicals of the early twentieth century, the time of most motorcycle construction in New York, are *Motorcycling* (later *Motorcycling and Bicycling*), *Motorcycle Illustrated* (later *Motorcycle and Bicycle Illustrated*), and the *Bicycling World and Motorcycle Review* (spelled "Motocycle" in the title until 1906). The early issues of the *Horseless Age* are invaluable. Another useful resource is the bicycle-derived *Cycle Age*, which in 1902 became *Motor Age*. The early issues of *Cycle and Automobile Trade Journal* have extensive industry coverage; motorcycle news eventually was abandoned, and the magazine retitled as *Automobile Trade Journal*. Also helpful for the early years are the *Cycling Gazette*, *Automobile Review* (later *Motor Way*), the *American Automobile*, the *Motorcycle Magazine*, and the *Dealer and Repairman*.

General periodicals (for example, *Scientific American*) also offer data. Newspapers are useful. The weekly *Hammondsport Herald*, for example, closely followed the activities of local motorcycle builders, especially Glenn H. Curtiss. Census records, city directories, patent data, insurance maps, and incorporation records maintained by the Division of Corporations in the New York State Department of State all provide useful information.

Since the activities of early motorcycle and automobile builders were similar—indeed, they often overlapped—historical surveys of auto makers have been helpful in preparing this encyclopedia. A vital reference has been Beverly Rae Kimes and Henry Austin Clark Jr.'s *Standard Catalog of American Cars, 1805–1942* (third edition, Iola, WI: Krause Publications, 1996).

Another valuable work is James F. Bellamy's *Cars Made in Upstate New York* (Red Creek, NY: Squire Hill Publishing,1989).

Motorcycle lists, surveys, and encyclopedias also have served as references. Striving to encompass all United States–built or even all the world's motorcycles, these compendia necessarily present limited material. Sometimes the information obviously is in error, but for initial, ready reference these works are worthy. Notable among them are the following:

Erwin Tragatsch, *The World's Motorcycles, 1894–1963* (London: Temple Press Books, 1964)

Erwin Tragatsch, editor, *The Illustrated Encyclopedia of Motorcycles* (London: Grange, 1991)

Michael Gerald and Jim Lucas, "The Complete Roster of Two-Wheeled Motorized Vehicles Made in the U.S.A., 1869–1979," *Road Rider* (1980)

Hugo Wilson, *The Encyclopedia of the Motorcycle* (New York: Dorling Kindersley, 1995)

Ron Christianson, editor, *1905 to 1985 Motorcycle Price Guide* (St. Paul, MN: Whitehorse Press, 1996)

M. Low, "A Comprehensive List of Names of American and Foreign Machines," *Motorcycle Illustrated*, August 1, 1909

Douglas J. Strange, editor, *The Antique Motorcycle Subject Index* (Maxatawny, PA: Antique Motorcycle Club of America, 1983)

Harry V. Sucher, *Inside American Motorcycling and the American Motorcycle Association, 1900–1990* (Laguna Niguel, CA: Motorbooks International, 1995)

Tod Rafferty, *The Complete Illustrated Encyclopedia of American Motorcycles* (Philadelphia: Courage Books, 1999)

Stephen Wright, *The American Motorcycle*, vol. 1, *1869–1914* (Fountain Valley, CA: Megden Publishing, 2001)

General, narrative histories of motorcycling or motorcycle construction, another type of publication, generally focus on geographic areas much broader than New York. Their treatment of New York's builders is necessarily cursory.

Material generated by motorcycle manufacturers is invaluable. This includes catalogs, brochures, dealer letters, and publicity photographs. Herbert Gale, Frank Westfall, Jim Dennie, and Bruce Linsday made available notes, photographs, drawings, and other material generated and retained by those active in the design, production, and distribution of New York–made motorcycles. Ken Philp kindly shared his unpublished article "Neracar Production in England" (1999). For active, contemporary motorcycle makers, their websites as well as interviews with their principals have proven informative.

It's not unlikely that readers of the encyclopedia are familiar with additional documentation of New York's motorcycle builders. The author encourages those readers to contact him, thus providing the basis for a more comprehensive and more accurate future edition of this work.

Resources for the Second Edition

The biggest difference between the late 1990s to 2000 and now is the vast number of resources available online. Here are some of the sources Brad Utter used regularly when researching for the second edition:

Ancestry.com

Business pages on social media outlets

Chronicling America: Historic American Newspapers (chroniclingamerica.loc.gov), sponsored by the National Endowment for the Humanities and the Library of Congress

HathiTrust Digital Library (hathitrust.org)

Internet Archive (archive.org)

Newspapers.com

New York Heritage Digital Collections (nyheritage.org)

New York State Historic Newspapers (nyshistoricnewspapers.org)

Old Fulton New York Post Cards (fultonhistory.com), an archive of newspapers and more

Organization of This Encyclopedia

Individual motorcycle enterprises are arranged alphabetically by builders' names. Sometimes the names are those of persons, and sometimes the names are those of companies.

Where corporate changes produced a new company name, a single entry in this book continues the history at one location. For example, the Auto-Bi Company succeeded the E. R. Thomas Motor Company, maker of the Auto-Bi motorcycle. Subsequent reorganizations produced the Greyhound Motor Company. In this volume, the chronology involving all those corporations appears in one place, under the "E. R. Thomas Motor Company" heading. The index at the back of this book will refer readers to the appropriate pages for data about companies for which there are no headings.

In this volume, trade names are subordinate to makers' names. While trade names are noted in boldface type within the entry headings (below the builders' names), readers seeking particular trade names should consult the index for references to the appropriate pages.

The dates listed at the top of each entry are those attributed to the period of activity [relating to motorcycles] by the individual or company listed. These dates may or may not coincide with model years.

For the purpose of this book, a motorcycle is defined as a motor vehicle with two tandem wheels. While in the twenty-first century such a definition seems obvious, in the late nineteenth the meaning of *motorcycle* was not so clear. In the 1890s, *motorcycle* or *motocycle* or even *automobile* might refer to a vehicle with two or three or four wheels. Early two- and three-wheeled machines, especially, displayed similar characteristics, both utilizing the same type of engine and both built much like the pedal bicycles from which they were developed. While a case might be made for including motor tricycles in an encyclopedia of motorcycles, for this work a strict two-wheel definition has been the guide in deciding which makers to include and which to exclude.

To clarify the nature of a number of New York's motorcycle enterprises, several of this book's essays deal with such entities as motorcycle distributors and sellers having names suggesting motorcycle manufacture and with foreign builders that maintained New York warehouses, salesrooms, or offices. Consequently, the reading of the essays, as well as of the index that follows, needs to be done carefully; a number of the names listed in the headings to the essays and in the index are *not* those of New York's motorcycle inventors, builders, and manufacturers.

Inventors, Builders, and Manufacturers

A

Rollin Abell
New York City (Brooklyn)?
1901

Rollin Abell (1880 to after 1939) lived in Dorchester, Massachusetts, in 1901. Yet the *Bicycling World and Motocycle Review* reported he had built a steam-powered bicycle in Brooklyn. Most likely, the *Bicycling World* confused Brooklyn, New York, with Brookline, Massachusetts. In any case, the *Bicycling World* said Abell's machine, one of few steam motorcycle designs at the turn of the century, was "not a bad looker."

Abell's motorcycle utilized a three-cylinder, rotary, single-acting engine of remarkably compact design. The 15-pound, 2-inch-wide power plant was mounted beside the rear wheel, which apparently was driven by a chain. A one-way clutch allowed the wheel to overspeed the engine and the vehicle to coast. A rotary valve directed steam flow to the cylinders. The engine developed 2 horsepower.

A 15-pound, 4-inch-wide boiler was fitted inside the frame triangle. A drawing of the motorcycle suggests a tank over the rear wheel, so perhaps gasoline or kerosene served as fuel.

Abell was issued several patents in the first decade of the twentieth century, but none for a steam motorcycle. A "back-pedaling brake and coaster" suitable for a bicycle or motorcycle was the subject of a patent application in 1900; the patent followed in 1903. Perhaps Abell utilized this invention in the motorcycle that, as has been noted, incorporated a one-way clutch.

Abell's steam motorcycle, with its diamond frame, resembled pedal bicycles and many contemporary motor bicycles of the day. Implementing pedal gearing for the rider to use as a supplement or alternative to the engine was also standard practice for early motorcycle makers.

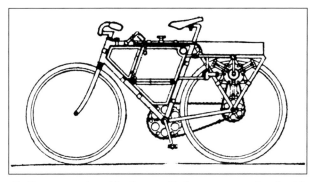

Abell motorcycle with three-cylinder steam engine beside rear wheel and boiler within frame triangle. From the *Bicycling World*, June 6, 1901.

Ed Allyn
Woodstock
1990s
Trade Name: **Harlvin**

Ed Allyn expressed his admiration for the English Vincent motorcycle by modifying a Harley-Davidson Sportster to resemble a British bike. Construction of his motorcycle took place over an eight-year period.

Allyn writes,

I've often thought the similarity of the vee motor shape of the Harley Sportster to the vee of the Vincent motor would make a[n] easy

Ed Allyn's Harley-Davidson Sportster model rebuilt to resemble a Vincent. Harl(ey) + Vin(cent) = Harlvin. Photo courtesy of Ed Allyn.

custom conversion to Vincentise the Sportster for the bike-builder. There have been at least two commercial kits from the USA and UK on the market to accomplish this but no longer available. These cosmetic kits were quite expensive but they never had a method [to] attach another carb to the rear of the rear head, like the Vincent. Nor did they provide an exhaust pipe coming out of the front of the rear head as with the original Vincent. After thinking about this a long time I started on the project without a kit, just used parts from British bikes and an idea. All available from parts right here in New York State. (Letter to the author, June 6, 2000)

The frame on Allyn's motorcycle comes from a Harley Sportster. The engine is a Harley V-twin with the rear head replaced by a front head from another engine. The exhaust is now located at the front of the cylinder in Vincent style rather than at the rear in Harley fashion. Allyn notes a considerable amount of reworking of the engine to make that change possible, including the rotation of the rear piston by 180 degrees and the fabrication of new intake and exhaust manifolds.

Parts from British motorcycles on the Harlvin include Amal carburetors from a Norton; fenders, taillight, and front wheel from Triumphs; headlight from a BSA; saddle from a Royal Enfield; and muffler from an Ariel. New rear fender braces were fabricated so that the fender would move with the suspension Vincent style (as opposed to fixed, in Harley fashion). Allyn selected a Harley-Davidson fuel tank similar in shape to that on a Vincent. He writes, "A front fender name plate was added to give a classic British touch. Finally a 'Harlvin' decal was made to mimic the style of Vincent tank decal which I will give free to anyone who does this to their Harley, good luck. Write me if you need further help on making your Harlvin" (letter to the author). Allyn says that unlike a show bike, his motorcycle is ridden often.

American Cycle Manufacturing Company
New York City (Manhattan)
1901–2

A subsidiary of the American Bicycle Company (ABC), the American Cycle Manufacturing Company had offices in the Park Row Building in New York City. After the testing of experimental machines in 1901, initial manufacture took place in 1902 at a Hartford, Connecticut, factory. Sales were made under a variety of bicycle trade names, all of which the American Bicycle Company (also known as the Bicycle Trust) had acquired at the time of its incorporation in 1899.

At the end of 1902, the ABC was in receivership. The successor, Pope Manufacturing Company, in Hartford, still had its "eastern" department offices at 21 Park Row in Manhattan.

In short, the American Cycle Manufacturing and successor Pope Manufacturing Companies' association with New York was the location of their offices.

American Hoffmann Corporation
New York City (Manhattan)
ca. 1950

The American Hoffmann Corporation at 621 West Fifty-Fourth Street imported the small, two-stroke, German-built Hoffmann machines.

American Motor Company
New York City (Manhattan)
1897–99

Stories in the *Cycling Gazette* and the *Horseless Age* noted the American Motor Company at 24 West Street (formerly in Hoboken, New Jersey) was building three-

and four-wheel vehicles as well as engines ranging from 0.75 to 5 horsepower. There are no mentions of two-wheel vehicles, i.e., motorcycles.

American Motorcycle Parts
Albany
1974–present

While trained in aircraft maintenance and experienced as an airport manager, William Nigro has turned a childhood hobby into a full-time profession as a builder of custom motorcycles based on Harley-Davidson technology. While most motorcycles are in the $20,000 to $30,000 range, some buyers spend up to $70,000 for their desired machines. Altogether Nigro estimates his American Motorcycle Parts business has built over one hundred custom motorcycles, including many "ground-up" builds. The challenge in assembling

Assembled by William Nigro's American Motorcycle Parts, this is a Harley-Davidson-based custom motorcycle called the XRTT 1750. It has a 100-cubic-inch S&S motor and was built for Reeves Callaway of Callaway Corvettes in 2005. Courtesy of American Motorcycle Parts, www.amcpchoppers.com.

such motorcycles from aftermarket parts, Nigro says, is massaging the pieces to make them work right. In addition to completely new motorcycles, Nigro also customizes production motorcycles and does restorations. In October 2021, Nigro submitted that he was close to retirement and that "there will probably not be too many more, if any [custom builds]."

A. P.
New York City (Brooklyn)
1900

"A. P." was the builder of the "Amateur's Motor Cycle" described in a letter from Brooklyn published in the *Horseless Age* on January 29, 1902. The writer claimed that he had built the machine nearly two years previously and had ridden it over 2,000 miles "with very satisfactory results." He could cover sixty miles on his two quarts of gasoline, climb a 6 percent grade, and cruise at 12 to 15 miles per hour on the level.

Utilizing an ordinary bicycle, A. P. installed a P. T. (q.v.) one-cylinder "type B gasoline motor," which powered the machine by a friction wheel on the rear tire. The roller itself was turned by a flat belt from a second pulley mounted on the end of the crankshaft. A coil spring held the friction wheel against the tire, while a cable was used to draw the roller to and away from the tire as required. A. P. claimed that his friction drive was a "great advantage" over belt or chain drive in busy city streets: "When I get in a tight place, I raise my friction wheel, let the motor run idle and pedal slowly, and as soon as I see my way clear I drop the friction wheel and away I go."

Photograph of A. P.'s machine published with his letter in the *Horseless Age*, January 29, 1902.

The writer noted that he had "built the entire motor on a 9-inch Star foot lathe, without the use of any special tools." A. P. claimed the innovation of a single-lever control that "holds the exhaust valve open, raises or lowers the same, and at the same time gives the circuit breaker a lead or lap, and thus regulates the speed. It also turns on and off the electric current at the proper time. This feature is, I think, original with me, although I have noticed lately that three makers of motor bicycles claim they are the originators of it."

Apex Wheel Company
Rochester
1900–1901

While developmental work on an Apex motorcycle engine took place at the Rochester bicycle factory, it is not known here whether any motor attachments or complete motorcycles reached buyers. By November 1900, James W. Shone of the Apex company, according to the *Cycling Gazette*, had "given his best time and attention to [the project] during the past year." His motorcycle would

> consist of an ordinary safety bicycle with what will appear to be an extra heavy mud guard over the rear wheel. This mud guard will contain everything essential to generate the propelling force for the machine with the exception of the battery for furnishing the spark which will be placed between the seatpost rod and the rear wheel.
>
> A small sprocket with a regular bicycle chain will connect the machinery to the rear hub, which will contain two sprockets, one on either side. The regular small sprocket will connect with the pedals as usual to furnish motive power should anything happen to the gasoline motor, and the sprocket on the opposite side of the rear hub will connect with the engine. The Apex Wheel Company will soon be in a position to supply these gasoline engines in any quantity to the manufacturer, by which he can list his regular stock bicycle as a motor cycle, without changing either gearing or lines of the frame.

However, in the Apex catalog that followed in February 1901, there was no motorcycle. Shone was "reportedly getting his motor cycle into shape and while it is not regularly listed in the Apex catalogues, the company will be ready to build this model in a short time."

James F. Bellamy notes that the *Motor Age* for March 1, 1900, said that the Apex Manufacturing Company (most likely referring to Apex Wheel Company), formerly the Shone-Hanna Company, had an experimental rotary motor. A rotary bicycle engine at the beginning of the twentieth century would have been a remarkable product "bound to become popular," as the *Gazette* suggested. That journal's description of a "sample engine . . . attached to the ceiling by two cords" running wide open yet "perfectly still" could describe a rotary design. An "ordinary gasoline engine . . . would have bounded up to the ceiling before half speed had been turned on."

Autocyclette Manufacturing and Sales Corporation
New York City (Manhattan)
ca. 1921–24
Trade Names: **Autocyclette**; **Pam**

Motorcycle and Bicycle Illustrated for July 28, 1921, announced the Autocyclette, the product of Victor Page Motors Corporation at 309 Lafayette Street in New York. Victor Page Motors promised "quantity production" of the $150 machine. However, a few weeks later, the journal reported that the Autocyclette Manufacturing and Sales Corporation at the Lafayette address claimed that Victor Page Motors, incorporated in Delaware but with a New York address on Fifth Avenue, was "an entirely separate organization with the exception of some of its personnel." It was the Autocyclette concern that was to build the Autocyclette with

The two-cylinder, two-stroke Autocyclette. From *Motorcycle and Bicycle Illustrated*, July 28, 1921.

American Motors Inc. at 100 Broad Street, to have responsibility for "exclusive sale and distribution."

As announced, the $150 Autocyclette was a "miniature car on two wheels." It had a two-cylinder, two-stroke in-line engine mounted on the floor of a pressed-steel, scooter-type frame with leaf-spring rear suspension. The engine was connected to a two-speed, sliding-gear transmission shifted by a foot lever. Primary drive was via bevel gears with a roller chain to the rear wheel. A magneto provided the current for the ignition system. Unlike most motorcycles of the day, the Autocyclette had a front wheel brake, operated by a hand lever, as well as a foot-controlled rear, V-band brake. The 80-pound machine rode on 18-inch wheels in a 52-inch wheelbase. Equipment included front and rear electric lights.

In February 1923, *Motorcycle and Bicycle Illustrated* published a chart of the mechanical specifications of American motorcycles, including two different Pam machines manufactured by the Autocyclette Corporation. Pam II featured the 12.56-cubic-inch, two-stroke engine, as in the original Autocyclette announcement. Pam I, on the other hand, used a 14.73-cubic-inch, one-cylinder, overhead-valve, four-stroke engine also of Autocyclette manufacture. The single was rated at 3 horsepower, while the twin was 2.5.

Both Pam I and Pam II used two-speed transmissions, although with different gearing. Wheelbases were now 58 inches. Weights were 175 pounds for the Pam I and 180 pounds for the Pam II. Wheels were 20 inches in diameter with 2-inch tires. The only brake was noted to be an internal expanding type.

David C. Leitner in April 2000 reported that he had a circa 1924 Autocyclette, designed, he noted, by Victor W. Page. He describes a two-cylinder in-line engine with a two-speed transmission and chain drive to the rear wheel. Disc wheels are used.

Victor Page (1885–1947), a mechanical engineer, is best remembered for his career as a writer of popular manuals on automotive and aviation subjects. Among his titles is *Motorcycles and Side Cars*, first published in 1914.

Michael Gerald and Jim Lucas have noted the Pam Autocyclette as having been manufactured in New York City in 1921 and 1922. In January 1925, *Motorcycling* claimed that the Pam was among a number of motorcycles "none . . . now made."

Automobile-Aviation Industries Corporation
Buffalo
1915

Motorcycle Illustrated reported that this company was organized in 1915 to "manufacture, sell and repair autos, bicycles and motorcycles." However, the certificate of incorporation does not mention motorcycles specifically; rather, it speaks of "cars, carriages, wagons, aeroplanes, air craft, hydroplanes, boats and vehicles of every kind and description." The certificate does mention motorcycles in regard to their being sold, rented, or operated.

Automobile-Aviation principals were Edward P. Leitze and Homer F. Sanford, who, with their wives, were the incorporators. Leitze (sometimes written "Leitz") was a mechanical engineer who operated the Leitze Automobile Training School and the Leitze Line Taxicabs, owned the U.S. Automobile Salvage and Reclaiming Company, and published the *Automobile Educator*. Sanford was also associated with the Corrugated Bar Company.

In July 1915, Leitze Inc., organized in 1913, was merged into Automobile-Aviation. At that point, the newer corporation owned all the stock of the older company and was "engaged in business similar to that of Leitze Incorporated," according to the merger certificate.

Automobile-Aviation Industries Corporation produced at least one plane and possibly two. Referred to as "Buffalo's new monoplane manufacturing company and school of aeronautics" by the *Buffalo Evening News*, the business was short-lived, and its property was sold at auction to satisfy debts in October 1915.

Autoped Company of America Inc.
(eventually a subsidiary of the
American Ever-Ready Company)
New York City (Manhattan; Long Island City)
1914–26?
Trade Name: **Autoped**

"Motor scooter" accurately describes the Autoped; with its small-diameter wheels and lack of seat, it resembles more a child's sidewalk scooter than a conventional motorcycle. Yet the Autoped led a rather long life for what the cycling press of the 1910s readily labeled a "freak" vehicle. While it was intended to provide handy transportation for urbanites running their errands, it's likely that most Autopeds served as recreational devices.

Hugo C. Gibson is credited with the Autoped's creation, although Joseph F. Merkel, one of America's best-known motorcycle designers, brought the machine to

Frances Smith and Florence Owens riding Autopeds on Long Beach, Long Island. From *Motorcycle Illustrated*, September 14, 1916.

a marketable state. At the time of the motorcycle's announcement, Gibson was president of the Autoped Company of America Inc. But by the fall of 1915, Gibson was promoting the similar Gibson Mon-Auto (q.v.). Succeeding Gibson as president of the Autoped Company was William B. Hurlburt, also president of the Hurlburt Motor Truck Company. A labyrinth of investors and officers involved with both companies extended to an Autoped Securities Company at the same 569 Fifth Avenue address as the Autoped Company of America.

In 1913 Merkel had left the Miami Cycle and Manufacturing Company of Middletown, Ohio, which built the Flying Merkel motorcycle. Of Merkel's work on the Autoped, it was claimed in 1917 that he "developed [it] from a crudity into a practical vehicle, which at the present time is making noticeable headway." Yet his stop with the Autoped was brief, and it's likely he undertook the job on contract or salary while he sought another business opportunity. In 1916 he incorporated the Merkel Motor Wheel Company (q.v.), which built a bicycle motor attachment in Rochester.

The first news of the Autoped came in early 1914, when it was to be 42 inches long and 9 inches wide, weighing 40 pounds. It was to cover up to 100 miles to a gallon of gasoline at up to 25 miles per hour. According to its adherents then—Gibson ("who has been identified as [an English] engineer and designer with both the automobile and aviation industries"), as well as Hurlburt and his "automobile men"—the Autoped could "be stored in the corner of one's house or office so that all storage expense is avoided; it can be carried in an automobile or car like a suitcase" (Autoped Co. of America, qtd. in the *Bicycling World and Motorcycle Review*, February 10, 1914).

In January 1915, the revised machine appeared at the New York motorcycle show; a reporter noted that Joe Merkel had no connection with the manufacturer, "but he designed and built [the Autoped]." And in fact, Merkel patented the Autoped design.

Patents 1,290,276 and 1,290,277, issued on January 7, 1919, describe the Autoped. Applications were filed on December 23, 1915, by Merkel, who gave a Flushing address. Patent 1,290,276 deals with the control lever, and 1,290,277 with the transmission, i.e., multiple-plate clutch and gear train. Merkel said his goal was "to produce a practical passenger-carrying motor of small size, compact, of great portability and of very light weight and inexpensive construction, primarily intended to carry a single person preferably in the standing position upon the vehicle, such vehicle being adapted to be pushed along or trundled by the dismounted rider and being adapted to be taken into the hallways of buildings and upon the passenger elevators thereof, if desired."

The Autoped Company of America had been incorporated in 1913 by the state of Delaware. By the fall of 1915, the Autoped office and factory were in Long Island City. In January 1917, the Autoped Company applied to the New York secretary of state to do business in New York. The company proposed to manufacture and sell "certain motor propelled vehicles known as Autopeds, and other similar devices." The principal place of business was to be at Thompson Avenue and Orton Street in Queens. By 1917, the American Ever-Ready Company of Long Island City had acquired the

Autoped business. The chief stockholder of American Ever-Ready was Conrad Hubert (1860–1928), an innovating Russian immigrant, who was credited with the invention of the pocket flashlight.

Among Autoped buyers in the late winter of 1917 were California operators who had secured fifty machines to be "rented out at the beach resorts next season." In San Francisco, "the Owl Drug Store, San Francisco News Bureau and Marks Bros" had all acquired Autopeds for "delivery and other utilitarian services."

Attached to the front wheel on the left side of the Autoped was a one-cylinder, 2.25-inch-bore-by-2.75-inch-stroke, four-cycle engine with an automatic inlet

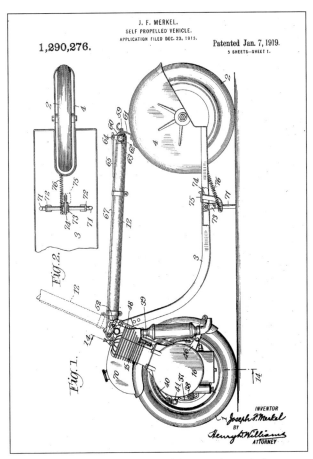

The Autoped design, as patented by Joseph Merkel in 1919, following a 1915 application.

valve. On the right was a flywheel incorporating the magneto. Controls were all located in the handlebars and stem. Pushing forward on the bars engaged the clutch. Pulling back applied the brake, fitted to the front wheel. The left grip adjusted the throttle, and the right the compression release. The rider stood on the platform between the wheels. The announced horsepower for the engine was 2. A five-plate clutch and 5:1 gearing connected the engine and front wheel. The 30-inch wheelbase Autoped frame was pressed steel. The steering column folded to the rear and clipped to the fender. While announced to weigh 40 pounds in 1914, the 1916 Autoped weighed 95. And while the anticipated top speed was to be 25, its actual top speed was 20.

In early 1921, *Motorcycle and Bicycle Illustrated* reported on the Wacker Motopede, which had "refined all of the crudities of its predecessor, the Autopede [*sic*], and it begins where the latter machine left off." The Motopede featured a leaf-spring frame, two-stroke engine, saddle (although the machine could be ridden while the operator stood), electric lighting, and a removable gasoline tank. By leaving the last "on the back porch" with the rest of the machine inside the house, "all fire risks are overcome." The Motopede was the invention of George W. Wacker of Rutherford, New Jersey.

Motorcycle historian Hugo Wilson notes that in the 1919–22 period the Krupp company in Germany built the Autoped under license; an engraving of the German machine shows a saddle mounted on a post. *Motorcycle and Bicycle Illustrated* for December 15, 1921, reports on the German motor scooter built by "Fried, Kupp, A.G." Perhaps this was a corruption of the well-known Krupp name. In any case, the Kupp machine appears nearly identical to the Autoped, a major difference being the provision of a saddle on a post. Erwin Tragatsch, who dates the American Autoped from 1915 to 1921 in his *Illustrated Encyclopedia of Motorcycles*, reports that it was built under license in Czechoslovakia by CAS as well as in England by Imperial Motor Industries Ltd. of London.

In September 1921, the Louis C. M. Reed Company at 230 Fifth Avenue in Manhattan advertised 25-miles-per hour, 100 miles-per-gallon Autopeds available to "Motorcycle and Bicycle Dealers [looking for] an opportunity for a right smart profit in quick time." In lots of ten, the machines were available at a cost of $43.50, freight prepaid—this on a motorcycle with a $125 list price. "This opportunity is possible only because of the slump in the export business. It left us with a little over five hundred Autopeds on hand. We are going to turn them into quick cash, regardless of the loss involved. Hence the low price . . . less than the original manufacturing cost."

In September 1925, *Motorcycling* reported that the Autoped "with larger wheels, now [is] being announced from 1974 Broadway, New York, by F. H. Ingerman, head of the Minute Man Motor Co." The machine was to be exhibited at the National Motorcycle, Bicycle, and Accessories Show in January 1926.

Tragatsch said, "like all other scooters of that period, the Autoped was not a commercial success." Richard Hough and L. J. K. Setright thought that the simple nature of the Autoped-style machine, with no seat and a single gear, "was its downfall, for it failed to be competitive with the motorcycle proper and cost far more [$95] than a push-bike."

One of several surviving Autopeds is in the collections of the National Museum of American History. The serial number D3210 for that 1918 model might indicate production numbers, assuming the *D* represents the fourth year of manufacture and the four digits the total number of all Autopeds. An Autoped sold at auction in July 1992 was called an "Eveready [*sic*] Autoped."

B

E. J. Baisden
New York City (Manhattan)
1914

E. J. Baisden (or Barsden) was a vaudevillian who specialized in trick-riding bicycles. Resident in Manhattan at the White Rats Club on West Forty-Sixth Street in early 1914, Baisden fabricated a battery-powered electric bicycle for use in his act. While intended for the stage, the motor bicycle was applicable to road riding, and Baisden reported that he was prepared to manufacture in quantity.

Starting with a bicycle from which he removed the cranks, Baisden installed a 6-volt Gray and Davis automotive starting motor just forward of the bottom bracket. A double chain reduction—silent chain to a countershaft and block chain to the rear wheel—gave a gear reduction of 8.5 to 1. Two sets of storage batteries were carried in wooden boxes low on each side of the rear wheel. The battery cases were removable for recharging or to lighten the load for someone to carry the more-than-125-pound vehicle. As built, the Baisden motorcycle had no motor control other than a simple on-off switch to vary speed, but Baisden claimed that "a series of coils in the tubing and handlebars will act as a rheostat, and that grip control will be arranged for."

Performance from the over-1-horsepower motor was impressive. Baisden claimed he could average 25 miles per hour for more than six hours, "taking the roads as they come." He also said that "in company with a rider mounted on a twin motorcycle, [he had] sustained a speed of forty-six miles per hour on the level road, and that the machine had climbed the slight grades encountered with no material diminishing of speed." *Motorcycling* thought that a touring radius of 150 miles would be practical for the Baisden motorcycle. The claims for the Baisden machine seem extravagant given the records of other electric vehicles in the 1910s and since.

Baisden electric motorcycle with automotive starter motor fastened to down tube and battery in portable wooden case. From *Motorcycling*, March 30, 1914.

E. I. Ballou
New York City (Brooklyn)
1905

A notice in the January issue of the *Motor Cycle Illustrated* reported a variety of new motorcycles "to be closed out at once" by E. I. Ballou, who listed a post office address at Station E in Brooklyn.

Two 1905 machines equipped with single tube tires and 1 1/4" wide flat belts. These machines are new and the tires are new, price $65 each. One second hand with single tube tires, tires new, $50. One 1905 fitted with G. & J. tires in the very best of condition, $62. One 1905, very fast machine, newly enameled and nickel plated, $62. One special racing machine, enameled red, weight 110 pounds, 5 h.p., has made a mile in 1.03 on a five-lap track, price $100. This machine is perfectly new. One special racer equipped with double grip control, enameled green, weight 96 pounds, has made a mile in 1.05 on a five-lap track. Will guarantee a speed of a mile a minute on the road; price $110. One special two cylinder, 9 h.p. racing machine, grip control, enameled blue, nickel plated cylindericaf [sic] tank with oil section, speed limit unknown: has made a mile in 40 seconds; price $150. Two exhibition machines, slightly scratched, at $75 each, latest 1905 models.

Certainly, it's likely that E. I. Ballou was only an agent for one or more motorcycle makers. If the journal notice had printed the trade names of the sale machines, the matter would be settled. On the other hand, the fact that there are special competition machines among the lot perhaps speaks in favor of Ballou-made, or at least Ballou-modified, motorcycles.

William Barber
New York City (Brooklyn)
ca. 1904
Trade Name: **Barber Special**

Bob Karolevitz in his *Yesterday's Motorcycles* notes a "Barber Special" built in Brooklyn, and Hugo Wilson in his *Encyclopedia of the Motorcycle* lists "Barber Brooklyn, NY c. 1900." The builder of the machines was William Barber. George Upington's city directory for 1901–2 lists William Barber as active in the bicycle trade on Coney Island Avenue. For 1905, but not 1906, there was a Barber Automobile Garage listed at 58 Schermerhorn Street managed by William Barber. According to Barber's obituary, he was "one of the first makers of disc wheels for automobiles and the inventor of many improvements on motor cars. One of his most important inventions was the overhead valve mechanism of the gasoline motor. . . . For many years he had a bicycle business on Ocean Parkway and manufactured his own motor cycle, the Barber Special." The nature of the motorcycles themselves remains to be discovered.

Sumter B. Battey
New York City (Manhattan)
1895

Sumter Beauregard Battey (1861–1934) was a surgeon born and educated in Georgia who spent his working years in New York City.

In addition to his career as a physician, Battey was a busy inventor. In 1895 he patented a rotary engine for bicycles, an imaginative work perhaps inspired by turbine technology and prescient in its anticipation of the mid-twentieth-century Wankel design. The *Horseless Age*, in its coverage of Battey's bicycle motor, noted that his inventions had covered "a wide range of thought" and that he had "not neglected the now popular subject of motors for road vehicles."

The heart of Battey's engine was a "revoluble cylinder," a rotor attached to the rear wheel. Adjacent to the rotor and emptying into it was a cylinder in which an explosive mixture was ignited. Combustion gases exited the open end of the cylinder and moved into pockets in the rotor, giving motion to the wheel as a turbine. A second cylinder, enclosing a piston given motion by a crank on the wheel, served as a pump to supply vaporized fuel to the "explosion chamber." Fuel was to have been gasoline, naphtha, "petroleum, or other like substance."

To put the engine into operation, the rider was to have begun pedaling. By doing so (and thus setting into motion the rear wheel in which the gears for the fuel pump were located), the rider would charge the combustion chamber. A battery ignition would fire the charge. The gases leaving the rotor were to assist in the vaporization of fuel in the carburetor.

Battey noted that his engine was not necessarily to be confined to bicycle use, for "it is plainly evident that my improved motor can be successfully used in connection with vehicles of any kind whatsoever." Whether any engines or vehicles were built according to Battey's design is unknown.

16 | Vincent H. Bendix

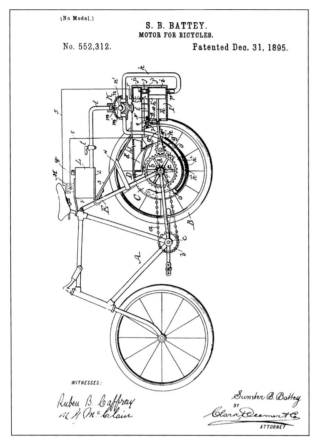

Patent drawing of Sumter Battey's engine fitted to a bicycle. The rotary piston, fitted with pockets to receive the combustion gases, is labeled D.

Vincent H. Bendix
New York City
1901–2

In the summer of 1902, "H. Bendix," the secretary of the New York Motor Cycle Club in New York City, visited motorcycle manufacturer Glenn H. Curtiss (q.v.) at the latter's Hammondsport home. Bendix, reported the *Hammondsport Herald*, wished to inspect the Hercules engine, which Curtiss and Charles B. Kirkham (q.v.) had developed, with an eye toward using it "for a new cushion frame motor-cycle to be put on the market next year." Bendix reportedly ordered an engine to try on a "sample machine." On September 1, however, Bendix rode a Kelecom motorcycle (s.v. "Albert H. Funke"), finishing second in a 10-mile handicap race at Ocean Parkway in Brooklyn; Curtiss was third

(although much faster) on his own Hercules machine.

A few months earlier, Vincent H. Bendix of the Bronx had received Patent 696,001 for an "improvement in motor-cycle frames, whereby the vibration caused by the motor is taken up and the objections largely done away with." The means was a modification of the basic diamond-style bicycle frame. The engine, according to Bendix's design, would be mounted in the rear triangle, which was separated from the main diamond by a spring at the top and an additional spring or hinged joint at the bottom. How Bendix would have dealt with the relocation of gasoline and oil tanks is not specified in the patent data. Vincent H. Bendix is likely the same Vincent Bendix (1883–1945) who led a creative, flamboyant, and productive life as an innovator in both the automotive and aviation field.

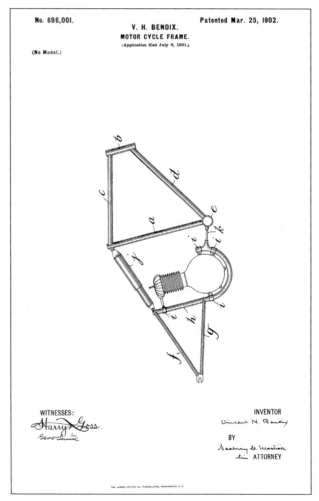

Patent drawing of Victor Bendix's motorcycle frame.

He had left his Illinois home for New York City in 1899; biographers note a joint venture with Glenn Curtiss building motorcycles shortly thereafter, a claim unsubstantiated through research on Curtiss's activities except for Bendix's visit to Hammondsport. By 1906, Bendix was in Chicago, where his first significant success was the "Bendix" self-starter drive for internal combustion engines, patented in 1914. The Bendix Aviation Corporation, founded in 1929, was a major developer and manufacturer of sophisticated transportation equipment by the time Bendix retired in 1942.

Joseph D. Bennett
Sidney
ca. 1908

In the fall of 1908, Joseph Bennett wrote to the *Cycle and Automobile Trade Journal* for advice about the "2-cycle, 2-port, 2-cylinder, air-cooled engine which I am building for bicycle use." He said that the bore was 3 inches and the stroke 3.5. He asked for advice about suitable dimensions for the ports, material for the crank, thickness of the proposed aluminum crankcase, and a need for piston rings below the ports.

"H. D." replied for the *Journal*, suggesting that the port lengths be increased over Bennett's proposed size, the shaft be made of tool steel, the crankcase be not less than one-quarter-inch thick, and a ring be installed below the ports to "save you a lot of lubricating oil and exhaust smoke." H. D. said such a power plant might be made to show 5 or 6 horsepower at 2,000 or 2,500 rpm—or "it can have such forms of ports and deflector as to give next to no power at all."

Whether Bennett finished this or any other engine has not been determined here.

Joseph "Joe" Berliner
Franklin Square (Town of Hempstead)
mid-twentieth century
Trade Names: **J. B. Special**; **JeBe**; **J-Be**

Michael Gerald and Jim Lucas cite the "J. B. Special" built in Franklin Square in 1950. Erwin Tragatsch notes the "Je-Be" motorcycle built in Germany circa 1960 for importer "Joe Berliner," for which Fichtel and Sachs, 100-cubic-centimeter and 125-cubic-centimeter, two-stroke engines were used. It is not clear whether Berliner actually made a motorcycle himself.

Joseph "Joe" Berliner established a motorcycle business in Manhattan around 1950. In 1951 his company, Berliner Motor Corporation, was the East Coast importer and distributor for Zundapp, based in West Germany. In 1957, Joe Berliner took over the International Motorcycle Company (q.v.), of which he was an investing partner. Berliner had a strong influence on the design of some of the motorcycles they imported for the American market. Some of the motorcycles his company sold had "J-Be" added in front of the brand name to signify his input to the design.

In 1959, the Berliner Motor company moved to Hasbrouck Heights, New Jersey, and continued to import and distribute European motorcycles, among them the Norton, Moto Guzzi, and Ducati trade names. The business folded in 1984.

Boisselot Automobile Company
alternatively,
**Boisselot Automobile and
Special Gasoline Motor Company**
New York City (Manhattan)
1901

A Boisselot Automobile Company advertisement in the *Cycle Age and Trade Review* in the late spring of 1901 boasted a 1.25-horsepower motor that would turn "Your Bike Into An Automobile." At under 20 pounds, the engine allegedly was the "lightest and most efficient Motor yet produced." The Boisselot company also produced larger, water-cooled engines, as well as "several types of Automobiles."

Advertising copy spoke of "valuable patents." Two were likely those granted to Jean Baptiste Boisselot, a French engineer living in Manhattan. The first patent, issued on December 24, 1901, was for an improvement in "Electric Igniters for Explosive Engines." Specifically, Boisselot said his invention dealt with the adjustment of the "sparking or electric igniting regulator or circuit breaker," which he noted "is preferably formed of indurated wood composed of pulverized ebony agglutinated and vulcanized under high pressure and heat with a mixture of beef-blood."

The second Boisselot patent, on February 11, 1902, was for an improvement in "Ignition-Plugs for

Explosive Motors." His idea was to provide an integral protective housing for a spark plug, all of which (plug and case) could nevertheless be readily dismantled for repairs. Both patents were assigned to Eduard Van Dam, a Dutch diamond cutter and merchant at the same 101 Beekman Street address as the Boisselot Automobile Company.

The Boisselot Automobile and Special Gasoline Motor Company, rather than the Boisselot Automobile Company, is listed on Beekman Street in *Trow's New York City Directory* for 1901–2. However, Beverly Rae Kimes and Henry Austin Clark Jr., in their *Standard Catalog of American Cars, 1805–1942*, state that the Boisselot Automobile and Special Gasoline Motor Company was in Jersey City, New Jersey. They note that in 1902 the Holland Automobile Company succeeded the Boisselot firm, apparently continuing manufacture of the bicycle engine into 1903.

A Boisselot tricycle and a "fetching 20-pound motor which certainly looks well, and which they say has brought them several healthy orders," was displayed at the Madison Square Garden cycle show in January 1901. What number of motor bicycle engines was built in Manhattan or Jersey City is unknown here.

Boller Brothers
Gowanda
1901

Boller Brothers in early 1901 was contemplating the construction of motor bicycles or "motocycles," according to the *Bicycling World and Motocycle Review* and *Cycle Age and Trade Review*, respectively. *Cycle Age* reported that a "new boiler for the work" had been installed, but whether any motorcycles were built is not known here. "Boller Brothers" was the name of a bicycle shop in Gowanda; the principal owner appears to have been Edward J. Boller.

John J. Bordman
New York City (Brooklyn)
1894–96

The *Horseless Age* in March 1896 reported John Bordman's patented "turbine or rotary principle" engine, which could be mounted in the "position of the ordinary treadle." Whether any bicycles were motorized with Bordman's engine—indeed, whether any engines at all were built according to his plan—is unknown here.

Bordman's patent, 457,414, for which he applied in 1894 and which was granted in 1895, describes an internal combustion engine in which a rotor called a "power wheel" covers and uncovers ports. Combustion was to occur in an annular chamber, from which the gases would flow to vanes called "buckets" on the periphery of the rotor. Bordman also described a make-and-break ignition system, a tank containing gasoline or some other hydrocarbon, and a water jacket for cooling the engine.

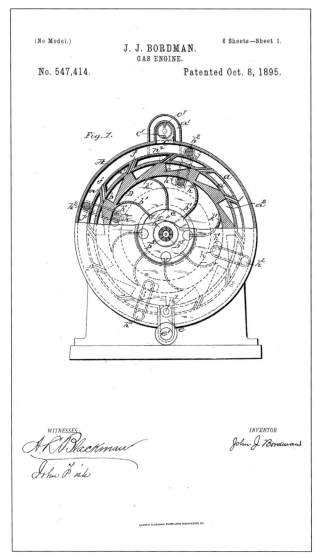

Patent drawing of John Bordman's gas turbine engine.

Bowman Automobile Company
New York City (Manhattan)
ca. 1905

The *Cycle and Automobile Trade Journal* in its January 1905 issue listed the Bowman Automobile Company, at 50-52 West Forty-Third Street, as a purveyor of motorcycles. Hugo Wilson in his *Encyclopedia of the Motorcycle*, perhaps using the *Cycle and Automobile Trade Journal* reference, notes "Bowman New York, NY c. 1905" as an "unconfirmed marque." Tod Rafferty's *Complete Illustrated Encyclopedia of American Motorcycles* (1999) notes "Bowman (1905) New York, New York."

The Sydney B. Bowman Automobile Company formed around 1903–5, to take the place of the failed Sydney B. Bowman Cycle Company. The cycle company formed around 1893 and sold bicycles. Around 1900, they started selling automobiles; in 1901, they added motorcycles, phonographs, motorboats, and a service area. The cycle company apparently ceased operations around 1902–3. It is not clear what type, if any, motorcycles they actually sold. Once the Sidney B. Bowman Automobile Company formed, advertisements, announcements, and articles in the *New York Times* suggest that they did not make or sell motorcycles.

Jay Brainard
Lewiston
1981–2011

Since 1981, Brainard, a motorcycle-component manufacturer doing business as JayBrake Enterprises Inc. has fabricated several extravagant custom motorcycles. All utilize longitudinally placed, Harley-Davidson-based, air-cooled, V-twin, four-stroke engines in elongated, tubular diamond frames. The lengths of the motorcycles are accented by long forks and significant fork rake. Many of the parts on the motorcycles, such as foot controls, brakes, and grips, are, naturally, JayBrake products, although often these are prototypical components. The wheels on some Brainard motorcycles have been turned from alloy billets. Flowing sheet-metal components, such as tank and fenders, combine with imaginative paint schemes and deeply polished bright metal to produce striking machines that are intended more to please the eye than to cover long miles. *VQ* magazine observed that on Brainard's "Orangegasm" motorcycle (1995) the "detail work is remarkable; the time and energy it took to hide, not only the wiring, but also the oil lines, borders on the fanatical."

Jay Brainard continued to innovate, holding numerous patents, until his retirement in 2011. In 2006, JayBrake Enterprises was purchased by Horschel Brothers Precision in Springville, New York. Jay Brainard stayed on and focused on research and development of performance motorcycle parts and accessories, while Horschel Brothers Precision / Horschel Motorsports focused on production and sales. In October 2011, SuperTrapp Industries of Cleveland, Ohio, purchased the rights to JayBrake products. Jay Brainard stayed on to help with the transition and retired shortly after. It is not known at this time whether JayBrake Enterprises produced any more complete custom motorcycles after 2000.

One of Jay Brainard's V-twin powered, custom machines. Photo courtesy of Jay Brainard, JayBrake Enterprises Inc.

Brandenburg Brothers
(Brandenburg Brothers and Wallace[?]; Brandenburg Brothers and Alliger[?])
New York City (Manhattan)
1901–?

Brandenburg Brothers and Wallace (later, Brandenburg Brothers and Alliger) at 56 Reade Street were merchants of bicycle and automobile parts and accessories, including the Thor hubs and hangers from the Aurora Automatic Machine Company of Aurora, Illinois. Joseph I. Brandenburg and his brother George founded the company. They had branches in Chicago and New York City.

With the introduction of Thor motorcycle engines, Brandenburg Brothers, according to a *Motorcycle Illustrated* story published in 1915, began "making motorcycles and putting their own label on them, as was the custom for some years afterward." Presumably, Thor engines powered the Brandenburg machines, apparently as early as 1901.

E. A. Brecher and Company
New York City (Manhattan)
ca. 1902

The February 1902 *Motor Age* directory of motor bicycle makers listed the Brecher firm. The principal was Emanual A. Brecher, whom the city directory for 1901–2 noted as being in the bicycle business at 95 Reade Street. For the 1900–1, 1902–3, and 1903–4 directory years (each beginning in July), Emanual Brecher and the Brecher company were shown to be in the "supply" business.

Bretz Cycle Manufacturing Company
Syracuse
1901

According to the *Cycling Gazette*, during the winter of 1901, Bretz company president John C. Bretz[2] was experimenting with motor propulsion for two-wheeled vehicles. "The whole problem in a motor cycle," he said, "is to get a good motor." Once he found an engine, he was going to sell his motorcycle (March 7, 1901).

A week later, Bretz said the motor was not going to be in shape, so there would be no motorcycle "this year." Besides, "the company is so busy with its regular work that it has not much time for the motor bicycle" (*Cycling Gazette*, March 14, 1901). The Bretz company remained active at least until 1905.

---

2. City directories list Jacob S. Bretz; some newspaper articles say James S. Betz was company president.

Patrick "Pat" Briggs
d/b/a **Briggs Custom Cycle**; **County Line Choppers**; **County Line Choppers by Briggs**
Phoenix
1996–present

According to an article in the March 2007 *V-Twin Magazine*, Pat Briggs started working on motorcycles professionally when he was just seventeen years old. With fifteen years of experience, he opened his own shop, Briggs Custom Cycle, in 1996, which, according to the article, changed its name to County Line Choppers three years later. The article states that in addition to being a service shop, "they build 10–15 bikes a year. They have a complete machine shop in-house and can fabricate anything. They also build motors and transmissions and have a frame jig that allows them to modify or build frames completely to their specifications."

Pat Briggs was certified as a level 2 master bike builder by the International Master Bike Builders Association. According to a newspaper interview with Briggs in 2019, he had "built nearly 50 custom choppers over the years and, he said, modified hundreds more." His work has been featured in numerous motorcycle magazines and he has won competitions for his builds.

County Line Choppers is also a licensed manufacturer, and in its online listing in *The Chopper Directory* County Line Choppers states, "We specialize in National show winning full custom bikes that are built to ride. Quality is never sacrificed and all of our bikes are warranted. From mild to wild, we can build a 'one of a kind' bike exactly the way you want it the first time. We can also customize your existing ride."

Broadway Choppers
Schenectady
1995–present

Lee Sikes is owner of Lee's Speed Shop Inc., which does business as Broadway Choppers. Sikes in 1998 bought out partner Mike Parisi, with whom he had founded the enterprise in 1995. At that time, the pair envisioned a motorcycle shop, a tattoo parlor, and a restaurant at a Broadway location. In 2001, Sikes employed a mechanic and operated a motorcycle business exclusively, at 1518 Bradley Street in Schenectady.

Sikes, a Florida native and former aircraft mechanic, has worked with motorcycles for thirty-seven years, turning an avocation into a creative, productive vocation. His business is confined to Harley-Davidson or Harley-Davidson-inspired motorcycles. Sikes both customizes extant machines and builds entire motorcycles to meet owners' requirements. For complete motorcycles, he starts with frames that, for liability purposes, he buys from outside suppliers rather than fabricating himself. Engines are all air-cooled V-twins, either actual Harley motors or power plants built from components obtained from other manufacturers. Sheet-metal work is done in-house. Painting is contracted. Several of Sikes's motorcycles have won prizes in competitive judging of custom machines.

While most of Sikes's work is customizing (and he estimates hundreds of such projects since he founded his business), he indicates his "ground-up" work averages two per year. In August 2000 he had four "builds going on."

Broadway Choppers changed its business to online new and used parts sales in 2016, focusing on parts for Harley and V-twin motorcycles.

Buffalo Motorcycle Works Corporation
Tonawanda
1981–90
Trade Name: **Buffalo**

The Buffalo idea originated on a cold November day in 1981 as three motorcyclists cut short their ride to chat at a hot dog stand. Mutually complaining about the quality of their motorcycles, they decided they could produce better ones. With two engineers and a "business-man" present, the three had the capacity to follow through with their ideas—so notes one of the engineers and former Buffalo Motorcycle Works chairman Ari Lehr.

Eventually, 136 people were involved with the Buffalo project, including thirty engineers, all of whom donated their time to develop new motorcycles; in fact, the only paid employee was a secretary. The enterprise was incorporated on November 25, 1983, by New York State. At that time there were 5,000 authorized shares with a par value of ten dollars each, but an undated stock certificate notes 99,950 shares, also with a par value of ten dollars.

With an interim location for the Buffalo company at 141 Niagara Street in Tonawanda, officials soon looked for a suitable production facility elsewhere. Officials in the states of Pennsylvania and Kentucky expressed interest and offered existing buildings. Development officials in Ontario acknowledged interest, also, but those in the namesake city of Buffalo did not.

Buffalo Motorcycle Works had the idea of a "hundred-year motorcycle," one built so substantially that it could be ridden indefinitely without repair. Stainless steel was envisioned for the cylinders, and appropriate chrome molybdenum alloys for gears and shafts. Buffalo's engineers produced single and dual overhead camshaft engines designed to omit gaskets above the crankcase; heads in three- and four-valve models were to be welded to the cylinders.

Development work produced two single-cylinder prototype motorcycles with three interchangeable engines in 500-cubic-centimeter (cc), 750-cc, and 1,000-cc size. The 1,000-cc single "ran great," said Lehr. The one-cylinder design, according to Lehr, was to go after the "commuter market."

Design sketch for the Buffalo single-cylinder motorcycle, 1985. Image courtesy of Ari Lehr.

There also were two-cylinder prototype motorcycles with 80- or 90-cubic-inch engines intended for more sporting use. The first machine suffered a failure of the nearly weldless frame during testing on the New York State Thruway. The engine on the second blew up in testing, indicating to the development engineers that the push-rod, V-twin, Harley-Davidson-style engine was not suitable for Buffalo use. The final of the three or four prototype twins, called the Buffalo Chief, had dual, chain-driven overhead camshafts. There was also a three-cylinder engine in "W" form installed in a chassis "not quite ready for the road" when development ended.

Word of the Buffalo motorcycles spread locally. Lehr says, "There were lots of fans." The Tonawanda police department helped by letting the Buffalo personnel test their machines on the streets. Enthusiasm for the new motorcycle was widespread away from the Niagara Frontier, too. The post office delivered mail addressed only to the Buffalo Motorcycle Company in Buffalo, USA, from as far away as New Zealand.

Lehr speaks of eight thousand orders for Buffalo motorcycles, but legal disaster ended the corporation's work. First, there was a disagreement on the board over the appearance of the motorcycles to be built. A majority favored a "classic" look, which would appeal to a conservative buying public. A minority favored a more "futuristic" style with enclosed engine, magnesium wheels, and electronic instrumentation.

Then, a stockholder who was not part of the original group of enthusiasts sought access to design drawings. Fearing that this individual was on the board of a competing motorcycle company, Buffalo management refused to share the requested information although required to do so by their by-laws. In the end, a state attorney general's investigation into the Buffalo operation forced the cessation of the corporation's activities as well as the destruction or sale of its designs and prototype materials. There never was, however, any proof of wrongdoing, according to Lehr. The Buffalo Motorcycle Works Corporation was dissolved by proclamation of the secretary of state in 1990.

William R. Bullis
Chatham
1897–99

William Bullis (1852–1915), a machinist living in Chatham, received Patent 597,389 for a "gasolene engine" intended to power "bicycles or other wheeled vehicles" in January 1898. He planned to utilize two horizontal cylinders extended beyond the rear axle, to which the piston rods were connected directly by cranks. The engine was a two-stroke affair with poppet valves, the intake of which was opened atmospherically. Perhaps the most significant Bullis idea was the encircling of the cylinders by the fuel lines twisted into coils. The purpose was to cool the engine while utilizing its heat to vaporize fuel. In addition, Bullis thought valuable his ignition trip actuated by a fitting on the tops of the pistons, i.e., inside the cylinders.

Bullis attached his patented gasoline engine to a railroad velocipede in 1899 "with most satisfactory results," according to the *Horseless Age*. Since the motor produced "unusual power," although weighing only 20 pounds, Bullis was said to contemplate "manufacturing them for bicycles." It does not appear that he manufactured them on a large scale, if at all. He did attach one to a tricycle, laying claim to the first motor tricycle in that "section of New York," according to one obituary.

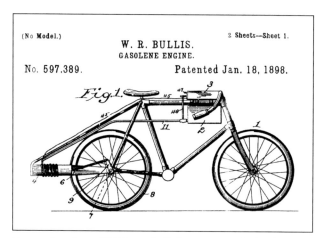

Patent drawing of William Bullis's engine with the fuel line wrapped around the cylinder to aid in vaporization.

C

Chain Bike Corporation
Rockaway Beach
ca. 1951–67

The *Thomas Register of American Manufacturers* in the 1960s period listed the Chain Bike Corporation at 350 Beach 79th Street as a manufacturer of "power scooters" and "gas engine motor bikes." The Chain Bike company, capitalized at over $500,000 at that time, was perhaps best known as the builder of Ross bicycles. The company started operation around 1951, and production moved to Allentown, Pennsylvania, around 1967.

Chaos Custom Motorcycle Corporation
d/b/a **Chaos Cycle**
Mastic (2004–18); Shirley (2018–present)
2004–present

George T. Stinsman spent most of his life around hot rods, muscle cars, and motorcycles, but his love of motorcycles really started when he bought his first one in 1995, a new Kawasaki ZX6 for road racing and later stunt riding. Stinsman reported that he was inspired by Jesse James and Indian Larry (Lawrence DeSmedt, q.v.) to build a bike from the ground up in 2002. He purchased most of the parts and fabricated unique features. Stinsman shared how this led to the beginnings of his own business that he runs with his wife, Dee:

> The first time I brought it to a car meet a couple of people asked me to build them bikes and that's how Chaos was born. Since those days I have competed around the world and have won the International Motorcycle Show in New York City 10 times of 11 entries. My Bikes have been featured in over 50 magazines, and I have clients with bikes I have built around the world. I was invited to display my bikes twice by Metallica at their Orion Festival.

Chaos Cycle offers hand-built one-off choppers, bobbers, cafés, baggers, and prostreet motorcycles, and, according to Stinsman, "anything's game." They fabricate frames, exhaust, handlebars, gas tanks, fenders, front ends, and many other parts as needed for their builds or clients. They use mainly Harley-Davidson and S&S motors. The key fabricators are George and his son Devin Stinsman. George estimates that they have built about fifty custom fabrications since 2004.

Tyvald Christensen
Port Richmond
1919

The patent office in July 1919 granted Tyvald Christensen, a Norwegian living on Staten Island, a patent

"Excelsis Deo" (Latin for "glory to God in the highest") was built by Stinsman for royalty, Princess Gloria von Thurn und Taxis of Germany, in 2011. At the time, she lived in New York City, and the bike was built to be ridden in the streets of NYC. The bobber features a one-off custom soft-tail frame, a 96-cubic-inch S&S shovelhead motor, and many little customized parts fit for a princess, including a Gucci-leather-wrapped seat and battery box with leather from one of the princess's old suitcases.

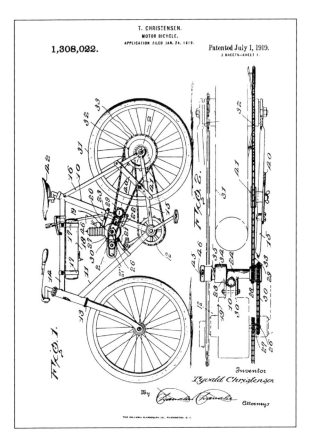

Tyvald Christensen's invention for converting a bicycle to a motorcycle, depicted in a patent drawing.

for a "motor-bicycle." Christensen claimed his goals were to "provide a novel and improved engine and driving means whereby the ordinary bicycle can be easily converted into a motorcycle" as well as a "novel and improved form of driving clutch and the means for attaching the same to the crank case of the engine and to the bicycle frame."

What Christensen patented was a disc clutch mechanism, which coupled or uncoupled adjacent sprockets on a common shaft. An engine was to be mounted on the forward edge of the seat tube and drive one of the two sprockets on the clutch mechanism, which was mounted on the rear side of the tube. The second sprocket on the clutch shaft was to turn a chain connected to the hub of the rear wheel. Christensen made at least one motor bicycle with his engine and used it to ride to and from work.

Edward P. Clark and William H. Brewster
Utica
1900

A physician and surgeon, Edward P. Clark of Utica attempted, apparently unsuccessfully, to patent a motorcycle design. Clark's idea was the modification of an ordinary bicycle frame by an extension of the top tube rearward combined with a new set of stays running from the extension to the rear fork. Attached to this new frame were the engine, gasoline tank, carburetor, and muffler. The advantage, Clark said, was the location of the engine heat away from the rider. In addition, the "whole can easily be removed in two minutes, leaving an ordinary safety bicycle, ready for riding."

Construction of the Clark motorcycle was undertaken by William H. Brewster, identified by the *Bicycling World and Motocycle Review* as "the John Street [bicycle] assembler." The machine was a Brewster "bicycle pure and simple until the back wheel is reached." There, the engine provided power via two sprocket wheels and a chain on the left side, leaving the ordinary bicycle pedals, crank, and chain on the right side. Clark said the Acme bicycle motor, made by Palmer Brothers of Miamus (*sic*), Connecticut, geared at 3:16 and turning 1,000–2,000 revolutions per minute, gave a top speed of 35 miles per hour, "all conditions being favorable." Clark, wrote the *Cycle Age and Trade Review*, claimed that his motorcycle "has proven satisfactory in every way." The *Horseless Age* noted that the "motor is over the rear wheel, and is said to weigh only 17 pounds." The *Bicycling World* reported a claimed steady speed of 30 miles per hour on the level and "fifteen miles an hour over the most hilly country. . . . The start is made with the feet on the pedals, and speed, braking and all parts of the motor are regulated from the handle-bars by three distinct levers." The aluminum gasoline tank on the right side of the rear wheel held a gallon of fuel, "enough to last for a 200 mile ride."

In June 1902, for the *Horseless Age*, Clark wrote of "My Experience with Motor Bicycles." In 1900, he "got the motor bicycle fever," and with the help of a "local bicycle manufacturer, who knew a whole lot more about bicycles . . . than he did about motors," he built an engine from a set of castings and put it on a bicycle. "This machine worked all right when run in

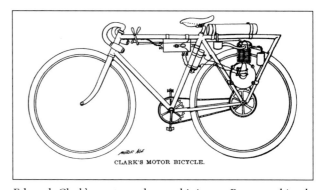

Edward Clark's motorcycle combining a Brewster bicycle with an Acme engine driving the rear wheel via a chain. From *Cycle Age and Trade Review*, August 30, 1900.

a jack on the shop floor, but when taken on the street absolutely refused to propel the bicycle."

Clark purchased a different set of castings and blueprints for a second engine. When "everything was favorable," the motor bicycle did run, "but lacked the power sufficient to ascend grades over 3 per cent unaided, and I abandoned that also and looked for a factory built machine." Perhaps this second iteration of a Clark motorcycle is the Brewster machine, which the trade press had described so favorably two years before. By 1902, Clark owned six different motorcycles.

Brewster was an inventive individual. In 1902, he was granted one patent for a planetary gear and a second (four years after his application) for a coaster brake design; by then he had abandoned the bicycle trade and identified himself as an automobile manufacturer.

Clement Motor Equipment Company
New York City (Manhattan)
1908–9

Clement bicycle engines, "Genuine French Clement Motors," likely were made in France, with the Clement Motor Equipment Company serving as a distributor from 1900 Broadway at Sixty-Third Street in Manhattan. However, *Motorcycle Illustrated* noted that the Clement Motor Equipment Company "*made* a motor attachment for bicycles" (October 15, 1909; emphasis added). The one-cylinder, four-stroke, 1.25-horsepower, 20-pound engines were advertised in 1908 and 1909. A complete kit, with tanks, pulley, idler, belt, and engine, was listed at fifty dollars (later sixty-five dollars), while the motor alone was thirty dollars (later thirty-five). A speed of 30 miles per hour was promised with an ordinary bicycle.

By October 1909, the Clement Motor Equipment Company had "silently vanished." According to a story in the trade press, the principals in the firm had been Howard Wray, "the well-known racing man," and "J. Elliott," both of Brooklyn. Earlier, there was a Clement factory in Hartford, Connecticut. That subsidiary of the French Clement firm built engines similar to those sold later by the Clement Motor Equipment Company as well as complete motor bicycles. The Clement factory in Hartford closed in February 1904.

Clement 1.25-horsepower bicycle engine, likely imported complete from France. From *Motorcycle Illustrated*, January 1, 1909.

Copper Mike (Michael Cole)
d/b/a **Gravesend Cycles Inc.**
Lindenhurst (2003–20);
Hawley, Pennsylvania (2020–present)
2003–present

Owner and builder Michael "Copper Mike" Cole reports he started riding dirt bikes when he was a kid and purchased a street bike as soon as he was old enough. According to Cole, his early career was spent in "high end retail construction," and he "brought a lot of that style" to his builds. He has been building motorcycles since 1995. In 2003 he started Gravesend Cycles, named after the neighborhood where he was born in Brooklyn.

Cole builds one-off motorcycles, which are Harley-Davidson-based in the bobber style. Each of his motorcycles are a "functioning work of art," and his work has been featured in magazines and art galleries around the world.

"The 60," built by Copper Mike in 2017. Starting with a 1960 panhead motor, he made custom exhaust pipes and the sissy bar (including an antique train reflector). Also, Mike reported that the bike has "Harley springer front end with Copper Mike custom ball milled front legs, Copper Mike handle bars," and "various pieces [are] antique copper plated." The motorcycle was purchased by a buyer in Australia. Courtesy of Copper Mike Cole, Gravesend Cycles.

Paul Cox
d/b/a **Paul Cox Industries, NYC**
Manhattan (ca. 1990–2000); Brooklyn (2000–ca. 2018); Port Jervis (ca. 2018–present)
ca. 1990–present

Paul Cox is a multimedia artist who builds motorcycles, leather products, knives, and more. Born and raised in Virginia, Cox came to New York City after graduating from Virginia Commonwealth College in 1998. Using his degree in fine arts, he found work in advertising but also found time to build choppers and specialized leather seat cushions in his apartment. He eventually started working at Sixth Street Cycles in the East Village (Manhattan). There he met his mentor and friend, Indian Larry (Lawrence DeSmedt, q.v.). In 1992, he started working at Psycho Cycles as a mechanic and fabricator. He also rented space in the basement to produce leather goods. He credits the crew at Psycho Cycles for creating the "NYC Chopper style," often described as a custom motorcycle that was stripped down, light, fast, rugged, nimble, and thin and having a shorter rake than traditional choppers and good ground clearance—all features designed to deal with NYC traffic, narrow streets, various street surfaces (like cobblestone or brick), and potholes.

In 2000, Cox and others formed the crew at Indian Larry's new shop in Brooklyn, Gasoline Alley. Larry was the main proprietor, and when he died in 2004 the rest of the crew changed the name of the shop to Indian Larry's Legacy. They continued to produce custom motorcycles following Larry's vision for a few years.

In 2007, Paul opened his own shop, called Paul Cox Industries. Located a short distance from the Legacy shop, Paul's shop included offerings that featured his wide range of interests and skill sets. In 2015, he told Bloomberg News that he produced four to six motorcycles a year, "including individually tanned leather and hand-hammered tanks." One of his most well-known custom motorcycles is the "Berserker," a 1958 modified 88-inch panhead, covered with leather, taking inspiration from Viking lore. His custom leather motorcycle seats are highly sought after and have been used by some of the biggest names in the custom motorcycle industry.

By July 2018, Paul Cox Industries had moved to Port Jervis (Orange County). The move has enabled Cox to expand his workspace, spend more time with his family, and find new inspirations.

Crescent Auto Manufacturing Company
New York City (Manhattan)
1902

A *Motor Age* trade directory appearing in February 1902 listed the Crescent Auto Manufacturing Company—not to be confused with the Crescent line of bicycles and motorcycles of Western Wheel Works in Chicago—as a source of "motors for cycles." Beverly Rae Kimes and Henry Austin Clark Jr., in their *Standard Catalog of American Cars, 1805–1942*, note that the company was incorporated in Delaware by 1900. The office and "small machine shop" were at 130 Broadway in Manhattan. Kimes and Clark say that the Crescent company had acquired the rights to the P. T. (q.v.) bicycle engine. The Crescent company also developed its own two-cylinder engine, which it installed in an automobile. Kimes and Clark quote the *Cycle and Automobile Trade Journal* in stating that stock was to be sold to permit the establishment of a factory to build the car.

Glenn H. Curtiss
1901–2
G. H. Curtiss Manufacturing Company
1902–9
Herring-Curtiss Company
1909–10
Curtiss Motor[cycle] Company
1911–13
Hammondsport
Trade Names: **Hercules**; **Curtiss**

Through his exploits as an aviation pioneer, Glenn Curtiss (1878–1930) is perhaps the best known of New York motorcycle builders. Yet by his motorcycle endeavors—his introduction to the United States of two- and three-cylinder motorcycles, his high-performance engines, his early tandems, and his record-setting rides in races and speed trials—Curtiss created a significant historical record before he ever left the ground.

In the 1890s Glenn Curtiss raced bicycles, and then in his Hammondsport hometown established Curtiss's Harness and Bicycle Store. By March 1902 he had opened additional shops in Bath and Corning. It was probably in 1901, after he visited the Pan-American Exposition, where motor vehicles were exhibited, that Curtiss decided to motorize a bicycle, ordering a set of engine castings from the E. R. Thomas Motor Company (q.v.) in Buffalo. The single cylinder measured 2 by 2.5 inches. Curtiss, according to Augustus Post in the *Century Magazine* in 1910, experimented with roller drive to the front wheel before settling on rear drive. He fabricated a carburetor from a tin can and used a medical generator for ignition. The next Curtiss motorcycle utilized another set of Thomas castings, these giving a bore of 3.5 and a stroke of 5 inches. The 190-pound machine "proved to be a terror" but produced a speed of 30 miles per hour and climbed the hills around Hammondsport.

It was after the construction of the second motorcycle, according to Curtiss biographer C. R. Roseberry, that Curtiss concluded that he "could make a better engine himself." According to Roseberry, the design principle was "maximal horsepower with minimal weight. From this formula he never wavered" (*Glenn Curtiss: Pioneer of Flight*).

At the end of April 1902, Curtiss had a "motocycle [probably a tandem] nearly completed," and on May 3, 1902, he and A. W. Stanton made what was reported as the "the first motocycle tandem trip ever taken in Steuben County." By mid-June, Curtiss was "meeting with quite a demand for motor cycles." In July, his own Hercules 2.5-horsepower, ball-bearing motor was available with a complete motorcycle, by itself "or Castings and Drawings." *Cycle and Automobile Trade Journal* described the Hercules frame as "16-gauge seamless tubing with double top tubes, heavy forks, crown and stem." The engine drove the rear wheel via a rawhide belt controlled by an idler. A coaster brake was fitted. The 40-miles-per-hour machine cost $180. A tandem version was $210.

It's likely that the engines for the Hercules motorcycles in the summer of 1902 already were being built for Curtiss by Charles Kirkham (q.v.), perhaps with his father, in Taggarts on Bath Road. It is known that the Kirkhams, along with Charles's brothers Clarence and Percy, built engines for Curtiss until 1905, but the very early (1902) involvement of Charles is suggested by an article in the *Hammondsport Herald* at the end of July 1902: "H. Bendix, secretary of the New York Motor Cycle Club, the largest in America, was in Hammondsport last Friday [July 25] to inspect the new Hercules motor, manufactured by G. H. Curtiss and Charles Kirkham, with a view to adopting it for a new cushion frame motor-cycle to be put on the market next year. He was pleased with the motor and left an order for one."

Another visitor to Hammondsport with an eye to adopting the Curtiss engine was Pulver G. Hermance of the Industrial Machine Company in Syracuse, which intended to market the 1903 DeLong (q.v.) motorcycle. The *Herald* noted "many sales" of Hercules motorcycles, "shipping some machines as far as California," and described Curtiss corresponding with interested parties in Nova Scotia, New Zealand, South Africa, "and other foreign countries."

Another query reportedly came from a "New York aeronaut," and in October it was reported that Curtiss "has been obliged to increase the facilities by the addition of more machinery, to meet the growing demand for these superior motors and motor cycles."

Glenn Curtiss was quick to take up motorcycle racing. On September 1, 1902, he rode in what has been designated the first "motorcycle handicap road race" on Ocean Parkway in Brooklyn. His Hercules, after starting with a two-and-a-half-minute handicap, was awarded third place for the 10-mile event.

According to Roseberry, the success of the Hercules motorcycle and the resulting demands on Curtiss's operation created a need for working capital. In response, the G. H. Curtiss Manufacturing Company, as the concern was known, received about $2,500 in investment funds from Hammondsport residents J. Seymour Hubbs, George H. Keeler, Victor Masson, and Jules Masson. Clara Studer, another Curtiss biographer, claims that the organization took place in 1901, with Hubbs staking $1,000 and Keeler, the two Massons, Henry Miller, and M. C. Plough each contributing $500, for a total of $3,000 (*Sky Storming Yankee: The Life of Glenn Curtiss* [New York: Stackpole Sons, 1937]).

1903 Model Year

In December 1902, the G. H. Curtiss Manufacturing Company advertised its 1903 model Hercules motorcycle, still with a 2.5-horsepower ball-bearing motor. "Special Features for 1903" included a "new throttle control" and "great strength of front forks [which remained unsprung] and frame." The Curtiss company also noted their automatic lubrication, a muffler with no back pressure, 100-mile gasoline capacity, 300-mile oil capacity, and speeds from 4 to 45 miles per hour. The wheelbase measured 56 inches. The motorcycle weighed 125 pounds.

After the racing defeat in Brooklyn in 1902, Curtiss had begun development of what was probably the first two-cylinder motorcycle engine. In format, he chose the "V," in which the cylinders lie parallel with the long axis of the frame. The displacement of the single was doubled, giving 5 horsepower. Announced in February 1903, the new engine differed significantly from its one-cylinder predecessor in the fitting of roller bearings rather than the ball type. The connecting rods were connected to a common wrist pin. A throttle was fitted. At a weight of 60 pounds, the new twin, with 3-inch bore and stroke, was capable of turning 3,500 rpm. The price of the engine alone was $150. When fitted to the Hercules motorcycle, the larger engine cost $75 more. Apparently, the one-cylinder engine was converted to roller bearings at the time of the twin's introduction; by March the Curtiss Manufacturing Company was advertising a "2½ H.P. Roller Bearing Motor." One-cylinder motorcycles remained in the Curtiss line to the end of production.

The two-cylinder motorcycle utilized a longer, 61-inch wheelbase frame with triple top tubes and double seat stays. The loop under the engine also was doubled. The *Dealer and Repairman* reported that Curtiss first used a V-belt on this twin, but it "slipped too badly to be of practical use," so he turned to a 2-inch flat belt. The journal said Curtiss built his first twin for competition but "early realized that the new machine was admirably suited for road riding and was of neat and attractive design and moderate weight, considering its power, so he immediately cataloged it and set to work to build others like it." An advantage to two cylinders, the *Dealer* said, was greater smoothness, not to mention greater fuel economy.

The *Automobile Review and Automobile News* in March 1903 said that among the many improvements to the Curtiss motorcycles for the season, the "novelty is introduced in the shape of a 5 h.p., 2-cylinder motor." The journal noted that the single-cylinder machine was driven by a "Corson round belt, with idler adjustment." The April 15, 1903, issue of the *Automobile Review* noted that a 160-pound "lady back" tandem was available with either one- or two-cylinder engine.

By April 1, due to the demands of the motorcycle trade, Curtiss gave up his Corning store. The *Hammondsport Herald* noted in April that "in the manufacture of the Hercules motor cycles G. H. Curtiss employs from four to seven people continuously. He is now about three months behind his orders. The Hercules is probably one of the best, if not the very best, motor cycle on the market. The new double cylinder machine which he recently finished is the first of its kind to be made in America."

On Memorial Day morning, Curtiss was in New York City with a 5-horsepower machine to take part in the New York Motor Cycle Club's Riverdale hill climb. The half-mile rise varied in grade from 5 to 12 percent (14 percent according to the *Automobile Review*). With the most powerful machine in the contest, Curtiss was the winner in fifty-one seconds with a margin of four and two-fifths seconds over the second-place rider. From Riverdale, Curtiss went to the Empire City racetrack in Yonkers to ride "in the five-mile motor cycle race for the championship of America." Again, he was victorious, this time against eight other riders. Again, Curtiss rode the only two-cylinder machine.

The *Hammondsport Herald* said, "Mr. Curtiss is certainly to be congratulated. From the most modest beginning, unaided by experts in motor building or skilled mechanics in bicycle work, he has developed a motor cycle which probably out ranks for road work and speed any and all others. With humble and unpretentious surroundings he has put upon the market this year twenty cycles and has many orders yet to fill."

Glenn Curtiss's Hercules was one of the first two-cylinder motorcycles sold in the United States and "the most powerful road machine regularly catalogued by an American maker," according to the *Dealer and Repairman*, July 1903.

In California, the balloonist Thomas Scott Baldwin chanced upon a Hercules twin motorcycle. With the idea of a light, multicylinder power plant for flying in mind, he soon ordered an engine from Curtiss for dirigible use. By year's end, the Curtiss Manufacturing Company had built other aircraft engines, and in late fall the basic two-cylinder engine design had been extended to a four-cylinder engine in "V" form installed on a lighter-than-air (balloon) ship built by "Professor Myers" of Frankfort.

1904 Model Year

The *Hammondsport Herald* claimed that Curtiss "wishes to state that a great deal of the success of the Hercules motorcycle is due to the superior construction and workmanship on the motors, which are built exclusively for him by Charles Kirkham of Cold Springs. Mr. Kirkham is a very talented young man, being a first class draughtsman and all around machinist. He has the best equipped shops in this section, and besides building the Curtiss motor, Mr. Kirkham also builds and markets the Kirkham 4 Cylinder Air Cooled Automobile engine."

Observers outside Hammondsport had noticed Curtiss's progress in the motorcycle industry. In mid-May, the Board of Trade and Business Men's Association of Owego "made him a very flattering offer to remove his motor cycle works to that place, which he is considering." And a week later, "Messrs Ives and Reynolds of the Reliance Motor Cycle Works, Addison" were in Hammondsport "concerning the consolidation and removal to Owego of the Reliance and Hercules works." At the end of July, Curtiss received a telegraphed order from San Francisco for five two-cylinder engines "to be used in a flying machine to enter the competition at the St. Louis Exposition. This is the largest C.O.D. order Mr. Curtiss has ever received" (*Hammondsport Herald*).

In September the *Herald* reported that Curtiss was building a motorcycle factory measuring 20 by 60 feet on "his residence property." A portion of the structure was to be two stories high. "It will be built with special reference to the requirements of his work, plenty of light being one of the principal advantages." They stated that orders for Hercules machines "continue to come in and the prospects for the future are very reassuring."

The *Automobile Review*, in reviewing the changes to the Curtiss motorcycles for 1904, noted "somewhat lower frames," shorter steering heads, and "a lower drop to the hanger." A second, lower top tube was added to the frame of the single-cylinder machine. The wheelbase on both one- and two-cylinder machines was 58 inches and the frame 22 inches tall. The one-cylinder engine, with its aluminum alloy crankcase "nicely scraped and polished," developed 2.5 horsepower at 3,500 rpm. The cylinder was cast "hard gray iron," and the cylinder head a "soft gray iron casting." The crankshaft was fitted with roller bearings, the other bearings being bronze. Drive to the rear wheel was via a 1.5-inch flat leather belt. The idler ran on a ball bearing. The engine was fitted with a throttle control on the carburetor and was fired by dry cells. The 120-pound motorcycle cost $210.

The 5-horsepower twin was "a most powerful road machine, and is the original double cylinder American machine," according to the *Automobile Review*. At 160 pounds and heavier than the single, the twin was "controlled as easily and can be run slower. The advantages claimed by the use of two cylinders are greater power for a given weight, absence of noise and vibration, and a greater range of speed on the direct drive," specifically 5 to 50 miles per hour with standard gearing. Stephen Wright notes in *The American Motorcycle* that Harry R. Geer in St. Louis, Missouri, sold the 1904 model 5-horsepower Curtis twin as the Geer "Green Egg" for $175.

1905 Model Year

In early January, the Curtiss company took part in the automobile show at Madison Square Garden. One of the two motorcycles displayed, still known as Hercules, was a 110-pound, two-cylinder racer demonstrating the efficiency with which the factory pared weight. The regular two-cylinder model, at 165 pounds, "also has had some 10 or 15 pounds of extraneous metal removed from it." Other changes for 1905 included cutting the frame height from 23 to 22 inches, a Breeze carburetor, "a considerably improved commutator," and "the first of the G. & J. detachable 2½ inch tires which have been turned out." It was claimed that the "roller bearings" had "given unstinted satisfaction" (*Bicycling World and Motocycle Review*, January 21, 1905).

Whatever the success of the Curtiss company in the spring of 1905, business was on a scale small enough to warrant Glenn Curtiss himself traveling to Albany to fix a motorcycle. His hometown newspaper reported that he "made a record trip . . . last week. He

Glenn Curtiss with his wife, Lena, on a two-cylinder Hercules. From the *Bicycling World and Motocycle Review*, October 15, 1904.

left home Tuesday night on his motorcycle, put in ten hours Wednesday in Albany, repairing and adjusting a motorcycle, and was home to begin work at seven o'clock Thursday morning."

Glenn Curtiss continued to participate in motorcycle competitions during the 1905 season. At the end of June, he had planned a Chicago trip to demonstrate one of his twins on the Fourth of July, when it was thought he might "enter one or more of the competitive races." A fellow contestant later recalled Curtiss's perfect score in a Federation of American Motorcyclists endurance run between New York and Waltham, Massachusetts, followed by a victory in a 25-mile road race on a two-cylinder machine, the only one in the race. At the state fair in Syracuse on September 18, six thousand people watched Curtiss "win everything and smash three world's records," his competitors "hopelessly out of the running."

According to Roseberry, representatives from other communities wooing Curtiss to move his factory raised local concern and resulted in the incorporation of the G. H. Curtiss Company on October 19, 1905, thus assuring the continued well-being of the motorcycle operation in its hometown. Capitalization was at $40,000, with $6,000 paid in. The certificate of incorporation notes the first-year directors and shareholders were Curtiss, Monroe Wheeler, G. Ray Hall, Lynn D. Masson, and Aaron G. Pratt. Four hundred shares of common stock, with a par value of fifty dollars each, were allotted to corporate president Curtiss, the other directors taking ten or fewer shares of preferred stock, also with a par value of fifty dollars. Llewellyn H. Brown, editor of the *Hammondsport Herald*, received five shares of preferred stock. Nine other local men also were shareholders. Soon it was announced that the Curtiss employment rolls would double—up to forty men. And the Curtiss company was to manufacture its own engines, displacing the Kirkham Motor Manufacturing Company in Bath.

1906 Model Year

In the fall of 1905, a new two-story, 20-by-50-foot building for the Curtiss Manufacturing Company neared completion, promising "nearly double the capacity of the plant." Calendar year 1905 ended with the Curtiss announcement that for the next season the price of its two-cylinder machine would be reduced by $25 to $275. The one-cylinder machine remained at $200. A Curtiss advertisement noted that "for 1906 all good features retained, others added."

A new trade journal, the *Motorcycle Illustrated*, observed that the machines were built "on the same graceful lines as in 1905" and so constructed that the one- and two-cylinder engines were interchangeable in any frame. There was a new "spring device" on the front fork, an option at extra cost, and a V-belt "copied after the most approved foreign designs, the top strand of which is composed of two thicknesses of mineral-tan leather."

Improvements to the two-cylinder motor included larger flywheels, wider connecting rod bearings, weight reduction, valve construction, and increased capacity. The roller bearings, "which have proved so successful in increasing the power by reducing the friction and permitting narrower bearings, are used on this year's machines." Also in the twin, a single gear, cam, and pushrods replaced five gears to operate the exhaust valves. In spite of the weight reduction of the engine to 55 pounds, the power was increased. The price of the engine alone was $150. The single-cylinder, 40-pound engine also saw improvements, including an increase in bore to 3.25 inches. Both motorcycles were fitted with a new, lighter coil and new carburetor. For fifty dollars, a Curtiss customer could have a sidecar with a two-bolt attachment to "any make of motorcycle" and an adjustable gauge "to fit wagon tracks on country roads." In early 1906, it was noted that the Curtiss Manufacturing Company employees were working thirteen-to-fifteen-hour days.

Glenn Curtiss continued to race his motorcycles during 1906. At Rochester, on the Fourth of July, Curtiss motorcycles "carried off their full share of prizes." Curtiss himself won the mile race, and Albert Cook of Hammondsport finished third. In the 5-mile race, Curtiss won by 300 yards. His hometown newspaper claimed that the Curtiss motorcycle had "demonstrated its ability to run rings around any of its competitors. The Indian was there in great force, with many machines and expert riders, but for accidents to the Curtiss machines they would not have been in the running." At the state fair in Syracuse later in the year, Curtiss established a new world record for a flat-track mile at a minute and one second.

1907 Model Year

On Friday evening, November 2, 1906, the directors of the G. H. Curtiss Manufacturing Company gathered at Hammondsport for the second annual meeting. The "regular dividend" was declared on the preferred stock. After one year in business, the Curtiss company had paid wages of $11,600. By mid-February 1907, there were forty men, "exclusive of the business office," at work.

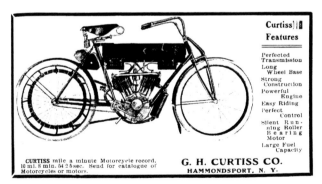

A 28-degree leather V-belt giving a single forward speed was the Curtiss "Perfected Transmission." The wheelbase was 58 inches, the horsepower rating 5, and the gasoline tank held two gallons. From *Cycle and Automobile Trade Journal*, May 1906.

The relative popularity of the Curtiss motorcycle, at least in Rhode Island in 1907, is indicated by a listing of the 407 motorcycles registered that year; there were six Curtiss riders, who rode the tenth-commonest machine. Among the agents for Curtiss machines in 1907, two were singled out in factory advertising. These were the New York distributor, Tiger Cycle Works at 782 Eighth Avenue, and the Whipple Cycle Company at 260 West Jackson Boulevard in Chicago. The former agency was operated by Harry Wehman, who maintained a close alliance with Curtiss. Larry M. Rinek, in his "Glenn H. Curtiss: An Early American Innovator in Aviation and Motorcycle Engines" (SAE Technical Paper 940571, 1994), has estimated that the Curtiss factory produced "500–600 motorcycle engines" for 1907.

In early October 1906 came news that the Curtiss facility was to be enlarged during the following winter and spring. In addition, Curtiss said he hoped to build one thousand motorcycles during the cold weather, keeping "a large force of men all winter." Six months later, the *Hammondsport Herald* reported that the Curtiss company had received a "large order . . . for double cylinder motors for the War Department." The Curtiss engine supposedly developed "a greater amount of power to the pound than any other known source of energy."

In February, the Curtiss Manufacturing Company was building a new machine shop, 20 by 75 feet, "in the rear of Mr. Curtiss's residence." By March it was reported that the Curtiss Manufacturing Company was building a 30-by-60-foot addition to its factory, which was operating twenty-four hours a day. In early February, the *Herald* reported that Curtiss had orders for seventy-five motorcycles to be delivered on April 1. Parts for four hundred machines were in process, "and there is little doubt that the demand will this spring greatly exceed the output." Most of the land on Curtiss's property had buildings on it.

For 1907, Curtiss motorcycles were little changed. The Curtiss company advertised "Increased power, reinforced fuel tanks, unbreakable handle bars, perfected valve-lifting mechanism, 30 degree [angle, changed from 45 degree] valve, hardened steel [instead of cast iron] pulley. Transmission can't be improved." Speeds of 60 and 45 miles per hour were claimed for the twin and single-cylinder machines, respectively.

Prices were $275 and $200. Extra equipment included spring forks, rear seat, combined luggage carrier, and stand, as well as a sidecar.

Of its motorcycles, the Curtiss Manufacturing Company said their aim was to build reliable, fast, powerful, strong, durable, and easy-riding machines. Of their frames, the Curtiss writers said their double top tube design had remained basically unchanged for five years. "We are always open for suggestions of improvements, but believe that our construction cannot be improved upon. The motor is in the only correct position, upright, and in front of the crank hanger."

Referring to the two-cylinder engine specifically, and the single by implication, the Curtiss company noted that "all parts are built to gauge and are interchangeable; the cylinders are ground to size, also the piston and rings; gears are hardened steel and designed for durability. The best materials, workmanship and methods are employed in the construction of Curtiss motors." A brochure titled "Achievement," probably printed in the second half of 1907, said that Curtiss "machines are especially adapted for the use of Police Departments, Collectors, Telephone Men, Mail Carriers and traveling men generally."

One each of the two Curtiss models was exhibited at the Grand Central Palace automobile show in Manhattan in early December 1906. There, Glenn Curtiss received an "armful" of orders for aircraft engines. An aviator of the period noted that "Curtiss could get twice as much money for an aeronautical engine as for a complete motorcycle." One aircraft engine developed in late 1906 was a V-eight model producing 40 horsepower. It was described as a thousand-dollar, 150-pound device with automatic intake valves and a hollow, 1.125-inch chromium nickel steel crankshaft, two carburetors, and a jump spark ignition system utilizing a distributor. With orders for two such power plants, Curtiss produced a third, which he installed in a special, shaft-driven motorcycle that he took to the Ormond Beach Speed Carnival in January 1907. On the hard sand, Curtiss rode a single-cylinder motorcycle three-fifths of a mile in a minute and five seconds. After setting a flying one-mile record of forty-six seconds with a two-cylinder motorcycle, he rode his eight-cylinder machine one mile in 26.4 seconds, or over 136 miles per hour. No man had ever traveled the earth as quickly.

On the Fourth of July, five factory employees raced Curtiss motorcycles at Penn Yan. Curtiss himself was in Clarinda, Iowa, assisting in a dirigible demonstration, and on at least three other occasions during the summer and fall was away from Hammondsport and his motorcycle manufacturing to work with aviators. Also in July for almost two weeks and in September and early October for over four weeks, Curtiss was at Cape Breton to assist Alexander Graham Bell with aircraft experiments.

1908 Model Year

Changes to the Curtiss motorcycles were few for 1908. Notable were an option for 26-inch-diameter wheels (instead of 28 inches), an oil gauge, a modification of the exhaust valve stem with the application of a hardened screw cap, double-grip control (doing away with a lever), a new style of muffler cutout on the single-cylinder machine, and enlarged rod bearings with a "hardened steel bushing . . . on the crank pin end." The cutout was moved to the muffler from the exhaust pipe, making for a quieter and safer arrangement in that "conflagrations are no longer possible in case the carburetter [sic] should leak or flood." Magneto ignition was made a forty-dollar option. And despite only minimal changes in construction, the power ratings of the two engines were revised upward to 3 and 6 horsepower, respectively. Glenn Curtiss was quoted as saying "the machines always were rated too low, anyway."

The lack of friction in its engines was a point pressed by the Curtiss company in its advertising. Of the roller bearing engines, it was said, "Like Tennyson's Brook, they go on forever." In the fall of 1907, there were several reports of the Curtiss company working on a two-speed gearing, but no two-speed transmission seems to have been advertised during the 1908 model year.

In November 1907, the Curtiss Manufacturing Company closed "for a few days for inventory." By early 1908, the Curtiss company, in the substantially enlarged factory, was operating twenty-two hours a day—a schedule maintained until July, when the night shift was "discontinued for the summer." Compared to other motorcycle builders, the Curtiss company produced many more of the components utilized in its products; frame lugs, crank hangers, carburetors, handlebars, belts, tool bags, battery boxes, and gasoline and oil tanks were all fabricated in Hammondsport. Within the 25,000 square feet of the operating room was a separate machine shop housing fifteen lathes, work benches, a drill press, a milling machine, and a planer. Forging and brazing operations were performed in a dedicated second building, while nickel plating and enameling were done in the main structure. Capacity for the operation was eight motorcycles a day. Figuring eight machines a day for three hundred workdays gives one an idea of the potential production for a model year in the vicinity of 2,400 motorcycles. It's likely that the actual figure for 1908 was considerably less.

One Curtiss rider in Milwaukee, Wisconsin, was Joseph Eckman. He told *Motorcycle Illustrated* in January 1908 that he had ridden a Curtiss motorcycle for two years. While he had sold that cycle, he intended to buy a new one in the spring, "as I consider them superior to any American-made machine. It is the most foreignized of any."

Glenn Curtiss busied himself with aircraft and flying during the 1908 motorcycle model year. As director of the Aerial Experiment Association organized with Bell and others interested in experimental flight, Curtiss built his first complete, heavier-than-air flying machines in Hammondsport. The Curtiss-powered Red Wing flew for the first time on March 12, 1908, thus beginning a new phase in Curtiss's professional life and the future for the Curtiss Manufacturing Company. Flights of other AEA-sponsored heavier-than-air craft, such as the White Wing and June Bug, followed. A July test of the June Bug won Curtiss the Scientific American trophy for a kilometer of flight.

Glenn Curtiss's motorcycle-building employees were now also working with aircraft. In July, the *Hammondsport Herald* identified Jay Safford and Tod Shriver as "members of Capt. Thomas Scott Baldwin's staff." Albert Cook, the superintendent of motorcycle construction at the Curtiss company, spent a week working "for the government on a balloon engine" in St. Joseph, Missouri, in September 1908, then went on to Girard, Kansas, to "work on a flying machine for Mr. Call," an inventor who sought to combine air, land, and water travel in one vehicle. During the summer, Cook also assisted Charles O. Jones of Hammondsport with his dirigible at Palisades Park in New Jersey.

1909 Model Year

Notwithstanding the myriad aviation pursuits in 1908, new motorcycle models marked the 1909 season for the Curtiss Manufacturing Company. An innovative three-cylinder engine developed 10 horsepower, while an optional low frame called the "Wehman" featured slightly more powerful and expensive single and twin engines (also available at extra cost on the older-style, taller frame). In all, said *Motorcycle Illustrated*, there were five Curtiss models—two singles, two twins, and the triple—for 1909, ranging in price from $200 for a 3-horsepower single to $350 for the triple.

The three-cylinder engine was constructed as a wide twin with two cylinders split vertically by a third at 50 degrees from the other two. Two carburetors were employed. Otherwise, the engine was similar to standard Curtiss motors of the period, with roller bearings, atmospheric intake valves, and separate heads. The Curtiss company claimed a top speed of 90 miles per hour for the 175-pound machine. But, a few years later, a trade press writer noted that one carburetor fed two cylinders and the other only one on the Curtiss three-cylinder motor, which needed "three revolutions . . . to fire all the cylinders in succession. It was not as successful as its designers wished, and was discontinued" (Leon Gibson, *Motorcycle Illustrated*, January 9, 1913).

The Wehman frame, merely 17 inches tall, was notable for employing only a single top tube. The absence of a second tube was reportedly ameliorated by reinforcement at the head as well as a "heavier main tube and a rigid truss fork. A new cushion device, however, is supplied as an option" (*Bicycling World and Motorcycle Review*, January 23, 1909). The Wehman frame was designed by Harry Wehman, a Curtiss motorcycle dealer in Brooklyn and "an uncommonly skillful motorcycle physician . . . called for consultation in a number of difficult cases" (*Bicycling World*, December 5, 1908). Curtiss advertising for 1909 emphasized record-setting performances of previous models as well as such venerable Curtiss features as the "trussed frame and fork," "upright motor position," "roller bearing engines," pioneering "double bar frame," "stripped [of cooling fins] cylinders," "long wheel base," "V-belt," and "numerous other so-called 'new' features which we have used for years."

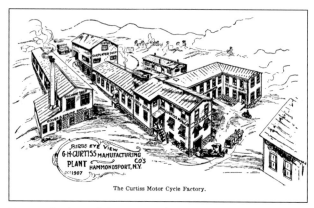

Vineyards abutted the Curtiss factory in the grape-growing area of Steuben County. From *Cycle and Automobile Trade Journal*, March 1908.

In early 1909, the Curtiss Manufacturing Company advertised that it had a distributor on the "Pacific Coast," George A. Faulkner in Oakland, as well as one for "New York and Long Island," the Wehman's Curtiss Motorcycle Company at 1203 Bedford Street in Brooklyn. Faulkner had been "one of the Curtiss company's best agents," ordering over two hundred motorcycles in the year ending in October 1908. Rinek, in his "Glenn H. Curtiss: An Early American Innovator in Aviation and Motorcycle Engines," has estimated "1000 motorcycles, about the same as Harley-Davidson" for 1909.

At a meeting of the Curtiss stockholders and directors on January 6, 1909, Curtiss was elected president and manager; Linn D. Masson, secretary and treasurer. The new directors were Monroe Wheeler, Thomas S. Baldwin, C. Leonard Waters, Masson, and Curtiss. Curtiss's longtime friend Waters, it should be noted, was in the motorcycle business, operating the Motorcycle Equipment and Supply Company (q.v.), which built and distributed the Erie motorcycle in Hammondsport.

In March 1909, a new firm succeeded the G. H. Curtiss Manufacturing Company. The Herring-Curtiss Company plainly focused on aircraft, although the manufacture of Curtiss motorcycles continued. Unfortunately, the partnership between Augustus M. Herring and Glenn Curtiss floundered, with disastrous results for the corporation. Herring was a figure involved with aerial experiments since the 1890s. To the new company Herring brought several aeronautical patents, as well as a contract from the United States Army for an airplane utilizing those patents. Curtiss contributed his G. H. Curtiss Manufacturing Company name and assets. Capital stock for the new corporation was $360,000—half preferred, and half common. By April 15, a certificate of payment of the capital stock was signed, indicating that $600 was paid in cash and $359,400 in property. Officers included Monroe Wheeler, president; Herring and Curtiss, vice presidents; and Masson, secretary.

On March 9, Curtiss noted that the consolidation was only for the "development and manufacture of aeroplanes." "It will in no way affect the Curtiss company's motorcycle industry," he said, "which will be continued under the same management and plans as heretofore" (*Hammondsport Herald*). In forming the Herring-Curtiss Company, Curtiss reported for Herring that during the calendar year 1909 he planned to build one thousand motorcycles as well as up to one hundred aircraft engines and ten airplanes. He added, "The Curtiss company's motorcycle business not only earns handsome profits now but is bound to grow. Our old agents are doubling their orders and, with several thousand machines on the road, the 'small parts and repair department' is showing a good profit."

In the summer of 1909, Glenn Curtiss became a director of the new Marvel Motorcycle Company, an enterprise managed by Leonard Waters. The new corporation, capitalized at $50,000, purchased a plot of land adjacent to the Herring-Curtiss factory in order to build its own production facility. Marvel motorcycles were to be powered by Curtiss engines. The Herring-Curtiss Company agreed to supply five hundred motors for the 1910 season, although it was later reported that the Marvel company began building its own Curtiss engines in December 1909.

Whatever the condition of his businesses in Hammondsport, Glenn Curtiss was away much of the time—involved in experimenting, flying, or helping other aviators. The climax of the Curtiss flying year may have been Curtiss's August trip to France, where, sponsored by the Aero Club of America, he flew in competition. Winner of the Gordon Bennett Trophy at Reims, Curtiss became "Champion Aviator of the World." Returning to Hammondsport, Curtiss was treated to a parade, fireworks, speeches, and a gold medal from his fellow Hammondsport residents. The motorcycle business must have seemed a small matter.

1910 Model Year

In the late fall, *Motorcycle Illustrated* said that during the calendar year 1909, the Herring-Curtiss Company completed two new concrete buildings: one 110 by 60 feet and the other 65 by 35 feet. Both were two stories high and to be used "exclusively for motorcycle manufacture." Also in the late fall, Herring-Curtiss installed a 100-horsepower, 18,000-pound boiler.

The company itself, as it was about to announce its 1910 models, was "making a splendid record in the motorcycle business and, although they are continually going ahead, they have refrained from splurging." Riders of the new machines were advised to "expect something . . . of a progressive nature."

The innovation that followed was an offset-cylinder design. This offset from the crankshaft was intended to lessen the side thrust of the piston "when the pressure within the cylinder is greatest"—on the downward, combustion stroke. The result was a reported increase in power as well as a decrease in cylinder wear and knocking.

The Herring-Curtiss Company simplified its motorcycle line for 1910. The three-cylinder was gone. Frames may have been limited to the 17-inch Wehman design. Despite extensive Curtiss involvement with aviation, the motorcycle engine design was extensively altered; one observer claimed it was "new throughout." New in addition to the crankshaft being offset was an automatic oil feed to the engine; a float valve in the crankcase maintained the requisite oil level for the splash lubrication system.

Other engine features of note were the revised 18-pound flywheels "with most of the weight in the rims—easy starting, no vibration"; the roller bearings; the hemispherical combustion chamber; and the overhead, 1.6875-inch-diameter valves actuated by a single pushrod and double arm rocker per cylinder.

The Herring-Curtiss catalog said the Curtiss was a "Machine That Has No Equal," being "A Powerful Combination of Scientific Principles worked out to the Highest Degree of Mechanical Perfection."

Unhappily, within a few months of the organization of the Herring-Curtiss Company, Glenn Curtiss realized that Herring had little to offer the corporation. In brief, Herring was a fraud who had no patents or any other assets. In the fall of 1909, the Glenn Curtiss–Augustus Herring relationship became completely adversarial. Business fell off, and Roseberry claims that in early 1910 Curtiss was using personal funds to pay his employees. Corporate bankruptcy soon followed, viewed favorably by the Curtiss faction as a means for being rid of Herring. Curtiss and his allies, meanwhile, assured their dealers that they intended to supply motorcycles and parts "through the parties who buy in the business at the bankrupt sale."

At the beginning of March, the Herring-Curtiss factory was closed for three days for inventory, with operations resuming on March 7. At that point, the *Hammondsport Herald* thought "the Curtiss motorcycle was never so popular as now." At the end of the month, eighty to ninety men were still at work, with a payroll "not yet . . . less than $1,100 per week." Editor Lewellyn Brown thought that Glenn Curtiss might "yet realize his ambition of building up an ideal motorcycle and flying machine plant in this community."

But by mid-June 1910, the situation appeared bleak, with "little chance for the Curtiss plant being opened as a motorcycle factory." The receiver, Gilbert Parkhurst, was "making up whatever stock is on hand." *Motorcycling* expected the plant to be sold when that work was finished. Were the Herring interests to acquire the Herring-Curtiss assets, there would be no motorcycle production. And if Curtiss were to prevail, he supposedly was "so absorbed in aeroplane work that he will not care to make the investment required to regain the motorcycle plant. And there is no sign of any public spirit in Hammondsport requisite to the formation of a syndicate to buy in the plant to keep the business there. Thus it seems likely that the machinery will be disposed of piecemeal, and the Curtiss plant will cease to exist" (*Motorcycling*, June 16, 1910).

In May 1910, Glenn Curtiss's fame broadened, and he won $10,000 by being the first flyer to go from Albany to New York City. Departing from an island in the Hudson, Curtiss made 137 miles in two hours and thirty-two minutes, beating the fastest railroad time. Yet in August, according to Curtiss's assistant, Jerome Fanciulli, the aviator wanted to retire from demonstration flights and concentrate on aircraft development and manufacture. At that time, Curtiss reportedly was building ten airplanes in Hammondsport despite his difficult situation.

1911 Model Year

During much of 1910, the Herring-Curtiss Company was in receivership. Production declined. In the fall the company was declared bankrupt, and in the winter the plant closed, "the greater number of the men being permanently laid off. A few men and a portion of the office force remain to take care of the mail orders that come in" (*Hammondsport Herald*, February 8, 1911).

Meanwhile, the Curtiss Aeroplane Company was incorporated. Capitalized at $20,000, its shareholders were Glenn Curtiss (195 of 200 common shares), his wife, and their Hammondsport allies G. Ray Hall and Monroe M. Wheeler. Another incorporation, that of the Curtiss Exhibition Company, had occurred in September. Organized to promote flying demonstrations and sell airplanes for exhibition use, the company had capital stock of $20,000. Directors were Curtiss, Wheeler, and Fanciulli.

Legal maneuvering over the remains of the Herring-Curtiss assets began in December, with Herring seeking to have Curtiss's earnings as an exhibition and competitive flyer added to the mix. A sale was advertised for February 11, 1911, when Curtiss's attorney, Monroe Wheeler, made an apparent winning bid of $18,418.75 and announced that the "Curtiss Manufacturing Company" would be organized "at once, for the manufacture of motors and motorcycles, and business will be resumed as soon as possible." This new entity would join the Curtiss Aeroplane and Curtiss Exhibition Companies. The *Hammondsport Herald* thought that together the three organizations, if successful, would "result in a business boom for the [Hammondsport] place." In the meantime, it was reported that the Curtiss Aeroplane Company would supply motorcycle parts while the Marvel company was building Curtiss engines and turning out Marvel motorcycles.

The results of the first auction having been aborted, in April 1911, Wheeler, acting for Curtiss, purchased at bankruptcy sale the assets of the Curtiss-Herring Company for $25,100. A major portion of the sum, $16,000 plus interest, was a mortgage held by Glenn Curtiss, so that only about $9,000 remained to be divided among creditors. When Curtiss returned to Hammondsport on April 17, he said he hoped to have the shops, in the *Herald*'s words, "running at full capacity upon aeroplanes and aeroplane motors." He mentioned building a 60-miles-per-hour speedboat but apparently said nothing about motorcycles. Still, the bankruptcy proceedings continued.

Whatever its official parent organization, by late spring of 1911, the presumably unincorporated Curtiss Motorcycle Company was advertising Curtiss motorcycles anew. A catalog including such accessories as a sidecar and tandem seating arrangement appeared by early June. A few months later, *Motorcycling* reported that the Curtiss Motorcycle Company had been "organized to make into complete for marketing the parts which fell to Glenn Curtiss when he bought the ex-Herring-Curtiss factory at public sale."

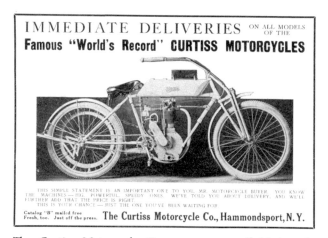

The Curtiss Motorcycle Company, an unofficial branch of the newly organized Curtiss Manufacturing Company, in 1911 offered this Wehman-frame model at $225. From *Motorcycling*, May 11, 1911.

That motorcycles were manufactured for the 1911 model year seems, at the vantage of over a century, remarkable. Glenn Curtiss in 1910 and 1911 had come to embody the spirit of aviation. Away from Hammondsport as much as he was at home, Curtiss was experimenting with new aircraft or flying demonstrations—earning fame and large sums of money in the process. Meanwhile, his work at Hammondsport had spawned a number of separate aviation enterprises, including that of his erstwhile colleague Charles Kirkham. That Glenn Curtiss accomplished so much in such a short period of time after beginning his bicycle business in Hammondsport is astounding. That he eventually abandoned motorcycles is understandable.

A surviving Curtiss Motorcycle Company catalog of the post-Herring period shows only one-cylinder machines available as the double-top-tube Cook model or the shorter Wehman style, both with mechanical inlet valves, i.e., the engine introduced for the 1910 models. The third offering for 1911 was the Model O, which had the old-style atmospheric inlet valve. In brief, the motorcycles were identical to the final offerings of the Herring-Curtiss Company, given the omission of the two-cylinder engine. Prices ranged from $175 for a battery-ignition Model O to $225 for either of the other models with magneto ignition. Spring forks and stands were included in the basic prices. Extra-cost accessories included a rear seat ($12), sidecar or parcel-delivery attachment (each $50), Eclipse free engine pulley ($15), and N.S.U. two-speed gearing ($40). Curtiss advertising for the 1911 models emphasized the design and power of the overhead valve engine—understandable given the lack of other changes in chassis or transmission for several years.

1912 Model Year

In October 1911 came a report of a merger between the Marvel and the Curtiss motorcycle companies, the former a "wide awake concern of which C. L. Waters is the leading spirit," taking over the assets of the latter. *Motorcycling* noted that it was "understood that the interests controlling both concerns were identical, anyway." Two weeks later, Waters reported continuing negotiations that "might not eventuate for two or three weeks, when 1912 prices will be announced." Meanwhile, the Marvel company continued to build and ship its own machines, while at the Curtiss factories, Harry Wehman, abandoning his Brooklyn motorcycle agency, arrived in Hammondsport to become "the office man" in a factory "devoted mainly to the production of aeroplanes." The proposed consolidation of motorcycle builders apparently was abandoned as Glenn Curtiss reorganized his companies. The Marvel company soon suspended production.

On December 19, 1911, the Curtiss Motor Company was incorporated to manufacture motorcycles, motors, motor vehicles, and engines for aircraft. In contrast to the capitalization of the Aeroplane Company at $20,000 and starting capital of $1,000, the Curtiss Motor Company had capital stock of $600,000, half of which was Curtiss's, and starting capital of $5,000. The initial directors and share subscribers for the Curtiss Motor Company were Wheeler, Fanciulli, Hall, Samuel D. French, and Philip B. Sawyer, an Elmira lawyer. Curtiss was not among them, but the *Hammondsport Herald* described the new Curtiss concern as a "large holding company for the several subsidiary companies under which Mr. Curtiss has carried on his extensive business . . . in aeronautical lines." To the new entity Curtiss "turns over . . . all his rights and holdings in the Curtiss Aviation School; the Curtiss Motor Company; *the Curtiss Motorcycle Company*; the factory and plant at Hammondsport, all patents secured and pending, contracts, good will, etc." (emphasis added). Glenn Curtiss was chosen as president of the company. By November 1912, the Curtiss Motor Company was able to file a Certificate of Payment of Half of the Capital Stock, signed by Curtiss as president, Hall as secretary-treasurer, and Wheeler. Cash and "good accounts receivable" amounted to $5,247.64, while "property purchased"—i.e., the assets of the Curtiss companies (including motorcycle materials)—totaled $294,752.40.

In late 1911, Hall, identified as manager for the Curtiss Motorcycle Company, said, "We have been so busy getting the aeroplane business organized that our motorcycle business for next season is not as far along as it should be. . . . In another month we will be under way. We will probably make some machines, but haven't decided yet how many. It will depend upon how things open up." When asked about a new 1912 model, Hall replied, "There will be no material change in our 1912 model. . . . We will elaborate the details of our 1911 machines considerably, but there will be nothing radically new in our next season's output, as no special changes in design have been found necessary."

After a final display in 1910, no Curtiss motorcycles appeared at the Madison Square Garden automobile (and cycle) shows of 1911 and 1912. However, one or more Curtiss motorcycles were at the Binghamton motor vehicle show in February 1912. Charles H. Wakeman, apparently the local dealer, was "present with that development from the early days of the motorcycles, the Curtiss." The reference to an antiquated design strikes the reader as a less-than-subtle indication of the unchanging Curtiss design.

1913 Model Year

On January 18, 1913, the annual meetings of the Curtiss Exhibition Company, the Curtiss Aeroplane Company, and the Curtiss Motor Company took place in Hammondsport. Glenn Curtiss was made general manager of all. The *Hammondsport Herald* in its report made no mention of the Curtiss Motorcycle Company, suggesting anew that the agency was a concept created in the aftermath of the Herring-Curtiss debacle solely to market motorcycles.

That there were no 1913 Curtiss motorcycles is suggested by a series of advertisements in the Hammondsport newspaper. In February and March, John A. Osborne declared that he had agencies for Thor, Yale, Excelsior, Henderson, Eagle, "or any motorcycle on the market." Conspicuously missing are Curtiss motorcycles, although in the same period Osborne elsewhere advertised two used Curtiss machines.

In the fall of 1913, the Curtiss Motorcycle Company advertised that it was selling its "complete stock of motorcycle parts, including designs, jigs, tools, good will, etc.," since the "rapid increase of our aeronautical business . . . requires our entire room and attention." In effect, the story of the Curtiss motorcycles came to an end. Glenn Curtiss's friend and colleague Harry Genung said, "We had a front-row seat in the motorcycle business when aviation came along and pushed the business out the back door" (qtd. in Roseberry, *Glenn Curtiss: Pioneer of Flight*).

The record-setting, eight-cylinder Curtiss motorcycle survives in the collections of the Smithsonian Institution. The Glenn H. Curtiss Museum in Hammondsport has a Hercules and several Curtiss motorcycles. Additional Curtiss machines remain in private hands.

Cycle Creations
Mineola
1994–2007

Dave Biagi and Eric Wolke were the partners in an enterprise at 133 East Jericho Turnpike, which as of August 2000 had built "thirty or thirty-five" custom motorcycles from the ground up over a six-year period. Biagi reported all were Harley-Davidson-based except for one machine, which used a Kawasaki Vulcan engine. The Cycle Creations shop, which employed two other people, also sold parts and repaired motorcycles. Their specialty was "Harley-Davidson and other American-made V-twin motorcycles," and the company advertised, "We can turn your dreams of owning an eye-catching custom bike into a reality."

Cyclemotor Corporation
Rochester
1915–24
G.R.S. Products Inc.
Menands
1924–26
Morley Machinery Corporation
Rochester
1926–47
Trade Names: **Cyclemotor**; **Evans Power Cycle**

1916 Model Year

The Cyclemotor made its American debut in the late summer of 1915 at the Rochester Industrial Exposition. Although the examples displayed came from a Canadian manufacturer—the John T. Wilson Limited company—local production was pending by the Cyclemotor Corporation. Manufacture of the Wilson Cyclemotor, reportedly underway for a year already, was to continue in Toronto.

The Cyclemotor was the brainchild of Canadian Douglas G. Anderson (1887–?) and American Leigh R. Evans (1885–?), according to Evans. Both were employed, as manager and chief engineer, respectively, by the Russell Motor Car Company of Toronto when "each began to think of the possibilities of a motor attachment for the bicycle." Evans, according to W. H. Parsons of *Motorcycle and Bicycle Illustrated* in 1922, was "convinced of the practical advantages of combining the two stroke and high speed principles in a small motor that would have sufficient power to propel a bicycle in the neighborhood of 20 miles an hour and still be light and compact."

Evans, a Pennsylvania native with extensive automotive engineering experience, claimed that the potential for the Cyclemotor in Canada was limited by its small population. So he and Anderson, "through their acquaintance with the directors of the General Railway Signal Co. . . . were induced to locate in Rochester," occupying a portion of the G.R.S. factory from 1915 to 1918.

The original Cyclemotor fitted to an ordinary bicycle. The fuel tank hangs from the top tube. From *Motorcycling and Bicycling*, November 8, 1915.

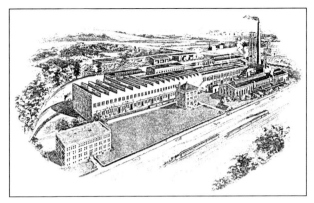

The General Railway Signal plant, where Cyclemotor production began in Rochester. From *Motorcycling and Bicycling*, November 23, 1915.

The Cady Street, Rochester, Cyclemotor factory. From *Motorcycling and Bicycling*, December 24, 1919.

As introduced in Rochester, the Cyclemotor was a two-stroke, 5.5-cubic-inch (91-cubic-centimeter) engine, developing 1 horsepower. Its top speed in a factory test was 33 miles per hour at 4,200 rpm, although the engine was sold to provide a normal 20-miles-per-hour cruising speed at 2,700 rpm. The 20-pound kit powered a bicycle via a chain-driven countershaft and a leather belt to a pulley on the rear wheel. A single lever and cable provided the only operator adjustment, effecting spark at the magneto and a compression relief for "starting and stopping." Installation, including tank, transmission, and control, was said to take one hour. The price was fifty-five dollars FOB (seventy dollars in Canada).

As organized, the Cyclemotor Corporation was a child of General Railway Signal Company officials. The three subscribers to Cyclemotor stock were Wilmer Wesley Salmon, G.R.S. president; John F. Braam, assistant secretary and treasurer; and Lyman E. Dodge, a G.R.S. patent attorney. The certificate of incorporation, filed on September 2, 1915, at the Office of the Secretary of State in Albany, notes capitalization of $500,000. The corporation began business, however, with working capital of $500. Officers of the new company were Douglas Anderson as president and general manager, Leigh Evans as chief engineer, and J. Arthur Fish as sales manager.

An early advertisement depicted the General Railway Signal Company factory on West Avenue at Buell Avenue along the main line of the New York Central Railroad. The text accompanying this Cyclemotor advertisement claimed the plant was "one of the largest and most completely equipped factories in the world." This Cyclemotor resource thus assured potential sellers "guaranteed exact deliveries covering any period desired during the entire year." A handbill claimed the factory had been established in 1904 and employed "more than one thousand skilled workmen." While initial production took place in the G.R.S. factory, Cyclemotor offices were in the Arlington Building in Rochester.

In September 1915, the Cyclemotor made its first appearance at a motorcycle show, a major exposition in Chicago. There, Fish was heard to say that the Cyclemotor Corporation had a capacity of fifteen thousand engines for the coming season; that there was a year and a half of manufacturing history in Toronto; and that production had been added at Rochester. A few weeks later, at least seven bicycles fitted with Cyclemotors were on display in New York City at the other leading show.

Full-page advertisements in both *Motorcycle Illustrated* and *Motorcycling and Bicycling* in September 1915 brought the Cyclemotor to the notice of the wider cycle trade. The slogan "One Horsepower for Every Wheel" in the advertisement was soon dropped in favor of "Wheeling Without Work," which became part of the Cyclemotor logo, the words appearing in the tail of the initial C.

The G.R.S. Products Company plant on Broadway in Menands, where the last Evans Power Cycles were built. From *Motorcycling and Bicycling*, April 2, 1924.

In the late fall of 1915, Burt L. Madden "of the Toronto office of the Cycle Motor Co." had moved to Rochester to work in the engineering department of the Cyclemotor Corporation. "Pressure of business in this country compelled the change." A few weeks later, Earl R. Perrin, who had been associated with the advertising department of the Taylor Instrument Company in Rochester, moved to the Cyclemotor Corporation to handle publicity.

Interest abroad in the Cyclemotor brought an order from Holland for 250 engines in the winter of 1916. Orders also came from the Hawaiian Islands, Cuba, Russia, and Spain. Requests for information reportedly had come from "every foreign and South American country"—this despite the company focusing on domestic business.

In the early spring, several changes were made to the Cyclemotor engine. Among the innovations was the adoption of die-cast aluminum for the crankcase, carburetor, and handlebar control. The fuel tank became "torpedo-shaped," while the crankshaft was bored to obtain better lubrication of the main bearing. Small changes were made, as well, to the control cable, the magneto, the drive pulley, the rear wheel pulley, and the flywheel, which was beveled "to improve its appearance." Beautification also came from "a cleaner appearance" overall due to "the installation of costly machines in the factory at Rochester and the branch at Toronto." The supplier of the cast aluminum-copper alloy parts, including the crankcase and carburetor body, was the Doehler Die-Casting Company of Brooklyn.

Cyclemotor advertising for 1916 appeared in such diverse journals as *Successful Farming*, *Farm Journal*, *Popular Mechanics*, *Popular Science*, and *American Boy*. As was customary in many fields, Cyclemotor utilized testimonial letters from dealers and riders. Among the latter were Edgar Wobig in Lincoln, Nebraska, who said he "wouldn't take a profit of ten dollars for my motor now"; salesman R. K. Kirby, who could "conserve about 2 hours' time daily for my other work"; and J. O. Metcalf in Daviess County, Missouri, whose machine was "the talk of the vicinity." He particularly liked the way he could ford a stream: "I picked up this outfit and walked right across. A motorcycle could never have been carried over it." Happy dealers were Snyder and Martin in Washington, Pennsylvania, who, in requesting their "next shipment" ("Send by EXPRESS. RUSH! RUSH!"), said, "The boys are all talking about them."

For riders, the Cyclemotor Corporation said its product was to be the link between bicycling and motorcycling, combining "THE ADVANTAGES AND CONVENIENCES OF BOTH and appeals to a larger class of riders." As with a bicycle, the lightweight machine could be taken into the house at night. And should the fuel give out, the rider could "pedal home just as easily as though there were no Cyclemotor attached."

1917 Model Year

Although in the summer of 1917 the complete motor bicycle known as the Evans Power Cycle joined the Cyclemotor line, for most of 1917 the Cyclemotor "Wheeling without Work" line consisted of the bicycle engine in two versions: one for bicycle frames with a single top tube, and a new style for the double-bar design. In the former Cyclemotor the fuel tank was suspended from the tube, while in the latter the tank was mounted between the tubes. The price for either was fifty-five dollars.

New for 1917 were a strainer in the fuel line and a carburetor valve utilizing a steel ball instead of a needle. Other improvements for 1917 included a crank forged by a new means, providing a 50 percent increase in strength; bronze main bearings replacing babbitt; grooves on the interior of the crankcase to direct oil to the main bearings; a "locking device" to keep the drive pulley attached to the shaft; a higher-speed magneto; a newly designed control cable for smoother action; a priming device on the carburetor; and a stronger idler pulley.

A *Motorcycle Illustrated* writer thought the Cyclemotor's fixed throttle and adjustable spark did away in "one fell stroke with the chief argument advanced against the employment of the two stroke motor on variable speed work . . . that a special carburetor is needed in order to provide a proper mixture at all speeds of the motor." With the Cyclemotor, "four-cycling" and "other irregularities" were eliminated. A single lever still controlled the engine by advancing or retarding the spark and relieving compression.

Motorcycling and Bicycling published an article by Cyclemotor sales representative Oliver W. Adams entitled "A Little Two-Cycle Dope" in the April 23, 1917, issue. In it, Adams claimed that a two-cycle engine, "on account of its simplicity, is the easiest engine to build, but is the hardest engine to build right" due to the need for precise engineering and machining. Unfortunately, he continued, mechanics used to four-stroke engines put their experience to bad use when encountering two-stroke machines. This had resulted in unwarranted prejudice against an engine style that produced more power for its weight and size.

At the Chicago cycle show in the Coliseum in November 1916, A. G. Kolkewyn (sometimes written "Koldewin"), general manager of the N. V. Algemeene Motoren Import Company in Apeldoorn, Netherlands, contracted to buy 1,500 Cyclemotor units. Kolkewyn said, "We have a level country and good roads and for this reason the big heavyweights do not appeal to our people." At the New York cycle show in December 1916, Adams claimed every 1917 engine was more powerful than any built for the previous season. At the show, Adams had a sales pitch "that can't be beat." As paraphrased by *Motorcycling and Bicycling*, Adam's argument was as follows:

> Take a look at the Cyclemotor. It's made at Rochester. You can turn your bicycle into a motorcycle in two jerks of a lamb's tail. All you need is a screw driver, a small wrench and a pint of gasoline. Clamp the pulley on the rear wheel of your bicycle, fasten the motor in the frame, spill the gas in the tank and away you go.

At the end of January 1917, the Cyclemotor Corporation produced the first of a projected series of eight three-color brochures to be mailed to ten thousand American motorcycle and bicycle dealers. A description of the Cyclemotor operation at the beginning of 1917 noted the installation of $75,000 worth of new machinery in the past six months, increasing capacity from about twenty-five units per day to between 100 and 150. A high-quality level in the production of Cyclemotors was achieved by "block-testing." This two-stage process assured low internal friction when the engines were started. In the first step, each of fifty belt-driven motors turn backward so "that the bearing pressures, pull on the driving chain and other internal forces shall be in the same direction as when the motor is operating normally." From the belting operation, which smoothed the rough spots "not visible to the naked eye and which cannot be detected with delicate measuring instruments," the engines moved to the second step in the testing process, running on their own—some "for hours at a stretch"—to assure defect-free operation. A Cyclemotor handbill claims each engine was belt-driven for ten hours "at high speed" and then run on its own for forty-five minutes "with full load," supposedly equivalent to 12 miles at 16 miles per hour.

With G.R.S. needing more space in its factory due to World War I demands, both Cyclemotor production and offices moved to a building at 149 Cady Street. This was a flat-roofed, two-story frame structure, which earlier had housed the Empire Pipe and Blower Company. Set back from the street, the plant also had frontage on Heisel Alley. In the spring of 1916, the Cyclemotor Corporation had begun to double the size of the building by adding an ell that stretched across the double lot behind the house at 151 Cady. The enlargement, the Cyclemotor Corporation explained, had been made necessary by a demand that had not allowed production to keep up with orders.

Manufacture in 1917 was probably still entirely at the General Railway Signal plant, even as the office staff numbers quadrupled to sixteen, resulting in a move from the Arlington Building to "quarters about four times as large over on Cady st." The sales staff were knowledgeable because, according to Anderson, "we are taking young men just out of college and putting them through the factory for a course of training. When they come out they can build a cyclemotor from A to Z and they can sell them because they will know what they are talking about." Of the engine, Evans said, "We started in to make a motor that would develop one man power and found we had made one that developed one horsepower."

In February 1917, Augustus "Gus" C. Rice (1886–?) became sales manager of the Cyclemotor Corporation, severing longtime employment with the Eclipse Machine Company in Elmira. *Motorcycling and Bicycling* said Rice was "one of the livest wires in the trade" as well as "one of those likable, refined chaps who always does credit to himself and the industry."

Cyclemotor trade journal advertising early in the 1917 model year emphasized the desirability of the product line to potential dealers. Cyclemotor territory could double a dealer's profits, enabling him to "re-sell many of your old bicycle customers and a large percentage of new bicycle purchasers." While the Cyclemotor was the "greatest value ever given to the riding public," the dealer "gets exceptionally liberal discounts." The dealer handling the Cyclemotor would "get a greater per cent of return from his capital invested than he can on any other cycle attachment or motorcycle." Adding a Cyclemotor dealership to a bicycle shop required no more floor space. "Sell Cyclemotor and Bicycle as a combination and get two profits."

In May, the Cyclemotor Corporation announced a price increase to sixty dollars, effective June 1. The rising costs of materials and manufacture were given as reasons for the raise. On the other hand, larger discounts to dealers were to give them a "substantial [13 percent] increase in percentage of profits." "Exclusive Selling Rights" in sales territories were valuable, the Cyclemotor Corporation maintained, since the engine had no "real competitors at its price or any other price!"

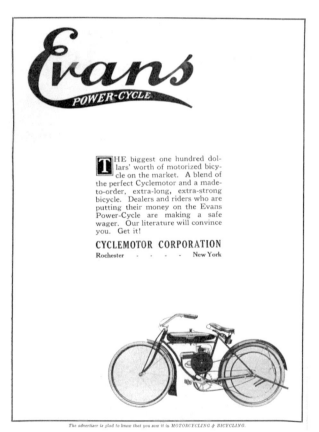

The first-generation Evans Power-Cycle, "the biggest one hundred dollars' worth of motorized bicycle on the market." Advertisement from *Motorcycling and Bicycling*, April 6, 1918.

Foreign sellers included the Marushi Shokai Company in Yokohama, which ordered one hundred units in December 1916 and again in January 1917. In August, Marushi Shokai ordered two hundred Cyclemotors and fifty Evans Power Cycles. Other winter sales included ten Cyclemotors to P. Anderson in Aalestrup, Denmark, and twenty-five to N. V. Algenillne (*sic*) Motoren Import Company in Batavia, Java. Other summer shipments included twenty-five machines to Australia and twenty-one Cyclemotors attached to Emblem bicycles sent to Colombia. Rice noted that shipping was easier for Cyclemotor than for some other manufacturers since the "neat compact cases in which we ship our machines . . . require the minimum space on steamships. Our best foreign business is naturally the Cyclemotor attachment for bicycles."

In the winter of 1917, Sam Bulley, an employee of the Planet Bicycle Works in Toronto, fabricated a bicycle frame specifically intended for Cyclemotor use. With strengthened head, heavier tubing, and wider rear fork, the bicycle reportedly had "shown well in numerous trials." How this experiment affected the development of the Evans Power Cycle remains to be determined. In any case, the Evans was announced in the early summer of 1917. The 65-pound machine combined a Cyclemotor engine with a bicycle-style frame to produce a 25-miles-per-hour motorcycle. It was named for Leigh Evans, the Cyclemotor engineer to whom design of the motorcycle was credited. Rice said that with the Evans, "we have finally struck the right note." The Evans appealed to a "wider field" than the Cyclemotor alone. "We are satisfied that what the American public wants is a machine all ready to go." In addition, the Cyclemotor people, he claimed, were "better qualified to pick out the right type of bicycle for the motor than the average dealer or customer": "This factor has already been recognized by many dealers throughout the country and they make a practice of taking in trade a bicycle owned by a customer for an Evans Power-Cycle. In other words, they prefer to turn over a complete machine rather than install a cyclemotor in the customer's bicycle."

Acknowledging a war economy, a full-page advertisement in the trade press in September 1917 said that the one-hundred-dollar Evans was the "Patriotic Vehicle" since its fuel consumption was so small: "Don't waste the nation's supply of precious fuel. Every time you take an aimless pleasure ride in a heavy gas-eating vehicle, you are a slacker."

1918 Model Year

For 1918 the Cyclemotor line incorporated the two-engine kits as well as the Evans lightweight motorcycle for one hundred dollars. The Evans frame was a double-top-tube type with a looping down tube. Twin trusses reinforced the front fork. For all Cyclemotor engines, there was a new link-belt drive for the National magneto, which was fitted with lighter, tungsten steel magnets. The Doehler-supplied crankcase was redesigned for increased rigidity. Engine balance was improved. The carburetor was redesigned to decrease the sound of air rushing into it. The cylinder was now "made under a special process" to increase uniformity and strength. A Champion spark plug was fitted.

For the Cyclemotor outfit, an endless Graton & Knight "Spartan" twisted-leather drive belt was supplied. The Evans, on the other hand, featured a V-belt. Other equipment on the Evans included a Troxel saddle and tool bag, Chicago handlebars, Federal tires and grips, Majestic pedals, Standard spokes, American wooden rims, a Wald stand, and an Atherton coaster brake.

In the fall of 1917, the Cyclemotor Corporation announced that much of their factory was being dedicated to production of aircraft parts for the war department. While orders for the Evans had been received "from all corners of the country," there were delays in shipments since "several lathes, drill presses and grinders" were "occupied with government work." *Motorcycle and Bicycle Illustrated* later noted that the Cyclemotor Corporation had made "aeroplane valves" during the war, "especially fine work" to which the facilities were dedicated "for many months."

The Cyclemotor machinery was probably still located in the General Railway Signal factory, as a journal article in *Motorcycling and Bicycling* claimed that until that point (October 1917), "the office has occupied the entire two story building at 149 Cady-st." But now "a large section" of the office was "giving way to space for several large turret lathes, milling machines, grinders, drill presses, heat treating furnaces, spot welders, riveters, cut off machines, tumbling barrels, buffers and an electric dynamometer and running-in stand."

In December 1917, Anderson, Rice, and Perrin (no mention of Adams) all reportedly "radiated optimism like a radiator with 20 pounds of steam pressure." As they added machinery to their factory, Anderson said, "We have been bothered in the past by getting out cyclemotors and Evans Power Bicycles due to slowness of material deliveries, but with our new facilities this has been obviated."

To reach their likeliest customers, "tradesmen who will have the actual need for the Cyclemotor or Evans Power Cycle for business uses," the Cyclemotor Corporation devised an improved time-payment scheme. Dealers were to be reimbursed for more than the wholesale price at the time that the final buyer made his first payment. Rice outlined the payment scheme in an undated letter to dealer H. D. Pickard in Rowley, Massachusetts. Rice noted that the Federal Financial Company of Indianapolis (FFC) carried out the plan; the Cyclemotor Corporation was not involved.

Utilizing the FFC scheme, the buyer paid a total of $107.50 over seven months—$35 down and $3 in weekly payments—which the dealer forwarded to the FFC. The dealer kept the $35 and also received $47.13 from the FFC. In addition, there was a $7.50 discount and a reserve of $17.87 for the dealer when the note was paid—i.e., the dealer eventually had $107.50 less his wholesale payment to Cyclemotor, a figure not specified but probably around $75.

This focus on "tradesmen" was based on a survey of records kept by the Cyclemotor Corporation. The check of several thousand buyer-registration cards revealed that 90 percent of riders—the majority reportedly skilled mechanics (predominantly machinists, electricians, and plumbers)—were looking for a quick and enjoyable way to work. In the war environment, Cyclemotor was able to claim that use of their products "greatly multiplies the personal efficiency of the owner and conserves fuel, rubber and man power" (*Motorcycling and Bicycling*, December 22, 1917).

In March, Earl Perrin left the Cyclemotor Corporation to become publicity manager and assistant sales manager of the Merkel Motor Wheel Company (q.v.), which also manufactured a bicycle-assist engine in Rochester. Cyclemotor distributors for 1918, including some of the agencies that had served in the previous season, were Baker, Murray & Imbrie Inc. in New York; the Hub Cycle Company in Boston; Johnson and Meyer in Memphis; the Walthour and Hood Company in Atlanta; the Hall-Williams Company in Minneapolis; the Washington Cycle and Supply Company in Tacoma; Whipple the Motorcycle Man in Chicago; the Saufley Supply Company in Kansas City; the George Worthington Company in Cleveland; the Pacific Motor Supply Company in Los Angeles and San Francisco; and the Simmons Hardware Company in St. Louis, Philadelphia, Toledo, Minneapolis, Sioux City, and Wichita. At the end of 1917, the Cyclemotor Corporation claimed two thousand dealers in the United States and Canada.

For 1918, the Evans remained one hundred dollars plus a 3 percent war tax. The Cyclemotor was still sixty dollars. Potential dealers were advised that "the way to be convinced that the Evans Power Cycle holds profits that will grow larger every year, is to tell us that you are willing to be shown." High wages of the wartime economy supposedly made the Evans "an exceedingly small consideration. Practically everybody can make this splendid investment."

1919 Model Year

For 1919, the Cyclemotor Corporation continued its emphasis on the Evans Power Cycle, although "for the rider who already has a bicycle, we have the Cyclemotor attachment." Dealers were advised to "Display an Evans in Your Window[.] Have a Demonstrator at the Front Curb."

1920 Model Year

The Cyclemotor Corporation announced delivery of 1920 model Evans Power Cycles in July 1919. Still, the effects of World War I lingered late into 1919 at the Cyclemotor Corporation. Rice, in a letter to a potential customer in October of that year, said it had been "only a few weeks" since the company had been "released from government work" and could resume production.

A story in the trade press at the end of 1919 noted that the Cyclemotor "people no longer push the bicycle attachment proposition, preferring to supply the complete Evans Power Cycle." The latter supposedly had parts designed specifically for motor bicycle use, unlike the average pedal bicycle to which a dealer or rider might add a Cyclemotor engine. In 1922, *Motor-*

cycle and Bicycle Illustrated reported that the Cyclemotor attachment for the past two years had been sold abroad exclusively and only the Evans had been distributed in the domestic market.

The Cyclemotor factory at that time (the Cady Street facility) was described as "well equipped with good machinery," although room "is rather at a premium because of the rapid expansion of the business, but there is no inefficient crowding." Cyclemotor cylinders were being "tested under water pressure for possible casting imperfections." The finish of the mechanical parts left "nothing to be desired." The crankshaft and its counterweight were a two-piece forging, "ingeniously welded together."

A *Motorcycling and Bicycling* writer met with Rice and Joseph Merkel, former manufacturer of the Merkel Motor Wheel and now new to the Cyclemotor staff. The two invited the reporter to take an Evans ride. "I was agreeably surprised with the pep of the tiny motor. The design of the Evans frame gives a low saddle position and the spring suspension of the saddle makes a very comfortable seat."

In March 1920, the annual stockholders' meeting saw Rice elected vice president for sales in recognition for "his marked success . . . in piloting the sales of . . . the . . . Evans Power Cycle." Rice credited his salesmen for their work. These were Adams in the eastern United States, W. M. Banning in the central west, Charles A. Merkel (the former Rochester dealer) in the South, and P. E. Snell on the West Coast.

1921 Model Year

The 1921 Evans Model G, announced in October 1920, was an almost completely new motorcycle. A different frame, with tubes more gracefully looping than the old, provided a more secure anchor for the engine. The power plant also was radically different. The spark plug now fitted at the top of the cylinder, allegedly contributing to a 50 percent increase in power. The crankcase was redesigned for improved lubrication as well as improved appearance. Now all engine parts were manufactured in-house rather than being supplied on contract.

Perhaps the most important additions to the Evans equipment were electric head and tail lamps powered by a Berling magneto. But other changes included a different, cantilevered saddle pivoting at the nose; new handlebars with a throttle control lever as well as a second lever for compression relief and ignition; a newly designed fuel tank; a new style of fenders; a new style of stand; reengineered eccentric adjustment of the chain; and a tool kit with tools.

The weight remained 70 pounds, but the price was now $165 FOB at the factory. The Model G operations manual claimed that the throttle control carburetor made "better" use of fuel, although more oil was consumed. An undated flyer claimed the "Electrically Equipped Evans" was as "Handy as a Bicycle[,] Efficient as a Motorcycle." A new price, effective July 1, was $140, a $25 reduction from the original list figure.

In early 1921, the Cyclemotor Corporation claimed that "in spite of general business conditions" Evans sales were exceeding production. The reason, according to an advertisement, was the need to increase "daily personal efficiency." Rice, in a separate statement as "vice-president in charge of sales," said that his "low-priced, ultra lightweight power two-wheeler" was meeting "with particular favor under the present economic conditions." His factory was behind on deliveries but working overtime to catch up.

1922 Model Year

An Evans sales folder for 1922 claimed that the Power Cycles were the "machines that are taking the American people off their feet." An overprint attests to a price reduction from $135 to $125. The convertibility of the Evans was noted; the drive belt could be disconnected "instantly" should the fuel supply run out, allowing the machine to be pedaled "as an ordinary bicycle." In addition, the engine could be removed via three bolts and a "coupling connection."

In the winter of 1922, T. J. Sullivan, editor of *Motorcycling and Bicycling*, visited the Cyclemotor factory on Cady Street. He observed that the building "might easily be mistaken for a two- or three-family dwelling house, setting back from the street with a good-sized yard." It was a factory, however, he noted by the sign, the "flock of Evans powercycles in the yard," and the noise "big enough to make all of the windows rattle." Inside, space was at a premium. "S.R.O. as far as the working men are concerned." The office was on the second floor. There, Rice told Sullivan that the production level stood at ten Power Cycles per day, six days per week. With the advent of the riding season, Rice expected to build fifty machines per day "as soon as . . . dealers abandon their buying from hand-to-mouth policy."

In the spring of 1922, W. H. Parsons of *Motorcycle and Bicycle Illustrated* paid a visit to Rochester. There, he found the Cyclemotor Corporation reorganized under the laws of Maryland, in anticipation of a move to a larger production facility. While the old Cady Street factory had a capacity of five thousand machines a year, the proposed new facility would turn out thirty thousand. In passing, Parsons noted that about fourteen thousand Cyclemotors and Evans Power Cycles together had been built to that point, eight thousand of which were exported. General Railway Signal officials and other Rochesterians dominated the board of the new corporation. G.R.S. president Wilmer Salmon, vice president George D. Morgan, and secretary John F. Braam were among the directors; Braam served as secretary-treasurer of the Cyclemotor organization, also. Anderson and Evans were on the board, too. Management for Cyclemotor included Anderson as general manager, Evans as factory manager, Rice as sales manager, and Joseph Merkel and Burt L. Madden (1886–?), also a veteran of the Russell Company, as engineers.

1923 Model Year

Motorcycling and Bicycling in December 1922 reported the resignations of "general manager" Anderson and "factory manager" Evans, "following the recent example of Sales Manager A. C. Rice." According to *Motorcycle and Bicycle Illustrated*, Anderson and Evans had moved to Hammondsport to become president (and general manager) and vice president (and factory manager), respectively, of Keuka Industries, a builder of aircraft engines and parts. While both men remained Cyclemotor directors, their departure left only Merkel of the "old timers." At the annual New York City cycle trades show in February 1923, new president Herbert W. Chamberlain, R. E. Morgan, and Merkel represented the company.

At a motorcycle rally in Rochester in the summer of 1923, Merkel was "busy all week seeing to it that every visitor to Cyclemotor town had a good time." A happy Evans rider in late 1923 was Homer Campbell of Rochester. He made his living as a special delivery mail carrier. Until buying his Evans from the local Towner Brothers firm, Campbell had averaged $26 to $46 a week covering 20 to 30 miles on a bicycle delivering 50 to 80 pieces of mail a day. After a month on an Evans, he was making $42 to $67, delivering 75 to 120 pieces over 40 to 60 miles. The motorcycle cost him $125. Service for the 1,000 miles he'd ridden was fifty cents, while gas and oil cost four dollars. Not getting enough riding on the job, Campbell took a trip to Binghamton, making 160 miles on five quarts of fuel and moving as "fast as was safe, legal and comfortable."

By the fall of 1923, Chamberlain, according to *Motorcycle and Bicycle Illustrated*, had spent the "past year laying the foundation for the future prosperity," with both domestic and foreign business "lined up." Merkel had the factory running "as close to 100 percent efficiency as is possible to have any factory." And improvements to the Evans had produced "a genuine lightweight motorcycle instead of a bicycle with a motor attachment."

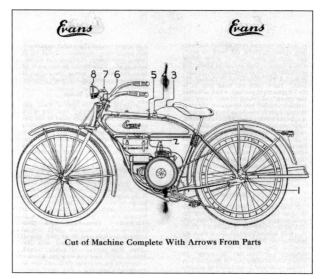

The "Sport Model" Evans as depicted in the owner's manual, ca. 1924.

1924 Model Year

A new corporation, a subsidiary of General Railway Signal called G.R.S. Products Inc., began building the Evans Power Cycle in the spring of 1924 in the town of Colonie just north of the Albany city line (an area incorporated as the village of Menands later in the year). The trade press reported that in the winter General Railway Signal had acquired the "business and property of the Cyclemotor Corporation." The explanation for the move to the former Federal Signal facility on Troy Road (now Broadway) in Menands was the buyout by General Railway Signal of competitor Federal, also in early 1924, which freed the Menands building for other use.

While G.R.S. Products built Evans Power Cycles, the company was known primarily as the manufacturer of G.R.S. washing machines, which had been manufactured in Rochester. At its incorporation on January 11, 1924, G.R.S. Products said its business would include washing machines, dishwashers, mangles "and other domestic appliances," "film detectors," *and* cycle motors. The initial board of directors, many of them lawyers, all had Rochester addresses. Capital stock was to consist of ten thousand shares with a par value of one hundred dollars and ten thousand shares with no par value.

The trade press noted that the Cyclemotor Corporation had been hampered by its small, overcrowded plant in Rochester. General Railway Signal, which reportedly had been "foster father of the Cyclemotor Corporation," now was to stand behind the motor bicycle "with ample resources and an organization made up . . . by big successful business men with full faith in the future of the reliable, easy-running and always delightful Evans."

The absorption of the Cyclemotor operation into G.R.S. Products brought Chamberlain to Albany, where he served as vice president and treasurer. Federal Signal veterans filled other offices; Alfred H. Renshaw was president and general manager, and W. Chester Vanderpoel was secretary. By 1926, Vanderpoel had been succeeded by Ambrose L. Herkert, who also became assistant treasurer. Burton K. Sheldon was the G.R.S. general sales manager responsible for the future of the Evans. With experience in the washing machine industry, Sheldon was said to be set to help Evans dealers sell the motorcycles that they had purchased from him. In a letter to potential dealers dated August 23, 1924, Sheldon said, "An Evans dealer tells us that his service costs on 85 Power-Cycles sold during 1923 averaged less than 50 cents each." Sheldon was going to place a franchise; "Will you be that dealer?" Thanks to branches in New York City, Rochester, Chicago, San Francisco, Montreal, and Melbourne, G.R.S. Products were "about to create a new era in the affairs of the Evans."

In the winter, Chamberlain as Cyclemotor general manager and Merkel as chief engineer had shown three Evans Power Cycles at the Chicago show. Never referring to the pending changes, Chamberlain said of Cyclemotor prospects that he was "very optimistic as to the outlook for 1924 and feels that sales this year ought to be considerably increased over 1923." New on the motor bicycles in Chicago were balloon tires in a 26-by-2-inch size and a spring fork.

By April, G.R.S. Products Inc., rather than the Cyclemotor Corporation, was advertising the Evans. One promotion noted that

Eight Years Experience Has Made Us Worthy of a New Factory-New Capital

We Are Indebted to Many Loyal Evans Dealers Who Have Made Our Increased Production Possible During A Period When Our Sales and Advertising Appropriations Were Being Conserved

These Dealers Knew That We Were Simply Resting a Little on Our Oars so as to Better Prepare for Big Future Operations

The G.R.S. advertising writer concluded by saying that "if the Evans Agency Does Not Put You on Easy Street It Will at Least Make a Few Hundred Dollars Extra Profit Each Season."

1925 Model Year

"One of the sensations" at the New York motorcycle show in February 1925 was the announcement of a decrease in the price of the Evans to $120. *Motorcycling* thought this had made the Evans "by all odds the lowest-priced motorcycle in the world, a real motorcycle and not a motorized bicycle." Chamberlain as "general manager of G.R.S. Products," Merkel of the "Engineering Department" and A. C. Morehouse of the "Sales Department" were on hand in New York with three machines in an attractive booth furnished with a carpet and a wicker settee.

An undated flyer marked by G.R.S. Products in Albany ("General Railway Signal Standards of Precision") and by Evans agent Meisel Cycle Exchange (Henry O. Meisel in Clintonville, Wisconsin) continued the theme that the Evans provided cheap transportation. Costing only one-third the price of a heavy motorcycle, the Evans would nonetheless "give you equally complete independence from street cars and busses." Averaging "close to 165 miles per gallon," the Evans was geared to run at 35 miles per hour, the limit in most states, "even on country roads." The Evans was "a common-sense method of transportation, proved in performance, and carrying the unqualified guarantee of a million-dollar Corporation." The specifications in the folder relate to only one model, the equivalent of the G Sport of 1924, equipped with spring fork and balloon tires. There is no model designation in the text, however.

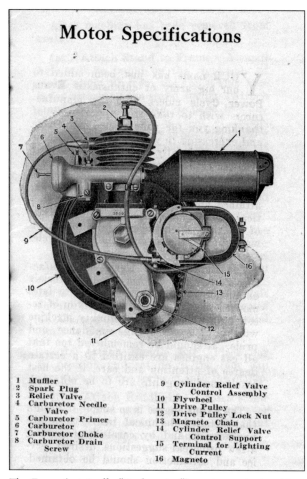

The Evans (originally "Cyclemotor") engine as depicted in a manual, *Operation, Care and Maintenance of "Sports Model" Evans*, ca. 1924. NYSM H-1990.96.4.

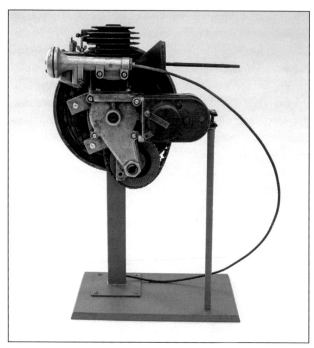

This ca.1920 "Cyclemotor" engine is similar to the one featured in the Evan manual from ca. 1924. NYSM H-1990.96.2.

In 1922, *Motorcycle and Bicycle Illustrated* announced that the Cyclemotor Corporation had arranged for the manufacture of the Evans by a "large German manufacturing concern, allied with the American Steel Export Company and Automotive Products Corporation. In 1925, the Kahn enterprise in Berlin began building a version of the Evans Power Cycle under the "Stock" trade name. Produced almost unchanged into the 1930s, the Stock differed from the American Evans in the use of a leaf spring for front wheel suspension, altered gearing, and a reserve oil tank. Electric lighting was 17.5 marks extra, while a German two-speed gear cost 90 marks. At a list price of 380 marks, the Stock was Germany's cheapest motorcycle, thanks, one writer notes, to large-scale production. Another German company, Pondorf, reportedly also built some Evans motor bicycles but "ran into license problems with Stock."

1926 Model Year and Later

G.R.S. Products Inc. voluntarily dissolved on November 27, 1926. At that time, the directors of the corporation were Salmon, George D. Morgan, J. N. Beckley, A. H. Renshaw, and H. W. Croft. Officers were Renshaw, president; Chamberlain, vice president and treasurer; and Herkert, secretary and assistant treasurer. Soon Chamberlain was back in Rochester, serving as assistant secretary in the General Railway Signal Company.

Whenever Evans production ended, it's likely that the remnants of manufacture in Menands were shipped to Rochester. There, the parts and tools came into the hands of the Morley Machinery Corporation, which was headed by Charles F. Morley.

VanBuren N. Hansford, whose Hansford Manufacturing Corporation succeeded the Morely Corporation in 1947, has written, "Anyone who runs a general machine shop aspires to having a project of his own which can be used to level out the dips of the machine shop business." For that reason, says Hansford, Fred Morley acquired the "Evans Motorbike."

Many Evans Motorbikes were made before the Morley acquisition. Morley never actually made any Evans Motorbikes, but they inherited many spare parts and, I presume, made some additional ones from the prototypes that they already had. Whenever someone had trouble with their Evans Motorbike, they would bring it to Morley and have it fixed . . . I doubt that Mr. Morley ever made a great many of the spare parts and when he gave out those that he purchased originally, it was the death knell for further repairing of Evans Motorbikes.

After taking over, I remember receiving several letters from people all over the world who had acquired Evans Motorbikes. I remember one individual in Norway who pled with me to furnish him the necessary spare parts for his bike. He had ridden to work on it everyday for so many years and relied on it so heavily that he just didn't know what he was going to do without it and would I please just take care of his needs. In each case, I wrote as courteous a letter as possible explaining that I had no further parts, that I had no drawings from which to make parts and that the era of the Evans Motorbike was over. These letters persisted into the 1950s.

Several Evans Power Cycles have survived in private hands. The New York State Museum collections include a Cyclemotor engine.

Cygnet Rear Car Company
(later the **Cygnet Manufacturing Company**)
Buffalo
1915–18?

This company manufactured only two-wheel passenger and freight trailers for motorcycles.

D

Day Manufacturing Company
Lake View
1900?–1903

The Day Manufacturing Company was incorporated 1898 but had been building bicycles since the mid-1880s and continued to do so until its demise in 1903. But motorcycles, too, figured in the company's activities.

In 1910 it was reported that John C. Glas experimented with engines as early as 1900, when he was employed by the Day company. In late 1902, a trade journal article said that several American "automobile manufacturers," including the "Day Manufacturing Company of Buffalo," were using the Belgian Kelecom motor. The Kelecom line, it should be noted, included engines suitable for both motorcycles and automobiles. And complete Kelecom motorcycles were marketed in Europe.

The *Cycle and Automobile Trade Journal*'s "Buyer's Guide," printed in the January 1903 issue, lists the Day Manufacturing Company as a source of motorcycles. But within a few months the Day company was bankrupt, and the assets liquidated. What motorcycles, if any, the Day firm produced remains to be determined. John Glas went on to the Emblem Manufacturing Company (q.v.) in nearby Angola—perhaps the most successful of all New York motorcycle manufacturers.

DeDion-Bouton Motorette Company
New York City (Brooklyn)
1900–1902

As early as 1896, motor tricycles powered by DeDion engines were imported by riders and entrepreneurs, including Kenneth B. Skinner in Boston, who subsequently acquired the rights to the American business for the French products. Then, in 1900, the DeDion-Bouton Motorette Company of Brooklyn purchased the DeDion rights for the United States from Skinner. At that point, according to the *Horseless Age*, twenty thousand of the DeDion-Bouton engines were in use in Europe and America, and further business was likely. While the "2 3/4-horse-power air-cooled motor of the deDion [sic] make" was "especially adapted and recommended for motor cycles, tricycles, and quadricycles," probably most applications to that point were in tricycles and quadricycles.

The new DeDion-Bouton Motorette facility was a "large building" at Church Lane and Thirty-Seventh Street, conducive for "general offices and factory." The Motorette Company was going to supply engines to "the motor vehicle and carriage trade for use on their makes of vehicles" as well as build its own lightweight automobile. It appears that the DeDion-Bouton Motorette Company, which was incorporated in New Jersey, and with which Skinner kept a connection, manufactured only three- and four-wheel vehicles. But, said the *Horseless Age*, they were reported to have made "special contracts with automobile, carriage and bicycle manufacturers to supply them with entire equipments, and under these conditions are licensing them to the use of many of the De Dion-Bouton [sic] detail patents on motor cycles, and also to some of the detail patents on carriages."

By 1901 the company was in financial difficulties. Three automobiles were seized by the sheriff on behalf of frustrated buyers. Additional judgments were found against the firm. Skinner served notice that he was canceling his agreement with the Motorette Company and utilizing a clause that allowed him to reclaim the patent rights. By the end of March 1902, Skinner again was acting as American agent. The extent of motorcycle-engine manufacture by Motorette in Brooklyn, or perhaps later under Skinner's direction, is unknown here.

G. Erwin DeLong
The Industrial Machine Company
New York City; Phoenix; Syracuse
1901–3
Trade Name: **DeLong Motorcycle**

George Erwin DeLong's idea was to incorporate the mechanical parts of his motorcycle within the frame tubes, producing a machine that, paraphrasing his patent claims, was lighter, more attractive, simpler, more practical, and more convenient. DeLong (1874–?) in 1896 was a partner in a Syracuse oil company but after a year or so left for New York City and the retail bicycle business. In Manhattan he developed his motorcycle design, and by late November 1901 he reportedly was working on "not a few other original ideas," including a button on the handlebar to cut out the ignition for starting and stopping the machine and a "fore carriage" that would add a second front wheel to a motor bicycle, thus creating a two-passenger tricycle.

DeLong's motorcycle patent, 703,769, issued on July 1, 1902, keys on the tubular diamond frame. Each of the three major tubes was assigned service as a container: the top (horizontal) tube served as the fuel tank; the down tube (head to bottom bracket) extended below the bracket and was capped there for access to the coil and battery housed within; the seat tube just below the saddle housed the carburetor, below which was the engine. The *Bicycling World and Motocycle Review* said the diameter of all the tubing was 16-gauge, 2-inch stock and the capacity of the fuel tank was two quarts, which the *Horseless Age* reported was enough to secure a 50-mile range.

The DeLong motorcycle drove the rear wheel through the same chain to which the pedal cranks were attached. The rider could choose between pedal-

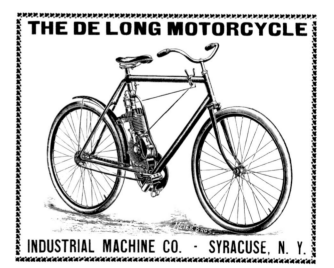

The *Motor Age* said the DeLong "had a clear cut, neat appearance that should make friends for it." This image of the motorcycle is from the *Bicycling World*, February 6, 1902.

ing or motoring, thanks to a clutch fitted to the cranks. In addition, the clutch allowed the cranks to be locked into a stationary position, providing a firm footrest. In late November 1901, the *Bicycling World* said that DeLong's motorcycle prototype had been on the road since May and had "rendered excellent service."

DeLong left New York to help incorporate the Industrial Machine Company in Phoenix (about ten miles north of Syracuse), where production of the motorcycle was to occur. One assumes that DeLong, in looking for a backer to help build his motorcycle, turned to his home city. Joining DeLong in the new concern were Syracuse businessmen William H. Haberle, secretary of the Haberle-Crystal Spring Brewing Company; Pulver G. Hermance of the Hermance Valve Company, manufacturers of beer pumps and bar fixtures; Edward Oswald, cashier of the brewing company; and the brothers August Finck Jr. and George Finck, partners in the firm A. Finck's Sons, wholesalers in shoes, leather, and findings. Also involved were J. I. Van Doren and Edwin B. Baker of Phoenix.

The certificate of incorporation filed on January 15, 1902, notes that the firm was to manufacture and sell "Automobiles, Motor Cycles, Coaster Brakes and Hardware Specialties," a statement corroborating reports of an automobile planned for early production. Although the company was capitalized at $25,000, $7,900 was paid in for shares valued at $100 each. Haberle was the largest holder, with fifteen shares, while DeLong was second, with fourteen.

By February the Industrial Machine Company had produced a "neat catalog." In response, the *Motor Age*, taken by "an original [motorcycle] production in many details," commented about the incorporation of the tanks and ignition components in the frame tubes. Altogether, the machine had a "clear cut, neat appearance that should make friends for it."

Industrial Machine planned for the "first run" to be turned out in February, but it appears no DeLong motorcycles were built in Phoenix. Perhaps Van Doren or Baker had found factory property, but in any case, the facility proved unsuitable. Probably in May 1902, the Industrial Machine Company moved to Syracuse, to the corner of Water and Grape Streets. The leased, second-floor facility promised to "give them larger and better facilities for the manufacture of their De Long [sic] motor bicycles." Another story noted that "G. E. DeLong is now getting up a new belt driven machine in addition to the regular [chain-driven] motor cycle that the company turns out."

By early fall, the Industrial Machine Company was insolvent. An offer of 35 percent to its creditors reportedly was the only alternative to bankruptcy. The company "despite considerable outlay failed to overcome the many difficulties incident to such production." It was understood that "some of the stockholders are willing to further contribute if the compromise with creditors can be effected," so there was a "possibility operations may be continued."

In October, Hermance met with Glenn H. Curtiss (q.v.) "to inspect his Hercules motor with a view of using it on the 1903 Delong [sic] motor cycle, which is manufactured by the company," according to the *Hammondsport Herald*. In a report dated December 20, 1902, the Industrial Machine Company still promised to build motorcycles; the *Dealer and Repairman* for January 1903 claimed that the firm "will be in shape to turn out machines in a short time, and it is expected to have a sample ready for the New York Automobile Show." A couple of 2.25-horsepower DeLong motorcycles were reported to have given "the best satisfaction" in use around Syracuse, but no DeLongs had been sold, "as the company found certain features that could be improved and did not care to sell a machine that, in its estimation, was not satisfactory."

With the beginning of spring 1903, there was news that the "Industrial Machine Co. . . . reports it will be filling orders within a month. It has been experimenting to get a good machine, and thinks it has a world beater." Whether after so many predictions of imminent production any DeLong motorcycles ever reached the public is unclear. Additional news after the winter of 1903 is lacking for the Industrial Machine Company.

By the time of the financial crisis in 1902, G. Erwin DeLong was already gone from the enterprise. Hermance, "a practical machinist," had succeeded him as general manager. The *Horseless Age* noted that "G. E. De Long [sic] of the Industrial Machine Company, Syracuse, N.Y. is endeavoring to organize a new company there to manufacture automobiles and motor cycles," while the *Dealer and Repairman* reported that he had "gone into the manufacture of automobiles with the J. S. Leggett Mfg. Co." Another report noted the Leggett company was to "manufacture automobiles and motor cycles after patents of G. E. DeLong, formerly with the Industrial Machine Company." A check reveals no patents granted to DeLong other than that for the motorcycle, which was assigned to the Industrial Machine Company.

The DeLong motorcycle reportedly weighed 60 pounds and provided speeds of up to 25 miles per hour. Industrial Machine Company advertising stressed the simplicity of the motorcycle. Ease of operation and cleanliness were other points raised, often to contrast the DeLong with heavier, more complicated, and ostensibly less reliable machines. Potential riders and dealers had been instructed to note that the two-hundred-dollar DeLong Motocycle was "not a lumber wagon" and "not an ice wagon."

Andrew J. Deninger
d/b/a **Deninger Cycle Company**
Rochester
ca. 1908–17
Trade Name: **Kulture**

Several motorcycle historians (Michael Gerald, Jim Lucas, and Hugo Wilson) have suggested that 1909 probably was the sole year of manufacture for the Kulture. On the other hand, reports in *Motorcycling* during 1913 and 1914 confirm continued Kulture distribution. And in anticipation of the Rochester automobile show in January 1917 it was said that "A. J. Deninger will show the Emblem [q.v.] and Kulture motorcycles, and Emblem bicycles."

Andrew J. Deninger (1870 or 1871–1940) operated the Deninger Cycle Company at 335 North Street. In the city directories, his stock was listed as bicycles and talking machines (the latter at 345 North Street), but *Motorcycling* in 1913 reported that "the Denninger [sic] Cycle Co. handle their own make of machine [motorcycle], the 'Kulture.' They have the name on the oil tank and instead of the usual name on the gas tank have a neat transfer showing a tandem pair in full flight. Mr. Denninger claims the distinction of selling anywhere in the United States, and has very strong opinions of the country garages who try to repair motorcycles."

Deninger advertised motorcycles as early as 1908, when he claimed that his company consisted of "agents for Manson [Chicago-built] motorcycles," while "all makes of motorcycles [were] repaired and overhauled." An undated Deninger handbill includes two photos of Manson motorcycles underneath a "Kulture Motorcycles" heading. The Mansons depicted are a 2.25-horsepower single with the engine in the seat tube and the 3-horsepower single with the engine in a loop frame introduced for the 1908 model year, the last year for Manson. On his handbill, Deninger said he was selling a new $210 motorcycle, apparently the lesser Manson, discounted 20 percent to agents—i.e., for "$168 net cash."

One wonders whether Deninger utilized the "Kulture" name for whatever motorcycles he sold, a theory reinforced in April 2000 when David C. Leitner noted that he had a 1911 Emblem two-cylinder motorcycle marked with the Kulture name. Leitner also has an undated Kulture Motorcycles catalog that depicts machines similar if not identical to the 1911 Emblem line. While the one-cylinder Emblems were advertised as 4- and 5-horsepower motorcycles, the comparable Kulture machines in the catalog are claimed to be 5- and 6-horsepower models. Frame construction is the same as the Emblem's, with reinforcement in the shape of an integral triangle inside the tube. The Kulture catalog notes the use of Emblem engines but also says the Kulture motorcycles are "made by [the] Deninger Cycle Co."

The catalog further claims,

> I have designed and built an every-day machine for the every-day rider, and I have eliminated all unnecessary features known to the trade as "talking points." . . .
>
> The "KULTURE" is not manufactured by a company who look to a superintendent to shade quality so that a fat dividend may be declared, but is made by me, in my own shop, under my personal supervision, and I take an honest pride in its manufacture.

DeSchaum-Hornell Motor Company
Hornell
1909

A report in the cycling press during the summer of 1909 noted the incorporation of the DeSchaum-Hornell Motor Company to manufacture bicycles and motorcycles as well as automobiles, boats, locomotives, and "engines of every description." Although capitalized at $150,000, the new company was to begin business with $1,500. Initial directors were William A. DeSchaum, Harvey J. Hopkins, William C. Paul, Hart H. Lincoln, and Judge Albert R. Smith. While all used Buffalo or North Tonawanda addresses, the principal office for the new company was to be at Hornellsville. A newspaper story reported that five acres were secured in North Hornell and that one hundred men were to be employed "at the onset, in the manufacture of automobiles." Construction of the factory only lasted a few weeks in November 1909 before workers went on strike for not being paid and creditors put a lien on what had been built. No vehicles were ever built, and the factory was never finished. In 1910, it was deconstructed.

James F. Bellamy as well as Beverly Rae Kimes and Henry Austin Clark Jr. have documented in brief William DeSchaum's career in the motor vehicle world. As William A. Schaum (without the "De" prefix to his surname), he presided over the Schaum Automobile and Motor Manufacturing Company in Baltimore, Maryland. Then, in Buffalo as "DeSchaum," he promoted the Rossler, DeSchaum, and Seven Little Buffalos automobiles. From Hornell, DeSchaum went to Detroit, where he was involved with two additional automobile projects before his death in 1915. The DeSchaum-Hornell Motor Company was dissolved by proclamation on March 10, 1926.

Lawrence "Indian Larry" DeSmedt
New York (Brooklyn, Manhattan)
1960s–2004

Lawrence DeSmedt (1949–2004) was more widely known as "Indian Larry," after the Indian Chief chopper he made and rode in the 1980s. He was born and raised in the Hudson Valley in the Newburgh area. He made his first motorcycle at the age of fifteen using parts from a lawn mower and tractor to motorize a bicycle. By the age of eighteen he was "officially in the business" of building motorcycles. Coming of age in the late 1960s, Larry was a fan of the style of stripped-down, stock-rake choppers popular at the time. Throughout his career he preferred tall handlebars, foot clutches with jockey shift, no front brake or fender, a small gas tank, open exhaust pipes, and a kick start.

Larry was an artist and saw his motorcycles as functioning works of art. He believed that building motorcycles is "one of the highest art forms, because it combines all media: sculpture, painting, as well as the mechanics." Art and performance "go hand in hand in my world," he said in an interview in June 2004, and he was "trying to perfect the motorcycle" ("Indian Larry Raw Interview & Building 'Chain of Mystery' for *Biker Build-Off*," YouTube video). With each motorcycle Larry built, he tried to make improvements on the things that he felt were not perfect. Usually starting with a panhead motor, he rebuilt his motors to ensure they could handle the performance that he required, often using older pro-stock technology and materials for his machines.

Along with the crew at Psycho Choppers, including Paul Cox (q.v.), Larry is credited with developing the "NYC Chopper style" in the 1990s, often described as a custom motorcycle that was stripped down, light, fast, rugged, nimble, and thin and having a shorter rake (than traditional choppers) and good ground clearance, all features designed to deal with NYC traffic, narrow streets, various street surfaces (like cobblestone or brick), and potholes.

While Larry worked in various shops in New York City, his work started to gain recognition by the late 1980s, appearing in magazines, and again in the late

According to Ted Doering of the Motorcyclepedia Museum, this motorcycle was Larry's first Knucklehead. He purchased the 1939 Harley-Davidson in 1965 for two hundred dollars. In 1971, the bike was "re-vamped . . . as a winter project after Larry returned to New York from California." Some of the custom features are the solo seat, spool kick start pedal, and axle plates featuring a "4-finger" design. The frame and transmission have "Larry's initials and quotes stamped on them." From the collection of Edward Doering, on display at Motorcyclepedia Museum, Newburgh, New York.

1990s. In 2000, Larry and others including Paul Cox and Keino Sasaki opened Gasoline Alley in Brooklyn. Shortly thereafter, he participated in the Discovery Channel's show *Motorcycle Mania II* in 2001 and three subsequent *Biker Build-Off* episodes. Larry died from an accident he had while performing his signature stunt, standing on his moving motorcycle with his arms outstretched.

After his death, his crew changed the name of the shop to Indian Larry's Legacy, and they continued to build Larry-inspired choppers until 2007. At that point, the name was changed to Indian Larry's Motorcycles, and the business is still run by Larry's former business partners Bobby and Elisa Seeger and builder and painter John Asarisi.

There are multiple long-format interviews with Larry, articles written about him, and two books about his life. Some of his best-known motorcycles are "Wild Child," "Daddy-O" ("Rat Fink"), "Mr. Tiki's Shop Droppings," and "Chain of Mystery," for which he used a welded tow chain for the frame.

George DeWald
New York (Brooklyn)
1901–8?
S. D. Manufacturing Company
Brooklyn
1909–11
Trade Names: **S. D.**; **S.D.M.**; later, **Peerless S. D.**

In a letter to the *Bicycling World and Motorcycle Review*, George DeWald in early 1908 said that beginning in the fall of 1901 he had built five different shaft-drive motorcycles. His incentive in writing was to join the list of claimants "to the production of the first shaft-driven motor bicycle." DeWald was a clever innovator who modified his approach to motorcycle design with each machine. The first used a 3½-inch bore by-4-inch stroke engine geared at 4.25:1. He judged it "quite a success," and he sold it. In the fourth motorcycle (1905–6), DeWald noted that "bevel gears were used with clutch to crank case and free engine started with a crank, the clutch being applied to get in motion." In the fifth machine (1906–7), "bevel gears were used for transmission, a compensating clutch being in the rear wheel."

DeWald said that at the time of his letter (March 1908), he was working on the sixth shaft-drive motorcycle "with compensating clutch and free engine,

Shaft-driven S. D. or S.D.M. introduced in mid-1909. From the *Bicycling World and Motorcycle Review*, June 26, 1909.

geared 3½ to 1. The motor will be powerful, 3⅜ by 3¼ stroke, 3,000 r.p.m."

DeWald was able to supply the *World* with photos of the fourth and fifth motorcycles, both neat machines on which the driveshafts are plainly visible at the left stay. He concluded, "All of my machines but one are chainless and pedalless. I think that I have said enough as to my claim for the credit of producing the first shaft-driven motorcycle."

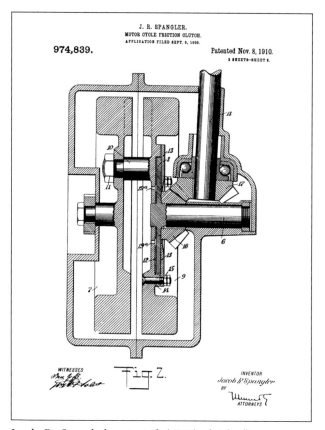

Jacob R. Spangler's patented (1910) clutch, "to overcome the shock and vibration in vehicles propelled by explosive engines," utilized on the S. D. motorcycles.

"S. D." denotes "shaft drive" according to advertising material distributed by the manufacturers of the shaft-driven S. D. motorcycles announced in 1909. By happenstance, "S. D." also denotes the names Jacob R. Spangler and George (alternatively Otto G.) "Dewald" (*sic*), the principals in the S. D. Manufacturing Company at 155 Ridgewood Avenue in Brooklyn. Each man alone, according to the *Bicycling World*, had "built two or more shaft driven motorcycles."

The "S.D.M." name was reported in the July 1, 1909, issue of *Motorcycle Illustrated*. The following January, the S. D. or the S.D.M. (both versions of the name appear in the press) appeared at the New York motor vehicle show in Madison Square Garden, one of three new makes among the nineteen on display in the basement area dubbed "Pneumonia Alley." The S. D. was not the first commercially available shaft-equipped motorcycle; it followed the four-cylinder Belgian FN (q.v.), which was imported by the Ovington Motor Company of New York City from 1905. The Buffalo-built, shaft-driven, four-cylinder Pierce (q.v.) arrived as a 1909 model. While a one-cylinder F. N. appeared in the winter of 1909, the S. D. *was* the first such domestic one-cylinder motorcycle.

More powerful (4 horsepower vs. 3.5), $260 "Special" version of the 1910 S. D. From the *Bicycling World and Motorcycle Review*, January 15, 1910.

The S. D. shaft-drive mechanism arrangement, fitted to a diamond frame, was enclosed in the left-hand, lower stay, with bevel gears running in ball bearings at both ends. To smooth the drive train from the pounding of an inherently rough single-cylinder engine, a friction coupling was fitted to the flywheel. The coupling itself consisted of a series of steel and composition disks, like a clutch. Tension adjustment was made by six screws distributed around the flywheel. The whole was splash-oil lubricated.

Spangler filed a patent application for the clutch with DeWald as a witness on September 9, 1909. The patent was granted on November 8, 1910, for a clutch to "overcome the shock and vibration in vehicles propelled by explosive engines, more especially motor cycles, incident to the firing of the charge when the motor cycle is first started or after it is started when the load is very heavy, as when climbing a hill." The patent describes a single disk rather than multiple friction disks.

An S. D. Manufacturing Company flyer for the 1910 models notes both 29.96-cubic-inch, 3.5-horsepower and 30.5-cubic-inch, 4-horsepower engines. Two versions of the smaller engine were available: Model D with battery ignition at $225, and Model E with magneto for $250. The larger, "special" engine was listed only with magneto, at a cost of $260. The S. D. Company claimed, "The most important feature in our motorcycles is a PATENT AUTOMATIC SHOCK ABSORBING DEVICE" that "works automatically in a splash of oil." The manufacturers said they were ready to build in volume, since "special machinery was designed and constructed. A process for manufacturing was brought down to a fine art." All S. D. motorcycles could be "equipped with spring fork if required."

Motorcycle Illustrated noted "many years in perfecting a single cylinder shaft drive together with other details in an endeavor to produce a motorcycle comparable in simplicity, strength and wearing qualities with the best in the market." The *Bicycling World* said the S. D. was an "excellent example of clean designing." *Motorcycling*, at the conclusion of the New York show, said, "During the week the mechanical excellence and neat, trim appearance of this, the only single-cylinder shaft-driven machine in this country, was impressed upon the public more and more. The simple,

The Peerless "S. D." (shaft drive) for 1911.

clever arrangement with disks, which prevent engine shocks from reaching the driving gear, and especially the dust-proof enclosing of the ball-bearing shaft, will interest any one who knows from experience . . . the comfort of a chainless bicycle. Rightly constructed, it is the ideal transmission." *Motorcycling* also reported "long, unusual road tests, both as to the shaft drive and shock-absorption." The *Cycle and Automobile Trade Journal* recognized in the new S. D. two "absolutely new and unique features." The first was the "neat and effective" shaft drive. The second was the "device of original design, which is claimed to give perfect shock-absorbing qualities, obviating any danger of sudden shocks to the gear teeth." The *Journal* also acknowledged the integral casting of head and cylinder with large cooling flanges, large bearings, and drilled piston, to allow lubrication of the cylinder wall.

Rather than take part in the Chicago show, which followed closely the New York event, an S. D. representative—specifically, Spangler's son Harry D.—traveled "to close with desirable agents after a strenuous week of explaining at New York." Apparently, the S. D. Company faced a challenge in gaining acceptance among dealers for its machines. It was mid-March 1910 before F. W. Sandruck of Baltimore, in becoming agent for the city and its environs, also had "the distinction of being the first representative of the makers of the S. D., a single cylinder shaft driven machine recently placed on the market." In May 1910, Harry Spangler completed a business trip to the "West," going as far as from Brooklyn as Nebraska. He noted "a very satisfactory experience both in respect to the general demand for machines and the character of the sentiment toward the departures embodied in the S. D." *Motorcycle Illustrated* reported that the S. D. company was demonstrating that its designs were practical and that the S. D. "folks [were] . . . willing to place themselves on record as confidently of the belief that the shaft-driven single will develop big selling possibilities."

Rider enthusiasm for the shaft-drive S. D. is recorded in a testimonial from Brooklyn dentist E. A. Gainsford, who by November 1910 had ridden his motorcycle 2,199 miles with no adjustment of the transmission. He had bought his machine at the Madison Square Garden show the previous January. Subsequently, he found

the transmission is surprisingly smooth, and when called upon, the machine always provides a continuous powerful pull. And I find it a pleasure to rub the road dust and dirt from a smooth tube rather than to keep a belt or chain in proper trim. I also appreciate the comfort while riding of not having to worry about the parts of the transmission rubbing my clothes and splashing grease or mud over me.

I know that a great many people are skeptical of the shaft drive when applied to a single cylinder engine, but I can only say to them that the shock absorbing device applied by the said manufacture has rendered me a service that I am grateful for.

Another enthusiast was Percy N. King of Brooklyn, who in early September reported that he had ridden a 3.5-horsepower S. D. 1,854 miles on business since April. In spite of "four bad spills . . . the gears make no more noise now than at first. The machine runs smoothly and quietly, and gives one that get-there-and-back feeling. I have not had to replace a part or make an adjustment of the transmission gear, and I lay this to the shock-absorbing device."

In February, advertisements for the S. D. began to appear in the motorcycling press. In *Motorcycle Illustrated*, the quarter-page ads likely represented a considerable investment. In September, the ad size decreased, and November saw even smaller blocks that promised "coming unusually attractive values in newly designed models." In December, the plan was to "get ready for originally new mechanically correct and tested features in redesigned models."

The 1911 models of the S. D. saw significant changes, including a modification of the name to Peerless S. D. A new looping frame design permitted the lower top tube to be removed and the tank to be swung aside, allowing the engine cylinder to be removed without disturbing the crankcase. The frame was fitted with springs in both the seat tube and the fork head. A mechanical inlet valve replaced the automatic type. Ball bearings were fitted to the main and connecting rod bearings. An auxiliary hand oil pump was new. A rider-operated clutch and a two-speed transmission were big news. And a $325, 7-horsepower twin joined the 4-horsepower single, the motorcycles being identical except for engines.

The new motorcycles were to be exhibited at the New York show in early January, but a truck accident in Brooklyn delayed the S. D. exhibit two days and eliminated the twin altogether, since it was "smashed." In fact, the *Bicycling World* reporter at the show never realized that a two-cylinder machine existed. Nevertheless, the $250, one-cylinder machine shown to the public made a favorable impression; according to the *World*, it no longer resembled "a push-bike with a motor, but is a full fledged motorcycle of first class appearance, rich in gray and nickel." The S. D. officials in Manhattan, George DeWald and Jacob Spangler, declared themselves "Pretty well pleased" with the show, as the single "attracted much attention."

In the spring of 1911, the S. D. Manufacturing Company was incorporated by Jacob R. Spangler, Harry Spangler, and George DeWald. Capitalization was $30,000, with $17,000 in capital available for the start of business. Corporate goals included the manufacture of automobiles and accessories as well as motorcycles. However, by the next New York motorcycle show in January 1912, the Peerless S. D. was gone from the ranks of show machines and the motorcycle world.

Edward N. Dickerson Jr.
alone:
New York City
1896–1901
with Joseph F. Raders:
1896–99

Son of a noted mechanical savant, Edward Nicoll Dickerson Jr. (1852–1938) combined a career as a patent attorney with that of an inventor. From the 1880s through the 1900s he acquired partial patent rights to the inventions of others. Several of those acquired rights, as well as his own inventions, were in the fields of steam power as well as gas (especially acetylene) production and use.

In 1896, Joseph F. Raders of Flushing, Queens, assigned partial interest to Dickerson in a patent application for a class of "Bicycles having Mechanical Means Assisting in their Propulsion." As opposed to providing a steady source of power, Rader's idea was to utilize compressed air periodically to supplement a bicycle rider's efforts. His mechanism combined an air compressor built into the saddle with a second compressor powered from the pedal crank. The compressed air was to be stored within a tank and used when the rider desired an assist. By moving a valve, the rider directed the air to three cylinders that were connected with the crank. One suspects the idea was not a great one and probably not realized even as a test vehicle. Edward Dickerson alone was granted a patent on April 30, 1901 (the application was filed in 1896), for an acetylene-powered motorcycle. *Cycle Age* called the design "theoretical," "hardly practical," and

Jospeh F. Raders's compressed-air, three-cylinder, bicycle-assist motor. Compressors were fitted to the saddle and the crank. Drawing for Patent 626,440, June 6, 1899.

"visionary." The journal continued by stating that the Dickerson invention "does not bear the marks of carefully studied design," yet, importantly, was "probably, the first patent claim for a motor bicycle having more than one cylinder, and the claim is broad enough to cover all forms of such motor bicycles in which the motor crank shaft drives the pedal crank shaft from which transmission to the rear wheel is effected in any desirable manner."

Dickerson's cylinders were each to be supported by a different tube in the frame—i.e., one on the top tube, one on the down tube, and one on the seat tube—"whereby the strain upon the frame and weight of parts are equally distributed." One wonders about the practicality of his design, with exposed piston rods, sprockets, and chain contained within the frame diamond, about which the rider's body was positioned. Dickerson's drawings and description lack any indications of carburation, ignition, and exhaust systems. In all, his work appears to be a less-than-comprehensive plan for a motorcycle. *Cycle Age* thought that "a practical pattern of double-cylinder motor, built into or detachably secured to the frame . . . is covered by the claim . . . as well as the queer three-cylinder affair. . . . The inventor may have a good thing in his patent if he holds onto it and does not try to manufacture acetylene gas motors."

Despite the *Cycle Age* analysis of the importance of the multicylinder motorcycle patent, Dickerson probably benefited little from it, perhaps because most multicylinder motorcycles did not use the pedal crankshaft to transmit power to the driving wheel. That is not to say that Dickerson did not live a wealthy, cosmopolitan existence before or after the granting of all his patents. In 1938, shortly before his death, he became a citizen of Monaco, where, according to the *New York Times*, he had "lived for many years and own[ed] considerable property."

James R. DiTullio
d/b/a **Race Visions**
Grand Island
1970s–2010

Doing business as Race Visons, James R. DiTullio fabricated drag-racing motorcycles. Nicknamed "Puppet," DiTullio noted he had been building drag-racing cars in the late 1970s, when Paul Gast (q.v.) came to him to have welding repairs done on a racing motorcycle. DiTullio wrote in a letter to the author that he turned to building motorcycles and by "the fourth chassis I had a good idea of how they worked and what happened when you moved the motor around and played with the wheelie bar length."

DiTullio passed away in 2010, and the many articles and tributes that followed in the motorcycle drag racing press referred to him as a "legend" in the business. He was a leading figure in the fabrication of the welded racing chassis and also offered a line of "hand made aluminum body parts custom made to fit your bike."

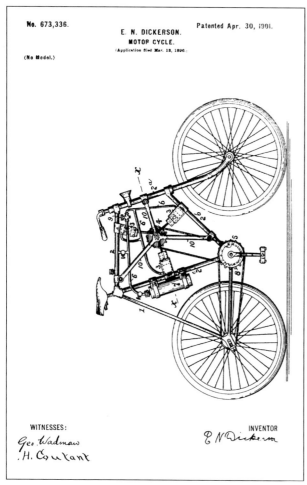

Patent drawing of Edward Dickerson's three-cylinder, acetylene-fueled motorcycle.

James J. Dragner
New York City (Manhattan)
ca. 1916–18

James J. Dragner (1893?–1980?) was an Italian-born chauffeur who filed a patent application in 1916 for "improvements in self-propelled vehicles." The patent, granted on December 3, 1918, covered elements of a motorcycle that was to "have greater stability than vehicles or cycles of similar character heretofore used, may be readily controlled; many of the parts usually employed in motor cycles will be eliminated and the vehicles will, therefore, be simplified and the cost of manufacture decreased." Dragner also noted that the rider's weight would be "distributed evenly upon the motor-driven ground wheel" for maximum traction.

Dragner's design utilized a horizontal tubular frame over the rear wheel. The wheel, with the engine attached directly to it, was suspended by a subframe composed in part of two leaf springs. The wide seat above the rear wheel also was fitted with springs to further "prevent vibrations from reaching the rider and to compensate for or absorb shocks due to uneven roadways." Forward of the engine, the frame resembled that of a motor scooter with a footboard.

To start the machine, the rider was to put one foot on the platform and then run with the other foot "for a short distance" before stepping onto the floor with the latter foot and simultaneously sitting down. The band brake, operated by a pedal, curved around the flywheel. Obviously, when the motorcycle stopped, so did the direct-geared engine. To restart, the rider would necessarily have had to run and jump again. Whether any motorcycles were built to Dragner's design is unknown here.

R. L. Dunn
Syracuse
1911
Trade Name: **Willbe**

In 1911, R. L. Dunn of Syracuse submitted a sketch to *Motorcycling* in response to a continuing debate on the best means to transfer power from a motorcycle engine to a driving wheel. At that time, proponents of belts competed with advocates of chains, each side claiming the merits of their preferred technology.

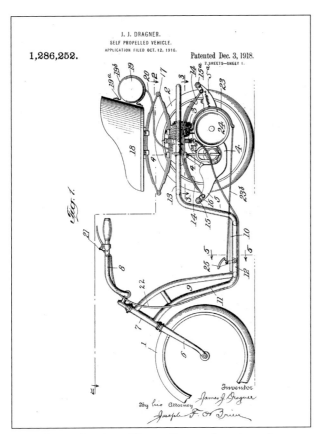

Patent drawing of James Dragner's motorcycle.

R. L. Dunn's idea for eliminating drive-belt and chain troubles was the "transmission in a nut-shell," building the engine into the rear wheel of his "Willbe" motorcycle. From *Motorcycling*, April 27, 1911.

Dunn noted that he rode "a belt-drive machine myself, and am satisfied with it." But he took up his pen to propose a system that would "do away with all transmission troubles," with "no chains to break, or belts to stretch." In essence, Dunn proposed putting the engine into the rear wheel, and in doing so "we have transmission in a nut-shell." He added that he would "gladly furnish the proper drawings" of his "Willbe" to anyone "willing to try my design." His sketch suggests a six-cylinder rotary installation.

Whether anyone took Dunn up on his offer is unknown here. But also in 1911, J. Newton Williams (q.v.) of Derby, Connecticut, who later worked in New York City, produced the first of several prototype machines with the engines built into the rear wheels.

R. L. Dunn may have been Royce L. Dunn or Ray L. Dunn—likely brothers—both of whom lived at 317 Center Street in 1911. The Sampson & Murdoch *Syracuse Directory* for 1910 gives Royce Dunn's profession as "gearmaker," a not-uncommon trade in a city that was home to several major manufacturers such as the Brown-Lipe Gear Company and the New Process Raw Hide Company.

E

Eastern Truckford Company Inc.
Buffalo
1916–18?

Motorcycle Illustrated in July 1916 noted the incorporation of the Eastern Truckford Company to manufacture "motor cars, motorcycles and motor equipment." The actual certificate of incorporation also included carriages, wagons, tires, bicycles, and "vehicles of every kind and description." Capitalized at $20,000, the Eastern company began business with $500 in capital.

The president of the Eastern company was Lincoln Green, who had been running an auto tire business called Buffalo Supply Company. The secretary was Charles P. Brady, who had worked at Buffalo Supply. The treasurer was E. Dunbar Sullivan. All three officers were also first-year directors of the Eastern corporation, as were John H. Sullivan, associated with the Michael Sullivan Dredging Company based in Detroit, and D. F. [Fraser?] Sullivan, who shared Dunbar Sullivan's 401 Delaware Avenue address. All three Sullivans also were the initial subscribers of stock in the corporation.

A newspaper article from April of 1917 describes the company as "general factory distributors for the Truckford one-ton attachment for Ford cars, . . . opening a branch at No. 1219 Main street." By the summer of 1917, the Eastern company was in the "auto trucks" business at 1219 Main Street, with an office at 927 White Building. The city directory lists the company under "auto dealers" rather than "auto manufacturers." There is no mention under the "motorcycles" heading. By the summer of 1918, the Eastern company, Green, Brady, and Dunbar Sullivan were all gone from the directory. John Sullivan remained associated with the dredging company and also with a White Building address.

The Eastern corporation was dissolved by the department of state in 1929. Motorcycle production by Eastern seems unlikely.

Eastern Wheel Works
New York City
ca. 1900
Trade Name: **Trenton**

The bicycle-manufacturing Eastern Wheel Works is listed in Manhattan directories from 1896 through 1902. A surviving motorcycle with Eastern's "Trenton" name on the head badge utilizes a diamond bicycle frame extended to the rear. Perhaps the maker shortened an existing double-diamond tandem frame, for on this motorcycle both the top tube and the chain stays intersect a second seat tube close behind and parallel to the first.

A vertical, two-stroke, air-cooled engine is mounted between the parallel tubes. A sprocket on the end of the crankshaft drives a one-inch pitch chain running to a countershaft mounted on the rear bottom bracket. From there, a second chain connects to a large sprocket on the left side of the rear wheel.

Clamps suspend the fuel tank from the top tube. A battery box is fitted to the seat stays and a coil to the rear seat tube. The forward bottom bracket is equipped with cranks, pedals, and chainwheel, allowing the rider to power the machine. The single saddle is located on the front seat tube.

Whether this survivor is an Eastern company product or the result of someone motorizing an existing Trenton bicycle, the workmanship is of high quality.

Brazed brackets for the engine, which is isolated at the bottom with a flat spring, were attached with care. The (front) seat tube carries the superimposed initials *C* and *B*, perhaps designating the original rider.

In 2000, the motorcycle in old paint remained as last used. Gregory Ostrowski owned the Trenton, having acquired it from a seller in New Jersey. Reportedly, there were two previous owners there, who had the machine for forty years or more each.

E. J. (Emma-Jane or Frank?) Edmond
Matteawan (now part of the city of Beacon)
1899–1900

In November 1900, after "more than a year's experimenting with motocycles," the *Bicycling World and Motocycle Review* said E. J. Edmond had "finally completed his bicycle, which is in shape for marketing." Utilizing a DeDion one-cylinder engine mounted behind the seat tube with the crankcase below the chain stays, Edmond effectively lowered the center of gravity as much as was practical. Drive to the rear wheel, judging from a small photographic image, was by chain.

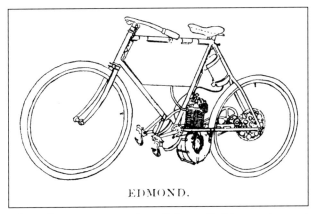

Edmond's 1900 motorcycle utilizing a DeDion engine and chain drive to the rear wheel. From the *Bicycling World and Motorcycle Review*, November 22, 1900.

The Edmond motorcycle was designed as a convertible machine to be made into a tricycle by substitution of two wheels for one in the front. A broad seat between the front wheels would make a "tandem tricycle." So equipped, and with a 2.25-horsepower engine, the machine was going to sell for $500. As a motor bicycle, the price was to be $175 to $300 depending upon the power of the engine desired. Edmond said that at the Danbury, Connecticut, fairgrounds horse track, a rough surface ridden "on the outer edge," his motor bicycle made a mile in a minute and forty-nine and a half seconds. Edmond apparently had a DeDion-Bouton motor tricycle to use for a pattern in his development work, for about the same time that he announced his machine, he advertised a DeDion-Bouton complete with trailer for two people and five new tires, "machine in first-class condition," for $300.

The couple most likely behind this motor bicycle is Frank and Emma-Jane Edmond. In 1900, Frank owned a bicycle-repair shop at 456 Main Street in Matteawan. The challenge is sorting out Emma-Jane's role, if any. "E. J. Edmond" most likely refers to Emma-Jane. However, is not clear whether Emma-Jane was an inventor or whether Frank just used her initials for his business dealings. Frank had at least one patent that he assigned to his wife. By 1910, Frank was involved in a few businesses, including selling automobiles and parts. He started a company called E. J. Edmond and Co. specializing in autos and later radios, based in Manhattan, which his nephew Claude helped run. Locally, Frank and Emma-Jane ran a lumber yard; Frank served as president, and Emma-Jane as vice president. Local newspapers at the time list multiple land transactions by Emma J. Edmond as well. What is clear is that Emma-Jane was outside of the social norms of the time with her business activity. It is possible that she was involved with the inventions and they kept it quiet; it is also possible that Frank was doing the business using Emma-Jane's name for some other reason. It is unknown at this time which role each played.

It should be noted that there was another E. J. Edmond working in the field of motorcycles. In October 1901, working for the E. R. Thomas Motor Company (q.v.) in Buffalo, this E. J. moved to the newly formed Auto-Bi Company, which assumed manufacture of the Auto-Bi motorcycle introduced by the Thomas firm. Edmond was to be assistant to the manager, E. L. Ferguson. In April 1902, the Buffalo Automobile and Auto-Bi Company, successor to the Auto-Bi enterprise, opened a branch office in Manhattan at 29-33 West Forty-Second Street, with Edmond as manager. A year later, Edmond was still on the job in New York. However, it is clear that he did not work or live in Matteawan.

Eisenhuth Horseless Vehicle Company
New York City (Manhattan) 1902
Trade Name: **Keating**

In early 1902, the Eisenhuth Horseless Vehicle Company of New York, the brainchild of John W. Eisenhuth, had acquired the "plant and business" of the bankrupt Keating Wheel and Automobile Company of Middletown, Connecticut, where a "much-heralded Keating motor bicycle . . . aroused considerable curiosity a year or more" earlier, according to the *Cycling Gazette*. Eisenhuth was "proceeding with its manufacture [in Middletown] and [would] soon have it on the market." The motorcycle, the design of R. M. Keating, used a single chain for both pedal and motor drive to the rear wheel, the pedals controlling a clutch and brake as well as being used for starting. The engine was mounted low behind the seat tube. The rear mudguard served as the muffler.

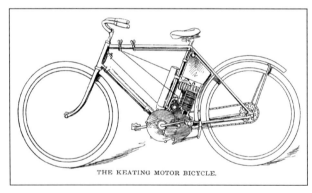

The Eisenhuth Horseless Carriage Company of New York acquired in 1902 the "plant and business" for the Keating motor bicycle, built in Middletown, Connecticut. From *Cycling Gazette*, February 1902.

In late 1903, the *Bicycling World and Motocycle Review* reported that the Eisenhuth company of Middletown had "an option" on a motor bicycle "designed by a well known New Yorker," whose identity, unfortunately, remains unknown here. Also late in 1903, the Eisenhuth company purchased the Graham-Fox Motor Company of New York with the intent of moving the Graham-Fox automobile plant to Connecticut. The Keating motor bicycle, "which we have described some time ago," said the *Cycle and Automobile Trade Journal*, also was to be manufactured.

It appears that in Middletown, the Eisenhuth Horseless Vehicle Company, later the Eagle Motor Car Company, concentrated on building automobiles, which were called first the Compound and later the Eagle. Beverly Rae Kimes and Henry Austin Clark Jr. sketch John Eisenhuth's long career as an automotive promoter.

Emblem Manufacturing Company
Angola
1907–25
Trade Name: **Emblem**

Perhaps the most successful of New York's motorcycle builders, the Emblem Manufacturing Company usually is identified with its president and manager, William G. Schack (1865–1941). A Buffalo bookkeeper in the 1890s, Schack also sold bicycles. By mid-decade, he had begun small-scale production of a bicycle he called the Emblem.

Following a depression in the bicycle industry at the turn of the century, Emblem production had lapsed, and Schack was traveling for the Day Manufacturing Company, a major bicycle builder with a factory at Idlewood in Erie County. Schack, already "one of the old-timers of the business," said *The Wheel* in July 1900, was "one of the best types of bicycle salesman. He understands bicycles, and he knows how to talk the inside and the outside of a bicycle. Beyond this, he has such a thorough confidence in his company and its product, so that, in his labors in its behalf, love walks arm in arm with the instinct of personal profit." At that point, Schack thought little of motorcycles: "No, I have not had or heard of any application from agents [bicycle dealers] for the motorcycles. It seems to be that this particular type of cycle has not the brightest future before it; its price and general character being against it, and, therefore, I cannot but figure a limited sale on them."

In the summer of 1903, the Day company was bankrupt, with liabilities of about $144,000. At auction of the assets, Schack bid over $7,000 but lost, perhaps "a bitter pill for Schaack [*sic*] or those who were alleged to be behind him. He appeared so certain of obtaining the property that only last week he sent out requests for quotations on material. His sudden rise from traveling salesman to the prospective proprietor of a considerable factory, caused considerable thinking all along the line," said the *Bicycling World and Motocycle Review*.

What funding Schack had secured has not been established clearly here, but it appears that he was working with John C. Glas (1874–1943), destined to play an important role at the Emblem Manufacturing Company. Both men, it was noted in 1904, had been "associated with the late and unlamented Day Mfg. Co.," where Glas reportedly had experimented with engines as early as 1900.

Schack and Glas moved on to Angola, perhaps having acquired some of the machinery from the Day factory. In early 1904, it was reported that the "little town" had raised $1,500 to assure the location of a bicycle factory, the Emblem Manufacturing Company.

In January 1904, the Emblem company was incorporated by Schack of Buffalo; Glas of Lake View; William J. Heil Jr. of Lake View; John Sykes, possibly a lawyer from Trenton, New Jersey; and Harry F. Seamark, a veteran of the bicycle trade since 1881 and eventual Emblem dealer in Washington, DC. Other local investors at this time or somewhat later included Albert W. Shepker of North Evans, John M. Warwick of Angola, and William Owen, probably of Angola. Donald C. Cook, writing in the *Evans Journal* in 1970, said Heil and Shepker, as well as Otto Waibel, who helped form the Emblem Company, had worked at the Day factory. Cook said Heil told him that the Emblem enterprise actually started in Heil's Lake View barn, operating there until the fall of 1904 before moving to Angola.

The Emblem corporate purpose was broad: the "manufacturing and selling for profit, any and all articles of merchandise of every kind and nature." The amount of capital stock for the corporation was forty thousand dollars, twenty thousand of which was designated for the start of business. Of the fifty-dollar par value shares, Glas subscribed 170; Schack, two hundred; Seamark, twenty; Sykes, twenty; and Heil, four. The Angola centennial booklet, *One Village through the Pages of Time* (1973), notes that Schack was Emblem president and Heil vice president at one unspecified time.

Emblem prosperity came quickly. During the season of 1906, Schack reported he built fifteen thousand bicycles, and the Emblem company had become important to the local economy. Using local labor, said the *Bicycling World*, Schack and Glas built a new concrete block factory:

> The same men who build bicycles drew the plans and dug the foundation of the building and then started the difficult and technical work of erecting the plant by a process thought to be understood by but few concerns in this country; but they did it, and did it well. They did more, too. They installed the plumbing and lighting, the boilers and engine, and electric lighting plant and telephone system, and when all was completed they moved the machinery and tools with practically little or no cessation of work.

From the beginning, the Emblem company advertised that its bicycles were the "Product of Co-operative Labor." At least some employees had a "stock interest in the company," which reportedly enabled Schack "to get a maximum amount of service for the least possible cost, and every step in the manufacture of his goods is under the watchful eye of a man to whom their excellence means something more than work well done."

1907 Model Year

As early as November 1906, the Emblem company advertised that they were "prepared to take orders for our Emblem Motorcycles." As did several other motorcycles of the day, the Emblem Model 100 used drive components from the Aurora Automatic Machinery Company of Aurora, Illinois. An illustration of the Emblem motorcycle appearing in early March 1907 shows the Thor engine incorporated into the seat tube of an Emblem-built diamond frame with a coil-spring front suspension. The fuel tank was suspended from the top tube, the coil on the down tube, and the battery box on the rear stays behind the saddle, in the pattern of other Thor-equipped motorcycles. The price for the Model 100 was $210.

64 | Emblem Manufacturing Company

The first Emblem motorcycle powered by a Thor engine supplied by the Aurora Automatic Machinery Company of Aurora, Illinois. From the *Bicycling World and Motorcycle Review*, March 2, 1907.

The *Cycle and Automobile Trade Journal* reported two months later that the engine was a 2.25-horsepower Thor "hung on a Thor special hanger, fitted with compensating sprocket" for the chain drive. The Emblem spring fork was a patented design, while the front hub was a Thor item. The rear hub was fitted with a coaster brake. The wheels were 28 inches with 2.25-inch G & J tires. A Thor carburetor was used. A force-feed oil pump was supplied, as was a copper fuel tank. Capacities were recorded as gasoline for 100 miles, oil for 200 miles, and speeds from 5 to 50 miles per hour. The standard finish was black; light and dark blue were also options. The Model 100 designation complemented the numerical designations given to the Emblem bicycles, with their numbers ranging from 25 to 63.

In early March, "Manager Schack" claimed that demand for the new motorcycle was "quite good." He had begun making deliveries at the end of February and expected to be able to "continue shipments on 10 days' time," said the *Bicycling World*. Advertising for the Emblem motorcycle continued at least to the end of April 1907. Some years later, *Motorcycling* reported that "nearly fifty" of the original model Emblems were built with Thor motors *in 1904*. That Emblem motorcycles were produced in 1904 or 1905 or even 1906 is questionable. Perhaps the production figure of fifty machines is accurate for 1907.

1908 Model Year

Data about the 1908 model Emblem motorcycles remains scarce at this juncture; it is likely that there were no motorcycles at all. In the fall of 1907, the Aurora Automatic Machinery Company introduced its own 1908 model motorcycle. While Aurora promised to continue to supply engines to other manufacturers, the announcement may have been the incentive (or additional incentive) for the Emblem Manufacturing Company to revise its motorcycle program by designing their own Emblem motors. The *Bicycling World and Motorcycle Review* in April 1908 listed the Emblem Company as a source of motorcycles but in January 1909 spoke of Emblem's "re-entry into the motorcycle industry." Unless evidence materializes to substantiate manufacture of Emblem motorcycles, one might assume the Emblem Manufacturing Company built only bicycles for the 1908 season.

1909 Model Year

"Well advanced" by early October 1908, the new Emblem motorcycle made its inaugural appearance during the New York City show in January 1909. A low top-tube height of 29 inches was achieved even when fitted with 28-inch wheels. The Emblem-fabricated tube members were reinforced internally with triangular braces, which reportedly made the frame "as strong as a solid bar of the same diameter. "Since the frame is braced from three points, twisting is practically impossible," reported *Motorcycle Illustrated*. Again, a suspended front fork was combined with a rigid rear wheel design, as usual for motorcycles of the period.

Mounted vertically at the bottom of a looping diamond frame, both 3.5- and 4-horsepower, single-cylinder engines were offered. Ball bearings were utilized for both crankshaft and connecting rods. The coil and the battery box were fitted above the top tube in front of the saddle, whereby "the rider may inquire within" by removing two nuts. The rounded tank sat between the two upper, parallel tubes. A toolbox was located behind the seat tube. Universal joints in the control mechanism allowed the handlebars to be turned without changing throttle or spark adjustment. The V-belt to the left side of the rear wheel featured layers of leather and linen to prevent stretching or breaking. Prices were $175 and $200.

An Emblem catalog appeared late in the winter of 1909. Emblem advertising mentioned the innovative or new qualities of the motorcycles for the 1909 season. These included the reinforced tubing ("Our Own Make"), the ball-bearing engines ("Of Our Own Make"), and the low frame. Emblem advertisements also prominently noted the "Product of Co-operative Labor." And after the Federation of American Motorcyclists' 1909 Cleveland-to-Indianapolis endurance run, display ads boasted of the perfect score achieved by George A. Heil on an Emblem.

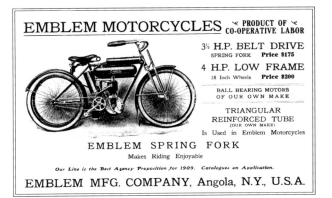

Emblem engines powered the second generation of Emblem motorcycles built by "co-operative labor" sharing profits. From the *Bicycling World and Motorcycle Review*, January 23, 1909.

1910 Model Year

In almost everything written about the Emblem Manufacturing Company, William Schack's name is prominent. The quintessential outside man, he was present at trade shows and meetings, on sales trips, and at public events of all types. His longtime colleague John Glas was much less visible but, as a designer and manager of factory operations, apparently was no less vital to Emblem successes. *Motorcycling*, in January 1910, identified Glas as "superintendent" and Schack as "manager" of Emblem operations, the two being "the constructive people here."

In the late summer of 1909, Schack was on the West Coast "closing contracts for 1910." At that point, he had distributors in Philadelphia (the Manufacturers Supply Company) for Delaware, Maryland, and southern New Jersey; in Los Angeles (John T. Bill and Company) for southern California; in Portland, Oregon (Ballou and Wright) for Oregon; and in Salt Lake City (Meredith and Guthrie Company) for Utah. Later it was reported that F. M. Spinning of Seattle had taken on distribution for Emblem in Washington State and W. D. Alexander of Atlanta for "several southern states."

In October Schack was in New York, where he stated "with but a faint reservation" that the entire Emblem motorcycle line for 1910 would be equipped with the Eclipse clutch ("free engine device"), which, it was noted, was "built into the engine pulley of belt-driven machines and, being very simple, has been tried out with marked success" (*Motorcycle Illustrated*, October 15, 1909). In the end, the clutch was made optional equipment.

Other major news about the pending Emblems included an option of magneto ignition at twenty-five dollars extra and the introduction of a 7-horsepower twin. Prices for the 3.5- and 4-horsepower singles as well as the twin were to be $200, $225, and $250 with battery ignition.

The 1910 motorcycles appeared within a few weeks, much changed from the old, with a new rectangular tank filling the space between the upper frame tubes and the move of the battery case to a spot between the seat tube and the rear fender. The *Bicycling World* said the new frame design had a "more graceful loop." The wheelbase for 1910, at 56 inches, was relatively long. The front fork travel was 2.5 inches. While the frame was brazed, the motor was bolted into place and easily removed. G & J or Empire tires of 2.5-inch diameter were fitted to 28-inch wheels. AV or flat belt delivered power. The copper tanks had a capacity of two gallons of gasoline and two quarts of oil.

The 1910 Emblem engines, featuring ball bearings in the crankshaft and connecting rod, used atmospheric intake valves. The 1.75-inch exhaust valves were cam controlled. Lubrication was the force-feed type, with a sight tube mounted on the tank. A Heitger carburetor was used, cable controlled by twist grip. Ignition was either battery and coil or magneto or both—the latter feature one observer called "radical

The lever-controlled idler served as a clutch on Emblems fitted with a flat belt. Alternatively, the V-belt model could be purchased with an Eclipse-made clutch for fifteen dollars extra. From *Motorcycle Illustrated*, January 1, 1910.

and original," with either system available "by altering the connection of the spark plug." The *Bicycling World* said the long stroke engine design "now is enjoying high favor with automobile engineers, and which principle the Emblem company is one of the first to apply to motorcycles. Increasing the expansion and reducing the crankshaft speed is claimed to reduce wear and increase economy."

Saddles for 1910 were Troxel or Mesinger. Colors were carmine or gray "with gold and green stripes." Weights were listed as 175 pounds for the 4-horsepower machine, 180 for the 5, and 200 for the 7 (twin). The least powerful of the Emblems ran 55 to 57 miles per hour on the road "while still 'green,'" according to Schack. Of the 1910 motorcycle line, *Motorcycle Illustrated* said it was "honest material, just enough ingenuity to produce up-to-date and at the same time thoroughly practical machines, and, finally, skilled and careful workmanship. The result is altogether fine."

Construction began in early April 1910 on a four-story, 75-by-40-foot addition to the factory. By that time, it was reported that the plant was thirty days behind in filling orders, although it is not clear whether these were for bicycles, motorcycles, or a combination of the two.

It's difficult to establish a clear picture of Emblem sales at this time. The identification of the distributors is plain from advertisements. At a glance it would seem that dealers were scarcer in New England, the lower South, the Plains states, and the Southwest than elsewhere. Detroit agent Robert Shattuck in August 1910 reported that he had sold fifteen Emblems in the city "and vicinity."

William Schack for many years was active in trade associations. In January 1910, the Emblem Manufacturing Company was elected a member of the Motorcycle Manufacturers' Association. In April, Schack attended an MMA meeting in Buffalo. In August, he attended an Atlantic City meeting of the MMA, where he was characterized by a *Motorcycle Illustrated* reporter as a man "who takes life just seriously enough to make him a crack-a-jack business man, the able representative of a firm with which it is a real pleasure to deal. Mr. Schack is a veteran, but one of the sort who is so many years young—not old. He has a fund of dry witticisms of the good natured kind, which he uses to excellent advantage."

Motorcycle racing and trials were important to riders and manufacturers of the late 1900s and early 1910s. While the Emblem Manufacturing Company never sponsored a team of racers, as some of its competitors did, Emblem advertising did benefit from the performance of Emblem motorcycles in races and endurance runs. Maurice E. Gale (1877–1936) of Angola was perhaps the best known of adventurous Emblem riders. In the late summer of 1910 on an Emblem twin, he delivered a letter from the mayor of Chicago to the mayor of New York. Departing on a Sunday morning and arriving the following Wednesday at noon, he set a fast-time record.

At that point, Gale probably was not on the Emblem factory payroll, but it's likely that his equipment was supplied and that he was reimbursed for his expenses, as well as for his time at trade shows and other venues where he represented the firm. Of the Chicago-to-New York jaunt, Gale said he spent thirty-five hours in the saddle. A full-page ad claimed the reliability of the Emblem, with "the machine in as good condition at the end of the journey as when it started. It's Emblem Quality That Counts, Emblem Perfection That Takes You Anywhere."

Track-racing successes also figured in Emblem advertising. For example, in Portsmouth, Ohio, on October 30, L. S. (Lee S., also identified as "C. S.") Taylor won both the 5- and 10-mile handicaps on an Emblem single. In a solo run, Taylor set a track record, taking fifty seconds from the previous 5-mile-time trial standard. Probably on another date, he covered 100 miles on a dirt track in 116 minutes, $57^{2}/_{5}$ seconds. According to *Motorcycling*, Taylor, an employee of American Machine Company, the Emblem agency in Columbus, had discovered the potential of the Emblem engine while riding a standard motorcycle. "The motor was put into a racing frame, to facilitate taking the short curves of a half-mile track at high speed; ports were cut and unnecessary equipment removed." Another Ohioan, George Evans, won a 100-mile race at Columbus on an Emblem.

Ira Swetland and Maurice Gale testing 1911 5-horsepower Emblems in the snow in Angola. From the *Bicycling World and Motorcycle Review*, January 14, 1911.

1911 Model Year

In the fall of 1910, William Schack claimed that he wanted to get away from the seasonal approach to motorcycle production and sales. He said that he saw "no reason why the trade should not buy and stock up with machines all the year through—this policy meaning, as it does, a greater economy for all concerned." He stated that the Emblem factory intended to operate at the same production rate all year around. Motorcycles not taken by sellers would be stocked, "ready for the first man who comes along with his money." *Motorcycling* magazine noted that dealers in the nonseasonal marketing scheme would have to invest in stock—something that smaller agents were not accustomed to doing.

The Emblem may well have "taken a distinct place in motorcycle product, a place of a sturdy, sensible machine free from any geegaws or attempt at being 'different,'" as *Motorcycling* declared in October 1910. The paper went on to report that Schack believed in "the road rather than in the track as a means of publicity promotion."

Emblems were prominent at both the New York and Chicago motorcycle shows in early 1911. In New York, there were four 5-horsepower machines, one of 4 horsepower, one stock twin, and a twin racing machine. The last, which Emblem advertising called a "Semi-Racer," was the first Angola machine available with chain drive as an alternative to a belt. The *Bicycling World* described the Semi-Racer as differing from the standard machines in that it had a "toboggan dropped frame—a sloping top tube at the rear-drilled cylinder flanges to reduce weight, auxiliary exhaust ports with bands, and will be furnished with either chain or belt drive." The free engine clutch "in conjunction with an idler on the flat belt model" as well as the spring seat post, which combined flat and coil springs, the pair providing an "exceptionally comfortable" ride, were features of the regular Emblem motorcycles for 1911.

In early 1911, the Emblem Manufacturing Company hired as its "publicity man" Frank Libbey Valiant,

Margelia Moreau of Buffalo riding her Emblem in Angola. From *Motorcycling*, February 16, 1911.

formerly an editorial assistant at the *Bicycling World and Motorcycle Review* in New York City. Valiant's job at the Emblem Company was described as "an executive position." Nevertheless, two years later he left for "a more responsible" role as advertising manager and assistant sales manager for the Miami Cycle and Manufacturing Company. While reportedly regretful at having to say goodbye to Schack, Valiant could not "conceal his delight at exchanging the muddy pikes of Angola, N.Y., for real paved streets in Middletown [Ohio]" (*Motorcycling*, April 11, 1912).

In the summer of 1911, the Federation of American Motorcyclists had their national meet in Buffalo. The Emblem Company exploited the event, inviting participants to Angola: "We'll see you in Buffalo, and we'd like to have you see us in Angola." Maurice Gale and his wife "attracted considerable attention" on their twin, modified for side-by-side seating.

For the 1911 season, Emblem distributors were John T. Bill & Co. in Los Angeles for California; Ballou & Wright in Portland for Oregon, F. M. Spinning in Seattle for Washington, the Meredith Cycle Company of Salt Lake City for Utah, and Henry Keidel & Company of Baltimore for the South. In addition, there were individual dealers, some of whom sought agency privileges on their own initiatives and some of whom were secured by the Emblem Company through its advertising: "Somebody's going to have the Emblem agency in your town. Will it be **you**? Write us please—we're waiting to hear—and we'll answer cheerfully." Emblem advertising was optimistic about the company's and their motorcycle's potential for success. In terms of their hopes, the 1911 season may have been the Emblem's high point, even if sales figures were greater in the 1912 and 1913 seasons. For 1911, Schack and his colleagues could claim that because of their

> joyous velvet-riding scenery changer we are not so haughty and arbitrary now as we soon may be, considering the flood of success that is attending the EMBLEM motorcycle. We are very approachable at present.
>
> Consider how the EMBLEM has jumped in a short time from an unknown factor to one of the recognized leaders. Do you like to pick winners? Then pick the EMBLEM. It has already won!

Valiant may have thought that images of women riders would increase the number of female enthusiasts. One photo in the trade press showed May E. MacClymont of North Evans riding a 4-horsepower machine fitted with a clutch. "Although she had not previously ridden a motorcycle, this charming motorcycliste states that she did not have the slightest difficulty in mastering the machine." As a private secretary, she was riding 20 miles each day, with Sunday outings of more than 100 miles.

Production estimates for the 1911 model year are lacking here. The Emblem Company at the beginning of the 1912 model year reported that it was "scheduled to reach 2,000 machines" for that season. Working backward from that figure, one might guess at 1,000 to 1,500 for 1911.

1912 Model Year

The 1912 Emblems were announced in September 1911 ("As to 1912 prices—later") and available in October 1911; fifty to seventy-five were sold "in various parts of the country" late in the month. The *Bicycling World* called the evolution "refinement of a pronounced nature." The most striking visual modification was the lowering of the top tube adjacent to the saddle, allowing the seat to be moved forward, shortening the handlebars, and thus lowering the center of gravity. *Motorcycling* claimed that the old-style frame would be available "if desired"; its advantage was a "very large accommodation for long-distance baggage carrying."

A tandem attachment was claimed to be the safest and most comfortable yet devised, fitted to lugs "firmly brazed on all 1912 Emblem models." Oil and gasoline compartments switched places in the tank. With the oil pump at the front and in a slanting position, the rider would find it "easy to oil on sandy or rough roads, as the rider holds the forearm against the left bar and works the oiler." A celluloid cylinder replaced a glass type in the pump. Engine modifications were minor, directed to greater reliability with longer intake valve guides, lighter cam gearing with longer bearing, and larger ball bearings for crank and connecting rod.

In November 1911, "drastic cuts" were announced for all models except the 7-horsepower twin, which was available only with magneto ignition still at $250. The 4-horsepower model was henceforth $175, and the 5-horespower was $200 for battery ignition; magneto was $25 more for either. Additionally, it was announced that every Emblem would be fitted with the Eclipse clutch "as regular equipment." *Motorcycle Illustrated* noted that the reduction in price did not connote a reduction in the quality: "Instead, just the opposite condition prevails. The very finest materials procurable in the market enter into the construction of Emblem motorcycle, and the reduction in price has been accomplished by systematizing the entire factory,

Emblem president William Schack with his omnipresent cigar, caricaturized in *Motorcycling*, February 8, 1912.

the employment of only the most skilled workmen, the installation of improved machinery, co-operative labor and increased factory facilities."

As in the previous year, Emblem motorcycles appeared at several motor vehicle shows. The first major event was at Madison Square Garden in January, where Schack, Valiant, Taylor, and W. H. Snyder represented the firm. Valiant showed a "neat handlebar mirror, of his own design," which he called the "reflectoscope." Taylor, it was learned in New York, had left the American Machine Company in Columbus to work for the Emblem firm. *Motorcycling* reported in 1912, "He is not only a racing man of resource, but a salesman and general helper, being now in charge of repairing and other work at the factory."

Although the managers counted on increased sales of Emblem motorcycles in 1912, bicycles still represented the "bulk of the Emblem business," where two hundred men were employed year-round, earning a payroll of $130,000 annually. With a total investment of $250,000, the Emblem factory reportedly was "the

mainstay of the town" (*Motorcycling*, November 26, 1911). In the summer, Schack was "very optimistic on trade conditions for 1913" (*Bicycling World and Motorcycle Review*, August 10, 1912). Speaking to a "*Bi-World* man," he stated that his company "would almost double its manufacturing capacity for next year and produce close to 5,000 Emblems," suggesting that he had reached his goal of 2,000 for the 1912 season. At that point, a fifth story on the existing 230-by-40-foot factory was being roofed, and a 105-by-40-foot addition was under construction.

Mattie Gale surveys the challenge of Kansas mud to her Emblem in 1912. Photo taken by her husband, Maurice E. Gale, and donated to the New York State Museum by her son, Herbert F. Gale. NYSM H-1992.68.40.

The relative popularity of Emblem motorcycles may be suggested by an informal census made at the Federation of American Motorcyclists tour in Columbus, Ohio, in July 1912. Emblems were the seventh most numerous of the seventeen makes recorded, comprising eleven of the 385 machines. A change in distribution of Emblem motorcycles was made in the spring of 1912, as Ballou and Wright of Portland, Oregon, replaced F. M. Spinning as distributor for Washington.

The large displacement engine of the Emblem twin served its builder to promote as much reliability as pure speed. In fact, the Emblem Company distinguished between engines that "show a wonderful burst of speed for a short time and then require a week to rest up" and those with the "power to take you there and back."

Aside from its encouraging words about Emblem reliability, the manufacturer backed its motorcycles with a guarantee. Typical for the period, the warranty was limited in scope, covering parts only for a period of a year. Repair or replacement was to take place only at the factory after the parts or machine was shipped prepaid by the owner. Tires, saddles, and magnetos were excluded since those pieces were covered by their individual makers rather than by the Emblem Manufacturing Company.

At the end of May 1912, the Motorcycle Manufacturers' Association met in Toledo, and Schack was on hand, "having never missed a meeting of the association" (*Motorcycling*, June 6, 1912). In addition to his membership in the Motorcycle Manufacturers' Association, Schack promoted the proliferation and use of cycles in other ways. He rode, himself, commuting to Angola from his Buffalo home from time to time. And he served as president of the Buffalo Motorcycle Club.

1913 Model Year

With its 1913 models, the Emblem Manufacturing Company may have reached the zenith of its motorcycle business. A new twin-cylinder model made Emblem the builder of the largest displacement motorcycle in the country. Asked about twins, Schack said he thought they would "be used very largely in the future and at least until a practical two-speed gear is brought out" (*Motorcycling*, October 3, 1912). Schack was referring to the greater torque of the twins, which allowed them to be ridden at low speeds without stalling and to accelerate without stumbling. But Schack thought a practical two-speed transmission would "undoubtedly be used on every motorcycle manufactured, especially those of large horsepower."

Interviewed by *Motorcycling*, Schack predicted, based upon information from his customers, "a materially increased business on motorcycles for 1913." He expected wider use by both pleasure and commercial riders. For the latter, he forecast the application of van bodies for delivery work. And he thought the use of sidecars would increase, too.

When asked about lighter motorcycles designed for city use, Schack said he thought it was "impossible to restrict the riding of any particular motorcycle to city pavements only. The use of two-speed gear would no doubt have tendency towards motorcycles of somewhat lighter weight."

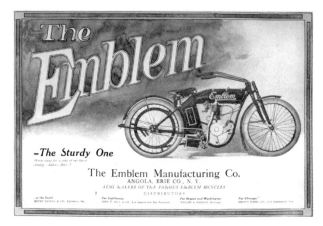

Advertisement for the magneto-equipped, belt-drive Emblem. From *Motorcycling*, January 9, 1913.

Having dropped the smaller single six months later, midway through the model year, Schack told *Motorcycling* that orders for twins were 75 percent of the Emblem's business. Trade, Schack said, was "certainly in a most prosperous condition," even "too strenuous"; demand had outpaced production since February. Customers were dissatisfied with thirty- to forty-five-day delays in shipments. It was perhaps the busiest time in the history of Emblem motorcycle production.

The Emblem distribution picture changed somewhat for the 1913 season. The Brown Music Company became the distributor for Chicago and the vicinity. Henry Keidel and Company in Baltimore remained the distributor for the South, but a list of leading dealers in Florida, Georgia, and South Carolina showed no Emblem representation. Ballou and Wright in the Northwest, on the other hand, noted that they had contracted for three hundred Emblems (and one thousand Indians) for 1913.

Increased demand for motorcycles resulted in an enlarged labor force compared to the previous year. The "average monthly force reported by concern" for 1913 was 260 men in the shop—an increase of one hundred—and eleven in the office, according to the New York State Department of Labor's *Second Annual Industrial Directory of New York State, 1913*. The shop workers averaged fifty-two to fifty-seven hours a week. In July 1913, a reporter for *Motorcycle Illustrated*, in visiting the Emblem factory, noted "16 departments on 5 floors utilizing a total of 66,000 square feet. On the lowest level was the heat treating department for frame tubing, which was bent (formed) in an adjoining area. On the second floor were the machining, polishing, plating and brazing sections."

On the third floor were the filing and enameling departments, both of which worked "in a manner indicative of the thoroughness which characterizes the whole establishment" (*Motorcycle Illustrated*, July 1913). Motorcycle frames received three coats of enamel, each being baked individually. Special color orders resulted in "even more pride than usual in turning out artistic and lasting work, and the durability and beauty of the Emblem finish testify to the company's complete success in this direction." The stripers worked quickly and accurately by hand.

Also on the third floor of the Angola factory was the shipping department. At the front of the building Emblem employees were able to slide the crated motorcycles (and bicycles) down a chute into a waiting freight car. On the fourth floor, above the shipping department, were the offices. Also on the fourth floor were the stockroom for motorcycle and bicycle parts, tracked with an "excellent system . . . to ensure accuracy and economize in time."

On the fifth floor of the Emblem factory were the assembly and crating areas for both motorcycles and bicycles. The motorcycle assembly was divided into sections for motor assembly, motor testing, final assembly, and final testing. The engines were run for twenty-four hours each "to ascertain whether they are giving perfect service." Having the Emblem factory on three railroads with private switches enabled the plant "to receive and distribute raw material and finished product in the most economical manner." The factory itself had been provided with "everything that money can buy or mechanical genius can devise in the way of modern tools and machinery." And "situated apart from the distracting influences of a large city, its employees are able to devote their undivided time and attention to the work in hand; coupled with this the workmen participate directly in the profits of the company, and a pride of workmanship is engendered in every man who assists in constructing Emblem-made wares which would be impossible under less favorable conditions."

Asked about notable features of the Emblem motorcycles for 1913, company representatives spoke of the large displacement of all three engines, the "balancing of the reciprocating parts . . . brought up to the highest standard," larger tanks, enlarged spring forks "to give greater strength and resiliency," and the mechanical inlet valves (*Motorcycle Illustrated*, October 31, 1912). The overhead intake valves were operated by the single cam working on pushrods and rocker arms. This arrangement of valve operation by one cam was unusual in the period, when a series of gear-driven cams for individual valves were common. With the Emblem system, accurate timing was assured as long as the cam gear was installed properly. "The perfecting of this valve gear must be credited to Superintendent J. C. Glas, who conducted an exhaustive series of experiments and tests."

Other changes in the engines for 1913 included plain bronze bearings replacing the balls of earlier Emblem models and cooling fins wider at the top than at the bottom of the cylinder. A larger intake manifold was also new. An aluminum, asbestos-filled muffler supposedly so quieted the exhaust flow "that the report is hardly audible, yet practically no back pressure is caused" (*Motorcycling*, October 24, 1912).

The frame of the 1913 Emblem was changed slightly, with a drop in the top tube farther toward the front of the machine compared with the 1912 style. The move to lower the saddle was typical of most motorcycle manufacturers. The top tube also was reportedly 2 inches taller at the front to allow larger tanks. The fork was modified with a packing to seal the spring housing and provide a pneumatic shock absorber. The fork was wider, to prevent "mud from jamming between wheels and forks. There is sufficient room for tire chains."

For 1913, an Eclipse disk clutch was standard equipment on all models. Larger tanks carried eight quarts of gasoline and two quarts of oil. Magneto ignition was standard except on the lowest price single, which had the magneto as a $25 option. Belt drive was available only on the single and smaller twin, with chain as an option. Color options were carmine, French gray, and maroon. Prices ranged from $175 to $300.

Emblem promotions continued to exploit the ventures of Emblem endurance riders, notably Gale, during 1913, maintaining a policy of advertising the durability and reliability of Emblem motorcycles. Early in the year, Gale rode a twin from Angola to the New York cycle show, "splash, slip, skid and paddle through icy puddles and slippery roads, then through a snow storm, all the way to Syracuse on Monday." Snow drifts marked the route to Schenectady on Tuesday. Gale reached New York City on Wednesday, where his motorcycle became part of the Emblem display. A few weeks later, Gale headed for the Chicago show on his 10-horsepower twin. Near La Porte, Indiana, his drive chain had broken, wrapping itself around the rear hub and shearing all the spokes. "Gale is now a strong advocate of the belt drive." In the summer "the well-known plumber and rider of Emblem motorcycles," accompanied by his wife, Mattie, took on a bigger challenge, riding from the Federation of American Motorcyclists meet in Denver to New York City, covering the 2,319 miles in eighty-seven riding hours over thirteen days. All Gale's efforts were praised in Emblem advertisements.

1914 Model Year

Changes to the Emblem motorcycle line for 1914 were few. Notable differences were roller bearings in the crankshaft ends of the connecting rods, blue paint, folding footrests, a revised suspension fork, reinforced frames, and rearrangement of the controls. Also of note was the availability of a two-speed transmission on all models.

In December Schack told *Motorcycling* that business was "great and looks like a fine year for the 1914 machines." The Emblem catalog for 1914 appeared in early February. Perhaps the most significant item in the catalog was the drop in price of the 10-horsepower twin from $300 to $275. This reduction followed an industry-wide trend begun vigorously in the fall of 1913.

The volatility of business affairs in 1914 affected the Emblem company with the bankruptcy at year's end of its central Ohio distributor, the American Machine Company. The Emblem Manufacturing Company was American's largest creditor at $7,000.

The unevenness of Emblem distribution remained a factor for the 1914 model year. At the end of August, the Los Angeles Motorcycle Club held its annual run to Venice. Of the 1,112 participating motorcycles, *none* was an Emblem. In the spring of 1914, Schack reported to *Motorcycle Illustrated* that during the past two months he had sold sixteen Emblem motorcycles to a

Ray Snyder, winner of a 5-mile track race in Toledo, Ohio, on a motorcycle powered by a modified Emblem engine. From *Motorcycling*, July 20, 1914.

Mattie, Edwin, Herbert, and Maurice Gale with their 1914 Emblem twin. Note seating for four, generator for electric lamps, speedometer, and, of course, umbrella. Photo courtesy of Herbert F. Gale. NYSM H-1992.68.42.

distributor in Portugal. In the summer, however, the European sales situation looked bleak with the start of the First World War. In the winter, *Motorcycling* said Schack noted that the rider-propelled machines "constitute the larger part of the Emblem factory production," estimated at thirty thousand units a year. His "list of bicycle dealers include many who don't sell motorcycles."

The 10-horsepower, 77-cubic-inch Emblem Big Twin had the largest displacement of any contemporary, regularly marketed American motorcycle. From *Motorcycling*, January 12, 1914.

Maurice, Herbert, Edwin, and Mattie Gale (*left to right*) posing in 1914 on their Emblem in Angola. Photo courtesy of Herbert F. Gale. NYSM H-1992.68.43.

1915 Model Year

The summer of 1914 saw the announcement of the 1915 Emblem motorcycles. Improvements to the same three basic machines included a step starter pedal that fit the standard Eclipse clutch. The new ratcheting device augmented the bicycle-style pedals and did not replace them, although, combined with footboards, the new starter made the pedals superfluous in case a rider wished to remove them. Also new were a hinged rear fender for ease of wheel removal, foot-controlled shift of the two-speed gearing, a battery-powered headlight, a Corbin-Brown speedometer, and an optional sidecar for seventy-five dollars. A van body for the same tubular sidecar chassis could be "be interchanged with [the passenger model] if desired."

The motorcycle catalog for 1915, subtitled *Class Power Speed Satisfaction*, claimed the Emblem was "in a class of its own," thanks, in addition to the footboards and two-speed transmission, to such features as

1. The largest bore and stroke "in motorcycle construction";

2. Valve mechanism that had been "accelerated" to give 5 or 8 miles per hour more speed; and

3. Grip ratchet control, a "most efficient method of regulating speed."

Each Emblem was "given a severe test by expert men, for speed, power and durability. Every Emblem twin motorcycle must be able to attain a speed considerably above the mile-a-minute mark." At the shipping department, "a final testing card" was attached, "giving actual top speed." The catalog noted that "the owner of a 1915 Emblem will feel himself the most splendidly mounted man on the road; but better even than this will be the assurance that, coupled with beauty of design, the Emblem has the material, the perfection of mechanical detail, and the power to bring him to his destination quickly, safely and comfortably."

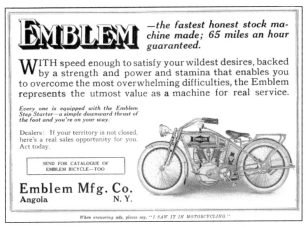

For the big Emblem twins, 1915 was the penultimate year. From *Motorcycling*, May 24, 1915.

Ted A. Hodgdon, writing for *Antique Motorcycles* in 1963, recalled the appearance of new Emblem motorcycles: the "*finish* and coloring and plating . . . were the envy of almost all manufacturers in those days. The color of the Emblem in the early years was a beautiful shade of French blue with dark blue striping, some gold decorations, all set off with a very large amount of nickel plating."

The 1915 season began in a positive fashion, according to William Schack, who told *Motorcycling* he

> would advise that orders for both bicycles and motorcycles are very satisfactory, and from all indications covering a recent trip from Coast to Coast, the writer is free to state that our business for 1915 looks very encouraging.
>
> We have more bicycles and motorcycles on actual specification today than a year ago, we are constantly adding to our force and expect that the season of 1915 will exceed that of 1914 by quite a margin.
>
> On motorcycles, the demand for two-speed is fairly good and seems to be quite popular. For sidecar or commercial van equipment it is really necessary to get the most satisfactory results.
>
> Our Kansas City agent, Fred P. Ames, has about ten of the 1915 machines and we understand that he has practically sold them all. Our Pittsburgh agent, T. J. Everwine, has also had a few of the 1915 machines. We are shipping samples each day. William G. Schack, General Manager

A few weeks later, Schack remained optimistic, saying he was shipping more machines since the Chicago show than he shipped last year at the same time. "Never a day at the Emblem plant without at least one machine being shipped out, he says, which is going some for these times."

A machine a day, of course, is far from realizing the goal of 3,000 or 5,000 motorcycles year, of which Schack had spoken not long previously. In fact, with a six-day work week, a machine a day barely would have topped 300 Emblem motorcycles for a year. One would think that Schack foresaw increased production further into the model year. In 1970, as reported by Donald C. Cook in the *Evans Journal*, a former Emblem employee, Percy Hoover, recalled the Emblem company building 25 motorcycles per week, i.e., 1,300 per year (as well as 125–150 bicycles per day). Hoover's statement came in reaction to seeing a photo of the Emblem factory interior in 1915, but he did not specify the exact year in which his remembered motorcycle-production figure was achieved. As far as factory capacity is concerned, a *Motorcycle Illustrated* writer in March 1915 said that the Emblem factory could turn out 7,500 to 10,000 motorcycles a year as well as 60,000 to 75,000 bicycles.

Comparing Schack's previous goals of 3,000 or 5,000 motorcycles a year with actual shipments of his largest competitors suggests the relatively small role Emblem played in the overall motorcycle market. The domestic industry leader, the Hendee Manufacturing Company, reported shipments of 13,000 machines by the first week of May from its 2,000-employee factory in Springfield, Massachusetts. By the end of the season, 16,418 Harley-Davidsons had been shipped by the 1,200-employee workforce in Milwaukee.

The Emblem lightweight twin, as announced in 1915. Three-speed gearing was not yet available. From *Motorcycling and Bicycling*, October 11, 1915.

Trade with Europe continued, despite Schack's fear expressed in 1914 that the outbreak of war would mean an end to transatlantic sales. In June 1915, Schack was able to report to *Motorcycling and Bicycling* the sale of nine motorcycles "to be shipped immediately" to newly appointed agents in neutral Holland as well as a contract for the sale of Emblems in Cuba. He went on to report that "demand for Emblems equipped with

Emblem sidecars far exceeds that of any previous year and is already beyond expectations." He anticipated that business in both motorcycles and bicycles would be "good" for the remainder of the 1915 season. Six machines were ordered from Johannesburg, South Africa. A photograph in *Motorcycling* attests to an Emblem motorcycle sale even in "Faraway Australia."

T. J. Everwine, the Pittsburgh "Emblem distributor and Merkel sub-agent," produced a design for a drop-frame motorcycle called a "ladies' machine," which was to be built by the Emblem factory. A photo of the machine shows a one-cylinder engine fitted under a shortened tank. A skirt guard covers the top half of the rear wheel. A number plate on the front fender suggests an intent to sell the machine in foreign markets. A caption under the picture notes that a two-speed gear was fitted in the rear hub.

For the motorcycle industry, 1915 was "undeniably a bad year," according to *Motorcycle Illustrated*. Unemployment conspired with poor weather to dampen sales. Yet the journal was hopeful for 1916, especially as several lightweight motorcycles were reaching the market. Schack on September 3, 1915, noted that his business was "quite satisfactory; looks much better for 1916."

1916 Model Year

Emblem's major motorcycle development for 1916 was a lightweight twin. The new machine was to endure longer than any other Emblem model, serving as the company's final offering in a diminishing motorcycle market.

As the demand for large motorcycles declined in competition with inexpensive automobiles, chiefly the Ford Model T in the mid-1910s, some manufacturers of two-wheel machines tried to undercut the dollar appeal of the cheapest cars. For most motorcycle companies, including Emblem, lightweights such as the $175 Model 106 proved to be only a temporary means of survival.

The Emblem company said their new motorcycle was designed to "meet the growing demand for a lighter and cheaper" machine. Upon its introduction at the Chicago automobile show in September 1915, the Emblem lightweight seemed an attractive buy. The machine offered a four-stroke engine, clutch, folding footrests, chain drive, spring fork, magneto ignition, and tool kit. A two-speed Eclipse hub was twenty-five dollars extra. *Motorcycle Illustrated* called the new Emblem "the most important . . . if, in fact, it is not the most interesting announcement that has come from a motorcycle manufacturer this year."

In Chicago, the Emblem Manufacturing Company announced a price of $150, but within a few weeks advertisements noted that "with the rising costs of labor and materials even the Emblem factory cannot do it. Even at $175.00 it is well-nigh a miracle machine, and the extra $25.00 means that we are able to include a beautiful finish, and to offer also generous equipment in the highest grade of tires and saddle."

In November, William Schack claimed in *Motorcycling and Bicycling* a "lively demand for the new Emblem lightweight which has made a marked hit with dealers and riders. [His] chief trouble is not to sell, but to make them fast enough." Yet an article in the same journal about motorcycle dealers in central California mentioned no Emblem agencies. Another story claimed that in San Francisco "no Emblem has been seen for months and no agency." The motorcycles "seen on the streets of Phoenix [Arizona] were Indians, Harley-Davidsons, Excelsiors, Merkels, and 'a few' Thors and Popes." A more promising West Coast note came from Los Angeles, where, for John T. Bill and Company in October 1916, John Bill reported that he had sold more Emblems than in any previous season "and attributes this to the lightweight Emblem, that has taken well with the messenger boys and those who preferred a four-cycle engine to the two-stroke."

Herbert and Edwin Gale ride a lightweight Emblem twin in the snow in Angola, ca. 1916. Photo courtesy of Herbert F. Gale. NYSM H-1992.68.41.

With the American motorcycle trade overall in decline, Schack turned to export. In New York City at the end of October 1915, Schack struck deals "with India, Scandinavia, China, Japan and England," with the lightweight motorcycle an "important part" of the orders. In December it was reported that Frank Edward Moriss in London would be the English distributor of Emblem, "the latest American motorcycle to invade the British Isles." Additional heavyweight machines were going to Holland and Norway. In January the Emblem company announced a shipment of motorcycles to Australia.

The Emblem motorcycle line for 1916 continued the three machines from 1915, in addition to the new lightweight Model 106. Changes to the Models 105, 108, and 110 were minor. Most improvements focused the performance and the reliability of the machines. New exhaust-valve action gave more power and speed. A new oil pump was driven by the same gear that operated the magneto. Piston clearances were decreased, "making them practically a tight fit when the motor is built up and are only worked down when running in a bath of oil until they run freely." A new grease injector was fitted to the clutch so that "all of the clutch trouble has practically been eliminated." As competitors began to fit three-speed transmissions to their machines, the Emblem company noted that there was less strain on the drive chain with their two-speed hub and that the high-power Emblem engines operated well without the extra gear. In appearance, the Emblem's most obvious change was a painted banner or ribbon on the tank, which served as the field for the Emblem name.

In the summer, H. S. Quine of the Million Bicycles Committee, a trade organization for promoting the use of bicycles, reported that the Emblem Company employed 150 men year-round. The total payroll for the past twelve years was approximately $1,200,000, "or $100,000 a year." Production ranged from 25,000 to 30,000 bicycles yearly.

In the United States, the lure of the versatile automobile had dimmed the attraction of motorcycles except for limited commercial use and recreational riding. Even the most successful of motorcycle makers, such as Indian and Harley-Davidson, now had bicycle companions in their product lines. While Harley-Davidson production neared 17,000 motorcycles for model year 1916, the Emblem number was far

The middleweight (née lightweight) Model 106 Emblem, manufactured from late 1915 to at least 1924. From *Motorcycling and Bicycling*, November 20, 1916.

smaller. Stopping in Chicago in the summer of 1916, Schack predicted a shortage of bicycles in 1917, while in the motorcycle world he thought there would be a "gradual lessening of the big machine demand in favor of lightweights."

1917 Model Year

For the 1917 model year, the Emblem Manufacturing Company dropped its larger twins and single in favor of the improved Model 106, now called a "middle-weight." The major changes were adoption of the cartridge style of coil spring used on the larger machines in the past, a new kick-starter that provided three revolutions of the engine with each kick, and an optional three-speed gearbox. A new standard color, carmine, served to distance the 1917 Emblem from its predecessors. Khaki was an optional color, and the formerly standard blue was available only by special order.

William Schack, according to *Motorcycle Illustrated*, claimed his one model would satisfy all motorcyclists: "By confining our efforts to one model . . . we approach an ideal in standardization. There is but one set of parts to manufacture, stock and assemble; it is simpler for the dealer as well as for the manufacturer. It has been the aim of the Emblem Manufacturing Company to standardize all constructions, whether of motorcycles or bicycles, and we feel that we have done so thoroughly in our 1917 policy."

Factory superintendent Glas said in *Motorcycling and Bicycling*, "Our many years of experience in building motorcycles and bicycles have convinced us that divided energy is wasted energy. . . . We are going to concentrate on just one model and make that the best that can be produced. By adopting this policy we are able to offer the riders a far better machine for $175 than could be produced for considerably more were we to divide our forces by putting out three or four different models."

A brochure entitled "The 1917 Emblem Motorcycle" claimed the Little Giant was "in reality a very light motorcycle" named for its "unusual power and speed." It was just the thing for "businessman, clerk, workman or sportsman."

The Emblem three-speed "made its bow" at the annual fall Chicago show held at the Coliseum. There, said *Motorcycling and Bicycling*, in "charge are William G. Schack, president; William G. Schack, treasurer; William G. Schack, secretary; William G. Schack, sales manager, Fred P. Ames, and R. Cunliffe."

One of Schack's contacts during the event was A. G. Koldewin [sometimes spelled "Kolkewyn"] of N. V. Algemeene Motoren Import Company in Apeldoorn, Holland. After signing for eighty three-speed and twenty single-speed Emblems, Koldewin said, "The Emblem twin will . . . be a good seller. It has plenty of power and speed and the upkeep will not be great, an important consideration with us in these times of war prices."

The Emblem Company used the pages of *Motorcycle Illustrated*, which evolved during 1917 into *Motorcycle and Bicycle Illustrated*, for a series of full-page advertisements praising the Emblem motorcycle. These apparently were the last such large-scale domestic efforts to promote the machine. As usual, much of the text of these advertisements, as well as those of the more common half-page appeals, was addressed in part to potential dealers. For example, the March 1 issue advised, "Get aboard, dealers! . . . The EMBLEM will not interfere in any way with your present line of heavyweight machines—it appeals to an entirely different class of people—so write to us today."

The Emblem Manufacturing Company in 1917, perhaps for the last year, maintained membership in the Motorcycle and Allied Trades Association. And in the summer of 1917 Schack was appointed to the manufacturers advisory board to the Federation of American Motorcyclists, the organization of motorcycle riders.

In 1922, *Motorcycle and Bicycle Illustrated* reported that for the 1917 season, the Emblem Manufacturing Company had produced 1,000 motorcycles (as well as 37,800 bicycles).

Emblem factory superintendent and shareholder John C. Glas, of whom *Motorcycle and Bicycle Illustrated* said he "works with his coat off and makes things hum" (May 4, 1922). NYSM H-1992.68.11.2.

1918 Model Year

Domestic sales of Emblem motorcycles continued during the 1918 season, but the Emblem company's focus clearly was on its bicycles. In September 1917, William Schack completed an "extensive trip" covering the western United States and Canada during which "he sold his usual carload of Emblem bicycles in every city he visited" (*Motorcycling and Bicycling*, September 24, 1917). With three West Coast distributors for the pedal machines plus "other jobbing channels" elsewhere in the country, Schack clearly was determined to secure wide dispersal for his bicycles. Motorcycles, on the other hand, were "marketed almost entirely by direct dealer connections." *Motorcycling and Bicycling* reported that the Emblem company claimed that motorcycle sales would be made "easily" due to their machine's long-established name, and discounts were said to be "liberal" to sellers.

The Emblem motorcycle line for 1918 continued the Model 106 exclusively and apparently unchanged. Prices, in an atmosphere of shortages due to the war economy, increased to $200 for the single speed and $225 for the three-speed version. Advertisements for 1918 spoke of the lightweight motorcycle "built right" so that it could carry a passenger in tandem or in a sidecar. With a 5-horsepower engine and a road speed of 45 to 50 miles per hour, the Emblem, they claimed, gave its buyer "more for your money than any other motorcycle purchase you could make." Emblem motorcycles and bicycles were described for potential buyers in a sixteen-page booklet. The Emblem engine, according to the factory's writer, was the "most wonderful ever constructed, containing fewer parts and developing more power and speed than any other motor." Exports remained a significant element in Emblem sales for the 1918 model year. In the late fall of 1917, for example, fifteen motorcycles were shipped to Australia "through the New York representative."

1919 Model Year

Emblem advertising in the trade press and Emblem news in the trade journals for the 1919 model year were almost, if not entirely, concerned with bicycles. In September 1918, Schack bought the assets of the bankrupt Pierce Cycle Company (q.v.) in Buffalo. While the Pierce company had once competed with the Emblem firm as a motorcycle builder (in 1909–14), in 1918 the Pierce equipment, parts, and labor for Schack meant a second, high-quality bicycle line. In short order, the Pierce operation was moved to Angola, where it survived as a separate company and manufacturer among Schack's enterprises until the demise of the Emblem company in 1940.

Apparently, the acquisition of the Pierce assets or the establishment of the Pierce operation in Angola required recapitalization of the Emblem company. In October 1918, when stock actually issued amounted to $29,450 of the $40,000 authorized, the shareholders—Schack, Glas, Seamark, Heil, Sykes, Owen, Warwick, and Shepker—agreed to increase the capital to $130,000. The new scheme provided for 800 shares of common stock with a par value of $50, and 900 shares of preferred with a par value of $100. The preferred shares were to be issued in seven series redeemable at $105, in succession from 1920 through 1926.

Shack, as well as Mr. and Mrs. John Sykes, represented the Emblem company at the Cycle Trades Association meeting in Atlantic City, New Jersey, in August.

The April 24, 1919, issue of *Motorcycle and Bicycle Illustrated* published specifications for the 6-horsepower, three-speed Emblem Model 106. Twenty-eight-inch wheels were fitted to the 52-inch wheelbase frame. Corbin brakes were used.

1920 Model Year

In August 1920, *Motorcycling and Bicycling* noted that the Emblem for the last three years had been a "medium-weight, two-cylinder machine" manufactured "exclusively for the foreign market." W. G. Paulson, a *Motorcycling and Bicycling* writer, visited the Emblem factory in December 1919. On the upper floors of the building he observed a "large number of middleweight Emblems . . . being built for the foreign trade." He noted frame lugs for fitting Rogers sidecars as well as a number of "detail changes" in the "little Emblem, all of which are improvements." Overall, however, there was little to distinguish the latest motorcycle, "with its pretty military drab finish and bright nickel trimmings," from its predecessors. Paulson, however, did record some of those changes, including a modification in the clutch pedal with the hand gear shift now incorporated, "making it necessary to throw the clutch before shifting gears"; step-cut, cast piston rings, the bottom one securing the piston pin; increased surface for the inlet rocker arms; hardened "plugs" replacing rollers on the cam followers to give a "snappier action" and "more pep"; and enlargement of the exhaust-valve stem with reconfiguration of the valve head. The kick-starter and the transmission were the same but now built by Emblem instead of outside suppliers.

For 1920, the Emblem Manufacturing Company published a joint bicycle and motorcycle catalog, a copy of which survives in the hands of a collector. But apparently there was little or no domestic advertising of Emblem motorcycles by their manufacturer. The Emblem booth at the Chicago Cycle Show in November 1919 had only bicycles in "a most attractive exhibit."

The catalog, *Emblem Motorcycles and Bicycles*, describes the motorcycle as "designed to meet the everyday requirements of the public. The practical and technical knowledge gained in ten years of motorcycle construction has all been drawn up in the building of this motorcycle." Potential buyers were advised, "If there is no Emblem agency in your city, write direct to us."

1921 Model Year

During the summer of 1920, the Emblem company advertised in *Motorcycling and Bicycling*, seeking "experienced motorcycle mechanics, also first-class production man."

In November 1920 at the annual cycle show in Chicago, the Emblem Manufacturing Company as well as the Pierce Cycle Company were represented by Schack, three colleagues, and about twenty bicycles. Of the Emblems, it was reported that all types were on hand except the "motorbike." The reference is likely to a pedal bike, the styling of which was inspired by motorcycles, rather than to the Emblem motorcycle.

1922 Model Year

The *Thomas Register of American Manufacturers* for 1922 to 1923, which was published in July 1922, lists the Emblem Manufacturing Company as a maker of motorcycles. Capitalization is noted as over $300,000.

Motorcycle and Bicycle Illustrated's W. H. Parsons visited Schack in the spring of 1922. Parsons noted that for the past ten years the "chief sales effort in the motorcycle line has been for foreign business, and that's why the fact that very good motorcycles are made at Angola are seldom advertised by the Emblem company on this side of the water." Foreign demand supposedly took all Emblem output, since Schack "sticks to 'Quality' as preferable to quantity." But the journal's readers were advised not to conclude that the Emblem motorcycles were "on the shelf. Some day 'Bill' Schack may take a good strong bite out of his cigar and start something that will make you sit up and take notice."

Emblem Manufacturing Company factory in Angola. From *Motorcycle and Bicycle Illustrated*, May 4, 1922.

Motorcycling and Bicycling listed the Model 106 in its "Motorcycle Buyers Guide" appearing in April 1922. The displacement of the Emblem engine was given as 32.4 cubic inches. The price was $250.

1923 Model Year

Motorcycle and Bicycle Illustrated listed the Model 106, with its 7-horsepower engine, in a compilation of "Mechanical Details of American Motorcycles" that appeared in the February 8, 1923, issue. While cylinder dimensions, at 2 ⅝ by 3 inches, are identical to those given by *Motorcycling and Bicycling* the previous year, displacement now was shown as 50 cubic inches. The weight of the three-speed Emblem was 217 pounds.

1924 Model Year

Although in response to a query in January 1923 *Motorcycling and Bicycling* claimed that the Emblem as a motorcycle manufacturer was "out of business," *Motorcycle and Bicycle Illustrated* continued to list the Model 106 for the 1924 season.

1925 Model Year and After

Motorcycling and Bicycling in January 1925 said that the Emblem, among a list of motorcycle trade names, was no longer made.

Allan D. Lehning in a letter to the author noted, "As a boy, I can remember as far back as 1925. I do not recall ever seeing an Emblem motorcycle on the streets of Angola."

Harry V. Sucher estimates that the Emblem Manufacturing Company produced about 2,500 lightweight twins between 1920 and 1925. These, he claims, "all were exported to Europe." Perhaps the reports of commercial attachés in European embassies might reveal the precise numbers of motorcycles received by the various countries.

Whatever the final date of Emblem motorcycle production, the Emblem Manufacturing Company's capacity for building motorcycles was noted as late as September 1932, when the *Thomas Register of American Manufacturers* listed the Emblem Manufacturing Company as a motorcycle builder.

Establishing total production of Emblem motorcycles is a speculative proposition since, to the author's knowledge, there are no definitive figures for any individual year, much less the entire run, from the Thor-engined Model 100 to the final Model 106 lightweight. It's likely as many as two thousand motorcycles may have been built for the 1912 season; figuring here arbitrarily an average of one thousand machines for the 1909–25 period, total production would equal twenty thousand motorcycles. The former Emblem factory building in Angola stood empty in the late 1990s.

F

Fabrique Nationale d'Armes de Guerre
New York City (Manhattan)
1906–9
Trade Name: **FN**

The FN was a Belgian motorcycle imported and distributed by the Ovington Motor Company in Manhattan between 1906 and 1909, when the Ovington company, a Maine corporation, was bankrupt. The larger FN, characterized by an in-line, four-cylinder engine and shaft drive, may have influenced the design of the Pierce (q.v.). There were also single-cylinder FN models, both belt- and shaft-driven. An unidentified "mechanical engineer" advertised in the trade press in November 1906 that he wanted to "interest capital in a Four Cylinder Tandem Motor to compete with the foreign product." In April 1909, the FN company (not Ovington) was elected to membership in the American Motorcycle Manufacturers' Association. In 1910, the American FN company was organized in Boston, Massachusetts, with Earle L. Ovington, Henry H. Wilcox, and Daniel B. Ruggles as incorporators.

William H. Fauber
New York City (Manhattan)
1914
Trade Name: **Fauber Bi-Car**

The Fauber Bi-Car was a single-track vehicle guided by a steering wheel from "a body . . . adapted to carry one or two persons" (*Motorcycle Illustrated*, April 30, 1914). "Spring stabilizers" kept the 66-inch-wheelbase machine upright at rest (Kimes and Clark). A drawing of the vehicle suggests a cross between a motorcycle and a small automobile.

Beverly Rae Kimes and Henry Austin Clark Jr. note a two-cylinder engine producing 8 horsepower and a $295 price, although "any man can save $100 by assembling the Bi-Car himself." According to Kimes and Clark, the Bi-Car and a cyclecar were built for Fauber by the Cyclecar Engineering Company of Indianapolis, although he made his office at 15 Murray Street in Manhattan. Fauber was an established inventor in the hydroplane field and reportedly "at one time well known in connection with the bicycle trade."

Daniel R. Fisher
Taughannock Falls (Town of Ulysses)
1912–13

In March 1913, Fisher patented an improved motorcycle frame. His idea was the addition of a suspension system to the rear wheel of the common diamond frame. Fisher added a second set of chain stays, the forward ends of which pivoted on the exterior of the engine. The rear wheel was fitted to the back ends of the movable stays. The fixed and movable stays were connected by two cylinders fitted with concentric coil springs. Fisher's patent states that he provided a "spring frame . . . which will be simple, strong, and durable in construction, efficient and reliable in operation, and which will not in any way interfere with the propelling mechanism of the motor." Whether any motorcycles were built according to Fisher's design is not known here.

Fleming Manufacturing Company
Brooklyn and Manhattan (1900)
Fleming Motor Vehicle Company
Ossining and Manhattan (1901 and 1902)
Ellis & Fleming Manufacturing Company
Manhattan (or Brooklyn, 1901)
1900–1902
Trade Names: **Fleming**; **E. & F.**

In the summer of 1900, the *Cycling Gazette* announced the Fleming "gasoline motor for bicycles, having 1.25 horse power." Standing only 13 inches high, the engine, with its aluminum crankcase, weighed 23 pounds. With the intake and exhaust valves opposite each other, "the makers are enabled to use extra large valves without having a large, clumsy cylinder head." Deep cylinder finning saw to sufficient cooling. The jump spark ignition eliminated the "noisy and complicated moving parts which are necessary when the contact or wipe spark system is used." The system also allowed a variation in engine speed from 500 to 2,500 rpm by adjusting the timing. In addition to complete engines, the Fleming Manufacturing Company at 90-92 Pearl Street in Brooklyn was prepared to furnish motorcycle builders with castings "and parts with full working drawings."

W. H. Wray Jr. later noted that during the summer of 1900, a "local [New York City] bicycle dealer made a motorcycle from Fleming castings, and it was such a success that he induced me to try it. From that time on I have not got rid of the [motorcycle] fever." By August 1900, the *Bicycling World* could write that not only "do the Fleming people impress one as knowing their busi-

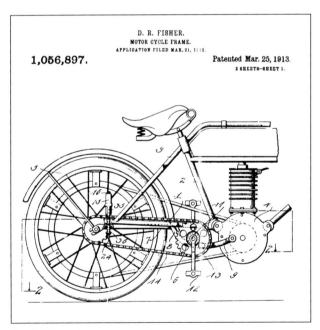

Daniel Fisher's rear-suspension system for motorcycles, seen in a patent drawing. Coil springs were to be fitted inside the small vertical cylinders.

ness intelligently, but the motor itself has features that commend it to notice." In the fall of 1900, the Fleming Manufacturing Company moved to 93-97 Elizabeth Street in Manhattan, "a change made necessary by their rapidly increasing business." The company now advertised 1.25-, 2-, 2.75-, and 4-horsepower engines for motorcycles and automobiles. Fleming agents were now reported in New York City, Philadelphia, and New Haven. In early November, the *Bicycling World* reported that the Fleming company was figuring on "running nights" to meet the demand for their engines: "They say there will be a much bigger call for motocycles next season than most people imagine; their experience and position give weight to the prophecy."

Records at the New York Department of State document the incorporation in January 1901 of the Fleming Motor Vehicle Company, with its principal office in Ossining. Although capitalized at $10,000, business started with $1,000 on hand. Among the three directors and subscribers, Peter G. Fleming, Angel Afanador, and William J. Brewster, the first took ninety of one hundred shares, which had a par value of ten dollars each. The *Horseless Age* noted the planned manufacture of "motors, marine and automobile, and complete motor vehicles." The *American Automobile* for February 1901 depicted one such complete vehicle, the Fleming "motor-cycle," with its engine mounted in front of the steering head and driving the front wheel via a belt.

In the late winter of 1901, the Fleming Motor Vehicle Company on Elizabeth Street continued to advertise the Fleming motor. Castings of the Fleming engine sold with blueprints were available at twelve dollars with an aluminum base and nine dollars in cast iron for the 1.25-horsepower model. The 3-horsepower versions were $27.50 and $22.50. In mid-May, the Fleming Company advertised that they were "now making deliveries of the 'Fleming' Motor Bicycle." The *American Automobile* reported that the Fleming engine, "having been in the market for the past year," had "proven itself equal to all the demands upon it."

The *Bicycling World* observed that, while bicycles with engines mounted on the front forks appeared to be the most popular type in Europe, the first American machine in that style was the Fleming. The *Cycle Age and Trade Review* said that the Fleming Motor Vehicle Company was "a devout believer in the desirability of front drive for motor bicycles." A drawing accompanying the story showed the Fleming motorcycle with its "specially constructed front fork." Transmission was by a half-inch-round belt, adjustable by a lever-controlled ratchet, "the driving tension being obtained after the motor is well started. Then, after the entire machine is under good headway, the belt can be slackened slightly, thus taking off some of the slight friction on the idler and tending to obviate stretching—a factor which in some instances has been the main source of trouble with belt-driven machines."

The battery switch on the Fleming motorcycle was in the twisting left grip. Speed control came through adjustments in the ignition timing. The battery and coil were suspended from the top tube of the frame, while the gasoline tank was mounted on the front fork with the engine. The muffler, situated in front of the gasoline tank, ensured "warm gasoline," with the exhaust gases directed down toward the road. All the equipment mounted on the fork meant that the engine and

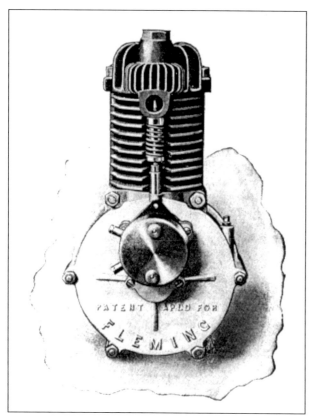

Advertising cut of the Fleming engine. From the *American Automobile*, March 1901.

The 1.25-horsepower Fleming engine driving the front wheel via a half-inch round belt. From the *Bicycling World*, March 7, 1901.

fork could be "readily attached to any strong bicycle." The complete motorcycle was listed at $200, while the fork, motor, and "all attachments" were available for $150. The Fleming company also had a 3-horsepower engine "for tandems and light carriages." *Motorcycling and Bicycling* in 1918 recalled that the Fleming fuel tank held two quarts, enough for 50 or 60 miles, but that an auxiliary, gallon tank could be mounted over the rear wheel "when desired."

In the summer of 1901, the city directory listing for the occupant at 93 Elizabeth Street was that of Afanador and Cooper in the machinery business. Meanwhile, the Fleming Manufacturing Company, in the "automobiles" trade, was at 43 Downing Street, with Fleming as president. In October 1901, it was reported that the Fleming Motor Vehicle Company "has during the past year been building motor bicycles with which it is satisfied, and it is now preparing to put them on the market in greater numbers" (*Cycle Age and Trade Review*, October 17, 1901).

In early 1902, the Fleming Motor Vehicle Company produced a catalog "describing the Fleming motor bicycle." The *Cycling Gazette* said, "Unlike most American machines of this kind, the Fleming has the motor over the front wheel. The makers claim that this simplifies the construction, and that the front position keeps the motor cooler. The machine can attain a speed of 25 miles an hour on ordinary roads."

Fleming, the Fleming Motor Vehicle Company, and the Fleming Manufacturing Company were missing from the New York City directory published in the summer of 1902. Manufacture after that time in Ossin-

ing is doubtful. At least one Fleming motor bicycle engine survives in a private collection.

In January 1901, an Ellis & Fleming Manufacturing Company motorcycle appeared in the New York Cycle and Automobile Show at Madison Square Garden. The *Horseless Age* said that the Brooklyn company's "motor is fastened to a pair of forks in front of the steering forks and drives the front wheel by a belt." The *Cycling Gazette* said five motor bicycles at the show, from various manufacturers, "had their good points and all were attractive." However, the *Bicycling World* said the Fleming "machine, which drives through the front wheel, is the nearest approach to the [French] Werner type seen at the show. It is heavy and not attractive looking, and the plan of carrying the motor in front of the handlebar is hardly likely to commend itself, although experience with the Werner has undoubtedly demonstrated that the objections to it are more theoretical than practical."

"Mr. Ellis" told the *Cycling Gazette* of the Madison Square Garden event, "The show is a great advertisement. It gives us the opportunity to show our motor bicycle. We will be able to turn out wheels in two weeks. We shall probably put out 1,000 this year. We have found the right place for the motor to be at the front of the machine. There has been no end of interest in motor bicycles. The business has a big future." The *Bicycling World* quotes "L. G. Fleming" of the Ellis and Fleming Company, who said that he was "very pleased with the show; we made a few sales, but had lots of visitors, and expect to reap the benefit when the retail trade starts up."

It would seem that the Ellis & Fleming Manufacturing Company and the Fleming Manufacturing Company were the same organization. "L. G. Fleming" is close enough in spelling to "P. G. Fleming" that one might ascribe the difference to an error in copying. (As for "Ellis," he has not been identified here; there are numerous possibilities, among them several machinists in Manhattan as well as Seele H. Ellis, a Brooklyn machinist, who in 1898, 1899, and 1900 was in the bicycle business at 819 Bedford Avenue.)

Evidence that the two companies were the same is found in two lists. The first document notes expected exhibitors at the New York show, among them the Fleming Manufacturing Company of New York in space 231. The second list, prepared a week later, reports the occupant of space 231, with one motor bicycle on display, as the Ellis & Fleming Manufacturing Company of New York.

Albert H. Funke
New York City (Manhattan)
1902–3 or later
Trade Name: **Kelecom**

Albert Funke, a gun dealer on Duane Street (later on Broadway), was the importer of Belgian-made Kelecom engines beginning in 1902. A 2.5-horsepower, air-cooled, side-valve unit was intended for motorcycle use, with larger, water-cooled models for automobiles. A one-piece cylinder and head were notable. In August of that year, Funke announced that he would be "able to make deliveries on a complete motor bicycle fitted with this well known motor." Whether the parts other than the engine were imported or domestic was not made clear. Funke did import one complete Kelecom motorcycle in 1902 "to demonstrate the qualities of the Kelecom motors" (*Motor Age*, August 7, 1902).

G

Paul G. Gast
d/b/a **Fast by Gast**
Grand Island
1973–present

Paul Gast (born 1949), as of 2000 a six-time national champion in drag racing, noted in a letter to the author that he built racing motorcycles exclusively. He estimated that between 1973 and 2000 he had turned out sixty machines. Until 1994 an employee, Joseph Wroblewski (q.v.), fabricated the chassis for the Gast machines. Since Wroblewski's departure, chassis have been purchased from outside suppliers. Four-cylinder Kawasaki and Suzuki engines were utilized, modified to turn out up to 320 horsepower. As of 2000, the quickest Fast by Gast "Pro Stock" category time from a standing start in the quarter-mile race was 7.17 seconds, reaching a speed of 190 miles per hour.

Paul G. Gast, whose company, Fast by Gast, manufactures components as well as complete drag-racing motorcycles, is seen here competing on one of his 320-horsepower Pro Stock–category drag-racing machines. Photo courtesy of Paul G. Gast.

Gast's Fast by Gast business is a "motorcycle drag race high performance company" distributing motorcycle parts. The business maintains a machine shop "specializing in transmission building and repair" as well as engine work. The *New York Manufacturers Directory 2000* reported that the privately owned Fast by Gast had ten employees and estimated sales of between $500,000 and $1,000,000.

Since the first edition of this book, Gast has continued to race and set the standard, winning numerous championships. Fast by Gast has also continued to produce performance parts for racing.

Gearless Motor Cycle Company
Rochester
1905–6?
Trade Name: **Gearless**

The Gearless Motor Cycle Company was incorporated with $50,000 capitalization in December 1905 "to engage in the manufacture, vending and selling of motor cycles and motors of all kinds, but it shall not manufacture automobiles," the last clause perhaps serving to distinguish the Gearless Motor Cycle Company from the Gearless Transmission Company of Rochester, which manufactured automobiles for three seasons before reported bankruptcy in 1909.

In the *Bicycling World and Motorcycle Review*, C. (Claude?) W. Miller of Rochester claimed in 1908 that he had "designed and built a shaft-drive motorcycle with friction transmission while employed by a firm then known as the Gearless Motorcycle [*sic*] Co. of Rochester." Miller went on to explain that he built the machine for the express purpose of powering a sidecar for delivery purposes: "I rode the machine both with and without the side car all during the latter part of the season of 1906—about three months. The speed ranged from nothing to 25 miles per hour, with about 7 to 1 gear on high, with 2½ horsepower motor with mechanical valves." Miller supplied two photographs of his machine to substantiate his story. The illustrations show a neat motorcycle with a large disk in the rear wheel, perhaps enclosing gearing or brake or both. A similar disk appears to be on the end of a shaft parallel with the wheel axle and behind a flywheel or disk mounted on the end of the engine crankshaft, which is apparently perpendicular to the axle (appropriate for a friction transmission arrangement).

The shaft-drive, Rochester-built, experimental Gearless of 1906. From the *Bicycling World and Motorcycle Review*, March 14, 1908.

Miller wrote of the Gearless Motor Cycle Company as a concern that if it had not abandoned its motorcycle-building ambitions or gone out of existence by 1908, at a minimum had changed names. The Gearless corporation was formally dissolved by proclamation of the New York secretary of state on March 13, 1926. The Gearless legacy remains the fabrication of an innovational motorcycle with a variable-speed transmission produced at a time (1906) when a single gear was the rather unsatisfactory norm.

Gibson Mon-Auto Company
New York City (Manhattan; Brooklyn)
1915–20
Trade Name: **Gibson Mon-Auto**

Introduced at the New York City motorcycle and bicycle show in the fall of 1915, the Mon-Auto was the brainchild of Hugo C. Gibson, an English designer and engineer. Earlier he had created the similar Autoped scooter and served as president of the Autoped Company of America (q.v.). Unlike the seatless Autoped whose engine was attached to the front wheel, the Mon-Auto provided a nicely sprung saddle over the four-stroke engine attached to the rear wheel. Lubrication was facilitated with a "splash wheel" rotating in the sump. The engine was rated at 2.5 horsepower and geared at 5:1 to the 14-inch rear wheel. Tires were 2½ inches in cross-section.

The Mon-Auto had a 4-inch-diameter, horizontal main tube in which the gasoline and oil supplies were stored. The controls, like the Autoped's, were ingeniously incorporated in the handlebar. Tilting the lever forward engaged the clutch and opened the throttle. Tilting back closed the throttle, disengaged the clutch and engaged the brake. An early report said the 4-foot-long, 45-pound machine could reach 25 miles per hour. The Gibson company advertised 120 miles to the gallon of gasoline. The motorcycle measured 48 by 9 by 18 inches.

An undated but probably pre-1917 Mon-Auto catalog, distributed by the Coalition Company at 50 Church Street in New York City, shows a photo of the Universal Machine Company factory in Baltimore, Maryland, which was "equipped . . . for manufacturing the Gibson Mon-Auto in quantities to meet the demand." On the other hand, a handbill for a Gibson stock offering, probably in late 1916, noted that the Mon-Auto factory was at 171-173 Lexington Avenue near Franklin Avenue in Brooklyn. And in August 1917, the Gibson Mon-Auto Company advertised that a factory in Elkhart, Indiana, built the Mon-Auto.

The Coalition Company, an automotive enterprise organized in 1915, apparently promoted the Mon-Auto

The 2.5-horsepower Gibson Mon-Auto with its four-stroke engine attached to the rear wheel. From *Motorcycle Illustrated*, July 17, 1917.

until November 1916, when the trade press noted that Gibson and "several automobile men" had incorporated the Gibson Mon-Auto Company in New Jersey with a million dollars "in common stock" (200,000 shares with a par value of five dollars). Offices for the new corporation were at the same 156 Broadway location as the Coalition Company. Gibson directors at that point were Gibson, president and chief engineer; the "capitalist" Abram Wyse, treasurer; Lewis R. Compton, secretary; George W. Wesley; E. A. Greene; Theodore E. Schultz; and George H. Bruce, general counsel.

In the summer of 1917, the Gibson company sought dealers from a Woolworth Building address (233 Broadway). Selling points for Mon-Auto agents included the motorcycle's size, which allowed it to "be picked up and carried into the home" as well as "lifted over obstacles." It was sturdy enough to "carry 300 pounds" (advertisement in *Motorcycle and Bicycle Illustrated*, August 9, 1917). The "accident possibility" was "so remote as to be negligible and simplicity is the keynote of its operation." One of the slogans they used to promote the value of the Mon-Auto was "The Hundred Dollar Car."

In 1917, the United States Navy tested a Mon-Auto for possible military applications. The Gibson company claimed that their scooter was used by "messengers, mail carriers, workmen . . . collectors, inspectors, clerks and by professional men" (*Motorcycle and Bicy-*

cle Illustrated, July 12, 1917). Into 1917, Hugo Gibson was president of both the Mon-Auto company and the Coalition Company. In 1918, Roy E. Harper was president of the Mon-Auto company. By 1920, offices for the Gibson Mon-Auto Company had moved to 1974 Broadway. By 1922, the Gibson company was gone from New York. Production numbers for the "Hundred Dollar Car" are unknown here.

Harry A. Gliesman
d/b/a **Tiger Cycle Works Company**
also known as:
Tiger Cycle Company
1903–10
Tiger Cycle and Aeroplane Company
New York (Manhattan), 1910–11
New York Motor Cycle Company Inc.
White Plains, 1911–?
Years of motorcycle manufacture: 1906–8?
Trade Name: **Tiger Special**

The *Motorcycle Illustrated* for April 1907 had a fine photo of Harry Gliesman on his "Tiger Special Motorcycle." This was a one-cylinder machine with the air-cooled engine incorporated into the seat post. With very long handlebars and the saddle over the rear wheel, the machine was fitted out as a pacer for a bicycle rider. The journal noted that their photograph of Gliesman showed him in September 1906 "on a machine constructed after his own design." He was then about to attempt to pace a bicyclist for 100 miles over Long Island roads to prove, in part, "that it was possible to ride a motorcycle for one continuous 100 miles (barring accident) without a dismount." Unfortunately, "the authorities" interfered with the unsuccessful project.

Gliesman, a veteran of the bicycle trade, was a pioneer rider and seller at various times of Rambler, Indian, Reading Standard, Curtiss (q.v.), Thor, Minneapolis, Racycle, and Merkel motorcycles on Eighth Avenue and later on Broadway and West Forty-Eighth Street. He was "ready at any time to lend a hand, or to support anything which has in view the advancement of motorcyclism." The January 1908 *Cycle and Automobile Trade Journal* lists Gliesman's Tiger Cycle Works Company as the source for Tiger motorcycles. Michael Gerald and Jim Lucas, in their "Complete Roster of

Two-Wheeled Motorized Vehicles Made in the U.S.A., 1869–1979," report the years of manufacture for the Tiger Special as 1906 to 1909.

Harry Gliesman, along with August E. Gliesman and Charles Jensen, incorporated his business as the New York Motor Cycle Company, capitalized at $10,000, in 1911. The $6,000 with which the company was to begin business represented sixty subscribed shares, of which Harry Gliesman took fifty-eight and the other two company directors one each. The principal office was to be in White Plains. Manufacture was among the corporation's contemplated activities, but whether any production was undertaken is unknown here. A check of the White Plains directories for 1910–11 and 1912–13 (the 1911–12 edition was not available) located no listings for the New York Motor Cycle Company, Jensen, or either Gliesman.

In 1914, Harry Gliesman and the New York Motor Cycle Company, according to the *Bicycling World and Motorcycle Review*, were at 1777 Broadway, with other facilities also in Manhattan. Activities included the sale, repair, and storage of motorcycles and parts; the journal made no mention of manufacture. The New York Motor Cycle Company was dissolved by proclamation in 1926. Probably before 1920, Gliesman opened the Summit Cycle & Auto Supply Company in Jersey City, New Jersey, according to *Motorcycle and Bicycle Illustrated* in January 1922. About 1904, according to the article, Gliesman had competed in bicycle races on his own make machine, the "Tiger Special."

Globe Cycle Company
Buffalo
1900

The *Cycle Age and Trade Review* in October 1900 reported that the Globe Cycle Company was "investigating the motor bicycle business and desires to correspond with makers of reliable motors." The Globe Cycle Company succeeded Globe Cycle Works in the 1890s. Both entities struggled financially at times. The Globe Cycle Company came out of bankruptcy in 1900 with new leadership. It is not surprising that they were exploring the motor-bicycle business; however, it does not appear that they produced or sold any. Remarkably, the Globe company had leased space and sold equipment to the E. R. Thomas Motor Company (q.v.), which in October 1900 announced two motorcycles with Thomas engines. According to *The Wheel* and the *Horseless Age*, when the lease was announced in the spring of 1900, the Thomas Company's operations were not supposed to interfere with the Globe works, "as the plant is a mammoth one."

In 1903 the Globe Cycle Company was selling Rambler automobiles and during the summer of 1904 stopped manufacturing bicycles.

Romaine Gressier
New York City (Manhattan)
1906

The *Motorcycle Illustrated* in July 1906 identified Romaine Gressier of 250 West Thirty-Eighth Street as a "manufacturer of motorcycles." He had just been fined two dollars for "running a cycle wildly through West 37th and 38th streets and Seventh and Eighth avenues without lights and nearly running down several children and adults." Gressier, a French citizen, listed his occupation as motor mechanic when he and his wife, Julia, immigrated to the United States from London in 1905. In 1907, he got another speeding ticket, but this time he listed his occupation as chauffeur. The 1910 census also listed his occupation as chauffeur. Around 1910, he opened the Opera House Garage Company, and he owned the shop until he died in 1919. The garage sold gas and repaired and sold automobiles. Whether he actually built multiple motorcycles is unknown here.

H

Charles Haberer
Buffalo
1903–8
Trade Name: **Yankee**

Charles Haberer told *Motorcycle Illustrated*'s G. W. Grupp in 1915 that he (Haberer) saw his first motorcycle in 1901 at the Pan American Exposition in Buffalo, where Oscar Hedstrom (q.v.) and Charles S. Henshaw demonstrated a motor tandem. Haberer subsequently acquired an Indian motorcycle powered by a Thor engine. By 1903 he was a Thor dealer.

At that point, the Aurora Automatic Machinery Company of Aurora, Illinois, manufactured Thor engines and associated components but no complete motorcycles. Consequently, according to Grupp, from "1903 to 1908 Mr. Haberer's company assembled the Thor parts into from six to 25 machines a year, calling them under their own name of 'The Yankee.'" It was then that the Aurora company began to build complete motorcycles, and Haberer became the Thor motorcycle agent in Buffalo.

Harberer was a copartner in the Globe Cycle Company (q.v.) until early 1900 when bankruptcy forced him out. Globe reorganized under new investors, while Harberer and G. A. Williston started Glouster Cycle Company at 71 Genesee Street in May. By 1907, Charles's brother George was a partner in the business, possibly replacing Williston.

Harper Engineering Company
New York City (Manhattan)
ca. 1911

No later than January 1911, the Harper Engineering Company at 50 Church Street announced a two-cylinder, air-cooled engine for motorcycles. The Harper engine was a 45-degree V-twin using atmospheric intake and mechanical exhaust valves. The latter were supplemented with auxiliary ports, which could "be opened for racing and kept closed for touring." The engine was unusual in that no gaskets or cylinder bolts were used, the cylinders being secured with a clamped band. The removal of seven bolts "takes apart the entire motor" (*Motorcycle Illustrated*, March 23, 1911).

The crankshaft was cast integrally with the flywheel. Bore and stroke were 3 inches. Ball bearings, magneto ignition, and semiautomatic carburetor were used. The advertised weight was 45 pounds, and the horsepower rating was 6. The company suggested in March 1911 that their engine was "especially suitable for Builders of Special Machines or for replacing other engines" and that it was "absolutely gas tight." The firm also claimed that due to the light weight of the motor, "it is adaptable to much lighter frame construction than is now the practice in the manufacture of motorcycles."

The first city directory listing for the Harper Engineering Company appeared in *Trow's General Directory of the Boroughs of Manhattan and Bronx* for the year ending August 1, 1911. William Harper Jr. was identified as president of the enterprise. He was an engineer with multiple patents and a keen interest in aviation. The business was housed in room 367 at the Church Street building. It's likely that the manufacturing of the engine took place elsewhere than in the Church Street area, which was known for its financial offices more than for its factories. Harper and his engineering company continued to be listed in the 1912–13 city directory and in the May 1912 telephone directory but were missing in the 1915 city directory (there is no 1914 edition).

Harper Motor Company
New York City (Manhattan)
ca. 1908

The *Cycle and Automobile Trade Journal* for January 1908 listed the Harper Motor Company at 20 Vesey Street among the manufacturers and importers of motorcycles. The company incorporated in 1906. *Trow's General Directory of the Boroughs of Manhattan and Bronx* for 1907–8 gives the motor company's address as room 610 at the Vesey Street location, suggesting an office rather than a factory. David Neil Harper was identified as the president. Both the preceding and following directories have no listings for either the Harper Motor Company or David N. Harper.

Advertisement from *Motorcycle Illustrated*, March 23, 1911.

Hartshorne and Battelle
New York City (Manhattan)
ca. 1921

A motorcycle designed by Fred Evans of Summit, New Jersey, was patented on February 23, 1921, following a November 1916 application. Evans assigned the patent to the investment firm Hartshorne and Battelle of New York City. Principals in the Hartshorne firm were Edward C. Hartshorne, Seavey Battelle, and Frederick W. Ludwig, brokers who had an office at 25 Broad Street in Manhattan. Whether Hartshorne and Battelle exploited Evans's invention is unknown here.

What Evans devised was a bicycle motor that would power the machine by means of a belt-driven roller engaging the top of the tire. What he claimed was unique was an L-shaped bracket by which the motor would pivot to engage or disengage the roller.

Haverford Cycle Company
New York City (Manhattan)
1911–20
Haverford Cycle Company of Buffalo Inc.
Buffalo
1924

Motorcycle and Bicycle Illustrated in May 1919 reported the incorporation of the Haverford company to "manufacture and deal in bicycles, motorcycles, hardware, etc." Capitalization was $350,000.

Eight years previously, the *Bicycling World and Motorcycle Review* also had reported the incorporation of a Haverford Cycle Company in New York with capital stock of $250,000. Entrepreneur Max M. Sladkin of Philadelphia, who operated with branches in New York and other cities across the country, was the "moving spirit" of the earlier Haverford operation. His company manufactured bicycles and distributed various brands of motorcycles, including a few in which Sladkin had a vested interest. His Haverford Big Four motorcycle was manufactured for him by the American Motor Company in Rockford, Massachusetts. In 1916, capitalization was increased to $350,000, and in 1920 to $500,000. Sladkin and his wife, Jennie, using a Pennsylvania address, were the sole shareholders of the company.

In 1920, the Haverford Cycle Company of New York was dissolved by the action of a meeting at the 120 Broadway office of the company. At that time, the sole stockholder was Sladkin, who owned 1,000 shares of common and 4,000 shares of preferred. All officers of the company except for one director used the same Philadelphia address, likely the main office for the Haverford operation. Next in 1920, the Haverford Cycle Company was incorporated in the state of Delaware, designating, in separate action, the 120 Broadway address in New York as the principal place of business within the state.

In 1924, the Haverford Cycle Company of Buffalo Inc. was organized under New York State law by Meyer Goldman, Annette Goldman, and Frederick C. Howard of Buffalo to deal in bicycles, velocipedes, motor-

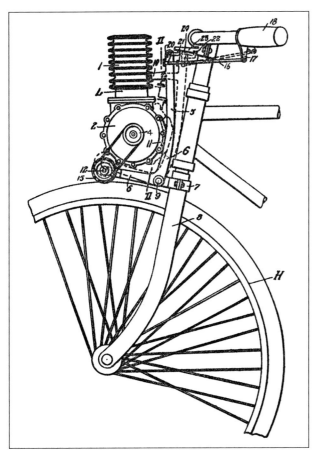

Patent drawing (1921) of Fred Evans's bicycle engine driving the front wheel by a roller atop the tire. His invention was the pivoting engine mount.

cycles, automobiles, and "vehicles of every nature." This business had been a branch of Sladkin's Haverford enterprise, and its incorporation came around the same time that Haverford in Philadelphia had ceased operations. By the time they incorporated, they had opened a special room to sell radios and related supplies. The Buffalo store burned in 1929 and bankruptcy followed shortly after.

It's unlikely that any of the Haverford operations manufactured any motorcycles in New York State.

Oscar Hedstrom
New York City (Brooklyn)
ca. 1898–1901
Trade Names: **Henshaw**; **Hedstrom**

Oscar Hedstrom's fame stems from his role as designer of the Indian motorcycles manufactured in Springfield, Massachusetts. His first notable effort at construction of a self-propelled, two-wheel machine took place, however, while he lived and worked in New York City. Growing up in Brooklyn, Hedstrom became a machinist and toolmaker. He also first became an amateur and then a professional bicycle racer, joining Charles S. Henshaw in the 1890s in tandem racing. At his Brooklyn bicycle shop, Hedstrom fabricated racing bicycles. Beginning in 1898, according to Victor W. Page (*Motorcycles and Side Cars*, 1921), Hedstrom produced several motorized pacing machines. Hedstrom said that he had been inspired by two motorcycles imported from France by Henry Fournier that year. These machines "gave considerable trouble, and I finally built some of my own to overcome the troubles," Hedstrom told *Motorcycling* in 1913.

Looking back that same year, the *Bicycling World and Motorcycle Review* thought the Henshaw and Hedstrom pacer "so much simpler and better appearing than the foreign machines which were in use at that time that it stood out like the proverbial house afire." At the Pan American Exposition in Buffalo in 1901, Henshaw, steering at the front, and Hedstrom, governing the engine, won the 10-mile tandem event "with the smallest motor in the race" (Hedstrom reported a 3.25-horsepower DeDion engine; *Motorcycling*, April 24, 1913). Hedstrom said they could cover a mile in one minute and eighteen seconds (*Motorcycle Illustrated*, January 23, 1913). A photograph shows Henshaw and Hedstrom "setting the Pace for a Boston & Albany R. R. Locomotive near Springfield, Mass., Anno Domini 1901" (*Motorcycling*, December 28, 1914).

The Henshaw and Hedstrom tandem used a double diamond frame, with an additional horizontal member (top tube) looping over the top of the engine mounted above the second sprocket axle. The second rider, over the rear wheel, was provided with his set of cranks connected to the bracket by a chain. The DeDion-style engine drove the rear wheel via a second chain. A panel between the rear handlebar and rear saddle was labeled "Built by O. Hedstrom New York N.Y." Actual manufacture, however, may have taken place at Middletown, Connecticut; an account in *Motorcycle Illustrated* says of Hedstrom that "in the plant of the Worcester Cycle Manufacturing Company . . . he had built racing bicycles and motor tandems."

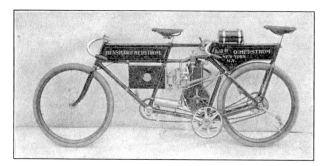

The Oscar Hedstrom–built, chain-drive tandem designed for pacing bicycle racers. From the *Horseless Age*, June 13, 1900.

At the New York Cycle Show in January 1901, James W. Grady, a veteran of the bicycle trade, said "he likes the ideas of Oscar Hedstrom better than others he saw." The location of the engine was protected in case of a fall, "and the only way it is exposed to injury is by a collision from either side." Another trade veteran was George M. Hendee, who brought Hedstrom and his pacing machine to Springfield "on account of the uncertainties of the pacemaking machines" Hendee had used in races there. Soon Hedstrom in Middletown was developing a new single-rider motorcycle for the Hendee Manufacturing Company in Springfield. The prototype Indian was finished in June 1901. Hedstrom moved to Springfield, eventually retiring in the mid-1910s from the Hendee firm as chief engineer. Henshaw also continued in the motorcycle world as a marketeer, working with the American concessionaire for DeDion products before moving on to the E. R. Thomas Motor Company (q.v.), builders of the Auto-Bi in Buffalo.

John O. Heitchen
Buffalo
ca. 1912

John Heitchen (1870–1944),[3] a German-born blacksmith, came to Buffalo in the 1890s. In the course of the next fifty years, he was employed by such local industries as the Buffalo Scale Company, the Buffalo Fire Appliances Corporation, and the Wire Wheel Corporation.

Heitchen, according to his daughter Cornelia Heitchen Quant, built several motorcycles. A surviving machine, perhaps dating from around 1912, utilizes a combination of salvaged and fabricated parts. The engine is a four-stroke twin with cooling fins resembling those on the heads and cylinders of the turn-of-the-century Curtiss power plants. The crankcase is iron and was cast at the Pohlman foundry in Buffalo, according to Quant. A battery powered the ignition system.

A hand-lever-shifted two-speed transmission in a two-piece cast-aluminum housing is notable among the apparently homemade components. A chain connects the crankshaft to the transmission with a second chain, on the same right side of the transmission case, turning a sprocket on the rear wheel. According to Quant, the Harley-Davidson Motor Company *in England*[4] was interested in acquiring Heitchen's transmission design, but, being German, he did not wish with to deal with the English.

Front suspension on the Heitchen motorcycle resembles the dual fork, with an enclosed coil spring system used on Pierce, Emblem, and Monarch machines. The rear wheel is rigid in the looping diamond frame.

The two floorboards are each fitted with a pedal. One pedal operates the contracting brake via a rod

The Heitchen motorcycle as it looked in 2000. Photo courtesy of Marv and Deb Moltrup of Genuine Cycle.

connection; the other pedal initially disengages the clutch and, when depressed farther, engages the brake. The engine is started with a hand crank since there are no rotary foot pedals. The combined fuel and oil tank is made of copper. The rear fender is hinged for removal of the 28-inch wheel. The front wheel is 26 inches in diameter.

Upon Heitchen's death and that of his wife, Frances, the motorcycle passed to their daughter. She related her knowledge of her father's motorcycle-construction activities to a neighbor and friend, Dennis Napora. She gave him a copy of a photo of Heitchen with another of his motorcycles, and she told Napora of her father riding motorcycles around the neighborhood. When Napora asked Quant if she had ridden the surviving motorcycle, she replied that her father would not let her do so.

Quant eventually gave the motorcycle to Napora, who after a number of years transferred it to Marvin Moltrup. Any other motorcycle documentation or parts that might have survived in the Heitchen-Quant house were lost after Quant's death in 1944 and the sale of the property. A search of patents for 1905 through 1918 reveals none granted to Heitchen.

William G. Henderson
Rochester
1910–11

The four-cylinder Henderson motorcycle established an envied reputation after its introduction by the Henderson Motorcycle Company of Detroit for the 1912 season. Production shifted to Chicago after the firm

---

3. On the 1900 census spelled "Heidchen."
4. Quant was mistaken; the Harley-Davidson Motor Company was based in Milwaukee.

was sold to the Excelsior Manufacturing and Supply Company in 1917. But to these Midwestern venues might be added a New York beginning to the Henderson motorcycle.

In 1910, William G. Henderson, the son of a Scottish immigrant, was employed as a draftsman by the F. A. Brownell Motor Company in Rochester. The company built four- and six-cylinder "Unit Power Plant type" gasoline engines for automotive and other applications. Henderson that same year submitted a drawing to the technical editor of the *Cycle and Automobile Trade Journal*, probably automotive pioneer Charles E. Duryea. Henderson claimed his four-cylinder motorcycle design met the objections the *Journal* had raised a few months earlier over contemporary motorcycles being based too completely upon bicycle construction. Henderson said, "I would be interested to know your opinion of the design I am sending you."

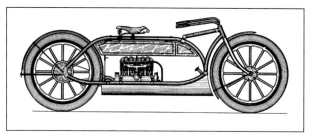

William Henderson's drawing of his proposed motorcycle, as published in the *Cycle and Automobile Trade Journal*, July 1910.

What Henderson described approximates the production Henderson of 1912, especially its long (66 inches) wheelbase, its four-cylinder engine, and its foot-pedal controls mounted on a floorboard. The *Journal* editor criticized the proposed pivoting of the head along with the front wheel, the result of which would have made the handlebars move up and down with suspension movement. He also suggested that the belt drive and idler be replaced by a "shaft running in oil or an enclosed silent chain with a free engine." And he pointed out that the seat mounted over the motor was an impractical idea, since the motor in the drawing was shown out of scale; in reality, the engine would have required the seat to be fixed too high to be practical. The four-cylinder engine itself was thought to be more powerful than necessary; "a smaller engine and two speeds will accomplish the same results."

When the Henderson appeared in Detroit, it was (except for a prototype) driven by a chain. A clutch was standard equipment. The front wheel was suspended in conventional fashion, moving vertically independent of the handlebars. The seat, however, remained above a four-cylinder engine, the feature by which all Hendersons were best known.

How much the *Journal*'s editor contributed to the evolution of the Henderson is a matter for speculation. Perhaps Henderson came to his design changes on his own after he submitted his drawings to the magazine. Perhaps he took Duryea's advice to heart. In any case, it's apparent that much of the Henderson motorcycle announced in Detroit was devised when its engineer resided in Rochester. Some historians have even suggested fabrication in Rochester: Bob Holliday, in his *Motorcycle Panorama*, claims that William Henderson "set up a business in Rochester, NY, to make and market his own design of machine." In *The World's Motorcycles*, Erwin Tragatsch lists William Henderson in Rochester as the first of four builders of Henderson motorcycles.

Arthur Herschmann
New York City (Manhattan)
or, more likely, Austria
ca. 1895

The *Horseless Age* for April 23, 1902, noted that Arthur Herschmann had built a motorized bicycle that he took to England "about seven years ago." That machine had two air-cooled cylinders mounted on each side of and parallel with the down tube of the bicycle. The engine crankshaft replaced the pedal crank. A second shaft, geared at half speed, was mounted forward of the bottom bracket and below the engine cylinders. This second shaft served two purposes: cam operation of the exhaust valves and drive for a sprocket connected by chain to the rear wheel. Intake valves were atmospheric. Ignition was by hot tube.

From 1901 Herschmann was a mechanical engineer with an office and a residence in Manhattan. A United States patent granted in 1900 also lists Herschmann as a resident of New York City, albeit as a subject of the Austro-Hungarian emperor. The *Horseless Age*

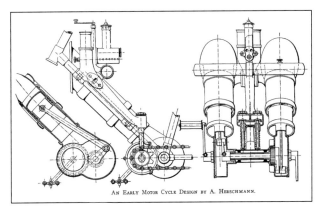

Arthur Herschmann's circa-1895 two-cylinder engine on the down tube of a bicycle. From the *Horseless Age*, April 23, 1902.

reported in 1902 that Herschmann was "working in the line of steam freight vehicles," implying that while the motorcycle being described was of interest, the designer had gone on to other matters. In fact, patents granted to Herschmann from 1898 through 1903 were for work with steam generators, clutches, gearing, and four-wheel vehicles, including a self-propelled truck with swing axles.

Left unsaid in the *Horseless Age* article is the place where Herschmann devised his motorcycle. The article may leave its readers the impression, since Herschmann's nationality is never mentioned, that he was an American who took his motorcycle from the United States to England. Likelier, however, was that he took the machine from Austria-Hungary to England as a way station on a journey to the United States. In fact, two Austrian patents were granted to him in Birmingham, England, in 1898, and a United States patent granted to him in 1899 also gives a Birmingham address.

Hilaman
Moorestown
ca. 1907

Bob Karolevitz's *Yesterday's Motorcycles* (1986) lists the Hilaman motorcycle of "Moorestown, N.Y." Karolevitz probably had in mind Moorestown in Burlington County, New Jersey. There, the A. H. Hilaman Company manufactured both one- and two-cylinder machines beginning in 1907.

Hitchcock Manufacturing Company
Cortland
manufacturing for the Motor Cycle Company
of Cleveland, Ohio
1894–95
Trade name: **Motor Cycle**

Caleb B. Hitchcock (1839–1918) began building sleighs in Cortland in 1877. The incorporation of the Hitchcock Manufacturing Company followed in 1884. By 1890, production reached 25,000 vehicles per annum—both wagons and sleighs—with 425 men employed. Henry P. Smith in his *History of Cortland County* (1885) said of Hitchcock, "Being a good judge of human nature enabled him to gather about him as employees men well fitted to aid him in his great enterprises. During his business career he has made no misstep through defect of his own judgement."

The Pennington (Hitchcock) motorcycle. The cylinders extend horizontally from the rear wheel with the piston rods attached to cranks on the hub. From *Scientific American*, February 9, 1895.

In 1894, Hitchcock reached an agreement with Edward J. Pennington (1858–1911) of the Motor Cycle Company of Cleveland, Ohio, to manufacture the motor vehicles designed by Pennington. These included one- and two-passenger (tandem) motorcycles as well as an automobile called the Victoria. The Pennington motorcycle, covered by patents granted in 1896 and 1897, was a simple design. It added to a safety bicycle frame an extra set of seat tubes, which supported two internal combustion cylinders beside the rear wheel. The connecting rods were attached directly to the rear hub. Spark came from a storage battery. Aside from the engine, the major contrast to pedal bicycles was the small-diameter wheels fitted with large cross-section tires, intended to provide a smooth ride as well as superior traction on soft surfaces. The whole of the drive mechanism weighed only 12 pounds. A gallon of gasoline, naphtha, or even kerosene would, so Pennington claimed, carry the machine and rider 100 miles. The cylinders operated independently of each other, so that, in theory, one could be removed. Pennington said that in a test made "in Washington, Oct. 3, 1894, in the presence of a large crowd. . . . In a distance of 390 feet on a two percent grade, the motor cycle from a standing start attained a speed of 30 miles per hour." He also claimed to have ridden "the motor cycle thousands of miles."

Pennington's career as an inventor and promoter is one of the most colorful and notorious in the history of late-nineteenth- and early-twentieth-century America. Among his specialties were promotions of purported inventions that would have revolutionized transportation. Among these were a near-magical aluminum airship and an electric railroad with special car-mounted motors free of wire contact to external power sources. Pennington's exploits were well documented by the press, yet he was able to operate fraudulent schemes for decades. The *New York Times* in 1893 quoted Charles E. Bleyer of the Chicago and St. Louis Electric Railroad on Pennington and his "Arabian Nights enterprises": "He is a glib, voluble fellow and a very smooth talker. Yet his reputation is worn so thin that I am much astonished at his finding investors."

While Pennington's involvement eventually spelled the demise of the Hitchcock concern, in late 1894, news of the contract between Hitchcock and Pennington brought much favorable anticipation of what the *Cortland Standard* called the "wheel of the future." The newspaper thought Pennington a "man of great inventive genius, a thorough mechanic and electrician. Besides this he is a business man in every sense of the word and with his fine presence will undoubtedly make many friends in this section."

Hitchcock told the *Standard* that he had made several trips to Cleveland to investigate the motorcycle. With his factory superintendent, Lewis B. Fairbanks, he "submitted the machine to every known test, examined the parts in detail both as to the possibility, construction and reliability to get out of repair, durability, skill, requirement to operate it, and after a number of days examination came to the conclusion that a motor cycle so strong, durable, simple, easy to manage, and so almost impossible to get out of repair, could not fail to be a success." As a result, Hitchcock contracted to build fifty thousand examples of the $275 machine. The *Standard* said, "If anything in the world can give a town the size of Cortland a boom this ought to do so."

After finishing the first motorcycle at the end of December 1894, the Hitchcock people in early 1895

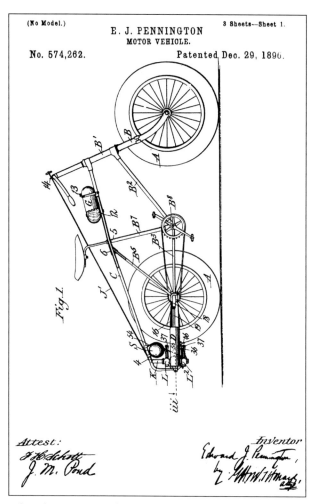

Edward J. Pennington's 1896-patented motorcycle, on which the Hitchcock Manufacturing Company placed unrealized hope.

were reportedly working on the first ten thousand machines, "running their factories day and night, the prospects are that there will be no hard times in Cortland for many years to come. All of the men who a year ago were walking the streets are now at work." In December 1894, a Toronto entrepreneur left an order for five hundred machines during 1895. In January 1895, Pennington displayed motorcycles at the Madison Square Garden and Chicago bicycle shows. And in February, Hitchcock sales manager William O. Niveson and Pennington demonstrated their motor vehicles in Elmira, where Grant and DeWaters had become their agent. The Elmira *Telegram* predicted "big success for the Motor 'Cycle.'"

In March came a rumor that the Hitchcock company would not be building motorcycles after all. Pennington denied this, saying that material for five thousand machines was on hand. In April, the Hitchcock firm added an agricultural implement department to their wagon, sleigh, and bicycle operations. Then, in July, the company was in receivership. "For some weeks rumors had been afloat of financial embarrassment in the Hitchcock Co. which was known all over the country." Liabilities totaled $189,887.67 with assets at $278,23.64, but in short order the Hitchcock real estate was sold by the receivers, who included Caleb Hitchcock. Pennington, who had left Cortland with several outstanding debts, was apprehended by the Cortland County sheriff in New York City in 1900. Rather than return to Cortland, Pennington paid the $750.06 due his creditors.

In 1900 the editor of the *Bicycling World* said that at the Madison Square Garden show in 1895 he had tried the Pennington motorcycle, which with its 4-inch tires "ran with far less vibration that the machines at present in use." The motorcycle itself was "a most ingenious contrivance, but it was in advance of the times; the public was interested in neither automobiles nor motorcycles."

One hundred years after its demise, the competence of the Pennington-Hitchcock motorcycle remains an enigma. To an extent, the uncertainty is grounded in Pennington's history of fraud. But there are testimonials to the successful operation of one or more of the machines. Some of the reports come from parties with interests in positive results—for example, Fairbanks, who claimed, "I have ridden it in the streets of Cleveland, up and down hill, among the usual crowd found on the streets of a busy city."

Perhaps a somewhat less biased report came from Ellis M. Santee, a Cortland physician and bicyclist, who, characteristically for Pennington inventions, tried a motorcycle under controlled conditions inside a Hitchcock factory building rather than on the streets, "as the roads were very slushy." Santee stated, "You can say anything you wish about the machine for me in praise of its merits. I will order one immediately for myself. Considering the power developed I have no doubt that it will go up the steepest hills round here at full speed. I expect within a day or so to give the machine a thorough test on the hills, but considering the power developed in the factory I have no doubt as to the result." "R. G. B." (probably R. G. Betts) recalled in the *Bicycling World* in 1909 a ride on a Pennington tandem with Santee in New York City in 1895: "Although we probably did not exceed a pace of 20 miles an hour, the speed seemed almost to take away my breath. I was glad to dismount and did not seek a second invitation. Neither the pleasures nor possibilities of motorcycling had been even faintly impressed on me."

It's likely that motorcycle construction in Cortland produced no more than experimental or "sample machines," according to Clara A. Elder in her "C. B. Hitchcock's Buggy and Cutter Factory" (*Cortland County Chronicles*, vol. 2, 1958). And those motorcycles, as with most of Pennington's creations, ran for short distances but failed to perform under everyday riding conditions. The *Cortland Standard* in 1900 said, "One or two motor cycles were built and they seemed to work perfectly on a run of four or five miles but on a longer run they would get hot and needed a supply of water constantly on hand to keep the machinery cool. In other words, the principle was all right but they had not then reached a state of perfection."

Hogle Motor Sales Corporation
Malone
1919

Motorcycle and Bicycle Illustrated for May 1, 1919, reported the incorporation of the Hogle company at $100,000 to "make and deal in motorcycles, automobiles, trucks, etc." Edwin E. Hogle, of Malone, president; J. Hubert Stevens, of Saranac Lake; and John A. Gallaway, of Malone, secretary, were the incorporators. Of the total capital, $54,000 was "paid in property," according to the certificate of incorporation.

The Hogle firm was dissolved in 1922, when the board consisted of Hogle, Stevens, and Frank P. Meehan of Malone (at that point the secretary), each of whom owned 180 shares of the company. Whether any motorcycles had been built is unknown here, but such manufacture would appear unlikely.

John Holtzman and Abraham Geffon
New York City (Manhattan)
1915–16

Patent 1,201,734, issued on October 17, 1916, deals with a motor attachment for "vehicles," although John Holtzman and Abraham Geffon described their invention as fitted to a bicycle. And a bicycle would have been the likeliest application, had the attachment been built.

Similar to the Smith Motor Wheel, perhaps the most popular such device of the 1910s, Holtzman and Geffon's machine added a third wheel fitted with an engine. Their novelty dealt with the attachment mechanism, which provided for all the wheels to stay parallel and for a spring to keep the drive wheel in contact with the road surface. Holtzman and Geffon signed their application in July 1915. Whether any motor wheels were built to their design has not been determined here.

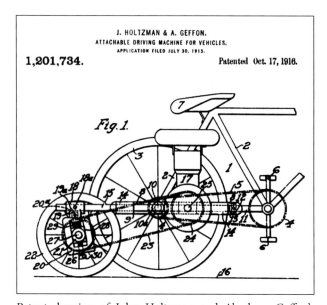

Patent drawing of John Holtzman and Abraham Geffon's motor wheel design.

Nelson S. Hopkins
Williamsville
1894–95

Nelson Hopkins (1870–1943) motorized a Columbia (Pope Manufacturing Company of Hartford, Connecticut) bicycle with the addition of an internal combustion engine mounted on the left side of the rear wheel. Spur gears engaged the rear hub, although the gearing could be disengaged by the removal of a pin "in case the engine should get out of repair," Hopkins noted in his patent description. A clutch allowed the pedals to be held stationary while the engine operated, although the rider needed to assist the motor for hill climbing.

Ignition came from a battery and coil, with current flow governed by a piston's movement. The additional weight of the engine on the left side of the bicycle was offset by moving the saddle to the right. The engine on the bicycle weighed 12 pounds, although Hopkins reportedly had a second engine weighing 8.5 pounds, which, according to *Scientific American*, would "propel a wheel and rider over moderate grades."

The Buffalo and Erie County Historical Society has preserved six sheets of mechanical drawings, dated June and July of 1894, which are labeled "Hopkins Cycle Motor" as well as "Columbia 91 Model," a reference to the bicycle. Probably done by Hopkins, the drawings note the dimensions of the engine parts as well as the materials used, for example, "machined steel," "wrought iron," and "phosphorus bronze" for bearings. On July 23, 1895, Hopkins received Patent 543,094 for his "improvement in motors for bicycles." Notable in the patented engine as on the motorized bicycle are the V-twin cylinders, one of which was used for compression and the other for combustion. In effect, the intake, compression, combustion, and exhaust portions of the four-stroke cycle were divided equally between the cylinders, both of which used poppet valves. Hopkins said that the acute angle of the two cylinders was critical; the pistons "although they are moved by the same crank-pin do not reach corresponding points in the two cylinders at the same time. The difference is due to the angle in which the cylinders are set to each other." Hopkins's carburetion consisted of a "small quantity of asbestos or other absorbent material," which would hold gasoline to be vaporized by air flowing through it en route to the compression cylinder.

Nelson Hopkins's motorized bicycle. From *Scientific American*, April 11, 1896.

Hopkins, according to an obituary in the *Buffalo Courier-Express*, became "widely known as a consulting engineer." In the 1910s, he managed the Curtiss Aeroplane and Motor Company Ltd. of Canada. Later, after developing a fireproof aircraft paint, Hopkins organized the Phoenix Aircraft Products Company in Williamsville to manufacture the coating. The Hopkins motorcycle, as well as the plans and associated papers, survive in the collections of the Buffalo and Erie County Historical Society in Buffalo.

I

Steve Iacona
d/b/a Iacona Custom Cycles
New York City (Brooklyn)
ca. 2005–present

Steve Iacona uses Harley-Davidson-based motorcycles to create one-of-a-kind custom builds. He has won numerous awards for his work. He began his business in his garage; in 2010 it had outgrown the garage, and he opened his own shop. Iacona Custom Cycles does everything from basic service to custom builds. They also produce in-house aftermarket parts, such as the "Fuggedaboutit Ignition Switch," designed for Harley Sportsters. According to the company's website, "there are no drawings or plans. Steve thinks up something in his head and gets busy on his lathe, drill press, English wheel and whatever else he can squeeze inside the diminutive shop."

A couple of Iacona's award-winning motorcycles are the "Challenger" and the "Phoenix," both modified Harleys.

International Motorcycle Company
New York City (Bronx)
ca. 1953

This company was apparently an importing operation using a 2432 Grand Concourse (Bronx) address. In January 1953, International Motorcycle Company advertised the Czech Jawa as well as the German Zundapp machine. The company dissolved around 1957, and the Zundapp agency and the entirety of the facilities were taken over by Joseph "Joe" Berliner (q.v.) of Berliner Motor Corporation. Berliner was a former partner in the International Motorcycle Company.

International Sport Motors Ltd.
New York City (Manhattan)
ca. 1950

This company at 111 Wall Street imported the Bee 100 (Imme R-100) motorcycle built by the Riedel Motor Corporation in Immenstadt, Germany.

J

Herman Jehle
New York City (Manhattan)
ca. 1900
Trade Name: **Spiral**

Herman Jehle (ca. 1869–1956),[5] an instructor at the Baron D. Hirsch Vocational School on Forty-Sixth Street in Manhattan in the 1890s, built a motorcycle for his own use. Harry Buck, the owner of that motor-

---

5. The 1900 census documents Herman Jahle, a twenty-six-year-old Swiss immigrant whose profession was listed as "instructor in mechanics."

cycle in 2000, learned the history of the machine from Jehle's niece, Pauline Neville, after Jehle's death in the 1950s.

According to Buck's account, Jehle was riding a bicycle on Fifth Avenue about 1895 when, for the first time, he encountered a man on a motorcycle. During the ensuing conversation, the motorcyclist made Jehle a gift of the German Daimler machine, which was taken to the Hirsch schoolyard. Subsequently, Jehle removed and studied the engine, while disposing of the wooden frame.

At the Hirsch shops, Jehle soon fabricated his own four-stroke engine, utilizing cast bronze for the crankcase and machined steel for the integral cylinder and head. The cooling fin is one continuous spiral, its form inspiring the name for Jehle's motorcycle.

The engine was mounted on a bicycle frame, with belt drive to the rear wheel. Jehle was unhappy with the arrangement, especially with belt slippage in wet weather, so he mounted the engine on a frame of his own design, incorporating double reduction chain drive. With the addition of a coaster brake, an acetylene headlamp, a speedometer, and a forty-dollar Bosch magneto, the turn-of-the-century Jehle motorcycle evolved to its present form.

Jehle was one of the first members of the New York Motorcycle Club, being photographed with his motorcycle among a group of riders in 1902 (see color insert for image). But he eventually left New York for Newark, New Jersey, where he operated an automobile parts store for many years and where the motorcycle was displayed. During the World War II gasoline shortage, Jehle intended to conserve fuel by riding the motorcycle but was unable to find a needed tire. After over half a century in Jehle's possession, the Spiral motorcycle met the half-century mark in Buck's hands, as well.

Jencick Motor Corporation
Port Chester
ca. 1912–14

The *Thomas Register of American Manufacturers* for 1914 includes among motor bicycle manufacturers the "Jencick Motor Company" of Port Chester. Capitalized at that point between $2,500 and $5,000, the Jencick Motor Corporation had been organized on January 23, 1912. The certificate of incorporation notes that the company was to acquire and take over the property, assets, and effects, "including the name and good will of the Jencick Motor Manufacturing Company, bankrupt, which were sold at public sale on December 8, 1911, . . . and purchased at said sale by Stephen Jencick."

Turner's Directory of Port Chester and East Port Chester for 1910–11 listed the Jencick Motor Manufacturing Company at 351 North Main Street. According to records in the Division of Corporations in the New York Department of State, the manufacturing company had been incorporated on October 20, 1906.

Jencick Motor Manufacturing Company president Louis C. Mertz was also president of the George Mertz's Sons contracting company in East Port Chester. The secretary of the Jencick firm was Leander Horton. Stephen Jencick was listed as the superintendent. Jenick was a well-known inventor, and he specialized in marine engines. He was trained at the Vienna Polytechnical Institute and worked for Daimler Motor Works and DeDion Company. The holder of many patents, Jencick worked at Climax Motors Devices Company of Cleveland and then Oldfield Motors Corporation of Duluth after the firm with his surname went under.

The corporate purposes of the Jencick Motor Corporation were manifold, including the manufacture, sale, lease, exchange, import, and export of motorcycles as well as of airplanes, boats, carriages, and "vehicles of every kind and description." The corporation ran into financial trouble in 1914 and was later dissolved by proclamation by the secretary of state in 1926. It appears unlikely that any motorcycles were fabricated by either the Jencick Motor Manufacturing Company or the Jencick Motor Corporation.

H. E. Jones (Harvey E. Toms)
Dansville
1906

In late 1906, Jones, who identified himself as an agent for Thomas and Indian motorcycles, submitted a drawing of a two-cylinder machine to the motorcycle editor of the *Cycle and Automobile Trade Journal*. Jones's major design innovation was an opposed engine with the cylinders running parallel to the long axis of the frame. The four-cycle power plant was to have battery ignition as well as an exposed flywheel on the left side, where the belt drive to the rear wheel would be located. The wheelbase was given as 56 inches.

The *Journal*'s editor, Charles H. Metz, himself a motorcycle pioneer, noted that the Jones design was "thoroly [sic] practical, and has the advantage of perfect balance in the motor, which the V-type cannot possess. It is advisable to design the frame so as to allow a low position of the saddle." In fact, Jones's top tube extended back horizontally from a tall head tube; a sloping top tube would have provided a lower saddle.

Jones claimed that he had built a four-cylinder automobile during the winter of 1905–6 and, as he wrote, was fabricating a 20-foot launch. Whether he built a motorcycle has not been determined here.

In the spring of 1908, the *Journal* reported that H. E. Toms (q.v.) of 10 Ossian Street in Dansville had designed "a unique but neat motorcycle with an opposed motor and V transmission." The identical initials in the Jones and Toms names as well as the similarity of the motorcycle designs suggest that Jones and Toms might have been the same person. Local newspaper ads and articles demonstrate that "Jones" was actually Harvey E. Toms. Toms was the owner and operator of a sporting goods store in Dansville. In addition to selling sporting goods, he had a machine shop where he repaired bicycles and automobiles. He was the agent for Thomas and Indian motorcycles and numerous automobile brands. Furthermore, he also built a boat and automobile in his shop. Toms also served as foreman for the short-lived Klink Motor Car Company (1907–10).

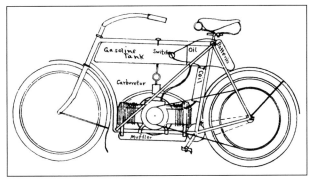

Jones's 1906 design for an opposed two-cylinder engine, perhaps realized on the H. E. Toms (q.v.) motorcycle in 1908. From *Cycle and Automobile Trade Journal*, March 1907.

K

John R. Keim
Buffalo
1901

In April 1901, *Cycle Age* reported that the John R. Keim bicycle manufacturing company of Buffalo "has taken hold of the Hafelinger [sic] motor bicycle." It was "known that several firms had made propositions to the patentee [Emil Hafelfinger], as the bicycle was neat looking and had all the ear marks of success." In a short article a week later, the magazine acknowledged a letter from John R. Keim denying that he had "taken hold of the Haffelfing [sic] motor bicycle" and claiming "he has no intention of doing so." The journal said that a recent report noted Keim would "manufacture the motor bicycle on royalty, but his statement disposes of the rumor effectually." Hafelfinger's Royal Motor Works (q.v.) eventually manufactured the Hafelfinger motorcycle in Manhattan.

Kiefler Motor Works
Buffalo
late 1907 or early 1908–1912 or later
Trade Name: **Kiefler**

The *Bicycling World and Motorcycle Review* in early February 1908 described the "Kiefer" motorcycle, "a local product fairly bristling with original features," which appeared at the Power Boat and Sportsmen's Show in Buffalo. The journal noted the engine set "at a forward angle," belt drive, band brake instead of a coaster, rubber-covered footrests, and no pedals. The saddle was mounted "directly over the rear hub resting on the top of a triangular truss." The handlebars were of "truly enormous length." The gasoline and oil tanks were separate, and the batteries "encased in an envelope-like casing." The price was $250. The article concluded that with "output . . . extremely limited it probably all will be absorbed locally."

The principals of the Kiefler motorcycle enterprise were the machinists Charles J. Kiefler and Henry J. Kiefler. The two brothers' motorcycle company was the Kiefler Motor Works, located no later than the first half of 1909 at 184 Broadway; Charles was the proprietor, and Henry was the manager. It's likely that the Kiefler business was small enough that both men were involved in a variety of administrative and production operations. The number of additional employees, if any, is unknown here.

In May 1909, the *Bicycling World* said the Kiefler motorcycle exhibited "several departures from general practice, its method of automatic lubrication being particularly notable." This lubrication system utilized engine vacuum to draw oil from a reservoir into the engine crankcase. Other noteworthy characteristics of the Kiefler were the 5-horsepower engine rating ("the most powerful of that [single-cylinder] pattern on the market"), created by a slow-turning, long-stroke design "mounted with a considerable forward inclination in a double bar loop frame."

The 5-horsepower Kiefler had the "most powerful . . . [single-cylinder engine] on the market," according to the *Bicycling World and Motorcycle Review*, May 29, 1909.

An automatic idler for the "chain belt" could be overridden with a pedal to provide slip for "steep hills or heavy roads." Spark and throttle levers were mounted on the top tube, with the left grip serving as an ignition cutout. A pedal operated the 4.75-inch contracting band brake with "metal to metal friction surfaces." A Mesinger saddle was mounted, as in the previous year, over the rear wheel. Two gallons of gasoline and two quarts of oil were carried in the double tanks housed in the torpedo-shaped container between the top tubes. The wheelbase was 53 inches. The 28-inch wheels were fitted with 2.5-inch tires.

In the summer of 1909, Henry Kiefler took part in a Federation of American Motorcyclists endurance contest between Cleveland, Ohio, and Indianapolis, Indiana. His score of 936 points earned him a silver medal in the class for trade riders of single-cylinder machines. Kiefler's endurance-run machine was later described as a "1909½" model, "a simplification of last season's machine." The engine, with dimensions of 3.75 by 4 inches, was "the largest single cylinder in the country." At the end of the year, *Motorcycle Illustrated* said the Kiefler engine developed "fully five horsepower."

The idler for the chain belt was released by a lever. The "Kiefer [sic] folks" manufactured their own "mixing valve" instead of using "the usual type of carburetor." Lubrication and valves were "automatic." The gasoline tank supposedly held two quarts, and the oil tank three pints. Two batteries took care of the ignition. The frame remained "double," and the handlebars "extra long." A Mesinger saddle was fitted. The price was $220. On the run, the Kiefler reportedly gathered "quite a little attention from the riders." Kiefler manufacture was described as done in "a small way" by the Kiefler Motor Works, still at 184 Broadway.

In November 1909, the *Cycle and Automobile Trade Journal* devoted a page to the Kiefler, including two photos of what was probably the 1910 model. In form, this Kiefler was much like its predecessors. The 5-horsepower engine remained the only power plant available, but buyers were offered the option of a two-speed gear (4:1 and 9:1 ratios), apparently a planetary type fitted on the end of the crankshaft controlled by a lever on the left side of the gasoline tank. The monthly reported that the "motor can be started with crank. Both clutches on gear are of the circular contracting band type, which does away with side thrust on bearings. The low speed is adjustable with a cone like a hub. All wearing parts are hardened and ground."

The *Journal* noted that engine-cooling flanges were "cut from the solid, making it possible to secure very thin and deep flanges." The intake valve remained automatic, mounted over the exhaust valve. The "automatic idler" adjusted the chain belt. Spark and throttle were controlled by "friction levers," and the ignition cutout still was fitted to the left grip. A foot-lever-controlled band brake was fitted to the rear wheel. The saddle remained mounted low over the rear wheel "on an auxiliary stay." Prices were $225 for the direct-drive, single-speed model and $260 for the two-speed.

A specification chart for the gray-and-red 1910 Kiefler noted that the cylinder dimensions were 3.75 by 4 and horsepower still rated at 5. The motorcycle was little changed from the previous year's offering. In fact, the Kiefler machine remained remarkably unaltered throughout its production run. In January 1911, *Motorcycle Illustrated* noted that the Kiefler motorcycle, presumably the 1911 model, was fitted with a one-cylinder engine and a two-speed planetary transmission. It listed at $275.

In 1912, the Kiefler company moved to 401 Sycamore Street. Production of motorcycles probably continued, as evidenced in part by a city directory listing of "motor cycles" as the business for the Kiefler Motor Works. Further evidence is a report in *Motorcycling* in April 1912 that the "Kiefler Motor Works are building a 10 h.p. twin for a would-be record buster."

By 1913 the situation at the Kiefler Motor Works had changed. Charles had departed the firm, and the directory no longer listed motorcycles as the company's business. A year later, "auto repair" was shown as Henry Kiefler's activity at the works. While the *Thomas Register of American Manufacturers* for 1914, which appeared in the fall of that year, still listed the Kiefler Motor Works at 401 Sycamore Street among makers of motorcycles, the next year Kiefler's name was absent from the *Thomas* annual.

Charles B. Kirkham
d/b/a Kirkham Motor Manufacturing Company
Cold Spring (sometimes listed as "Taggarts" or "Taggerts") and Bath
ca. 1903–7

Charles Kirkham, his father, and his brothers were known as machinists and manufacturers of engines, including motorcycle power plants for Glenn Curtiss (q.v.), maker of the Hercules and Curtiss motorcycles in Hammondsport. The *Hammondsport Herald* in 1904 said that to Curtiss himself is attributed the statement that "a great deal of the success of the Hercules motorcycle is due to the superior construction and workmanship on the motors, which are built exclusively for him by Charles Kirkham of Cold Springs [sic]." The *Herald* continued by noting that "Mr. Kirkham is a very talented young man, being a first class draughtsman and all around machinist. He has the best equipped shops in this section, and besides building the Curtiss motor, Mr. Kirkham also builds and markets the Kirkham 4 Cylinder Air Cooled Automobile engine, which is one of the best designed and most efficient air cooled engines on the market."

The "Buyer's Guide" printed in the January 1903 issue of the *Cycle and Automobile Trade Journal* listed Charles Kirkham as a source of motorcycles. In May 1904, it was reported that Kirkham was about to take a "motor bicycle of his own invention and manufacture" to Dayton, Ohio, for a "trial." "Should it meet with the approval of Mr. Kirkham's customer, an added increase to the business of the firm will be the outcome. Fifteen men are employed at their factory which is running night and day."

A year later, the *Bicycling World and Motocycle Review* reported that "L. J. Kirkham" of Bath was the "practical man" in an effort to establish a motorcycle factory in Bath to operate under his name. Five thousand dollars had been subscribed, half the amount needed. It was proposed to employ forty men at the beginning of the operation.

It's likely that "L. J. Kirkham" was Charles B. Kirkham, who had assumed the management of the machine shop founded by his father, John. Charles's brothers, Clarence and Percy, also had joined the firm. The Kirkham Motor Manufacturing Company was organized in early 1905. The New York State certificate of incorporation for the Kirkham company lists the purposes of the new organization in part as the "manufacture, purchase, use, leasing and selling of self-propelling vehicles, motors, engines." Of the $25,000 in authorized capital stock, the Bath enterprise began its business with $16,975. Charles Kirkham was the principal stockholder, with 150 shares of preferred and 100 of common. Other shareholders were the four remaining directors of the corporation, Charles A. Ellis, W. L. Dolson, Mathew E. Shannon, and David L. Stewart, all of Bath.

In early March 1905, the Kirkham Motor Manufacturing Company "began operations in the Hardenbrook block, Bath . . . with several hands. Half of the machinery has been installed. The remainder will be taken from Taggarts as soon as possible, when it is expected that the number of employees will be doubled," according to the *Herald*.

A 10-mile road race in or near Bath on June 28, 1907, was won by C. B. Kirkham, "riding a machine of his own manufacture," in 17 minutes and 28 seconds. He had been passed by Albert Cook on a Curtiss, but the latter fell on the muddy road. A crowd of about four thousand people saw the race "and worked up considerable over it" (*Hammondsport Herald*).

In the summer of 1907, the Kirkham company signed a contract to provide one hundred four-cylinder automotive engines at a cost of $25,000 to the York Motor Car Company, makers of the Pullman car in York, Pennsylvania. This was the "second order from this company, attesting to the merits of the motors after a year's experience," said the *Herald*.

How many complete motorcycles were fabricated by Charles Kirkham and the Kirkham Motor Manufacturing Company remains unclear. It seems likely that the number was small and that after 1907 the Kirkham company focused on automotive and aircraft engines, as well as complete aircraft. In 1909, according to the *Herald*, the Kline Automobile Company of York, Pennsylvania, acquired control of the Kirkham concern, with Charles Kirkham remaining until 1910 as manager of the "mechanical department," after which he manufactured aircraft engines in Savona. James Bellamy in his *Cars Made in Upstate New York* (1989) reports that the Kirkham firm failed in 1913 and was succeeded by the Kirkham Machine Company. The *Hammondsport Herald* at the time (1913) noted the organization of the Kirkham Aeroplane and Motor Company taking over the business of Charles Kirkham of Savona and the Rex Monoplane Company of New York. The new stock company, with Kirkham as president, was to build Kirkham motors as well as flying boats and "flying machines." A late-twentieth-century observer, Kevin Cameron, claims that Charles Kirkham, in designing an engine for fighter airplanes in 1916, "made the four-valve DOHC concept a part of his epoch-making V-12. . . . Its reverberations were complex, but one clearly traceable result was the Rolls-Royce Merlin V-12. which powered the Hurricanes and Spitfires that won the Battle of Britain in 1940."

Kenneth Klingerman
New York City (Brooklyn)
ca. 1955–60

In December 2000, Gordon Bensen of Rensselaerville reported that he owned a custom motorcycle built by Kenny Klingerman of Coney Island in the second half of the 1950s. Klingerman, in the auto body business, modified a Harley-Davidson motorcycle to produce a 10.5-foot-long machine he called "Hot Lips." Bensen notes the motorcycle won "first place" at a competition in the Coliseum in Manhattan in 1961 and was last registered for road use in 1970. Bensen planned to display the motorcycle for a fee at such venues as the Altamont (Albany, Greene, and Schenectady combined) Fair.

Samuel B. Kurtz
New York City (Brooklyn)
1907–15

Samuel Kurtz patented a hybrid motorcycle-automobile, the purpose of which, he claimed, would be to provide "a high-power, high-speed motor-vehicle which will be light and capable of easy manipulation; to provide a motor-vehicle having all the advantages of the motorcycle and none of its disadvantages, and all of the advantages of an automobile and none of its disadvantages"

Kurtz meant specifically to combine the "high power and speed" of an automobile with the "mobility" and "easy manipulation" of a motorcycle. He also would have provided convertibility to use on runners as well as wheels, cheapness of construction, and a unique transmission.

Two retractable outriggers, each fitted with a wheel (or runner), were to provide stability for the vehicle at rest or at low speed but were to be drawn close to the frame for general travel. In effect, the vehicle was transformed from two-wheel motorcycle to four-wheel automobile at the driver's whim.

Kurtz had a drive shaft from the engine run to a clutch and transmission giving one reverse and two forward gears. Another shaft ran from the transmission to a bevel gearing arrangement near the rear wheel. A split drive in this second transmission would have allowed the rider to power the rear wheel by either of two chain wheels fitted to the ends of the driven shaft in the bevel gear mechanism. In effect, there were two additional gear choices, since different-sized chain wheels on the shaft ends and on both sides of the rear wheel gave the vehicle four speeds ahead and two in reverse.

Wheel steering, a ladder-type frame, elliptical (or semielliptical) springs, and a bench seat were all automobile-style components, but basically Kurtz's vehicle would have operated as a motorcycle. Whether any were ever built is unknown here, as is the reason it took the patent office almost eight years (from the application filed on December 20, 1907, to issuance on September 5, 1915) to grant Patent 1,152,821. Several of Kurtz's ideas were realized on similar vehicles, such as the wheel steering and outriggers on the Militaire (q.v.).

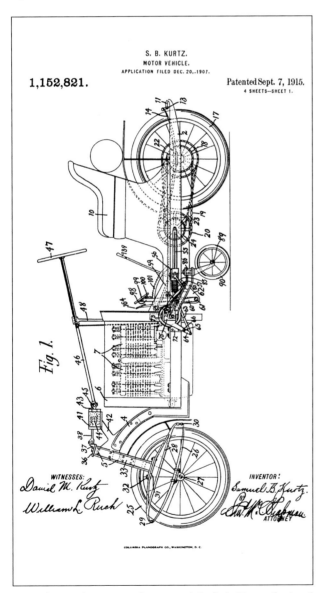

Samuel Kurtz's motorcycle-automobile hybrid, as depicted in a patent drawing.

L

Lomart Engine Products
part of **Lomart Perfected Devices Inc.**
New York City (Brooklyn)
ca. 1967–71
Trade Name: **Cheeftah**

Martin Hoffinger was an entrepreneur who started Lomart Industries in 1954 in Brooklyn. Lomart Industries eventually specialized in swimming pools but had subsidiary businesses, including Clinton Engine Corporation, purchased in 1967. Around the same time, Lomart Engine Products, another subsidiary, started producing mini-bikes. The brand name was Cheeftah, and they featured Clinton engines. At least six models of Cheeftahs were available for customers to choose from. According to available advertising, engines a came in 3, 3.5, or 4 horsepower.

The business was located at 980 Alabama Avenue in Brooklyn. It is not clear how many mini-bikes were produced or the exact start and end dates for production. Advertising suggests that the Cheeftah was produced from around late 1967 through 1971.

Lomart Perfected Devices Inc., a Delaware corporation, was authorized to do business in New York on October 26, 1961. The devices, according to the "Statement and Designation" filed with the New York Secretary of State, were "swimming pool filters and accessories for pool filters, metal stampings and metal products and by-products and mechanical devices for translating any type of drawing into an optically correct perspective drawing and mechanical, electronic and electro-mechanical devices of every class, kind, type and description." Martin Hoffinger was the corporate president.

In 1983, the corporate name became Hoffinger Industries Inc., as Martin Hoffinger still served as chief executive officer. Apparently, the Alabama Avenue operation in Brooklyn survived to 2000, manufacturing swimming pool accessories and metal stampings. In that year, Hoffinger Industries of Rancho Cucamonga, California, surrendered its authority to do business in New York. The number of mini-bikes produced in Brooklyn is unknown here.

Long Island Choppers
Freeport
ca. 1995–present

The Facebook page for Long Island Choppers describes the company as follows: "LI Choppers is a full-service motorcycle service specialist and custom motorcycle manufacturer. In addition, we offer parts and accessories from leading vendors and manufacture custom parts as well." LI Choppers is owned by John Jordan.

Lozier Motor Company
Plattsburg
1900–1901

In 1900, the Lozier company moved from Toledo, Ohio, to Plattsburg, where motorboats were to be built. The *Bicycling World* in late summer reported news of a motor tricycle: "That George W. Burwell is its designer, coupled with the name Lozier, is sufficient to give it immediate standing; it was Burwell who did so much to make Cleveland bicycles what they are."

The next January, there was a rumor of a chain-driven motor bicycle. E. R. Lozier in New York City "would not deny that a number of Lozier agents had urged him to make a move of the sort." He went on to confirm that when the Lozier motorcycle appeared, it would list at more than two hundred dollars. "Such a bicycle as we will turn out . . . cannot be made and marketed for any such sum, and we desire the fact known in advance," the *Bicycling World* quoted him as saying.

With Burwell still employed, the *Bicycling World* thought that "whether it be chain or motor driven, or both, the future of the Lozier bicycle is not in doubt for a moment." Whether any motor bicycles or tricycles were built is unknown here. A Lozier automobile was introduced in 1905 in Plattsburg, and production ended in Detroit in 1918.

George V. Lyons Motor Company
New York City (Manhattan)
1905–9
Trade Names: **Wagner**; **Minerva**; **Motosacoche**

Starting in 1905, George V. Lyons was the agent for Wagner Motorcycle Company based in St. Paul, Minnesota. In 1907, the Lyons Company, at Eighty-Seventh Street and Broadway, had "the American agency" for the Minerva motorcycles, built by Minerva Motors Ltd. of Antwerp, Belgium. In 1909, Lyons imported the Motosacoche "lightweight" from Switzerland, but by October 1909 it was reported by *Motorcycle Illustrated* that Lyons "quit" the business and the old store was occupied by the McLaughlin & Ashley Motor Company (q.v.). George V. Lyons Motor Company did not go out of business but rather transitioned to automobiles and later trucks, surviving into the 1920s.

M

Frank D. Maltby
d/b/a **Maltby Automobile and Manufacturing Company**
New York City (Brooklyn)
1901

Frank D. Maltby was an active, lifelong inventor with several patents to his name. From as early as 1895 to 1908, he was involved with numerous Brooklyn-based companies featuring his surname. Starting around 1899, Frank's business ventures focused on internal combustion engines. While some of the businesses overlapped, they all appear to have been short-lived.

In the late winter of 1901, forty-six-year-old Maltby, in the bicycle business at 10 Clinton Street, had finished building a motor bicycle after three years' work and was "endeavoring to secure capital for the purpose of exploiting it." The engine of Maltby's machine was mounted "just above" the pedal crank in "a nearly vertical position." Chain drive was used to power the rear wheel. A container for gasoline and battery was in the "forward portion of the frame." Attached to the top tube was the coil. "It is claimed for the carburreter [*sic*] that it is not affected by the changes of the atmosphere," according to the *Bicycling World*.

The Automobile for June 1901 printed a photo of the Maltby motor bicycle, "made by F. D. Maltby, 10 Clinton Street, Brooklyn." According to the report, the crankcase "is built into the lower frame, and the motor, which is rated at 1¼ HP., is attached by a system of clamps and locking sleeves. The crank case has lugs which support an eccentric sleeve carrying the pedal cranks. A half turn of the eccentric sleeve disconnects the pedals from the motor." The wheelbase was noted at 54 inches. A 1.25-gallon fuel tank was mounted to the interior of the frame triangle.

A scrapbook dating from the 1900s of motorcycle images and descriptions assembled by G. N. Rogers includes a clip from a periodical showing the Maltby motorcycle. The printed data notes the machine was available from by Frank D. Maltby at 10 Clinton Street for $250. The 1.25-horsepower engine operated at 800 to 2,200 rpm, and the speed was controlled by adjustments to the timing and the throttle.

Published in 1901, *Horseless Vehicles, Automobiles, Motor Cycles Operated by Steam, Hydro-carbon, Electric and Pneumatic Motors*, by Gardner Dexter Hiscox, featured an entry on "Vehicle Motors of the Maltby Automobile and Motor Company," which was incorporated in 1900. According to Hiscox, they were producing "gasoline motors with water-jacketed and rib-cooled cylinders for bicycles, tricycles, carriages and launches."

In July 1901, the Maltby company reorganized and incorporated as the Maltby Automobile and Manufacturing Company. Automobiles, bicycles, motors, and launches, but not motorcycles, are mentioned in the articles of incorporation. In May 1902, they were advertising as the agents for Oldsmobile and National Electric Vehicles. The *Cycle and Automobile Trade Journal* "Buyer's Guide" that appeared in the January 1903 issue lists the "Maltby Auto. & Mfg. Co." at 10 Clinton Street as a source of motorcycles. The 1903 Brooklyn city directory lists the Maltby Automobile and Manufacturing Company at 70 Montague Street, where Frank Maltby is also shown to be in the automobile business. In 1903 Frank D. Maltby claimed bankruptcy, and, late that year, all of the Maltby Automobile and Manufacturing Company's equipment was auctioned off, including "several finished motors, automobile running gear and a complete motor cycle." The Maltby Automobile and Manufacturing Company is not listed in the city directory for 1904, and Frank Maltby does not have a trade listed with his name. It is possible that the company regrouped and produced brakes up until at least 1908, as listed in *International Motor Cyclopaedia—Year Book 1908*. In 1909, Maltby moved to Battle Creek, Michigan, where he married for a second time and had a successful business life running a machine shop and inventing.

The Maltby Automobile and Manufacturing Company was eventually dissolved by proclamation in late 1930. What motorcycle production the Maltby enterprises achieved is unknown here.

George W. Manson
New York City (Manhattan)
ca. 1897–1904

George Manson, in the bicycle business at 181 Broadway in Manhattan, was granted numerous related patents that together produced a unique motorcycle design. The first patent, issued in December 1898 for a bicycle design, encompassed the essential parts of the motorcycle less the engine. A key feature was the open frame in which parallel, twin members in elevation approximated the front portion of a drop-frame bicycle of the period less the seat tube and stays. The rear section of the frame consisted of double, parallel, horizontal members extending from the bottom of the down tube to the rear axle. Other significant Manson ideas were foot levers instead of rotary cranks and a two-speed, spur-gear transmission located between the pedal crank and final chain drive to the rear wheel.

Three years later, on July 23, 1901, after a November 1900 application, Manson received a patent for a motorized version of the bicycle. The patent description mentions that the engine to be used was "the well-known DeDion-Bouton motor." The rider was to have the option of assisting the engine by means of pedals attached by the levers first mentioned in the 1898 patent. Remaining patents in the series granted from 1900 through 1902 dealt with the gear-change mechanism, a "bicycle driving mechanism" incorporating a clutch, and a modification of the frame.

Cycle Age reported the motorcycle patent in the summer of 1901, calling Manson's design a "Strange Motor Cycle." The journal took note of the frame construction again—the clutch, transmission, and the cranks that "may be left in gear or thrown out as desired, being provided so as to start the motor, to propel the vehicle without aid of the motor or remain stationary while the machine is in motion."

The Manson Bicycle Company was organized in New York in May 1902 with $250,000 of capital stock.

The principal directors were Manson, George W. Clark, and George E. Clark, who took 39,000; 7,000; and 3,500 of the 50,000 shares, respectively, with par value of five dollars each. Whether any motorcycles of Manson's design were built by him or the Manson Bicycle Company in New York is unknown here. Production of a Manson motorcycle did take place at the Fowler-Manson-Sherman Cycle Manufacturing Company in Chicago. While George Manson was a principal of the Chicago enterprise, the motorcycle was entirely unlike the one he had sketched in New York. The Manson in Chicago used Thor engines built by the Aurora Automatic Machinery Company of Aurora, Illinois, and an ordinary diamond frame substituted for the style that had occupied George Manson's creative mind in New York. Jerry H. Hatfield notes that the Chicago Manson was manufactured from 1905 through 1908 (*Illustrated Antique American Motorcycle Buyer's Guide*, 1996).

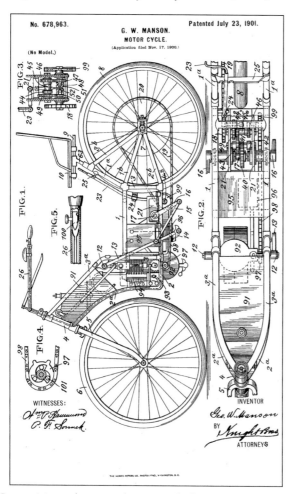

George Manson's patented motorcycle design of 1901, a variation of his earlier bicycle invention.

John F. McLaughlin
1907–8
McLaughlin & Ashley Motor Company
1909–?
New York City (Manhattan)

The *Cycle and Automobile Trade Journal* in December 1907 listed "J. F. McLaughlin" of 149 East Forty-Ninth Street among motorcycle exhibitors at the Madison Square Garden automobile show. While the *Journal* does not specify which motorcycles McLaughlin represented, *Motorcycle Illustrated* reported in the same month that John F. McLaughlin was the New York agent for the German-built N.S.U. at 148 East Forty-Ninth Street. Specifications appearing in the *Bicycling World and Motorcycle Review* in April 1908 for the 1.25- and 3-horsepower singles, the 4- and 6-horsepower twins, and the 6-horsepower "tri-car" of the 1908 N.S.U. line match exactly McLaughlin's offerings otherwise unidentified by the *Journal*. McLaughlin also raced N.S.U.s in New York City–area races in 1908–9.

In 1909, McLaughlin partnered with George A. Ashely to form McLaughlin & Ashley Motor Company. As reported by *Motorcycle Illustrated* on October 19, 1909, they had taken over the former store of the George V. Lyons Motor Company (q.v.). Lyons had transitioned to automobile sales. Also in the same issue *Motorcycle Illustrated*, an update was given on the fairly new business: "McLaughlin & Ashley Motor Company, of 206 West 76th street, has removed to 2384 Broadway, near 87th street, where it will carry a complete line of new and second hand motorcycles and accessories, and be prepared to do lathe work and brazing, together with repairing of every description."

Meadowbrook Cycle Company
alternatively, **Meadow Brook Cycle Company**
Hempstead
1904–6
Trade Name: **Meadowbrook**

In December 1904, the *Cycle and Automobile Trade Journal* said that the Meadowbrook, a "new make recently put out," was "very neat in appearance and light in weight, and the operating mechanism is responsive as well as simple to operate." The rider controlled the machine by "varying the spark from the switch grip and by one spark advance lever." Another lever operated a compression-relief valve. Equipment included a "spring handle bar" and a spring seat post.

Photos of the Meadowbrook depict a frame closely resembling that of a bicycle of the period, with the vertical, four-stroke engine mounted at the base of the diamond. The battery and coil apparently were suspended from the top tube, while the fuel and oil supplies were fitted behind the seat tube. Specifications for the 60-pound Meadowbrook include a 22-inch frame with a 44-inch wheelbase as well as 26- and 28-inch wheels with 1.5-inch tires.

The engine cylinder measured 2.1875 by 3 inches. Splash lubrication, battery ignition, and "automatic" carburetor were used. With 1.5 horsepower, the Meadowbrook was capable of 30 miles per hour as well as 70 miles on a tank of gasoline, 90 miles on a tank of oil, and 1,000 miles on the battery before replacement.

The Meadowbrook (a.k.a. Meadow Brook) Cycle Company at 137-141 Jackson Street in Hempstead organized in 1895. The manager was Frederick W. Werner, who was an "experienced machinist." According to Werner's obituary and local newspaper accounts, he designed and built "The Meadow Brook Bicycle," which was the main product of the company. His obituary did not make a reference to a motorcycle. Werner did have a few patents, including one for improving combustion engines in 1900. It is worth noting that local press spelled the company and bicycle "Meadow Brook" and trade magazines spelled it "Meadowbrook," though both used the same address for the company. It is possible that the bicycle and company name was two words, and the motorcycle name was one.

The Meadowbrook Motor Cycle, as depicted in the December 1904 issue of the *Cycle and Automobile Trade Journal*.

The February 1897 Sanborn-Perris insurance map shows the Meadowbrook concern in the business of "repairing and setting up bicycles." The "Meadow Brook Cycle Company" appears in the 1901–2 and 1903–4 Hempstead directories. The 1904 insurance map indicates that a "cycle shop" was located on the second floor of the Jackson Street building, adjacent to the Long Island Railroad tracks. While the *Cycle and Automobile Trade Journal* "Buyer's Guide," which appeared annually in the January issue, includes the Meadowbrook motorcycle for both 1905 and 1906, it's likely the Meadowbrook motorcycle enterprise did not survive into 1907.

Mears Cycle Machine Works
alternatively, **Mears Cycle Machine Company**
New York City (Brooklyn)
ca. 1901–3

The Mears Cycle Machine Works, at 712 Bedford Avenue, noted as "makers of cycle motors," had added storage and repair capabilities to their facility at the end of October 1901, according to the *Horseless Age*. A charger for electric vehicles complemented the capacity for fifty stored machines, presumably automobiles. A year later, the Mears Cycle Machine Company was listed at 712 Bedford Avenue in the *Cycle and Automobile Trade Journal* "Buyer's Guide" as a source of motorcycles.

John W. Mears (1855?–?) was the man who lent his name to the business. In the 1899–1900 *Lain & Healy Brooklyn Directory*, he was listed as being in the bicycle business at 270 Broadway. After a year at 685 Bedford, he landed at 712 Bedford and in the automobile trades, according to the 1901–2 *Upington's General Directory of Brooklyn*. For the following few years, he was in the automobile business at various Brooklyn addresses; there is no mention of the Mears Cycle Machine Works or Company in any city directory.

Merkel Motor Wheel Company Inc.
New York City (subsequently, East Rochester and Rochester)
1916–18
Trade Name: **Merkel Motor Wheel**

The Merkel Motor Wheel converted a pedal bicycle to a motorcycle through the installation of a replacement rear wheel complete with engine, fuel tank, drive train, coaster brake, and fender. The Merkel Wheel in the 1910s competed with other motor attachments, such as the Cyclemotor (q.v.), also built in Rochester, and the Okay (q.v.), built in Brooklyn, as well as complete lightweight motorcycles.

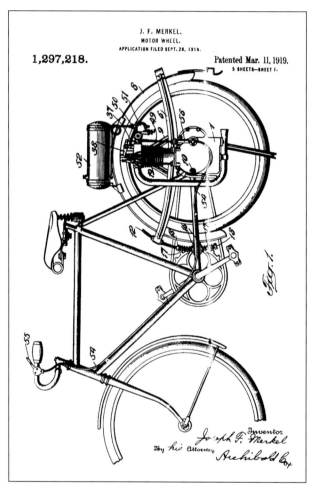

Patent drawing for the Merkel Motor Wheel, 1919.

Joseph F. Merkel was a talented motorcycle engineer. His Merkel Manufacturing Company in Milwaukee introduced a belt-driven, one-cylinder motor bicycle in 1901. By 1904, the firm had become the Merkel Motor Company and briefly added automobiles to its line. In 1908, the Merkel company merged with the Light Manufacturing and Foundry Company in Pottstown, Pennsylvania. Joseph Merkel became vice president of the new firm, moving to Pottstown to build one- and two-cylinder motorcycles called "Flying Merkels." In 1911, the Miami Cycle and Manufacturing Company of Middletown, Ohio, purchased the Merkel-Light concern, and soon Joseph Merkel was in Middletown. By 1913, he had introduced a spring starter, two-speed gear, and mechanical inlet valves to a ten-model line.

Merkel Motor Wheel Company secretary-treasurer William W. Shoemaker drives a golf ball. Such publicity photos were intended to promote upscale Merkel use. From *Motorcycle and Bicycle Illustrated*, August 30, 1917.

The next year, he was in New York City, engaged by the Autoped Company of America (q.v.) to redesign its prototype seatless motor scooter. In 1916, according to *Motorcycle Illustrated*, "some months" after Merkel left the Autoped company to devote "his entire time" to a new project in "a laboratory which was established in Corona, L.I., and which he is still maintaining until plans for the manufacture of the device are fully consummated," Merkel's new creation, the Motor Wheel, was at hand. In August, an organization to build it had been incorporated with capitalization of five thousand dollars.

In September, Joseph Merkel applied for a patent for the "motor-wheel." Unfortunately, when granted on March 11, 1919, the patent had postdated both Merkel's involvement with his invention and the operational life of the corporation created to manufacture the device. In his patent description, Merkel said his objective was to "provide a motor-wheel which may be readily attached to an ordinary bicycle in place of one of its wheels. An additional object of my invention is to provide the bicycle to which it is attached with what is in effect a spring frame":

> My motor-wheel consists of a framework comprising the engine crank-case on one side, an end-plate on the other side and a rigid sleeve extending between the crank-case and the end-plate. Upon the outside of this sleeve and between the crank-case and the end-plate is mounted the road-wheel, and within the sleeve is the crank-shaft of the engine. The frame is pivoted to the rear forks of the bicycle at a point forward of the axis of the road-wheel. The motion of the frame of the motor-wheel upon this pivot is limited by the frame sides, which are attached to the frame and extend substantially horizontally surrounding the road-wheel. The frame sides are elastically connected at their inner end to the frame of the bicycle.

In October 1916, the Motor Wheel Company was reorganized with authorized capital of $215,000. A *Motorcycle Illustrated* report said that "not a hint of the real backers of the venture is to be gathered from the incorporation papers, the corporators in this latest instance, as in the first, being Merkel himself . . . Huntington and . . . Schreiber, New York corporation attorneys with offices at 20 Broad Street."

The 57-pound motor wheel itself appeared in November 1916. The cylinder of the 2.5-inch square engine was outside the left side of the wheel, and the flywheel and magneto were outside the right. A gear train provided an 8:1 reduction in crankshaft-to-hub speed. The float-feed carburetor was controlled by the single handlebar lever, which simultaneously worked the compression release. The ignition was nonadjustable. A mechanical oil pump was fitted.

Opposing coil springs at the front of an arm, by which the Motor Wheel was bolted to the bicycle frame, provided cushioning. The pivot point was at the end of the rear forks, with the springs mounted just behind the bottom bracket. An early test by a motorcycle journalist showed a speed of 42 miles per hour "before he had gone half a block, and its real possibilities for speed were not even tested."

In the fall of 1916, Merkel said that the new corporation contemplated the purchase of components, which then would be assembled in a Motor Wheel factory. The idea was to avoid equipping a plant "when both machinery and materials are so costly." The Merkel facility had not been chosen at that point. Distribution was to be direct to dealers where "practicable or advisable." Otherwise, distributors would be used "in remote districts."

When the seventy-five-dollar Motor Wheel was shown at the New York cycle show in early December, Merkel, as president and chief engineer of the company, was joined in the booth by William Walter Shoemaker, identified as treasurer and sales manager. Shoemaker had gone to the Merkel operation from the Graton & Knight Company of Worcester, Massachusetts, best known in the motorcycle world as a supplier of drive belts.

Early advertisements for the Merkel company used Flushing as an address—probably Joseph Merkel's residence. By the end of December 1916, however, offices had been established in the Circle Building at Sixtieth Street and Broadway in Manhattan. Shoemaker said it was "practically certain" that deliveries would begin in February 1917 (*Motorcycle Illustrated*, December 28, 1916), but a factory was not acquired in East Rochester until March 1, 1917. The structure was described as a "brand new, thoroughly modern fireproof building of concrete and steel construction, affording a floor space 100 by 150 feet, with every convenience even to a railroad siding entering directly on to the company's property" (*Motorcycle Illustrated*, March 1, 1917).

Meanwhile, Robert A. Hoppe had joined the Merkel company as vice president in charge of production. Joseph Merkel had known Hoppe at the Autoped concern, where Hoppe had been involved "with the production end of the business."

An improvement to the Motor Wheel design in this period was the incorporation of a generator into the magneto design with the capacity to illuminate "a liberally sized headlight and also a tail light." Lamps were not supplied with Motor Wheel outfits.

Now deliveries, at ninety dollars rather than seventy-five, were seen in the middle of April, after component suppliers had promised that their parts would be available before the first of that month. Letters to the Merkel company indicate components for five thousand units were to be provided. These included disc coaster brakes from the Eclipse Machine Company in Elmira; rims from the Mott Wheel Works in Utica; magnetos from the Splitdorf Electrical Company in Newark, New Jersey; 26-by-2-inch "Corrugated Motor Bike" tires from the United States Tire Company in New York City; and engine units from the Hendee Manufacturing Company in Springfield, Massachusetts.

Joseph Merkel posing with a Merkel Motor Wheel fitted to a bicycle. From *Motorcycling and Bicycling*, September 17, 1917.

In June 1917, the New York office of the Merkel company at 1834 Broadway, which had been run by Shoemaker, closed, and he moved his operations to the East Rochester factory. During the summer of 1917, with the factory building Motor Wheels, the Merkel company reportedly had "rounded out its organization and elected a strong directorate to guide its future progress" (*Motorcycle and Bicycle Illustrated*, August 9, 1917). The board consisted of Merkel as president and "moving spirit in the enterprise," Hoppe as vice president and "works manager," and Shoemaker as treasurer and "sales manager." Also on the board were Jacob C. Myers, "co-owner" of the Hotel Chelsea in Atlantic City, New Jersey; Joseph H. Tunley, "an influential member of the New York Produce Exchange"; George L. Miner, a cycle jobber and dealer in Rochester; and H. R. Van Deventer, "connected with the Sumter, S. C. plant of the Splitdorf Electrical Company." Miner, according to *Motorcycling and Bicycling*, was an "enthusiastic booster for the new power plant, and the only conveyance Mr. Miner owns is Pierce bicycle with Merkel motor wheel." The Merkel company was "now tuned up to concert pitch" and "'confidently asserted'" it would exceed the "proposed 5,000" production figure.

In August 1917, *Motorcycling and Bicycling* editor T. J. Sullivan visited the Merkel factory, which he found "well-lighted, commodious and in every respect admirably adapted to every requirement." He was taken by a testing device, which he did not describe. Riding a Motor Wheel, the reporter confirmed it was "Joe Merkel's Best" design, there being "no hill too steep or sand too deep within a radius of 10 miles around the factory for the machine to vanquish." The writer said he "lifts compression, pedals, closes compression and opens throttle—Motor parades gently along—Gives 'er more gas—Machine hits 'er up to 40, calls for more, but Editor holds 'er down to 30—'Oh Boy, Oh Joy, Where will we go to now?'"

Of Motor Wheel prospects, Joseph Merkel said,

> We have every reason to be optimistic. The out look for business is fine. We are receiving returns by every mail inclosing new contracts and new connections with bicycle and motorcycle dealers. Export business is especially good. We are laying a splendid foundation for future business while the laying is good. Foreign customers that we are getting now are of a class that will stick when the war is over.
>
> Shipments are going out regularly. We are out after fall business. . . . There is no reason why dealers should wait until spring to sell Merkel Motor Wheels. . . . We started deliveries on July 1st and find business increasing steadily up to date.

Merkel Motor Wheel advertising in 1917 seems to have been inspired by competitor Cyclemotor's layouts, which featured motor-bicycle owners enjoying such recreations as tennis and fishing, with their motorized bicycles parked nearby. A fine photo of Shoemaker shows him having completed a drive on a golf course accompanied by a caddy and his Motor Wheel–equipped bicycle.

Shoemaker noted that at the end of 1917, "After unavoidable delays the Merkel Motor Wheel Co. are just getting into their stride." He mentioned shipments of five Motor Wheels to Hawaii, twenty-five to Japan, thirteen to Surabaya in Java, and 120 to the Iberian Peninsula. These were, he said, 1918 models with "drop forged gears." He said,

> We have never felt as optimistic as we are feeling today in view of the fact that the Merkel Motor Wheel is at last coming through in the shape that we wanted it, and is being recognized as the best motorized bicycle proposition possible. We might have begun filling orders earlier but both Mr. Merkel and myself felt that we could not afford to let the Merkel Motor Wheel go out until it was absolutely right. Now we know that it is right and what is more every dealer knows that it is right and it is nothing to apologize for when he places it in the hands of a buyer. (*Motorcycling and Bicycling*, December 29, 1917)

A month later, Shoemaker said the "greatly refined" Motor Wheels were being shipped. The factory was busy despite the winter weather. "Business looks good and we have a lot of orders ahead both for spring and present delivery." Among those ordering was Merkel shareholder George Miner, who contracted for one hundred Motor Wheels for 1918 and said he thought he could "sell 50% more than our contract" (*Motorcycling and Bicycling*, February 2, 1918).

In San Francisco, the Pacific Motor Supply Company became the Merkel representative for California, Arizona, and Nevada. Pacific management thought the Merkel would ease the challenge of San Francisco hills and California heat for bicycle riders. The distributor had it "tested out on the steepest hills in San Francisco and Los Angeles and the results were so satisfactory that Mr. Freed decided to back this motor vehicle to the limit" (*Motorcycling and Bicycling*, October 29, 1917). By the end of October, Pacific had signed at least two dealers who contracted for twenty-five Merkels each. By December, a San Jose dealer had contracted for fifty.

In the winter of 1918, the Merkel company moved its factory to a "two-story, modern, fireproof structure" at 1139 University Avenue in Rochester (*Motorcycling and Bicycling*). By February 5, all the machinery had been shifted to the new facility, which "in the best manufacturing center in the city" offered superior shipping facilities, according to a journal report. Joseph Merkel said the new location offered a day's quicker shipping than East Rochester. "We are now making deliveries on the same day we receive the orders," he said, "and are all set for business to a fare-ye-well." Meanwhile, Shoemaker had returned from a New England sales trip with "practically all the business that [the factory] can take care of during the next two months, even if it does not receive another order." Distributorships for several areas in the northeastern United States had been assigned.

In the late winter, Earl R. Perrin, who had been assistant general manager for publicity at the Cyclemotor Corporation, moved to the Merkel company as manager of publicity and assistant sales manager. He was said to "promise big things in the way of sales stimulators, publicity campaigns and other dealer helps. . . . His slogan now is, 'Get Merkel-wise and motorize'" (*Motorcycling and Bicycling*, March 23, 1918). Perhaps at this point internal relationships among the principals at the Merkel company took a turn for the worse. Whether the conflict had Perrin and Shoemaker on the same or opposing sides has not been determined here.

In the spring of 1918, Joseph Merkel "and his engineers" reportedly examined the Motor Wheel with an eye to improvements. Their sole change, however, was a breather pipe leading from a valve in the crankcase to the exhaust pipe that doubled as a muffler. The trade press noted that the alteration would enhance engine cleanliness.

Sales reports remained positive in the spring, especially from foreign distributors. In Pittsburgh, T. J. Everwine sold Merkels to "two young lady riders," expected to triple his contract quota, and became distributor for six Pennsylvania counties. But by the summer the Merkel Motor Wheel Company was in financial difficulty. A receiver, John H. Keef, called a meeting of creditors for September 6, 1918, at the Merkel office on University Avenue. Two months later, another meeting, this time before Federal District Court Judge John R. Hazel, determined that the assets should be sold. The problem, according to a report in the trade press, was a "quarrel between the two ownership interests," headed respectively by Merkel and Shoemaker. *Motorcycling and Bicycling* said they were "temperamentally incapable of pulling together": "With an excellent product and a ready market, the prospects of the company at first seemed excellent; but an unfortunate division of opinion between the two parties resulted in such a disagreement that neither side would or could raise the funds sufficient to tide over its owings, and the receivership resulted."

Sold on December 12 were accounts receivable, patents assigned to the Merkel Motor Wheel Company by Joseph Merkel, tools and office equipment, patterns, models, drawings, and stock on hand for about three hundred Motor Wheels, all at the Rochester factory, as well as tools, jigs, dies, and other materials in possession of the Hendee Manufacturing Company in Springfield, Massachusetts, where the Merkel engines had been assembled. Among the accounts receivable was a $2,700 claim against C. V. Graw of Westchester, Pennsylvania, for the balance of a $3,000 subscription for preferred stock.

The Hendee Company bought the assets for $1,700, with Joseph Merkel as underbidder at $1,650. The auctioneer's last words were "seventeen hundred dollars for assets worth near $17,000" (*Motorcycling and Bicycling*, December 14, 1918). By February 1919, the Hendee Company was advertising "service for the Merkel Motor Wheel": "Let us know what you require to fix up any Merkel Motor Wheel you may have around your place of business, or any Merkel Motor Wheel you may know of that can be put back into use and we'll cooperate to the fullest extent of our vast resources."

In April 1919, receiver Keef issued his final report on the Merkel Motor Wheel Company. Assets had been converted to cash totaling $2,043.53 against claims of $69,833.12. Creditors were notified of a hearing in federal district court in May 1919.

In the spring of 1921, the Hendee Company promoted the $110 Merkel Motor Wheel, now improved with a lever-operated disc clutch, which, according to *Motorcycling and Bicycling*, allowed the "motor to run free without driving the bicycle or driving wheel." The journal reported that "during the war the Wigwam [Hendee] had too many other problems to occupy attention without adding the Merkel Wheel to the list. Now, however, sensing the demand for cheap transportation of this kind . . . it looks as if bound to make a go." In the summer, a number of dealers "signed up for the Merkel Motor Wheel," according to *Motorcycle and Bicycle Illustrated*. In February 1922, the Hendee Manufacturing Company still was listed as manufacturer of the Merkel Motor Wheel. And in the first half of 1924, Donald Kleitsch sold ten Merkel Motor Wheels in Duluth, Minnesota, "forced to put in a small shop at once at his home till future arrangements could be made."

By the summer of 1919, Shoemaker, Hoppe, and Perrin were gone from Rochester. Joseph Merkel went to work for the Cyclemotor Corporation. Promoting the Evans Power Cycle at the New York trade show in January 1923, Merkel was identified by one wag as having been "in this business for years—I think he's the man who invented gasoline."

A check of the secretary of state's records in September 1999 resulted in a certificate attesting that "so far as indicated by the records of this Department, such corporation [Merkel Motor Wheel Company Inc.] is a subsisting corporation." Several Merkel Motor Wheels, at least one of them assembled in Rochester, survive in private collections.

Militaire Autocycle Company of America Inc.
Buffalo
1915–16
Trade Name: **Militaire Autocycle**
Militaire Motor Vehicle Company of America
Buffalo
1916–17
Trade Name: **Militaire-Car**
Militor Corporation
New York City (offices; factory in
Elizabeth, New Jersey)
1917–20
Trade Name: **Militor**
Sinclair Motors Corporation
New York City (offices; factories in Springfield,
Massachusetts, and Bridgeport, Connecticut)
1920–23?
Trade Name: **Militor**
Sinclair Militor Corporation
New York City (offices; factory in Bridgeport,
Connecticut?)
1923
Trade Name: **Militor**

William G. Moore was credited with the invention of a "two-wheeled auto," which reached the market in 1910. Moore claimed he was combining the "convenience, safety and luxury of a four-wheeler, the economy of the motorcycle, and the flexibility and ease of control of a bicycle" (*Motorcycle Illustrated*, June 1, 1910). The means was a one- or two-cylinder, water-cooled engine driving the rear wheel of a low motorcycle through a two-speed transmission. Wooden artillery wheels were fitted—the front guided by a steering wheel. Two idler wheels offered support for the vehicle at low speeds or at rest. A wide, upholstered seat together with a footboard offered comfort beyond that of an ordinary motorcycle. Production of the 260-pound, $300 or $350 machine was by the De Luxe Motor Car Company of Cleveland, Ohio.

By March 1911, the Militaire Auto Company of Cleveland was manufacturing the "De Luxe Two Wheeled Auto." For 1912, the aluminum body was gone, as was the upholstered seat, replaced by a bucket on long, cantilevered sprung arms. The low frame, wooden wheels, idlers, and steering wheel remained.

In the spring of 1913, the Militaire company "first began to feel the pinch" of financial crises in Cleveland, and by July 1 a receiver was appointed. Liabilities of $15,000 to $20,000 far outweighed assets, according to the *Bicycling World and Motorcycle Review*.

Militaire publicity photo taken overlooking Delaware Park Lake in Buffalo. From *Motorcycling*, December 13, 1915.

The successor, American Militaire Cycle Company, was incorporated in Cleveland in the spring of 1914 with a capitalization of $100,000, although less than a year later the "patent rights" covering the idler wheels, kick-starter, front fork, and cantilevered seat supposedly were acquired by a "new syndicate" headed by John Richter. Meanwhile, in St. Louis, the Champion Motor Car Company introduced its three-hundred-dollar Champion with four-cylinder engine, two-speed gearing, shaft drive, wooden wheels, and low tubular frame with idler wheels. Steering was by handlebar. *Motorcycling* reported that the Champion machine was the "Militaire motorcycle with many improvements" being manufactured under the "sole license" for the United States from the American Militaire Cycle Company.

In the summer of 1915, a new company, "backed by substantial and leading capitalists of . . . [Buffalo] . . . and Toronto, Ont.," was organized in Buffalo to manufacture and sell the Militaire (*Motorcycling and Bicycling*, August 30, 1915). Ten thousand dollars of the $250,000 capitalization was paid in, according to the certificate of incorporation filed on August 30. The president of the new concern was Neil R. Sinclair, former assistant manager of the Traders Bank of Canada. Other investors included

Harry T. Ramsdell, vice president and cashier of the Manufacturers and Traders National Bank of Buffalo (Ramsdell was elected president of the bank in October);
Robert W. Pomeroy, director of the Erie Railroad, of the People's Bank of Buffalo, and of Buffalo Mines and trustee of Fidelity Trust Company of Buffalo;
Edwin (Edward) McM. Mills, attorney for the Manufacturers and Traders Bank, director of the Houck Manufacturing Company, and director of Buffalo Copper and Brass Rolling Mills;
Carlton M. Smith, vice president of the Bank of Buffalo and president of Smith, Fassett and Company (another source says vice president of the People's Bank of Buffalo);
George C. Miller, director of Buffalo Mines (another report says vice president of Fidelity Trust Company);
William A. Morgan, president of Buffalo Copper and Brass;
Ward A. Wickwire, president of Wickwire Steel Company;
Edward W. Streeter of the Buffalo Express;
Gideon Grant, of Toronto, solicitor for the Royal Bank of Canada;
W. Frank Goforth, president of Ladies' Wear Ltd. of Toronto;
R. T. McLean, president of R. G. McLean Ltd. of Toronto; and
J. Robert Page, Elgie and Pate Ltd. of Toronto.

Officers included Miller as vice president, Mills as treasurer, and A. N. McLean, formerly associated with the Bank of Nova Scotia in Toronto, as secretary. *Motorcycling and Bicycling* thought, "Never before in the history of motorcycle production has such an eminent array of financial men placed their influence and means back of any motorcycle organization."

Building on the efforts of the Cleveland Militaire, which "died a-bornin for lack of responsible financial backing," and the St. Louis Champion, "which . . . failed when its backers found they couldn't do business on a shoestring," the Militaire Autocycle people buttressed their new company with the purchase for $175,000 of rights and patents "to protect the public against buying an experiment when they buy the Militaire." In addition, "thousands of miles" of testing had proven the strength of the newest Militaire, noted *Motorcycling and Bicycling*.

W. (William?) F. Miller, identified as "formerly with the Maxwell Motor Car Company," was superintendent for the Militaire company. C. T. Schaefer, formerly of the St. Louis Car Company, was to be chief engineer. The Militaire offices were located in the Fidelity Bank Building in Buffalo, but soon the company purchased a 300-by-100-foot factory on Kensington and Clyde Avenues near the Delaware, Lackawanna and Western Railroad.

The Militaire was shown at the October New York and September Chicago trade shows, resulting in "a large number of orders." Sinclair hoped to start deliveries by the beginning of 1916, although since the company planned to assemble its motorcycle from parts purchased from outside suppliers it was dependent upon the timely receipt of those components.

The motorcycle that the Militaire company introduced for 1916 had a low, pressed, 2.5-inch channel steel frame. At the front was an artillery-style wooden wheel mounted on a pivoting axle supported by leaf springs. The design of the fork was patented—number 1,089,647—by David James Johnston of Toronto and assigned to the Militaire Auto Company of Cleveland in 1914.

Fitted to the frame was an 11-horsepower, 65-cubic-inch, L-head, four-cylinder engine. The crank was supported by three main bearings. Lubrication came from a gear-driven oil pump. Ignition was by Bosch magneto. A Schebler carburetor provided the fuel mixture. A step

Militaire Autocycle Company advertisement showing the "two-wheeled automobile" and the factory on Kensington Avenue. From *Motorcycling and Bicycling*, December 13, 1915.

starter had an automatic disengagement in case of a backfire. Behind the engine was a multiplate dry clutch operated by a foot pedal. The selective shift transmission had three speeds ahead and one in reverse. Drive to the rear wheel was by shaft. A double expanding and contracting 7-inch brake was fitted in the rear wheel.

Idler wheels were lowered or raised by a foot lever adjacent to the brake pedal on the left side of the machine; Johnston in 1913 had been awarded Canadian Patent 145,511, assigned to the Canadian Militaire Auto Company Ltd. for the idler-wheel arrangement. The Militaire saddle was mounted on cantilevered arms fitted with coil springs at the rear of the frame. This arrangement also was a Johnston invention, for which he received United States Patent 1,088,028, assigned to the Militaire Auto Company in Cleveland, in 1914.

The Militaire factory on Kensington Avenue in Buffalo. From an advertisement in *Motorcycling*, December 13, 1915.

The Militaire came supplied with 28-by-3-inch tires, electric lighting, and a horn powered by a battery and generator, which one report said was to be an extra-cost option. A speedometer was standard. The Militaire weighed 382 pounds, distributed over a 65-inch wheelbase. The list price was $335. By comparison, a Ford Model T roadster automobile for the 1916 model year listed at $390.

A note in the trade press in October 1915 said that the Militaire Autocycle Company of Buffalo was going to establish an assembly plant in Canada to avoid an import duty. Whether any such Canadian factory was created is doubtful.

In November, Sinclair said that deliveries from the Buffalo factory were to begin at the end of January 1916. Meanwhile, he had three hundred dealer applications on file. Material and parts had been ordered for 2,025 motorcycles, of which fewer than five hundred were scheduled for export.

In January, the Militaire at the New York Auto Show at the Grand Central Palace was "the center of an admiring crowd at all times and the staff of attendants is kept busy explaining the functions of the idler wheels and other features." Later in the month, Sinclair said, "We will be turning out Militaires not later than the second week of February . . . and production will reach an output of eight machines a day by March 1. The first machines completed will be distributed among our dealers for demonstration purposes. War orders will be served after the regular dealers" (*Motorcycle Illustrated*).

In February, the trade press noted that the Militaire Autocycle Company of America Inc. had applied in the state supreme court for a name change to Militaire Motor Vehicle Company of America Inc. The reason for the change, according to the application, was that "the name desired tells more accurately the purposes and activities of the corporation as set forth in the incorporation papers." Action of the supreme court in Buffalo granted the change effective June 1, 1916.

In June 1916, the Militaire Motor Vehicle Company said that a contractor for aluminum crankcases had failed to make deliveries and "finally confessed that because aluminum went up to 60 cents a pound they could not carry out the contract." As a result, Militaire production had been "embarrassed and hindered." In October, the Militaire Motor Vehicle Company claimed to have solved its material supply problem and was "planning optimistically for the 1917 season." A "selling problem" also was solved, "the New York agency having made the requisition for the great portion of the 1917 output," although arrangements were to be made to supply other agencies around the country with increased output "if necessary."

A stockholders meeting on September 20, 1916, voted to increase the capital stock to $650,000; the $400,000 increase was to be preferred shares, and the outstanding $250,000 was to become common stock. At that point, $180,000 of the original capitalization had been paid in. The shareholders meeting also voted on a proposition to mortgage the real estate and factory for $75,000, according to the Certificate of Increase and Classification of Stock.

The increase in capital did not help the Militaire Motor Vehicle Company. At the end of 1917, a post-bankruptcy reorganization of the enterprise saw the creation of the Militor Corporation, with capital of $1,000,000 (although beginning business with $500). Sinclair was president, and George W. Dunham, president of the Society of Automotive Engineers, served as vice president; Campbell Scott was vice president and general manager; and Robert L. Notman was secretary and treasurer. Among the directors were Edward Mills, the former secretary of the Militaire company, and Notman—both of Buffalo; the other directors all had New York City addresses. A factory was secured in Elizabeth, New Jersey. The motorcycle also was renamed "Militor."

In November 1918, the Militor Corporation was reorganized, with an increase in capitalization to $1,625,000.

At that point the sole stockholders were Sinclair, Mills, Dunham, and Clyde S. Thompson.

In April 1919, *Motorcycle and Bicycle Illustrated* reported that the Militor Corporation had taken over the Springfield, Massachusetts, factory of the Knox automobile company, where the Militor concern, then reportedly organized at $2,500,000, would build its motorcycle as well as a "light passenger car," four-wheel-drive truck, and tractor designed for army use, "and all of the familiar Knox models." The Jersey City plant was to be retained as "a development department." At the end of 1919, H. A. Goddard, sales manager of the Militor Motors Corporation factory in Springfield, reported orders for four thousand Militor motorcycles at the Chicago vehicle show. In January 1920, the Militor Corporation, with "General Sales Offices" at 115 Broadway in New York, advertised three models of their shaft-drive machine: a solo version, a sidecar passenger type, and a sidecar delivery style. All were fitted with the three-speed forward and reverse transmission and a 68-cubic-inch, overhead-valve, four-cylinder engine (the lower crankcase of which was integral with the stamped steel chassis). Now, the front suspension utilized coil springs in the fork tubes. The cantilevered seat suspension had been replaced by quarter-elliptical leaf springs separating the rear axle from the frame. A generator was now standard, with the magneto an option. The price was $450, with the idler wheels a $25 extra. With a two-passenger sidecar, the price was $575 FOB Springfield. By comparison, a Ford roadster was $395.

In January 1920, the Militor Corporation, at a special meeting of the shareholders at its New York City office, reorganized again. The number of shares was increased from 40,000 to 56,000; the classifications (preferred and common) of the shares were changed; and the "stated capital" was reduced to $850,000. At that point, Sinclair as president and George Nicol as secretary attested that the corporate debt amounted to $50,000 in accounts payable; $55,000 in notes payable; and $8,000 in deposits on contracts. The next month, the Militor Corporation became Sinclair Motors Corporation. L. M. Bradley, a "veteran of the automotive industry," was appointed as advertising manager and immediately started "on an extensive advertising campaign." In February, at the Chicago vehicle show, Goddard announced to *Motorcycling and Bicycling* appointments of four for a combined total of eighteen states as well as "8,000 machines have actually been sold and deliveries will start about April 15th." In March, a dealers meeting in Springfield brought an enthusiastic group from as far away as Italy and Norway to view the 1920 Militors. On hand were Goddard and Bradley as well as "Vice Presidents G. W. Dunham and R. L. Notman; J. M. Hollett, assistant to the president; N. S. Lincoln, purchasing agent; C. G. Minor, chief engineer, and J. A. Bennett, factory manager." In the spring, the company leased a 4,000-square-foot office space in the new Marlin-Rockwell Building at Forty-Sixth Street and Madison Avenue in Manhattan.

In the winter of 1922, the "stocks" of the Sinclair Motors Corporation were moved from Springfield to the facilities of the Bullard Machine Tool Company of Bridgeport, Connecticut, which had acquired the "rights and patents" to the Sinclair Militor motorcycle, according to *Motorcycling and Bicycling*. Parts for more than ten thousand machines were to be shipped, and production was to start about April 1. The same journal in another story said that the Sinclair Militor Corporation "continues as the selling organization," and while "the machine has never been extensively produced, we are now assured, however, that production on a large scale has been started and deliveries can be confidently expected early in April." Offices remained in New York City, where the Sinclair Molitor (*sic*) Corporation advertised in mid-March for "a few reliable dealers." Officers at this point included the president, Sinclair; the first vice president and sales director, Goddard; the second vice president and treasurer, E. R. Mulcock; and the secretary, F. G. McGuire. Sinclair, Goddard, Mulcock, Mcguire, E. P. Bullard, and L. A. Van Patten were directors.

In March 1922, the Sinclair Militor Corporation, a Delaware corporation, received authority to do business in New York, the principal location being New York County. The service of process address was that of Samuel B. Howard and George V. Reilly at 65 Cedar Street; both were subscribers and shareholders in the incorporation of the Militor Corporation five years before. Goddard announced the first shipment of motorcycles from the factory on May 24. An extensive advertising campaign in the trade press took place during the summer, when the Sinclair Corporation noted the shipments of motorcycles numbered 151 through 160. But in the fall of 1922, Goddard left the Sinclair Militor offices at 347 Madison Avenue. *Motorcycling and Bicycling* hoped that the "motorcycle industry will not lose his activities permanently."

In January 1923, *Motorcycle and Bicycle Illustrated* said the Sinclair Militor remained the only shaft-driven motorcycle manufactured in the United States. *Motorcycle and Bicycle Illustrated* in February 1923 said that the Sinclair Militor Company continued to build the Militor. But *Motorcycling* reported in December 1924 that the Sinclair Molitor "is not now being made, according to our latest information." In June 1925, after the journal had reported that the Militaire and successor motorcycles had "not been made in a number of years," Joseph Matt of Buffalo wrote that he could provide new parts for Militaire motorcycles, since he had "bought up several hundred dollars' worth of these in 1918 and had a service shop on these at that time until the latter part of 1922." Three years later, he had everything available "but the wheels or the frame, but [knew] where [he] could get them if needed." The Sunbeam Motor and Cycle Company in Buffalo also said in 1925 that they could furnish new and used parts for "Militor, Militaire and Sinclair-Militor machines." In November 1999, the New York State Department of State still had the Sinclair Militor Corporation on "active" status as a corporation, although the biennial statement was "Past due—undeliverable."

Total production for all versions of the Militaire motorcycle has been estimated at no more than a few hundred. Several machines have survived, although probably none in public venues.

In 1903 the 1.25-horsepower bicycle motor cost "complete, as shown in cut, with spark plug, $40.00." From *Cycle and Automobile Trade Journal*, April 1903.

Charles E. Miller
New York City (Manhattan)
1900–1903

Charles Miller, at 97-101 Reade Street, identified himself as a "manufacturer, jobber, exporter and importer" and as operator of the "largest cycle and automobile supply house in America." The *Cycle and Automobile Trade Journal* thought he might have the "largest collection of automobile parts, fittings and sundries to be found in the world."

In April 1900 the *Journal* reported that Miller had on display a P. T. (q.v.) motor attached to a bicycle. A month later, however, Miller had "given up the United States sales agency for the P.-T. motor," adding the "McCullough and Buffalo [q.v.] Motors for bicycles, tricycles and carriages." In February 1901, *The Automobile* reported that the Holley "Autobike" was "built by the Holley Motor Co., Bradford, Pa., and Chas E. Miller, 97 Reade St., is the New York agent." In 1902 and early 1903, Miller advertised an 18-pound, 1.25-horsepower, four-stroke bicycle motor complete with spark plug, at first for less than thirty-five dollars, then for thirty-five, and later for forty dollars. Cylinder dimensions were 2.125 by 2.875 inches, while the exterior was 14 by 6.5 by 6.875 inches. Running speed was 2,500 rpm. A photograph of the Miller engine shows what appears to be a vertically divided, cast-aluminum crankcase with four strengthening ribs in a cross pattern. An iron cylinder has horizontal fins. The head, secured to the crankcase by bolts outside the cylinder, also is finned. The stem of what is likely an atmospheric intake valve is shown in the illustration.

Miller claimed the engine was "constructed along the lines of the best French types . . . and the equal of the best foreign makes." Where the engine was built is not revealed in Miller advertisements, but he reported, "We control the sale of this motor and have no agents." A visual comparison of photos suggests the engine was neither the locally built P. T. nor the Fleming (q.v.).

The Miller Motor was available at discount "to the trade and special prices to manufacturers." In addition to the engines, Miller carried accessory parts such as rim pulleys, belts, carburetors, and spark plugs for the motorization of bicycles. He priced the pulley at $1.50, a coil at $6, and the "generator valve" at $1.50. Special prices could be quoted for quantity purchases. In the late fall of 1902, Miller's motors reportedly were finding a "ready sale." He suggested that buyers "Get the Best[.] Shun the Rest[.] Order by Name. Substitutes Cost Same."

Herman L. Moody and Albert Solvay
New York City (Brooklyn)
1906

The *Motorcycle Illustrated* in July 1906 printed a photo of Herman Moody seated on the motorcycle that he reportedly designed and Albert Solvay ("the French racing motorcyclist") built. A tall diamond frame has its down tube looping around the front wheel for a shorter wheelbase. The fork is rigid with a strengthening truss. Very long handlebars end behind what normally would be the seat tube, the saddle on this machine being mounted above the rear fender directly over the rear axle.

The engine is a one-cylinder DeDion-Bouton mounted at the bottom of the diamond. The journal noted that the motorcycle weighed 190 pounds and could reach 65 miles per hour. Other equipment included "band brake [on] rear wheel; gasoline capacity, 10 quarts; storage battery. Control by throttle, spark and exhaust."

The 1906 Brooklyn directory notes that Moody's business was "automobiles."

Herman L. Moody on his 65-miles-per-hour motorcycle. From *Motorcycle Illustrated*, July 1906.

Morgan Motor Company
New York City (Brooklyn and Manhattan)
1901–2
Trade Name: **Morgan**

"After considerable experimenting," said *Cycle Age*, the Morgan Motor Company at 55 Furman Street of Brooklyn in the spring of 1901 had "on the market complete motor outfits ready for attachment to bicycles." The 1-horsepower, 1,000-rpm engine was to be mounted inside the frame triangle on the down tube and drive the rear wheel, either by belt or chain. When the former system was purchased, an "adjustable idler pulley for tightening, and to be attached to the seat mast, [was] included." The gasoline tank was suspended from the top tube, the coil fitted behind the seat tube, and the battery box was on top of the seat stays under the saddle. Instructions for mounting were included with the complete outfits. Alternatively, the purchaser could acquire castings or "finished motors" separately.

Upington's General Directory of Brooklyn for 1901 and 1902 (but not the following three editions) listed James F. Morgan Jr. in the motor business at 55 Furman Street. In August 1901, the trade press reported that the Morgan Motor Company had added a department "for the furnishing of transmission gears of all descriptions" as well as other motor-vehicle parts. The firm shortly was to sell both gasoline and steam automobile runabouts complete or in pieces. "Mr. Wyatt at 50-54 Columbia Heights" was in charge.

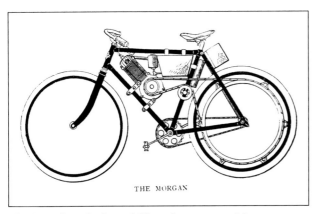

The $175 "standard model," 1.5-horsepower Morgan motor bicycle with twisted rawhide belt drive. From the *Dealer and Repairman*, April 1902.

In April 1902, the Morgan Motor Company at 54 Columbia Heights offered a complete twisted-rawhide-belt-drive, 1.5-horsepower motor bicycle for $175. The Morgan engine was still available by itself, as were "complete motor outfits ready for attachment to bicycles." There was also a 2.25-horsepower engine for motor bicycle, tricycle, and automobile use. If a purchaser wished to build or finish his own engine, drawings and castings were available.

In July and August 1902, the Morgan Motor Company, at 114 Front Street, advertised "Motors and Motor Castings. All accessories for Motor Cycles. Pulley Rims of steel. Motors from 1½ H.P. to 9 H. P. Complete Outfits."

Cycle Age in the summer of 1901 said, "Among the manufacturers who have decided to market the small motor designed by the *Motor Age* and described in its columns is the Morgan Motor Company, of 91 Cliff Street, New York. This company will also sell castings to those who desire to finish and assemble the motor themselves."

In March 1902, the *Motor Age* said the Morgan Motor Company was planning a new building in Worcester, Massachusetts, for manufacture of an "auto truck." There was also talk of a "movement . . . at Detroit for the organization of a company . . . to engage in the manufacture of automobiles." Ralph L. Morgan and Charles H. Morgan were the principals. Whether the Cliff Street, Manhattan, and the Massachusetts Morgan Motor Company were associated with the Brooklyn Morgan Company has not been determined here.

Joshua M. Morris
Morris and Corkhill Motor Cycle Company
Morris-Corkhill Motor Company
Rochester
1900–1903
Trade Name: **M. C.**

At the beginning of the twentieth century, Joshua M. Morris manufactured gasoline engines in Rochester, possibly at 368 State Street. One of his motors was used on the Sager (q.v.) "Regas" motorcycle built nearby.

In early 1901, the Morris operation was purchased by Fred Patee and moved to Indianapolis, Indiana. There, the newly organized Patee Bicycle Company planned to manufacture both bicycles and motorcycles. Morris, the "inventor and former manufacturer" of the Morris engine, was to manage the motor department for three years. Fred Patee, according to the *Cycling Gazette*, said the Morris engine was "a motor that will run . . . and what is more it will run all the time." An engraving of the Patee motor shows an air-cooled engine with a tall cylinder and finned head. The Patee motorcycle had the engine mounted low behind the seat tube with the crankcase below the pedal axle to provide for a low center of gravity and to get the engine heat and odor behind the rider, said the *Cycle Age and Trade Review*.

The Patee enterprise was not a success, and Morris was back in Rochester by September 1901. Joining Thomas Corkhill in a partnership at 43 Central Avenue, Morris was soon building complete motorcycles, specifically a road machine, a racing machine, and a tandem with a combination drop and diamond frame.

The frames as well as the engines were fabricated in-house. On all models, the air-cooled motor drove the rear wheel via a chain. On the touring motorcycle, the down tube curved around the front wheel and under the engine to the crank axle. The engine was mounted, unlike the Patee, in front of the seat tube. The *Bicycling World and Motocycle Review* said the long wheelbase would "give easy riding over the average country roads." One gasoline or oil tank was fitted inside the frame triangle forward of the engine, and the other tank was mounted over the rear wheel. The city directory that appeared in the summer of 1902 lists Corkhill as superintendent and Morris as vice president of the Central Avenue operation.

The Morris and Corkhill Motor Cycle Company survived into 1903 and was included in the January 1903 *Cycle and Automobile Trade Journal*'s "Buyer's Guide" to motorcycles. In the same month, the Morris-Corkhill Motor Company was incorporated by the secretary of state for the "manufacture of gas engines and their accessories, and the manufacture of motor vehicles." Capitalized at $5,000, the company began business with $1,000. First-year directors, all from Rochester, were Morris (forty shares with $25 par value); Corkhill (forty shares); Charles L. Reed, a salesman (forty shares); Frederick H. Clum, a stenographer in the Rochester Savings Bank Building (forty shares); and Samuel Kay, president of the J. R. and S. P.

Joshua M. Morris (*right*), Rochester engine manufacturer and later partner in the Morris and Corkhill Motorcycle Company, posing in Indianapolis with Fred Patee (*left*), who adopted the Morris engine for the ill-fated Patee motor bicycle. From the *Bicycling World*, May 23, 1901.

Kay Contracting and Elevator Company (ten shares). H. Clifford Spurr, the attorney who handled the incorporation, also subscribed two shares (valued at $50; perhaps these were in exchange for his work).

The Rochester directory, appearing around July 1, 1903, listed the Morris and Corkhill Motor Company at the Central Avenue address. However, in August, Morris and Corkhill Motor Cycle Company consolidated with H. L. F. Trebert and Company, incorporating as the Trebert Gas Engine Company, located at 163 Main Street, Rochester. They were set up to build "water and air cooled motors for automobiles, marine and stationary." Both Morris and Corkhill were among its directors. For 1904, the Rochester directory lists Corkhill as the superintendent. In 1908, a "John Morris" is mentioned as the superintendent of the company in a newspaper article. It is possible that John was actually Joshua. In addition to building and selling motors, the company sold automobiles of various makes until mid-1908, but by 1909 the company was bankrupt. In 1910, the company emerged from bankruptcy and was enticed to move to Butler and later Terre Haute, Indiana. There, they continued to make motors and coin-operated popcorn machines.

Joshua M. Morris stayed in Rochester and continued inventing improvements for motor vehicles. Two highlights are an electric cigar lighter and a motor starter for automobiles. In 1920, he had a business called Morris Auto Cold Starting Company, in Rochester.

Motorcycling for August 8, 1912, refers to the M. C. motorcycle built in Rochester in 1901 by F. H. Clum and "Morris Corkhill." In 1912, Clum was involved with the Crawford motorcycle enterprise in Saginaw, Michigan.

Motor Bicycle Equipment and Supply Company
1905 model year
Motorcycle Equipment and Supply Company
1906–9 model years
Marvel Motorcycle Company
1910–12 model years
Buffalo (1904–6); Hammondsport (1906–12)
Trade Names: **Mesco**; **Erie**; **Marvel**
1905 Model Year

The Motor Bicycle and Equipment and Supply Company of Buffalo in late 1904 announced the "Mesco motorcycle outfit for application to the ordinary pedal propelled bicycle. The outfit includes a motor 1¾ h.p., designed for either chain or belt transmission." C. L. (Leonard) Waters was identified as manager of the new firm, which was located at the corner of Main and Allen Streets. Waters had left his home village of Hammondsport for Buffalo, where in the spring of 1904 he was reported to be a "successful practitioner of Mechano-Therapy, or muscle manipulation, embracing the most modern methods of scientific physical culture." In the Queen City he "'just happened' to offer certain motorcycle specialties, by advertising, as a side issue," said *Motorcycling* in 1911.

The Erie was available with either belt or friction drive for the same price in 1906 and early 1907. From the Motorcycle Equipment and Supply Company's "Agent's Net Price List of Motorcycle and Bicycle Accessories."

As built, the Mesco outfit offered either a "chain belt" (belt with chain-link core) or friction drive. The Mesco equipment included a 2.75 inch bore-by-2.625-inch stroke air-cooled engine with splash lubrication, transmission (belt or friction pulley on the top of the rear tire), gasoline and oil tanks, spark control in a handlebar grip, and other control levers. The outfit weighed 50 pounds, cost $75, and permitted a speed of 30 miles per hour, said the *Cycle and Automobile Trade Journal*. Within a short time, the Motor Bicycle Company was advertising a complete motorcycle priced $125 to $135, perhaps varying upon the type of transmission desired. An advertising image shows an ordinary diamond frame except for a reinforced front fork. The drive pulley for the friction-equipped machine is chain (or perhaps belt) driven from the engine, which lies parallel with the down tube inside the frame. A lever on the right side of the gasoline tank (which is hung from the top tube) controls the pulley on the tire. Mesco parts were "sold separately," and there was a "liberal discount to agents." Stephen Wright notes in *The American Motorcycle* that many Mesco products, including the roller-driven motorcycle for the 1905 model year, were manufactured by the Reliance Motor Cycle Company (q.v.).

1906 Model Year

In December 1905, the *Hammondsport Herald* reported that Waters was moving to Hammondsport, where he was to be "connected with the Glenn H. Curtiss Manufacturing Company" (q.v.). He supposedly had "developed a profitable business in the Buffalo Bicycle Supply company, which will be conducted with the Curtiss business. Mr. Waters is also a motorcycle expert, and will be of great service to Mr. Curtiss in placing on the market the product of the works." Certainly, there was close association between Waters and Curtiss, who was in the motorcycle manufacturing business. But it's unlikely that Waters ever went to work for the Curtiss firm.

By January 1906, the Mesco had become the Erie, and the Motor Bicycle Equipment and Supply Company was the Motorcycle Equipment and Supply Company, still, according to the *Cycle and Automobile Trade Journal*, at 934 Main Street in Buffalo. The engine output for the new model year climbed to 2 horsepower with a "new bearing composed of a special hardened tool steel sleeve forced over the crank shaft and running in phosphor bronze bushings in the crank case." Main bearings were 1.1875 inches long. The crankshaft was 0.75 inches in diameter. The sight-feed oiler was fed from a tank large enough to hold a 150-mile supply, up from 100 for the 1905 model.

The fuel tank on the Erie motorcycle was attached to the top tube. A steel battery box was fitted on the seat stays. The spark advance lever was attached to the tank, while the "grip [ignition] switch" was on the left handlebar. The truss fork continued. A Mesinger saddle was fitted, as were 1.75-inch Goodrich tires. The wheelbase measured 50 inches, and the frame 22 inches. Weight for the complete machine was 85 pounds, the engine accounting for 25. Again, both belt-

and friction-drive models were offered, the pulley of the latter driven by a chain. Both machines could reach 32 miles per hour. An undated sheet titled "Directions for Maintaining the Erie Motorcycle" advised riders with the friction system, "When driving, force the roller on the tire good and hard." A 1906 Erie catalog with the Buffalo address notes that for either the friction-drive or belt-drive motorcycle the dealer price was $100 and the customer cost $135.

An "Erie 1906 Power Outfit" was available for converting an ordinary bicycle into a motorized machine. The Motorcycle Equipment and Supply Company also advertised "unfinished sets furnished for building your own motorcycle from special frame or bicycle." And they offered 2-, 3-, and 5-horsepower "cyclemotors" complete or as castings.

By March the Motorcycle Equipment and Supply Company had moved to Lake Street in Hammondsport. There, it appealed to "Repair Men . . . [to] Build Your Own Motorcycle." In June 1906, the makers claimed that the Erie "fills the requirements of ¾ of your Customers." Also mentioned were the 1-inch flat-belt drive and the "silent" nature of the machine.

1907 Model Year

The two motorcycle styles continued apparently generally unchanged into 1907. Compendia of motorcycle specifications for the 1907 model year, which appeared in the March issues of the *Cycle and Automobile Trade Journal* as well as the *Motorcycle Illustrated* indicate models similar to those of 1906. The frame was described as 21.5 inches and made of 1.125-inch tubing. The motor dimensions were given as 2⅔ inch bore by 2¾ inch stroke. It was fitted with an Erie carburetor and three dry cells for ignition. Fuel range was given as 100 miles, and speeds were up to 35 miles per hour. A Morrow brake was fitted, as well as G & J or Goodrich tires. The motor outfit alone for either belt or friction drive was offered at eighty dollars and consisted "of every part of the complete motor cycle except the parts represented by the bicycle." The friction-drive unit required no alteration of a bicycle frame. The belt-drive conversion did, however, "and the manufacturers supply frame offsets for brazing into the frame of the bicycle."

Then in April, a radically different Erie motorcycle reached the market. The engine was square, with 3-inch bore and stroke, and rated at 3 horsepower. It rested at the bottom of the looping frame triangle with the cylinder upright and drove the rear wheel via a 1.25-inch, double-ply flat belt. A halftone of the $175 machine shows a torpedo-shaped tank fitted between parallel top tubes. Speed was up to 45 miles per hour. G & J tires of 1.75 inches were mounted on 28-inch G & J steel rims. A Morrow coaster brake was used, as were a coil-spring Mesinger saddle, jump spark (three dry cell) ignition, and sufficient fuel and oil capacities for 150 miles.

The 2-horsepower (at 2,000 rpm) engine continued at sixty dollars for installation on bicycles; a 3-horsepower version was also available. An advertisement in August 1907 claimed that one thousand 2-horsepower attachments were in use.

1908 Model Year

The 3-horsepower Erie apparently continued largely unchanged for 1908, while the 2-horsepower machines were dropped. Possible problems with the Erie carburetor were alleviated with the adoption of the "Curtiss compensating float feed carburetor" produced by the Curtiss Manufacturing Company. The Motorcycle Equipment and Supply Company also advertised "Bowden Wire Grip Control" and "choice of tires and saddles," as well as a one-year guarantee and immediate delivery for the $175 machine. The company claimed that "More Agents [were] Wanted."

In December 1907, the *Bicycling World and Motorcycle Review* announced an Erie two-stroke lightweight, to be built with an engine produced by the G. H. Curtiss Manufacturing Company. It was said to be one of the lightest and most "ingenious little engines that has been produced for many a day," and Glenn Curtiss was "reported to have fallen in love with it." In May 1908 the new lightweight Erie appeared. The engine was available by itself for motorizing bicycles, as its predecessors were. It reportedly "fits any size or make of frame and is attached without a particle of alteration to the bicycle frame, except slightly bending the narrow makes of cranks." Speeds of 4 to 30 miles per hour were promised. The "heavy tin" tank would hold sufficient fuel for 80 to 110 miles and enough oil for 100 to 150. The drive belt was an "Erie flexible waterproof, gray, tanned V-belt." For ninety dollars, one received the engine, clamp and pulley, coil, switch grip, muffler, carburetor, control lever, tank, battery box, three dry cells, belt, oiler, and valve. For fifty-five dollars (sixty according to an Erie catalog), the motor was offered by itself.

For $150, the buyer had the complete lightweight Model 1 Erie motorcycle. Options included a spring fork for $3.50, mudguards at $2.50, grip control for $4.50 ($3.50?), and 2-inch clincher tires on steel rims (instead of single tube tires on wooden rims) for $7.50. An engraving shows the machine with tank mounted over the rear tire, truss fork, and large flywheel. Another image, in the *Motorcycle Illustrated*, depicts the engine with finned head as well as cylinder. The Model 2 Erie, at $130, was similar to the Model 1 except, according to the Erie catalog, for the "heavy bicycle frame, wheels and tires—extra long frame." Either motorcycle was available "knocked down" for six dollars less. There was also the 3-horsepower special motorcycle "for rough use" with a $175 "special price to introduce it."

An undated (but likely 1908) "Agent's Net Price List" showed the $150 Erie available alternatively with belt and friction drive to the rear wheel. The engine is shown mounted within the standard bicycle-form frame triangle with the cylinder parallel to the down tube. The idler on the belt-drive model is fitted to the seat tube.

"C.L. Waters, Sec'y & mgr." of the Motorcycle Equipment and Supply Company, said among the reasons the Erie was cheaper were

- large capital allowing the company to "buy when and where" it wished;
- saving, for example, on foundry costs;
- buying crude material in bulk;
- being the largest maker of attachments in the country;
- selling direct to agents with no intermediaries;
- no traveling salespeople;
- selling for cash only; and
- "one profit cash price."

Erwin Tragatsch, in his *Illustrated Encyclopedia of the Motorcycle* (second edition, 1977), claims that Erie motorcycles, in addition to Curtiss engines, used "Spake [*sic*]" and Minerva (Belgian) power plants during the 1905-to-1911 period of activity, which Tragatsch ascribes to Erie manufacture. Unfortunately, the source of Tragatsch's information is lacking in his compendium. He does not mention Erie-built engines.

1909 Model Year

The last models sold under the Erie name were 3.5-horsepower motorcycles for 1909. One machine continued the single-speed transmission, while the other was equipped with a clutch ("free engine") and two-speed gear.

The Erie frame reportedly was strengthened for 1909, while the rigid truss fork continued. An overhead, rocker-actuated intake valve ("one cam to operate both valves") replaced the former atmospheric type, perhaps accounting for the increase in horsepower. A V-belt replaced the flat belt, "and the idler has been dispensed with; a wide range of adjustment for taking up slack in the belt is provided at the rear stays." Double-grip control supplanted the single-grip system, 2.25-inch tires replaced 2-inch equipment, and wider fenders were fitted, according to the *Bicycling World*. The price advanced to two hundred dollars, one presumes for the single-speed version. Apparently, a 2.5-horsepower "aluminum base motor" with tank oiler and V-belt-drive bicycle attachment was still available during the 1909 model year.

Jerry Hatfield notes among 1909 Erie models a "semi-racer" and an "R.F.D.," the latter equipped with a planetary two-speed transmission for use by rural free-delivery agents (*Illustrated Antique American Motorcycle Buyer's Guide*, 1996). Hatfield also claims that the lightweight Model A Reliance (q.v.) "appears to be an exact duplicate of the Erie Lightweight model."

1910 Model Year

Although an advertisement for the 3.5-horsepower Erie appeared in the August 1, 1909, issue of *Motorcycle Illustrated*, the Erie motorcycle name disappeared during the summer of 1909 as the Motorcycle Equipment and Supply Company reorganized. A new Motorcycle Equipment Company was to market motorcycle supplies. In October 1910, the Motorcycle Equipment Company was incorporated with $14,000 in capital. A second, separate firm, the Marvel Motorcycle Company, was incorporated to produce motorcycles. The latter organization was capitalized at $50,000, with C. Leonard Waters, Elizabeth H. Waters, and Glenn H. Curtiss as incorporators. Curtiss, of course, was already in the motorcycle manufacturing business in Hammondsport, but it was reported that "his interests in the new company are merely nominal and in no way affect his connection with the Herring-Curtiss Co" (successor to the G. H. Curtiss Manufacturing Company). Curtiss was also an old friend of Leonard Waters (nicknamed "Tank" and "Lee") from youthful bicycle-racing days, says C. R. Roseberry. Lee Waters, who "built up the supply company from a very modest beginning," was to head both the Marvel Motorcycle Company and Motorcycle Equipment Company. Clarence P. Rudd was to be superintendent of the Marvel operations, "which will market a motorcycle of that name and which Waters states will be worthy of it." A new 30-by-115-foot plant was being built for Marvel production and Motorcycle Equipment operations; the old building was to be sold for a wine cellar. The *Hammondsport Herald* noted in November that the new Marvel factory was "admirably lighted" and equipped with wooden floors, "which have proved preferable to cement to work on."

The "leading motorcycle experts" were Glenn Curtiss, who "originated" the Marvel engine; Henry Kleckler, who designed the motor; and Clarence Rudd, who designed the "frame and fittings." Image from *Motorcycle Illustrated*, February 15, 1910.

According to the records of the New York Secretary of State, the distribution of stock in the Marvel concern was 75 shares of preferred and 249 of common to Lee Waters, 75 of preferred to Curtiss, and 1 share of common to Elizabeth Waters. In the list of first-year directors, Elizabeth Waters's name is written above that of Clarence Rudd, which is crossed out. The new company began business with $15,000 of capital, which might be the paid-in value of the preferred shares at a par value of $100 each. Holders of the preferred stock were to receive a dividend of 6 percent per year, payable before the distribution of any other profits.

Lee Waters told *Motorcycle Illustrated* in late July 1910,

I found my business, that of the Motorcycle Equipment and Supply Company, increasing so rapidly that I needed additional capital and incorporated with a view of selling stock. Mr. G. H. Curtiss, being some time ago interested with me in the motorcycle business, gladly consented to act as an incorporator and director. He has not severed his connections with the Herring-Curtiss Company, and his small connection with this company in no way affects his other interests. Mr. C. P. Rudd, one of the stockholders, will be superintendent.

The Motorcycle Equipment & Supply Company will be known as the Motorcycle Equipment Company. The amount of business this company is now doing will surprise you. We keep three men busy shipping goods to all parts of America and Canada. The name "Marvel" is used because the new motorcycle will be a wonder. Nothing we have been able to coax to go up against it has anywhere equaled it for power per cylinder capacity.

The Marvel name, according to Lee Waters and reported in *Motorcycling*, came from Curtiss, who was suitably impressed by Waters riding the first such machine up a local grade called Mount Washington. The makers of the Marvel claimed it was the design of "three of the leading motorcycle experts in the country," initially unidentified. Later, Waters said that "Curtiss originated the motor, Henry Kleckler designed it and C. P. Rudd designed the frame and fittings, 'while riders all over the country, by their persistent call for a frame that was without leaky, rattling tanks, certainly helped originate the tankless frame.'" *Motorcycle Illustrated* noted the similarities in the Marvel and Wehman-model Curtiss frames, the latter designed by Henry J. Wehman.

Lee Waters, in adopting a Curtiss engine, took advantage of the Herring-Curtiss Company's name and capacity for turning out strong power plants. The Model 4 Curtiss overhead valve motor used on the Marvel was called "the latest creation of Glenn H. Curtiss, the successful aeronaut," by *Motorcycle Illustrated*. Before becoming a flyer, Curtiss had acquired a reputation as a builder and racer of fast motorcycles. And of the new Model 4 it was said that it developed more horsepower than any previous engine of the same displacement. "On hills, it is reported to have done as well as the average twin of a year ago."

The engine was notable for the offset head and cylinder "said to do away with one-fifth of the strain on the running parts," roller bearings, pushrod-operated overhead valves (the intake of which was 1.625 inches in diameter "to prevent overheating"), domed piston head to assist in evacuating burned gases, integral cylinder and head to provide a smooth combustion chamber, and deep sump complementing an automatic lubrication system. While an early report about Marvel motorcycles mentioned a twin-cylinder model, only single-cylinder machines were offered. The "Marvel 1910 Advance Circular" listed among the motorcycle's features "A GRIP CONTROL that has an adjustment so it will stay put 99 years from now regardless of wear."

The Marvel frame was innovational. The top tube, "18-gauge [said *Cycle and Automobile Trade Journal*; 16-gauge in other reports] Shelby seamless turned steel tubing, 5 inches in diameter Oxy-Acetylene welded to a malleable cast fitting," served as the gasoline tank. The 16-gauge, 4-inch-diameter oil tank was similarly built into the seat tube. The engine served as a stressed frame member, and there was no direct connection between the down and seat tubes. The frame was described by *Motorcycle Illustrated* as "simple, handsome in appearance and strong," giving a low saddle position and long wheelbase (58 inches). The *Bicycling World and Motorcycle Review*, on the other hand, said, "Except for a slight difference in the frame lines which will be of the loop type, it [the Marvel] practically will be a replica of the Curtiss and will employ that make of engine and carburetor."

In February the Marvel company responded to speculation about the agency situation. In doing so, the Marvel people told *Motorcycling* that 250 of the 500 motorcycles they intended to build for the year had already been sold. "Also, we are not starting out in a small way. We own a concrete building, 30 x 115 feet, two-story, and attic, and storage room and sheds elsewhere. We have contracted with the Herring-Curtiss Co. for 500 motors, and [have] orders in for 500 sets of tires, hubs, brakes, rims, pulleys, motors carburetors and saddles." The rumors had suggested to some "large dealers" that mere riders could become agents. The Marvel company wanted it understood, however, that it wanted no rider-agents and that "no one, not even a small dealer, can obtain a Marvel representation, unless he has arranged to purchase at least two machines." Still, the Marvel Company sought representatives, in January inviting queries "regarding our agency proposition" and during the winter and spring in *Motorcycle Illustrated* advertisements telling "Why You, Mr. Dealer, Should Sell the Marvel." In January 1910, the Motorcycle Manufacturers Association admitted the Marvel Motorcycle Company to membership.

In April 1910, with the Herring-Curtiss Company bankrupt, Waters, now "secretary and manager" of the Marvel firm, noted in *Motorcycling* that while Glenn Curtiss was a director of the Marvel Company, which had bought a number of Curtiss engines, the Marvel operation "is in no way involved in the affairs of the other company, has ample capital to pay for its entire season's purchases, and is rushing deliveries on its sales, which have been exceptionally good."

1911 Model Year

The next Marvel closely resembled its predecessor. The most striking change was in the front fork, where a Curtiss type replaced the Sager. The new one, reported the *Bicycling World*, had "a very smooth and soft action. The webbed crown forms a support for the truss leading from the lower tip to the handle bar clamp, and long supple springs are carried in an independent front member." *Motorcycling* said a reshaping of the handlebars "greatly improves the riding position and is claimed to practically eliminate fatigue from that cause." While "the actual changes in the Marvel have been minor ones, in appearance the machine suggests a radical difference there has been added to the Marvel that something called finish, that touch that proves the part the tailor has in making the man; the part that is worth many dollars by increased sales made through its effect on the mind through the eye." A less effusive analysis in the *Bicycling World* said that the Marvel "in its 1911 dress differs chiefly in detail refinements from its predecessors," although its "distinctive and original features [are] calculated to place the machine in a class by itself." Some modifications affected the engine, including a revised cam, which "eases the exhaust valve to its seat," and two-piece valves consisting of cast heads with "half-inch nickel-steel stem."

If alterations to the motorcycle were few, there was a major change in the way the Marvel came together. The engine, which previously had been purchased from the Herring-Curtiss Company, now was assembled in the Marvel's new factory. In fact, there was no alternative for Waters and his colleagues since after the Herring-Curtiss bankruptcy production had ended there. Glenn Curtiss purchased the assets of the defunct concern at auction in February 1911, but the new Curtiss Aeroplane Company planned to emphasize aircraft production. Exactly when the Marvel company began to build engines is not clear. A *Motorcycling* report in February 1911 claimed that the Marvel firm "will continue to manufacture the Curtiss overhead-valve motor and make Marvel motorcycles in this new factory, the same as they have been doing for some time."

Another view in *Motorcycle Illustrated* suggested that the Marvel company would continue to produce motorcycles in the factory "where the Curtiss motor has been turned out for more than a year." The separation between the Curtiss and Marvel companies was emphasized, this time with a note that the Marvel firm had made "great strides . . . in the development of its product over the old Curtiss machines" by "avoiding the careless assembly that in some instances adversely affected the old Curtiss product."

The Herring-Curtiss bankruptcy proceedings affected the Marvel company directly in the spring of 1911. In a May hearing, the Herring-Curtiss trustee, Gabriel H. Parkhurst, offered a $2,000 claim against Marvel for "goods furnished and work done," one assumes on engines. The Marvel company in turn offered a claim of $1,000 "for alleged non-fulfillment of a contract by the Curtiss Company. Evidence was . . . taken in this matter, but no conclusion reached," said the *Herald*.

Even with numerous agencies announced, and "every 1910 agent . . . back for 1911 and some . . . contracted for four times as many Marvels," the Marvel Motorcycle Company reported in the spring of 1911 that "a few more desirable agencies will be placed." Still, the company claimed it had "expected this big Spring rush and prepared for it last Winter. Our Agents, because they have the machines to deliver, have more than doubled their sales. Write today for our contracts and let 'immediate delivery' boost your sales." If a doubling of sales for the entire 1911 season was realized, then production for the year probably totaled about one thousand machines. In January, the Marvel company reportedly had five hundred engines on hand "for immediate delivery."

The Marvel company took part in the Madison Square Garden motor vehicle show in January 1911. The Marvel representatives told *Motorcycling* they "did nothing last year. Did very well this year." On hand at the show, displaying two of their machines, were Waters, identified as "secretary-treasurer and manager"; "C. P. Pond [likely Rudd], superintendent"; C. Edward Clark, "manager assembling department"; and Harry E. Longwell, "sales manager." The *Bicycling World* in its show report noted as new features "in order of importance" the spring fork, chain idler, and oil pockets in the piston bosses. A sectioned motor "fitted with hand crank to show the action of the mechanism, also was in evidence."

For the 1911 motorcycle, the Marvel company advertised the Glenn Curtiss design of its engine as well as the "up-to-date" frame "designed by C. P. Rudd." The outstanding feature of the frame likely remained its incorporation of fuel and oil tanks, the former in the 5-inch-diameter top tube (holding two gallons), and the latter in the 4-inch seat tube. With Curtiss motorcycles gone from the market, at least temporarily, the Marvel company was happy to advertise the Curtiss engine in its product. In fact, the largest and boldest type in a January display advertisement for Marvel motorcycles was the word "Curtiss" as in introduction to the information that Curtiss engines

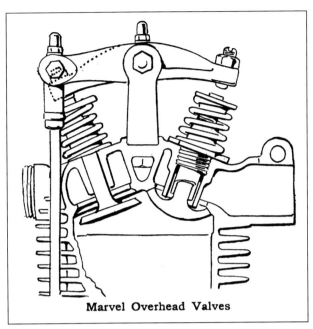

The Marvel (and Curtiss) overhead valve mechanism used a single pushrod to move two joined rocker arms. From *Motorcycling*, January 11, 1912.

were used "exclusively on Marvel motorcycles." In other words, those riders who would have looked for a Curtiss motorcycle now might better turn to a Marvel.

1912 Model Year

In October 1911 came rumor of a merger of the Marvel Motorcycle Company and the Curtiss Motorcycle Company. The latter, it was reported, "was organized to make into complete machines for marketing the parts which fell to Glenn Curtiss when he bought the ex-Herring-Curtiss factory at public sale." The proposed combination, reported in *Motorcycling*, was deemed a "benevolent assimilation of the Curtiss by the wideawake concern of which C. L. Waters is the leading spirit. It has been understood that the interests controlling both concerns were identical, anyway. Manager Waters promises details of the merged company's 1912 program within 30 days." Two weeks later, the negotiations continued, with Waters claiming it might take two or three weeks more to "eventuate," at which time 1912 prices would be announced. In the meantime, "Marvels are being turned out, tested on the road, and shipped," while the Motorcycle Equipment Company facilities were being enlarged. At the same time, it was reported that Henry Wehman, who was "originator of ideas used on both" the Curtiss and Marvel motorcycles, had given up his New York City shop and moved to Hammondsport, where he became "chief office man in the Curtiss plant."

The next news was the surprising announcement that Leonard Waters had resigned from the Marvel company to "accept a position as general manager of the Motorcycle Equipment Co." He said that the rapid growth of the Equipment company required "all his attention," with the offices and warehouse being doubled in size and the value of the stock increasing from $15,000 to $25,000. "H. E. Longwell, formerly with the Curtiss Motorcycle Co., will become manager of the Marvel," reported the *Bicycling World*.

Leonard Waters, interviewed by the *Herald* in the spring of 1912, suggested that "in a few years, the high-water mark in the manufacture of motorcycles will be attained," while, on the other hand, there would be a "general demand for parts for renewal and repairs." In effect, he was indicating that the Marvel enterprise was less promising than his Motorcycle Equipment Company. The latter, "in the big cement building of the Curtiss Company, on the hillside, paralleling Lake street," had mailed fifty thousand fifty-page spring catalogs.

It appears that the idea of a merger of the Curtiss and Marvel operations had been given up before the end of 1911. G. R. Hall, identified as manager of the Curtiss Motorcycle Company, in December was quoted in *Motorcycling* as saying that, for the 1912 season, "we will probably make some machines, but haven't decided yet how many. It will depend upon how things open up." Longwell was as pessimistic as his Hammondsport colleague, Hall: "Our business is dull now. . . . We haven't decided how many motorcycles we will build this year. We are watching the situation and governing our policy accordingly. We will be in a position to make all the motorcycles we can sell. We look for an unsteady year in the business. We have cut the price of the Marvel motorcycle from $225 to $200. We have enough stock on hand with which to fill early orders. I think the cut in price regrettable."

Perhaps it was a disappointing 1911 season as well as, or as much as, the promise of expansion for the motorcycle supply business that helped Waters decide to abandon the management of the Marvel company. For 1912, the Marvel motorcycle remained nearly identical to its predecessor, "no radical changes having been found advisable." The relative perfection of the motorcycle might be one justification for such a statement. The alternative, of course, is a lack of incentive to improve it in the face of flat or decreasing demand. The failure of the smaller motorcycle manufacturers to profit in a world increasingly filled with economical automobiles was a reality of the period.

The Marvel company passed on the Madison Square Garden show in January 1912. Longwell did announce in March that he had patented and was selling an attachment "that can serve as both a tandem seat and luggage carrier." The 1912 Marvel motorcycle reportedly had a spring fork of the same design as before, but with a "stronger tubing to eliminate the chance of breakage." Possibly some other parts had a "change of metal . . . to make the machine stronger and more durable than ever."

Motorcycling magazine in January 1912 published a concise, explicit description of the Marvel overhead-valve arrangement:

> A notable feature of the Marvel motor is the overhead valve system, and the form of the exhaust valve. The valves are placed at opposite points in a domed cylinder head and are actuated by rocker arms pivotally secured to a supporting post in the center of the head. The exhaust valve is operated by an upward thrust of the push rod, which, being transmitted through the rocker arm, presses down on the valve stem. The intake valve is operated by a downward pull on the same rod, which is transmitted through a single crank to the intake valve. The exhaust valve is of the mushroom type, that is, with a cup shaped head. A sleeve cast integral with the cylinder head surrounds the valve stem, passing into the hollow valve head far enough that when the valve is open the escaping gases strike this sleeve instead of the valve stem, which to a great degree prevents heating of the valve stem and fouling with oil or carbon. By this method both valve springs are fully exposed, which should be a further aid in cooling and preserving their temper.

Clark, who had managed the "assembly department," apparently had left Marvel employment by the fall of 1911, when he departed for Russia to deliver a Curtiss airplane. By February the "expert mechanic" moved to Owego, where he joined the Ives Motorcycle Corporation (s.v. "Reliance Motor Cycle Company"), maker of the Monarch motorcycle.

1913 Model Year

Apparently, Marvel motorcycle production ended sometime during 1912. A report under the heading of "Important Business Changes" in the *Herald* for November 6, 1912, notes that Clarence Rudd, "former superintendent of the Marvel Motorcycle Works," had left his job as foreman in the "Curtiss Works," where he had gone after "the discontinuance of the Marvel shops." One concludes that Marvel production had ended some months before. Rudd's departure was also reported by *Motorcycling* in December 1912. In April 1913, the *Herald* said that "Harry Longwell . . . is making good as a traveling representative of the Hammondsport Wine Company." Another indication of the Marvel's demise came at the end of July 1913 when J. B. Brewer, a Rochester motorcycle dealer, was identified as a Marvel agent "until they ceased to be manufactured." He was seeking another make to sell.

The Motorcycle Equipment Company continued its mail-order business for several years after the demise of the Marvel. A new Harley-Davidson motorcycle dealership in Hammondsport in 1926, whose principals were Equipment Company veterans Warnie L. Hayes and B. L. Casterline, operated under the Motorcycle Equipment Company name. The successor company to the Curtiss Aeroplane Company, the Curtiss-Wright Corporation, has survived to the beginning of the twenty-first century, albeit in New Jersey. Several Marvels and at least one Erie motorcycle survive in private hands.

Motorcycle Car Corporation
Buffalo
1914–15

Motorcycle Illustrated in November 1914 noted the organization of the Motorcycle Car Corporation at 253 Utica Street, "manufacturing motorcycles, appliances, etc." Incorporators were father and son Arthur

E. Bennett and Edmund W. Bennett, both of Grand Island. Initial capitalization was $10,000, increased in late winter or early spring of 1915 to $100,000.

Arthur submitted a patent application in November 1915 for a "car attachment for motor-cycles." The patent, granted in November 1918, was assigned to the Motorcycle Car Corporation of Buffalo. According to the patent application, the main objective was "to provide a wheeled body or chassis which is so constructed as to be easily attached to any motor or other cycle in such a manner as to bring the seat of the attachment directly in the rear of the motor or other cycle, the attachment being provided with a steering wheel and other controlling levers which are connected to the respective controlling devices of the motor or other cycle." It is not known how many, if any, of these car attachments were made.

Arthur E. Bennett started his working life as a carpenter, but he expanded into many different businesses. With multiple patents to his name, he was involved in a few different business efforts. He ran a specialty manufacturing company, a confectionary store, and, in the 1910s, a marine and auto supply business at 1231 Niagara Street with his son. By 1916, that operation apparently was defunct. What motorcycle production there was, if any, by the Motorcycle Car Company is unknown here.

Charles and William Murphy
New York City (Manhattan)
1902

Charles M. "Mile a Minute" Murphy gained fame by drafting a Long Island Railroad train for a mile in 57.8 seconds on a bicycle. His brother "Billy" was "almost as famous as a cycle racer," according to *Motor Age*. By the spring of 1902, together they had built a steam-powered motorcycle, with which they planned to set a straightaway mile record. The machine utilized twin boilers, tested at 360 pounds per square inch each, to power two double-acting cylinders. Bores were 2.5 and 3.5 inches, with a common stroke of 3.5 inches. Drive to the rear wheel was by chain, with the gearing at one to one. Capacity for the engine was 2,500 rpm.

A photo shows a long wheelbase machine with a very heavy frame. The rear rider, who probably controlled the engine, was mounted over the back wheel. The boiler and engine were fitted between the wheels, the front rider being seated on the boiler housing. The Murphy brothers dressed in road-riding clothes, posed with their machine on a city street. A horn fitted to the front handlebar also suggests road use.

Charles and William Murphy's steam motorcycle that covered a half mile in 27 seconds. From the *Motorcycle Illustrated*, July 1906.

In early April the brothers said they had ridden a half mile in 27 seconds, "and think that with confidence that will come from further practice they will have the nerve to pilot their wonder under 40 seconds for the mile. They do not doubt its practically limitless speed and declare it is only a question of letting out and holding to the road without accident." While they hoped to set a world record at the Automobile Club of America time trials on May 31, 1902, the *New York Daily Tribune* has no notice of their participation at the Staten Island event. Charles H. Metz recorded the fastest time on a gasoline motorcycle at one minute and twenty and two-fifths seconds.

Terence "T" Musto
d/b/a **Fabbro Industries, LLC**
Voorheesville
2013–present

Terence "T" Musto remembers seeing *Motorcycle Mania* on the Discovery Channel while in sixth grade and that it was a transformational moment for him. He thought, "This is what I am here to do." That spark inspired Musto to learn as much as possible about motorcycle building. In 2007, while in college, he had saved up enough to build his own chopper, which he admits was a "death trap." He graduated from Babson College in 2010 with a finance degree but knew he wanted to build motorcycles. Turning away from the finance world, he started his own shop called V&V Cycles. The venture was short-lived, as he decided that he was not ready to build and sell a custom-built motorcycle. After some searching, Musto found an apprenticeship with Copper Mike (q.v.) at his shop, Gravesend Cycles on Long Island.

At Gravesend Cycles, Musto says he "spent every hour of every day in that building," learning and building as much as possible. After completing his apprenticeship, he stayed on and worked his way up to lead fabricator and shop foreman. While working at Gravesend, he noticed that "no one had really figured out how to develop the rigid frame line with a comfortable ride," and he set his sights on developing one.

In 2013, Musto moved back to the Capital District and started his own company, Fabbro Industries, with his sister Alexis Musto, who serves as chief marketing officer. Their main goal was "creating innovative parts for the industry that were rooted in vintage design—providing an updated functionality to classic style." The first challenge was to develop an integrated suspension frame. Musto named the frame the Type 57x and has built one complete prototype. For development of the Type 57x, Musto has built his own testing devices to measure the strength and effectiveness of the suspension system, including a shock dyno and a road simulator that looks like a treadmill, which replicates hitting different sizes of bumps in the road. The frame system has two patents and another one pending as of April 2022. Musto's complete prototype has been in major motorcycle magazines and was part of the prestigious Michael Lichter exhibit in Sturgis, South Dakota, "Old Iron, Young Blood," in 2017. Lichter, a famous motorcycle photographer, curated the annual show with the work of forty custom-motorcycle builders and eighteen artists under the age of thirty-six, highlighting the future of the field.

Some of Musto's best advances in design have come from prototyping the same frame system for bicycles. This process has allowed for easier monitoring of the suspension's reactions to the road. The design is such that one bicycle utilizing the Type 57x frame can be used for different applications, from trail racing to taking a family ride on the local bike path.

Musto is also exploring using the frame for an e-bike setup. However, his first love is building motorcycles, and with the lessons he has learned from bicycle testing he is building a new prototype motorcycle with an improved Type 57x frame.

Fabbro Industries has built four custom motorcycles since opening. They fabricate most of the parts from the frame up in-house, excluding the driveline. Musto has developed a new style of handlebar that will

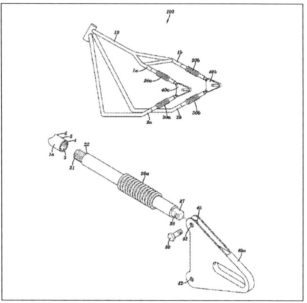

Patent drawing for Type 57x frame. Courtesy of Terence Musto, Fabbro Industries.

Close-up of patent frame components. Photography by Michael Lichter. Courtesy of Terence Musto, Fabbro Industries.

be produced for sale, as well as a line of home goods and artwork, which are available for purchase. Fabbro is also a research and design shop, and they work with companies or individuals to produce "small batch, high quality manufacturing of metal components."

N

Ner-A-Car Corporation
Syracuse
1920–28
Trade Name: **Neracar**

The Neracar was a distinctive motorcycle utilizing a low sheet-metal frame and body, drag-link steering, two-stroke engine, and a friction-drive transmission. Designer Carl A. Neracher's surname may have helped prompt the trade name, Neracar, which suggested the machine was "almost a car." The motorcycle was promoted as clean, safe, and suitable for riders who might otherwise prefer an automobile. The Ner-A-Car Corporation was capitalized on a large scale, and the Neracar reached many markets, but its makers ended production in the face of disappointing sales.

Carl Neracher (1882–1969) came to the Neracar motorcycle with broad motor-vehicle experience. In 1914 he had been sales representative for the Smith Motor Wheel Company, manufacturer of a motorized third wheel for bicycles. Neracher next went to the Cleveland Motorcycle Manufacturing Company as chief engineer (reportedly designing a lightweight, two-stroke motorcycle) and then, in 1916, to the Essex Motor Truck Company of New York.

How much, if any, the Neracar was influenced by similar motorcycle designs remains a question. Certainly, the Neracar had antecedents in earlier low motorcycles with the saddles mounted on platforms, in contrast to the more usual diamond frames adopted from bicycles.

Numbers on a surviving 1922 Neracar refer to patents granted to John J. Chapin (1866–?). In 1911, the Detroit Bi-Car Company, of which Chapin was president, announced their motorcycle, which resembled the Neracar in appearance. Like the Neracar, the Bi-Car, according to the *Bicycling World and Motor-cycle Review* in 1911, was "an attempt to construct a two-wheel vehicle embracing many desirable features of the automobile." Both machines utilized an automotive-style frame with the front splayed for a link-steered, suspended wheel. Both used a sheet-steel panel and footboards beneath the saddle. And both omitted the rotary pedals common to motorcycles of the 1910s. For rider comfort and safety, both featured a low center of gravity.

The *Bicycling World* reported that the Detroit Bi-Car Company was to begin delivery of their motorcycle in March 1912, but few if any Bi-Cars were sold. By 1914, Chapin was working as an engineer for the Lincoln Motor Car Company. Nevertheless, Neracher or others associated with the Neracar project obviously were familiar with the Bi-Car and utilized elements of Chapin's design, apparently secured by license, in the construction of the Neracar.

United States Patent 1,547,157, granted to Neracher but assigned to the Ner-A-Car Corporation, might be considered key to both the idea and the construction of the Neracar chassis. While the application was filed on June 27, 1921, the patent was not granted until more than four years later, on July 21, 1925. In volume, this patent is unusually extensive, incorporating nine sheets of drawings, thirteen pages of text, and *ninety-eight* separate claims of improvement in motorcycle design, excluding the engine, transmission, and controls, which were covered by other patents.

Neracar prototype in New York City, ca. 1918. Note the faired headlamp, disc wheels, and imperfect sheet-metal work. Photo courtesy of Bruce Linsday.

Carl A. Neracher, the Neracar's designer, posing for a publicity photo ca. 1922. Photo courtesy of Bruce Linsday.

The Neracar as built in 1922 utilized a combined sheet-metal chassis and body. A handlebar, rather than a steering wheel, controlled the drag-link steering mechanism on the suspended front wheel. A one-cylinder, two-stroke engine mounted in the center of the chassis had its crank longitudinal to the direction of travel. A sliding friction wheel moved along the face of the flywheel to give the rider five forward speeds selected by a lever. A chain provided final drive to the rear wheel. The 175-pound machine was equipped with two electric headlights and one tail lamp.

In 1922, Ner-A-Car Corporation president, J. (Joseph) Allan Smith (1872–?), recounted the origin of the Neracar. He said he and Neracher began about 1918 to discuss the development of a lightweight motorcycle, "resulting in the gradual evolution and development of the machine known as the 'Neracar.' The problem confronting both at all times was to build a machine weighing less than 200 pounds which could be ridden by either lady or gentleman in any costume without injury to their attire from mud or grease. Development has been going on over a period of years, each step being covered by suitable patent application" (*Motorcycling and Bicycling*, March 29, 1922).

News of these machines "percolated over to England," thanks to Smith's former business association with Harry Powell, who facilitated manufacture by Sheffield Simplex Motors Ltd., which obtained a license to manufacture and sell the Neracar in Great Britain and the British colonies "excepting Canada." Both Smith and Neracher were on the board of a Sheffield Simplex subsidiary, the Inter-Continental Engineering Company Ltd. Production in England began on September 1, 1921.

The Ner-A-Car Corporation was incorporated by the New York secretary of state on April 1, 1920. Within two weeks, the Ner-A-Car stockholders held a meeting to increase the number of preferred shares to ten thousand, with a par value of $1,000,000. Total capital was to be $1,100,000, up from $400,000. The *Bicycling World* said, "None of the stock has been offered for public subscription." Two years later, a special meeting of Ner-A-Car stockholders voted to allow the president, Smith, and his appointees to manage the affairs of the corporation between board meetings. The secretary at that point was Chauncey L. Lane (1878–?), Smith's former associate at the United States Light and Heat Corporation in Niagara Falls, which produced automotive systems.

The Ner-A-Car directors impress with their executive titles and the names of their enterprises:

Frederick P. Assmann, first vice president and general manager of the Continental Can Company operation in Syracuse

Dana R. Bullen of the General Electric Company in Schenectady

Alexander H. Cowie, a Syracuse lawyer. He was president of the Rochester and Syracuse Railroad Company and of the Empire State Railroad Corporation. His name appears as the lawyer on the Ner-A-Car incorporation certificate, and his practice provided legal services for the corporation through its existence.

Huntington B. Crouse, president of the Crouse-Hinds Company in Syracuse, manufacturer of electrical apparatuses

King C. Gillette, president of the Gillette Safety Razor Company in Boston

Edwin K. Gordon, vice president of the Ner-A-Car Corporation and probably a veteran of the advertising world

Egbert H. Gold, president of the Vapor Car Heating Company in Chicago

Carl A. Neracher, whose city directory listings in the early 1920s give his primary occupation as vice president or chief engineer of the New Process Gear Company, a manufacturer of automobile components in Syracuse. Given his position there, it's not likely that Neracher played a full-time role in day-to-day Ner-A-Car activities.

J. Allan Smith, president of the Ner-A-Car Corporation. Smith, with postbaccalaureate study in electricity, was a manager and leader who moved quickly from one significant position to another. In 1909 he became vice president and general manager of the United States Light and Heat Corporation. He was elected president in 1913, and by 1918 was also president of the New Process Gear Corporation in Syracuse. With the incorporation of Ner-A-Car, Smith severed his connections with United States Light and with New Process.

Publicity shot for the Neracar, 1922. Ner-A-Car vice president Edwin K. Gordon is in the center. Photo courtesy of Frank Westfall.

The first American Ner-A-Car offices were in the Onondaga Hotel in Syracuse. In May 1921, a factory building at 196 South Geddes Street was occupied. The flat-roofed, trapezoidal brick structure offered three 12-foot stories plus a basement. Neracar production scheduled for November 1921 to prepare for the 1922 season was delayed by tooling problems. In the meantime, testing of prototypes continued.

Interviewed by *Motorcycle and Bicycle Illustrated* in the fall, Smith was generous in sharing his views of the Neracar. It was not a "sporting proposition," as many motorcycles were. Its top speed was limited to 35 miles per hour over Smith's objection; he would have preferred 30 but was overruled by his associates. "What we started out to do was produce a car that anybody from 9 to 99 of either sex could ride, and I think I have done it." Beyond the initial motorcycle, Smith also had plans for a two-passenger, three-wheel machine in which the driver and passenger "will sit side by side as in an automobile."

The Ner-A-Car Corporation in the fall of 1921, according to the *Bicycling World*, had a capacity of 150 machines a day, with plans for 25,000 motorcycles in 1922. "At present it is largely a matter of assembly, many parts being made in outside factories." Distribution of the first five hundred machines was planned for an area near the factory, it being Smith's aim to "have the first lot of American built machines under his close observation."

In March 1922 Smith said that the Ner-A-Car Corporation was prepared to meet both large and small orders. "All that we require from any dealer is a small initial order as an evidence of good faith, provided he is in shape to give good service." Smith said that both motorcycle and automobile dealers were appropriate Neracar agents, although he preferred motorcycle enterprises, "provided they are worthy of their calling."

Smith told W. H. Parsons of *Motorcycle and Bicycle Illustrated* that the Ner-A-Car Corporation had had "a little trouble convincing some of the people who are manufacturing parts for us that we are just as particular about the appearance of the Neracar as we are about its performance, but now they are coming along the way we want them to." With many parts being fabricated by outside contractors, the quality of the materials was vital, of course. Smith said his style of manufacture led to greater "economy and speed" compared to greater in-house production.

Parsons and a colleague, after interviewing Smith in Syracuse, visited the new Neracar agency operated by L. M. Thorn. "It was one of the most attractive motorcycle agencies I had ever seen," Parsons reported. The show window held a single black Neracar against an orange background. Another machine occupied a "big rug" in the center of the store. "To one side was a comfortable settee where you could sit and look it over while the salesman told its fine points." At the conclusion of a sales effort, "we had to disclose our identity. He [the salesman] laughed and said it was good practice anyway, and invited us to call every time we came to town. We surely will, for I intend to watch the progress of that store."

The now-demolished Neracar factory at the northwest corner of Geddes and Fayette Streets in Syracuse. From *Motorcycle Illustrated*, April 13, 1922.

A cross-country trip in 1922 perhaps brought the Neracar to its zenith of renown. The well-known endurance rider and racer Erwin G. ("Cannonball") Baker in October and November journeyed via Neracar from New York to Los Angeles in 174 hours of riding over twenty-seven days. He averaged 19.5 miles per hour, using 38.5 gallons of gasoline in the 3,400 miles. Baker arrived in Los Angeles at the time of an automobile show there, and "machine and rider were the lions of the show" (*Motorcycling*, November 22, 1922).

In the spring, *Motorcycling and Bicycling* published L. E. Fowler's "Road Test of the Neracar." He was impressed by the ease of handling and the cleanliness of the Neracar on muddy roads. At the conclusion of his trip from Syracuse to Auburn and Skaneateles, Fowler was able to ride the machine standing, using no hands.

In the summer of 1922, the Ner-A-Car Corporation announced a retail price reduction from $225 to $185. Smith said, "A short time ago, we were able to effect savings in manufacture which we immediately passed on to the dealer in the shape of an extra discount, making an increase from 20 per cent to 25 per cent. Now, with additional economies, we are passing the saving to the public. We are doing everything that we can to get more people into the two-wheel habit and we believe that this reduction in price on our electrically equipped [electric lamps] machine will mean a very large sale of Neracars."

Sometime before the fall of 1922, Gordon succeeded Lane as Ner-A-Car vice president. By then, J. Allan Smith Jr., Smith's son, had gone to work for the company as a salesman. John F. Emiliussen (1879–1963) was corporate secretary, and Morton Frick served as treasurer while maintaining the position of comptroller at the New Process Gear Company. When Frick died in April 1923, his Ner-A-Car position was combined with that of the secretary, and the enlarged post was held for most of the company's existence by Emiliussen.

Motorcycle and Bicycle Illustrated in February 1923 reported minor changes to the Neracar, emphasizing "more safety and satisfaction to the rider." These modifications included ball-and-socket joints on both ends of the drag link, an adjustable steering post, heavier brake mounting, a change in the piston pin, and an Eisemann flywheel generator as standard equipment.

In 1923, when Neracars were being "sold in France in quantities," the local Neracar distributor announced that the "police department of France" had approved the Neracar for registration, an event that relieved owners from getting lengthy individual approval for their imported motorcycles. Franklin Chase, in his *Syracuse and Its Environs*, said that "the Ner-a-Car manufactured in Syracuse had become popular with the Arabs and the Moors in 1923, because its construction permitted riding in native costume." The *Syracuse Herald* noted that Syracuse's "latest emerging automotive industry" had "found rapid favor in foreign cities with their narrow streets and highways; and is meeting an expanding market here as congestion makes parking increasingly a more difficult problem."

In the summer of 1923, J. Allan Smith Sr. wrote an article for *Motorcycle and Bicycle Illustrated* entitled "Are Motorcycle Prices High?" In his essay, Smith endeavored to demonstrate that even a $440 car was too expensive for most people with incomes of less than $3,000. And with most cars being used to carry only one person, the $207.50 Neracar, with operating expenses of $70.50, according to Smith, offered the average person a much more economical form of transportation than the $440 car, at $278 per year, and much pleasanter travel than did the $75.50-per-year trolley, with its "waits, transfers, crowded, foul air cars."

The 1924-model Neracar, called the Series 3, was introduced in August 1923. Changes to the engine included added cooling fins, interior ports, increased compression, a one-piece crankcase to prevent leakage, and relocation of the carburetor to the left side of the engine to provide a cooler mixture. Other improvements included larger, more resilient springs for the

J. Allan Smith, Ner-A-Car Corporation president, caricaturized by *Motorcycle and Bicycle Illustrated*, February 22, 1923.

front wheel and a new Eisemann magneto, which provided three times the wattage compared to previous equipment. The modifications combined with an increase in labor and material costs resulted in an increase in the list price with standard luggage carrier to $200 from $190 with the carrier or $185 without. A second, internal expanding brake on the left side of the rear wheel and operated by a lever on the right handlebar, "required in many overseas markets," was available in the United States for an additional ten dollars.

An August advertisement noted that four hundred dealer franchises had been awarded in 1923. An advertisement in the *Saturday Evening Post* said the Neracar was "Motoring on Two Wheels," giving 300 miles for one dollar, 85 to 100 miles per gallon of gasoline, and a speed of 35 miles per hour to the general public, who could "lunch at home and live where rents are cheaper. Available to both sexes, any age."

At the February 1925 National Motorcycle, Bicycle, and Accessory Show in New York City, the Ner-A-Car Corporation introduced a three-wheel delivery vehicle called the Type CB. The prototype was painted with the name and logo of the Crouse-Hinds Company, the electrical apparatus manufacturer of which Huntington B. Crouse, a Ner-A-Car shareholder, was president.

For regular 1925 Neracars, the second brake as well as balloon tires, speedometer, and tandem seat were optional "at slight additional cost." A Type B engine promised enough power to eliminate downshifting on hills while maintaining 85 to 90 miles per gallon of gasoline. The "new price" for the 1925 Neracar was $175, a reduction the company thought would "get large sales for live dealers." With the second brake, the cost was the old price of $185. An undated sales letter to dealers from Gordon announced the price reductions. For the $175 Neracar, dealers would pay $131.25, so gross profit for the dealer was $43.75. On the double-brake model, the dealer paid $138.75. Net to the dealer was $46.25.

A report in the spring of 1925 indicated great success for the Neracar in Japan. The distributor, Pappadopoulo and Company, had placed their first order in January 1924, receiving six machines the following April. Orders had grown per month from ten, to twenty, to thirty, to eighty in March 1925. Overall, the Ner-A-Car Corporation reported at the end of August 1925 that, while domestic sales were "far from what they could wish," some "noteworthy progress" had been made in "certain districts." If "they could just get hold of the right type of dealers who appreciate the opportunities in the Ner-acar line," then the "possibilities are very good indeed" (*Motorcycling*, September 2, 1925).

Carl Neracher, who had been employed by the New Process Gear Company, in the summer of 1925 was treasurer of the National Twin-High Sales Corporation, an automotive transmission company with offices in Syracuse. Within a year, Carl Neracher was gone from the city but remained associated with the Ner-A-Car Corporation, serving as a director to the dissolution of that company.

While starting production with the same 13.5-cubic-inch displacement as the American engine, the English Sheffield-Simplex factory had increased displacement to about 16 cubic inches in 1922 and then in 1925 offered a four-stroke engine and three-speed transmission. At the New York City motorcycle show in late January 1926, a prototype four-stroke American Ner-A-Car appeared. The 21-cubic-inch, 6-horsepower engine reportedly allowed a top speed of 55 miles per hour for the machine, which was built with a strengthened frame to handle the additional power. An English Binks carburetor and a Bosch magneto were fitted. Deliveries were promised for May. Whether any other such motorcycles were built has not been determined here. At the show, Smith spoke of a "steady and healthy growth" in Ner-A-Car business. On hand at the Ner-A-Car booth were Frederick E. Spicer, sales manager, and Frank Engle, "Works Manager."

In February 1926, Spicer distributed a mimeographed sales letter to dealers, in which new prices were announced. The elimination of the Type A (the less powerful model) was mentioned, as was standardization of 26-by-3.3-inch balloon tires. The single-brake model henceforth was $190, which, compared to the similarly equipped balloon-tire model the year before at $195, was actually five dollars cheaper. Meanwhile, "a few" Type A motorcycles and Type B machines with the high-pressure tires were to be sold at the old prices.

As late as April 1927, the Ner-A-Car Corporation was advertising to the cycle trade, seeking dealers for a "new and better proposition." The idea, still, was for motorcycle sellers to "complete" their lines by selling a lightweight motorcycle to "get the volume of business to which you are entitled." But in a letter dated February 29, 1928, the Ner-A-Car Corporation gave notice that production, "sales, service, etc.," had been suspended as of that day. It was noted that "F. E. Spicer" at the Geddes address would be operating a "parts service business," which was to have "no connections or relation whatever with the affairs of the Neracar Corporation."

On October 2 the stockholders voted to dissolve the Ner-A-Car Corporation. At that point the officers were Smith, president; M. (May) Arter Smith (J. Allan's wife), vice president; Neracher, vice president; and James F. Buckley, secretary and treasurer.

Cowie, Crouse, and Assmann maintained their several employments and directorships through the 1920s. An obituary for Gold when he died in November 1928 said, "He was very wealthy." One assumes that most Ner-A-Car investors wrote off their Ner-A-Car experience. Smith and Gordon, on the other hand, were both Ner-A-Car officers and managers. With the Ner-A-Car enterprise failing to realize dreams of large income, Smith secured other employment sometime in 1926 at the latest. While remaining president of the Ner-A-Car Corporation, he went to work as the eastern representative for the bus manufacturer Twin Coach Company of Kent, Ohio. Gordon's fate has not been discovered here; he had left the Ner-A-Car Corporation in August or September 1924.

Spicer's Neracar parts business apparently ended by the summer of 1930. A researcher in the 1940s noted that the Syracuse Chamber of Commerce told him at that point that the "Spicer Manft' Co." took Neracar parts to Toledo "about '29. Ans to Inquiry out there was vague—gave impression they knew nothing of it."

A number of Neracars have survived to the end of the twentieth century. Among those in public venues are the Syracuse-built version in the collections of the Buffalo and Erie County Historical Society in Buffalo as well as an English model at the Science Museum in London.

Christian Newman
d/b/a **CT Newman Engineering**
Buffalo
2011–present

Christian Newman has been tinkering with machines since he was a kid. By the time he was in college, he was modifying imported cars. A chance purchase of an old Honda CB550 at a yard sale turned out to be his father's old bike. He took it apart and rebuilt it, and, according to Newman, during that process he realized how much he "loved working on motorcycles because every mechanical piece needed to have both function and form."

Newman is a trained mechanical engineer, and his full-time job is designing mining and oil-field equipment. He opened CT Newman Engineering in 2012 to build one-off custom motorcycles and custom motorcycle parts, "as a hobby." As of April 2022, he reports that he has built five complete custom and ten "normal" motorcycle builds.

Newman's background in engineering comes through in his builds. In 2021, he said that he had over five hundred hours of digital design time before he started to build his one-off, award-winning Custom Twin Turbo 8 Valve Harley-Davidson ULH. One of his recent builds included all custom parts except the crankcase. He also offers computer numerical control (CNC) machining services and mass-produces headlights, taillights, frame fixtures, and other tooling.

A 1940 knucklehead built in 2017 by Christian Newman. It is completely hand-polished stainless steel, including frame and girder fork. Newman notes that is not chrome. Further, he wrote that "the sprocket and rotor sit outside the frame. Transmission narrowed by 3" by making custom kicker side. All the oil flows thru the frame. I could go on and on. There's a lot of engineering there."

Nioga Cycle Works
Whitney Point
ca. 1903

The "Buyer's Guide" printed in the January 1903 issue of the *Cycle and Automobile Trade Journal* lists the Nioga Cycle Works as a source of motorcycles. A year later, the Nioga company's entry was in the "bicycles" and not "motorcycles" section of the *Dealer and Repairman* "Classified Buyers' Guide." The Nioga name is likely a variation of "Tioughnioga," the river merging with the Otselic at Whitney Point.

Norsman Motorcycles
Webster
1999
Trade Name: **Norsman**

Mark Anderson has been involved with motorcycle sales, repair, and fabrication since 1980. From 1997 to 1999 he worked with David Robinson (s.v. "Robinson Cyclenet"), building AR Streetracker motorcycles in Scottsville. Anderson states he did the construction, turning out nine identical, 650-cubic-centimeter, Yamaha-based motorcycles plus a number of custom machines.

In October 1999, Anderson left Robinson to pursue his own path as a motorcycle manufacturer. As a start, Anderson built a prototype Norsman TL1000SST. Like the AR Streetracker, the Norsman resembles a dirt-track racing motorcycle but is designed for street use. In 2000, Anderson expected the selling price to be around $19,500. The Norsman was intended to be a high-performance, high-quality iteration of the Streetracker theme. The 340-pound machine utilizes a 1,000-cubic-centimeter, liquid-cooled Suzuki engine, which delivers 115 horsepower. With components from a number of United States sources, the Norsman had few Suzuki parts other than the engine and radiator. Anderson's goal in 2000 was an independent operation of sufficient size to turn out one to two hundred high-end motorcycles annually. After test-driving the completed prototype, Anderson felt that it was too powerful to be placed on the open market and decided not to market the Norsman. He did build one more for a dirt-track racer.

Anderson took a break from direct involvement in motorcycle sales and fabrication to build Adirondack guide boats from 2009 to around 2021. In 2022, he reports that he has located and purchased the Norsman flat-track racing motorcycle and is working on making it street legal. He also is planning to revive the Norsman project in some fashion in the next couple of years.

North American Motor Corporation
Stapleton
ca. 1909

In late spring of 1909, the North American Motor Corporation was organized in Manhattan, although the principal business office was to be at Stapleton on Staten Island. The *Bicycling World and Motorcycle Review* observed that the manufacture of motorcycles was included among the many diverse purposes of the corporation. While capital stock amounted to ten thousand dollars (according to the certificate of incorporation), the company began business with five hundred dollars, corresponding to five shares with a par value of one hundred dollars each. The incorporators and subscribers were Chauncey Cleveland (two shares), H. Bernard Layman (two shares), and Priscilla Wallace (one share). These three individuals, all with a 68 West Ninety-Sixth Street address, served as first-year directors, as did J. Robert Rubin and John E. Davies, the latter of 534 West 135th Street.

It is unlikely that any motorcycle production occurred. Company advertising focused on marine and automobile engines. One should remember that in the early years of motor-vehicle transportation many corporations were organized with extremely inclusive statements of purpose, including manufacture as well as purchase, sale, operation, lease, repair, and mortgage of many forms of equipment. Often, trade was the principal activity of such companies, with little or no manufacture. The North American Motor Corporation was dissolved by proclamation in 1926.

N.S.U. Motor Company
New York City (Manhattan)
1908–1911 or 1912
Trade Name: **N.S.U.**

The N.S.U. was a German motorcycle imported by the N.S.U. Motor Company of New York City. Eugene C. Kircherer, a "factory representative," arrived in New York in January 1908 to "establish an N.S.U. depot . . . of which he will be manager" (*Bicycling World and Motorcycle Review*). The N.S.U. Motor Company subsequently was located at 206 West Seventy-Sixth Street in Manhattan. Later in the year, a Chicago agency was added. While the N.S.U. Motor Company joined the (American) Motorcycle Manufacturers Association, N.S.U. motorcycles were built by the Neckarsulmer Fahrradwerke in Germany; the New York operation remained an import, distribution, and sales center. The N.S.U. Motor Company yielded as American importer to the Sun Motor and Supply Company by January 1912.

Apparently, export efforts to the United States began as early as 1906, when the N.S.U. Cycle and Motor Company of London, England, advertised in American journals. In 1907, the Leader Specialty Manufacturing Company of Bradford, Pennsylvania, sold N.S.U. motorcycles, and in 1908 John F. McLaughlin (q.v.), identified as the "New York agents of which company," sold them at 148 East Forty-Ninth Street in New York (*Motorcycle Illustrated*, December 1907). The Sun Motor and Supply Company, managed by Kircherer, first at 206 West Seventy-Sixth Street and subsequently on Amsterdam Avenue in New York, dissolved at the end of 1912. Kircherer then worked in Detroit for the Haverford Cycle Company, to which he "turned over N.S.U. parts" (*Motorcycling*, November 28, 1912). *Motorcycle Illustrated* in August 1916 said there was no American agent for N.S.U. "at present."

Okay Motor Manufacturing Company Inc.
New York City (Brooklyn)
1916–17
Trade Name: **Okay**

In a time of bicycle motors competing for public favor, the Okay figured among the lightest, simplest, and cheapest. Complete with gasoline tank, the two-stroke, 2,000 rpm, 2-inch bore by-2-inch stroke, 1-horsepower engine measured 6 inches wide by 12 inches high and weighed 18 pounds. Driving the front wheel via a roller resting on the tire, the thirty-five-dollar engine could propel a bicycle at over 20 miles per hour.

Steel head and cylinder were integral and attached to the aluminum crankcase by four cap screws. A counterbalanced crankshaft ran on *one* main bearing to reduce "the possibility of the mixture escaping from the crankcase through the bearings." A single piston ring was "found quite sufficient to hold the compression in a motor of such small size." Ignition

The original Okay bicycle engine, showing the flywheel, roller atop the tire, rectangular fuel tank, exhaust pipe serving as muffler, and hold-down spring. From *Motorcycling and Bicycling*, October 16, 1916.

season approaches." Woodruff had just returned from a "flying trip" to the Midwest and was headed for New England. Meanwhile, the Pacific Motor Supply Company in San Francisco had ordered fifty units for their "territory," which included the coast states, Nevada, Arizona, and the Pacific Islands.

In late 1916, the Okay was improved with a new muffler and device for lifting the roller from the wheel. From *Motorcycling and Bicycling*, November 6, 1916.

came from three dry cells and a coil housed a metal box attached to bicycle frame behind the seat. The fuel tank was fitted to the left side of engine, counterbalancing the crankcase mass. The throttle control incorporated a compression release for starting. With no muffler, the exhaust pipe was flattened "to break up any sound waves." A spring supplemented the weight of the engine in maintaining roller and tire contact. The Okay prototype had a wire to lift the engine and its roller from contact with the tire.

The major Okay figure was Lee S. Woodruff, who sold a sporting goods store in favor of the bicycle engine enterprise. In the incorporation of the Okay company in September 1916, Woodruff took fifty shares with five-dollar par value, as did G. Kenneth Fisher. Ralph E. Bates subscribed one hundred shares. Woodruff became company president, and Fisher secretary-treasurer of the Okay Motor Manufacturing Company Inc. at 713 Flatbush Avenue.

The first announcement of the Okay motor came in August 1916 at the Atlantic City convention of the Cycle Trades Association, when *Motorcycle Illustrated* reported plans to turn out thirty motors a day. By early October 1916, the Okay company was at a new facility at Second Avenue and Thirteenth Street. Machinery to permit production of ten motors a day was being installed, with plans for additional output "as the 1917

Improved Okay with new muffler visible on the right. From *Motorcycle Illustrated*, November 9, 1916.

In November, the Okay company began to use one of the showgirls at the Winter Garden in Manhattan as "Miss Okay" in photographic promotions. At the national cycle show in Chicago, the Okay was "displayed in a gold frame, the motor being placed on the platform of a spotlessly white scale to impress the visitor with its extremely light weight." Nearby, Woodruff and Fisher predicted that they would be making deliveries at a rate of ten to fifteen motors a day by January 1, 1917. New on the Okay was a spring arrangement to allow the rider to disengage the engine via a "toe lever," so the rider could "pedal along without interference when the traffic is heavy." Also new were a muffler and a priming cup. Woodruff reportedly was "kept busy demonstrating his very unique device, and had to answer a million questions. Leave it to Woodruff." In addition, a Boy Scout–model Okay in "drab color" was fitted to a Harley-Davidson motorbike. Application of the Okay engine to canoe or rowboat use was also promoted.

Eighteen-pound, 1-horsepower Okay engine fitted to a bicycle. The man may be Lee S. Woodruff. From *Motorcycle Illustrated*, August 24, 1916.

At the New York show a few weeks later, additional changes included an aluminum cylinder lined with a steel sleeve for reduced weight and better cooling; a strap holding the fuel tank securely to the cylinder; and two different attachment brackets for use respectively on bicycles with and without reinforced forks. Woodruff, accompanied by Fisher and "Engineer Ralph E. Bates," still expected to begin production by January 1. Of the cycle show, Woodruff told *Motorcycling and Bicycling*, "We are young in the field and it certainly requires the pep of youth to keep up with the pace set here this week."

By the end of February 1917, Woodruff had left the Okay company to become sales manager of a motor truck and tractor manufacturer. A dearth of information about further Okay activities suggests the demise of the operation then or shortly thereafter. The Okay corporation was dissolved by proclamation of the secretary of state in 1929.

Andrew H. Oldfield
Waterloo
1946
Trade Names: Oldfield; Barney Bike

Andrew Oldfield (1920–70), according to his friend Lloyd D. Washburn, was an "extremely capable person" whose career as a mechanical engineer encompassed optical lens grinding machinery design, aeronautics, and toolmaking. In the late 1940s, Oldfield was a machinist at Synchro-Master in Seneca Falls. At the time of his death, Oldfield's daughter, Kathleen J. Oldfield, notes he was president of Senoptics Inc., "a company which designed and marketed lens grinding machines." He had built an airplane, "the plans for which are still marketed today," Washburn said in 2000. And "Barney" Oldfield (nicknamed after the unrelated automobile racer) had fabricated a motorcycle. Kathleen further noted that her father "also designed and marketed a miniature motorcycle called the Barney Bike in the late '40s." Whether any were actually produced and sold is not known at this time.

In the military at the end of World War II, Oldfield had acquired in Germany a two-cylinder opposed Zundapp motorcycle engine, transmission, and shaft-drive unit, all of which he brought home to Waterloo. There, he mated his running gear to the frame of a

The Oldfield motorcycle, ca. 1946, combining an Indian frame with Zundapp engine, transmission, and shaft drive. Photo courtesy of Lloyd D. Washburn.

1940 Indian Sport Scout motorcycle. In Washburn's words,

> this required redesigning the frame from the original . . . wherein the engine was part of the frame, to . . . [a frame] . . . which looped down under the engine and attached to the rear frame section. This meant cutting off the existing tube and replacing it with a double down tube under the seat. The frame at the rear had to be redesigned to accommodate the rear drive unit and the rear wheel hub redesigned to accept the smaller space available to it.
>
> Andy had the Indian factory make up a special set of extra large gas tanks (Daytona) with no oil compartment, to fit the Scout frame. As another example of his varied skills, he made the pattern and sand cast the aluminum nameplates (OLDFIELD) script and attached them to the tanks.

After Oldfield's death, his family gave the motorcycle to Washburn, who previously had expressed interest in acquiring it. In the summer of 1999, Washburn rode the Oldfield machine in a three-day antique motorcycle club "road run" in central New York. Washburn notes that as a long-legged person, he finds the machine uncomfortable, since his knees contact the carburetors. Lloyd Washburn passed away in 2006. The whereabouts of the Oldfield motorcycle is unknown at this time.

Olive Wheel Company
Syracuse
1901

The Olive Wheel Company, a major manufacturer of bicycles in the 1890s, survived an end-of-decade decline in the bicycle industry as well as the creation in 1899 of a bicycle trust; the American Bicycle Company consolidated many of the other leading Syracuse factories.

The Holley motorcycle, with frame supplied by the Olive Wheel Company in Syracuse. From the *Horseless Age*, vol. 7, no. 3, 1900.

In Bradford, Pennsylvania, meanwhile, George M. Holley developed a motorcycle and organized the Holley Motor Company to build it. His design attached a one-cylinder engine to the seat tube of a diamond frame, the engine's crank displacing the pedal crank usually fitted to motor bicycles of the era. Ignition and fuel supply were mounted to the engine within the diamond or fastened on the outside of the seat tube. The *Bicycling World* in 1900 thought the $150 machine had "a clean and compact appearance, while the use of the familiar chain and sprocket gearing instead of the belt and pulley is another item that will command attention."

Don B. Smith, manager of the Olive Wheel Company, reportedly had a financial interest in the Holley company, and in the late winter of 1901 the *Bicycling World* reported the Olive Wheel Company was going to fabricate frames "and many of the parts" of the Holley motorcycle "and thus get them on the market in quantities early in the season." The *Cycling Age* said that the arrangement was to last only "until about the first of August," by which time the Holley company was to have finished its new factory. The *Cycling Gazette* in its story said that the Olive factory was to turn out "200 or 300" complete motor bicycles before June 1 and in September noted that such motorcycles had been built. Another story said that the bicycles were shipped to Bradford, "where the motors are put on." This split manufacture is confirmed by a *Cycling Age* report that claimed, "As is well known, the company is having frames built at Syracuse by the Olive Wheel Co., while the motors are made at Bradford under the supervision of the young inventor, George Holley . . . just twenty-two." A year later, an observer noted that "something less than fifty" Holley motorcycles were built the first season.

Francis W. Gridley, president of the Olive Wheel Company, contemplated manufacturing complete Olive motorcycles for 1902, independent of the Holley operation. He reportedly "had several conferences with a New York man who has a motorcycle, and if a deal is made motor cycles will be turned out at the factory." The Olive company had previously announced its intention to build steam-powered automobiles.

Smith, who was said to be contemplating a move to Bradford, died suddenly in June 1901. Further misfortune saw the Olive plant dormant by October and bankrupt by December. In 1902, the remaining bicycle stock of the Olive Wheel Company was purchased by P. A. Williams and Company and moved to Springfield, Massachusetts. The Holley Motor Company discontinued the manufacture of motorcycles in 1903.

Orange County Choppers
Rock Tavern (1999–2008); Newburgh (2008–21);
Pinellas Park, Florida (2021–present)
1999–present

Like many of his generation, Paul Teutul Sr. ("Paul Sr.") got the bug for motorcycles when he saw the movie *Easy Rider* in 1969. By 1972, he had a secondhand 1971 Triumph that he used to get around. He made a living as a welder, first working for others, then partnering with Fred Gerini and forming P & F Ironworks. In addition to ironwork, Gerini built choppers. Paul Sr. took it all in as Fred showed him how to stretch frames and fabricate most parts on a motorcycle. Soon, Paul Sr. purchased a new 1974 Harley-Davidson Superglide.

It wasn't long before Paul Sr. started customizing the Superglide, following Gerini's example. He named it the "Sunshine bike" and still owns it today.

Eventually, Paul Sr. would strike out on his own and form Orange County Ironworks. In the 1990s, his son Paul Jr. started working at the ironworks. With the ironworks doing well, Paul Sr. started taking time to build motorcycles in his basement. In 1995, Paul Sr. and Paul Jr. built their first bike together, a chopper featuring a custom frame and EVO motor. Over the next few years, they built a few more and started to get a little recognition for their work. Paul Sr. decided that he wanted to build motorcycles and sell them full-time. So he took his retirement savings to fund a set of new custom builds that he and Paul Jr. made together. In 1999, Paul Sr. started Orange County Choppers (OCC), working out of the basement at the ironworks. Paul Jr. was the lead designer, and, using the bikes financed by Paul Sr.'s retirement savings, which they call "the Basement Bikes," they set out to promote the new company. According to Paul Jr., each of the six bikes built were prostreet style, with modern engines and parts, as opposed to the old-school-chopper style that Paul Sr. preferred. But they also brought some chopper-style bikes that they built for themselves to shows.

Starting in the fall of 1999, motorcycle magazines started to take notice and featured some of OCC's bikes. In 2001, Paul Jr. built his first theme bike; it would be called "Spider Man." The Spider Man bike was a huge hit at all of the shows they brought it to.

Starting in 2000, the Discovery Channel was airing new shows about custom motorcycles, the first of which was *Motorcycle Mania* featuring Jesse James of West Coast Choppers. The popularity of choppers was starting to make a comeback, and OCC was finding its groove at the right time. In 2001, the Discovery Channel was looking to make a documentary about an East Coast custom-motorcycle builder. OCC was on their list and was eventually selected after the producer felt their first choice was wrong.

The show *American Chopper* was born, first with two pilots and then a series that lasted over ten years—longer if you include spin-offs and web-based programing. The stars of the show were many, including the theme bikes, but the father-son relationship was one of the main draws of the show, which went on to air in over two hundred countries and territories. The crew at OCC became famous very quickly, and their staff continued to grow. The theme bikes and family relations struck a chord with entire families. The show didn't just appeal to motorcyclists; it went mainstream. In the process, along with other Discovery Channel shows, the chopper was brought back to the public's eye and grew in popularity.

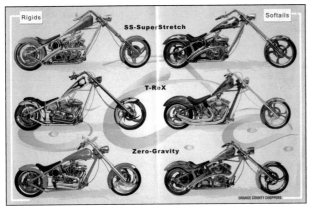

Sections of an Orange County Choppers brochure showing examples of some of the custom motorcycles they were offering in 2003. NYSM H-2022.11.1

While continuing to build custom bikes for customers, the Teutuls made a new business model by building custom theme bikes on commission. Companies would pay to have a custom motorcycle built as an advertising tool. Some of those builds were featured in the television series, giving the sponsor of the bike an hour-long commercial and, after, a radical advertisement piece to be displayed at events. Most of the theme bikes were about form over function, meant to be displayed at media events and only driven short distances. Others built by OCC were more about function and were built to be used on the road.

In addition to Paul Sr. and Paul Jr., the OCC crew during the height of the show included other mechanics, fabricators, and designers; notable on-screen appearances were those of Vinnie DiMartino, Rick Petko, Cody Connelly, Craig Chapman, Jason Pohl, Jim Quinn, and Mikey Teutul (Paul Sr.'s youngest son), who helped run the office and provided much-needed comic relief.

In the early days of OCC, most of the parts were purchased and modified as needed; however, as the company grew, more parts were made in-house, and computer numerical control (CNC) machines were added to help produce new one-of-a-kind parts. They also used those machines to turn out a line of OCC-brand motorcycle parts. In 2006, they were building over one hundred bikes per year, with prices starting at around $39,000 and ranging up to over $200,000 for the high-end theme bikes. In 2007, they produced a limited-edition line of production motorcycles that started in price at $31,000.

In April 2008, OCC moved to a brand-new, 92,800-square-foot facility in Newburgh, right along the New York State Thruway. The building included a store, restaurant, offices, and a production area where visitors could watch the crew work from behind glass. To Paul Jr., this seemed like a mistake, and he did not support the move. That September, the father-son volatility that viewers liked to see on screen took its toll, and Paul Sr. fired Paul Jr. from the company. Paul Jr. went on to form his own company, Paul Jr. Designs (q.v.). The shows continued in various forms and with various levels of success through 2020. Eventually, their popularity waned, and OCC had to downsize. In 2020, Paul Sr. announced that he was moving the company to Florida, citing New York State's high taxes, among other reasons. In 2021, OCC opened a new headquarters in Pinellas Park, Florida.

Alden E. Osborn
New York City (Bronx)
1909–13

Alden Osborn's work, according to the *Bicycling World and Motorcycle Review*, was the "improvement of motor vehicle patents." Beginning in 1909, he filed patent applications for several versions of sliding-valve mechanisms for internal combustion engines. In the patent specifications for one such invention (Patent 987,164, granted on March 21, 1911, following a 1909 application), Osborn said that poppet valves "at best, are noisy, unreliable and unsatisfactory in almost every respect." While previous slide-valve engines had not been successful, Osborn said his invention would "provide an efficient valve mechanism of this character."

Two other slide-valve patents are 985,198 (February 28, 1911) and 1,011,480 (December 12, 1911). The former apparently guided Osborn's modification of a Pierce (q.v.) motorcycle engine so that it would operate with a single sliding valve. The new valve mechanism utilized a small-diameter piston, whose crankshaft was gear driven at half engine speed. The rising and falling small piston would cover and uncover ports at the appropriate time to service the four-stroke engine.

The Pierce motorcycle modified in 1911 to run with Alden Osborn's patented slide-valve system. From *Motorcycle Illustrated*, March 20, 1913.

The *Bicycling World* thought the "real novelty . . . is the fact that the valve cylinder is offset with relation to the center of the shaft which carries the half-time wheel." With increased angularity of the valve piston, the speed of the valve movement was irregular; lags at the top and bottom gave "the necessary time for the passage of the gases" at the bottom as well as for ignition and expansion of gases at the top. A floating, V-section ring blocked the inlet port to prevent exhaust gas from entering. Suction lifted the ring to admit the incoming charge. *Motorcycle Illustrated* in March 1913 noted that Osborn's motor was "brought out in January 1911" and was running still in the original Pierce frame.

By 1913, Osborn, of 2058 Valentine Avenue, also had "perfected a belt transmission system which is intended to eliminate the most detrimental features of the orthodox belt drive." His means (Patent 1,049,260, December 31, 1912) was the separation of the gear-reduction and belt-drive functions. The former was performed by an internal gear mounted in the rear wheel hub. The belt drive was freed to utilize pulleys of near-equal size, thus achieving "a belt speed more closely approximating the ideal 'mile-a-minute' mark which is laid down in the text books, when the motorcycle is traveling under ordinary conditions and at average speed," according the *Bicycling World*. As an alternative design, Osborn provided for a clutch a belt shifter and two differently sized pulleys, each with attached gearing at the rear wheel to give his motorcycle two forward speeds. Osborn was a prolific inventor, with patents granted to him over a fifty-year period. Whether any motorcycles were built to accommodate Osborn's power-train ideas is unknown here.

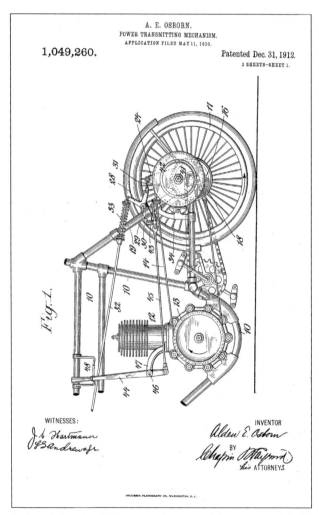

Alden Osborn's 1912 patent drawing of his improved belt-drive system, which utilized equal-size pulleys, thus "more closely approximating the ideal 'mile-a-minute' mark which is laid down in the text books" (*Bicycling World*).

FRONT ROW—E. F. Willis (President) Henry Allmen (Leutenent) Fred'k Thourot, M. E. Toepel, F. B. Widmayer, Hngo Bendic (Secretary.)
REAR ROW—R. G. Betts, Chas. Theile, Henry Glade (Treasure) Geo. B. Jenkins, E. L. Fergerson, D. D. Miller, F. E. Moskovics (Captain) W. F. Widmaysr, H. Jehle, Raymond Douglas.

"A Sunday Run of the New York Motor Cycle Club" The club was formed in late May of 1902. They organized various events to test motorcycles (and riders') abilities. They also advocated for motorcyclist's interests, like better roads. Many of the men listed in this image are also mentioned elsewhere in this book.

Although not an inventor or builder, Ritchie G. Betts, was an editor who wrote for bicycle and motorcycle magazines, he also helped to organize numerous local and national motorcycle organizations. In 1902, the Brooklyn based editor was writing for *The Bicycling World* and a member of at least three motorcycle organizations. His reviews of motorcycles and more are quoted throughout this work. The only woman in the picture is likely R.G.'s wife Susan Betts. Image from *The Bicycling World,* October 30, 1902.

Herman Jehle was a member of the New York Motor Cycle Club and is in the picture above. He is known for his one-off motorcycle that he called "Spiral." Starting around 1896, it is believed that the Spiral evolved and improved with Jehle's interest and abilities. The motorcycle in the 1902 image above appears to be a different machine. This is a picture Jehle's Spiral as it looks today. From the collection of Edward Doering on display at Motorcyclepedia in Newburgh, New York.

Assembled by William Nigro's American Motorcycle Parts, this entirely chromed motorcycle has a 127ci engine and was built in the 1990s. Courtesy of American Motorcycle Parts, www.amcpchoppers.com.

Chaos Cycle's "The Hate Tank," 2013–2016, featuring a rebuilt 1983 80" shovelhead engine sitting in the modified 1937 VL frame. Some of the custom fabricated parts include, gas tank, fender, oil bag, handlebars, jockey shift, foot controls and struts all built by Chaos Cycles' George Stinsman and Patrick McColgan. Courtesy of Courtesy of George T. Stinsman, Chaos Cycle.

Charles Clifford "Cliff" Coleman Jr. and his father Charles C. Coleman Sr. went on a motorcycle trip from Albany to Niagara Falls, sleeping in barns along the way. The Emblem belonged to Cliff and his father rode in the sidecar. According to family, the trip was around 1911–1912. NYSM H-1998.49, H-2021.36.53

Another person who often rode with Cliff was his future wife. Family lore states that Cliff proposed to Stella on this motorcycle ride in 1914, "near Troy Schenectady Road." NYSM H-2021.36.77

Cliff had at least two Emblem motorcycles, the twin cylinder (with sidecar) is a 1914 model and the single cylinder is a 1913 model. NYSM H-1998.49.28

Copper Mike Cole, Gravesend Cycles, built this bike in 2005. Mike named it the "Coppa Choppa," and says that the engine is a "rare 1939 knucklehead motor with a Panhead wishbone frame." He hand hammered the gas tank, fenders and oil tank out of 16 gauge copper. According to Mike the bike was sold to the artist David Uhl and is in his Art studio in Golden Colorado. Courtesy of Copper Mike Cole, Gravesend Cycles.

The "Type57x® Mark I" motorcycle features Terence Musto's (Fabbro Industries) patent integrated suspension frame. This chopper built by Musto has a 1966 Harley-Davidson flatside shovelhead engine and serves as the prototype for the patented frame. The bike also features numerous custom parts designed and built at Fabbro Industries. Photography by Michael Lichter, Courtesy of Terence Musto, Fabbro Industries.

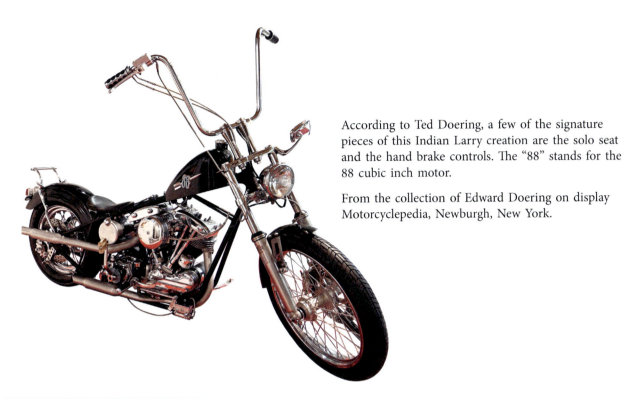

According to Ted Doering, a few of the signature pieces of this Indian Larry creation are the solo seat and the hand brake controls. The "88" stands for the 88 cubic inch motor.

From the collection of Edward Doering on display Motorcyclepedia, Newburgh, New York.

Completed in 2021, CT Newman built this award-winning bike from scratch. Newman notes that "The whole top end of the engine is built from scratch my design, the bottom end is a side valve case. Brake pedal flips up to become [the] Kickstarter." The twin turbo, all stainless-steel motorcycle features 8-valve top ends with a ULH bottom ends, with the heads exposed for viewing with a clear top. Courtesy of Christian Newman, CT Newman Engineering.

Orange County Choppers (OCC) brochure from 2003 (one side of brochure). Note the original Spider-Man bike on the bottom right. Designed by Paul Teutul Jr., this is the motorcycle that kicked off the themed bike movement for OCC. NYSM H-2022.11.2.01.

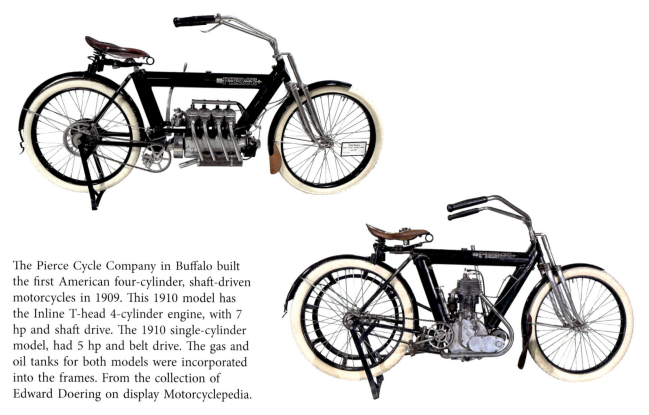

The Pierce Cycle Company in Buffalo built the first American four-cylinder, shaft-driven motorcycles in 1909. This 1910 model has the Inline T-head 4-cylinder engine, with 7 hp and shaft drive. The 1910 single-cylinder model, had 5 hp and belt drive. The gas and oil tanks for both models were incorporated into the frames. From the collection of Edward Doering on display Motorcyclepedia.

The first mass produced motorcycle made in New York State, the Thomas Auto-Bi in 1901 and one of the newest brands to design a motorcycle to be mass produced in America, Tarform Luna.

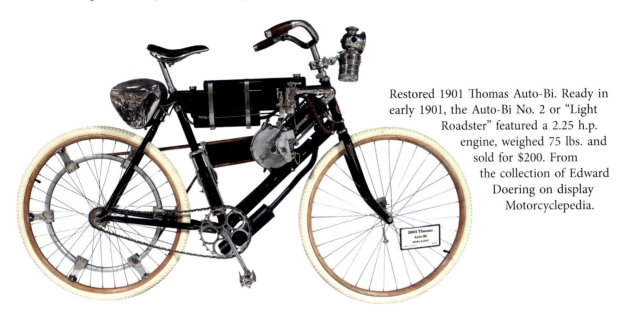

Restored 1901 Thomas Auto-Bi. Ready in early 1901, the Auto-Bi No. 2 or "Light Roadster" featured a 2.25 h.p. engine, weighed 75 lbs. and sold for $200. From the collection of Edward Doering on display Motorcyclepedia.

Tarform Luna electric motorcycle. Photograph by Ryan Handt, courtesy of Tarform.

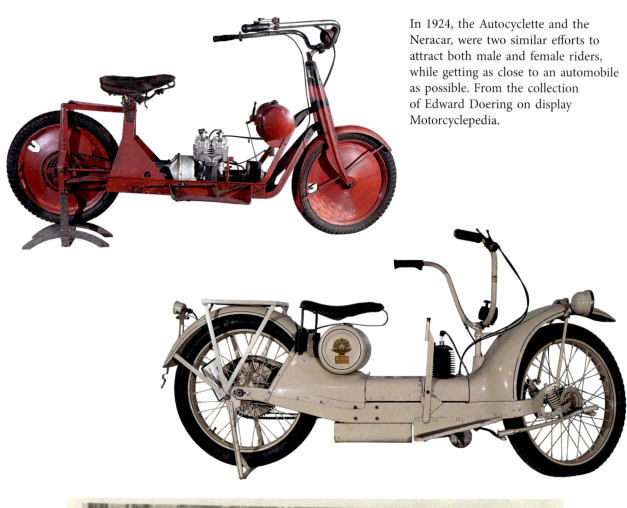

In 1924, the Autocyclette and the Neracar, were two similar efforts to attract both male and female riders, while getting as close to an automobile as possible. From the collection of Edward Doering on display Motorcyclepedia.

Riders lined up with their Emblem motorcycles around 1913, possibly in Albany. Charles Clifford "Cliff" Coleman Jr. of Albany is one in from the right. Note on the far left the motorcycle is equipped with a side-by-side seating arrangement and a single seat on the gas tank for a toddler, complete with foot straps. NYSM H-1998.49.163_01

P

Ira C. Palmer
Buffalo
1912

Motorcycling in the summer of 1912 published a photo of a motorcycle built by Ira C. Palmer (a bicycle and motorcycle repairman at 112 Rodney Avenue) for tandem travel with his wife. The forward part of his machine resembled that of the common diamond-frame-style motorcycle of the day. But where the rear wheel would normally be placed vis-à-vis the front, the Palmer motorcycle inserted additional tubing in the form of a drop-style frame segment for the second rider. The wheelbase measured 82 inches.

Palmer used a 9-horsepower, two-cylinder Spacke engine but fitted his own two-speed transmission, perhaps a planetary type; *Motorcycling* said, "with two large friction discs, the gears are enmeshed at all times." The three-stop lever provided a neutral position. Gear reduction for the chain-drive machine was 7:1 in low and 3.5:1 in high.

Ira Palmer's self-made, 290-pound, chain-drive motorcycle, utilizing a 9-horsepower Spacke engine and Palmer's own two-speed transmission. From *Motorcycling*, August 2, 1912.

Mrs. Palmer had a lazy back attached to her saddle and her own handlebars. The front fork was trussed, but without spring suspension. A band brake was fitted to the rear wheel. The wire spoke wheels had 28-by-2.75-inch tires. An acetylene generator and headlamp provided illumination for night riding. Fenders, a rear stand, and a luggage carrier over the back wheel were additional equipment. *Motorcycling* reported that the Palmers had covered 225 miles a day "with ease" in the course of a 2,000-mile year "thus far this season" in 1912.

Newspaper accounts suggest that Ira may have built at least two other tandems around 1903–7, while living in Fulton, New York.

Paul Jr. Designs
Rock Tavern; Montgomery
2010–present

Paul Teutul Jr. ("Paul Jr.") started working at his father's ironworks in his early teenage years. There he learned the ins and outs of welding and fabricating. In 1995, Paul Jr. and his father, Paul Teutul Sr. ("Paul Sr."), built their first motorcycle together. After five years, Paul Sr. opened Orange County Choppers (q.v.); Paul Jr. served as his lead designer.

In 2001, Orange County Choppers was featured in a television documentary called *American Chopper*. The episode was so popular that it was turned into a series for the Discovery Network. Each episode featured a custom motorcycle build and a volatile father-son dynamic that made for popular TV. Most of the motorcycles Paul Jr. designed for OCC were theme bikes; many credit him for starting this trend.

In 2008, Paul Jr. was fired from OCC by his father. Contractually, Paul Jr. still had to appear on the show, so he served as a consultant for a while. In the meantime, he started Paul Jr. Designs (PJD) out of his home. Due to a noncompete clause in his contract with OCC, he could not build motorcycles for one year. He found work designing products for the Colman Company, who specializes in outdoor recreation products. The main product was a portable grill.

In 2010, Paul Jr. decided he was ready to build custom motorcycles again. At the same time, the producers of *American Chopper* were looking to keep the series going, but without the father-son dynamic it was going to be cancelled. So, they came up with a new format and called it *American Chopper: Senior vs. Junior*. The show now followed both companies as they built a custom motorcycle for each episode and followed the ongoing drama within the family.

Since he decided to get back into the business of building one-of-a-kind motorcycles, Paul Jr. found a shop in Rock Tavern. Running the company with his wife, Rachael, he hired former OCC staff members Vinnie DiMartino, Cody Connelly, Joe Puliafico, and his brother Michael "Mikey" Teutul. Brenden Thomas, a sheet-metal specialist, rounded out the fabrication team. Their first two builds were the "Anti-Venom" and a theme bike called the "GEICO Armed Forces Bike" for the insurance company. Paul Jr. won two Discovery Channel "Biker Build-Offs" and continued to play a role in new variations of *American Chopper* through to 2020.

PJD continues to produce theme bikes, custom motorcycles, and merchandise and will work with customers on unique design needs. In 2021, PJD partnered with Ruff Cycles of Germany to produce an e-bike (electrically powered bicycle). The e-bike was designed by PJD, while the engineering and production was done by Ruff Cycles. The limited-edition e-bike sells for $6,500 in the United States.

Pennsylvania Motor Car Company
New York City (Manhattan)
1910

In September 1910, the *Bicycling World and Motorcycle Review* reported the incorporation of the Pennsylvania Motor Car Company of New York City with "the manufacture of motorcycles as one of the objects of its business." However, the certificate of incorporation, filed on August 22, 1910, notes the manufacture of "cars, carriages, wagons, boats, aeroplanes, dirigible balloons, and vehicles of every kind and description," but not motorcycles specifically. Despite the company name, the principal office for the corporation was in Manhattan. Incorporators and first-year directors were D. Hamilton, A. A. Russell, and L. H. Denny, all of whom had New York City (Bronx and Manhattan) addresses.

Philip Perew
North Tonawanda
ca. 1899

In early 1899, the *Cycling Gazette* reported that Philip Perew was having a motorcycle built "under his direction," which was to use gunpowder as fuel. The description of the motor suggests an internal combustion engine in which "a few grains of the explosive . . . fall into a plunger as the wheel moves along. In the latter is an electric spark, which causes a regular explosion of the powder. . . . The force drives a piston rod, which is attached to the rear wheel. The speed is regulated by the amount of powder allowed to run into the plunger."

According to the story, Perew had patented his invention. A check with patent records, however, fails to find it. There *are* patents granted to "Louis P. Perew" of North Tonawanda in 1899 for a towing system for canal boats, and for a cigar cutter and lighter in 1901. In 1900, the *American Automobile* reported that Louis Perew of Tonawanda had constructed a mechanical man, 7 feet and 5 inches tall: "When properly wound up and connected with an engine the man can walk at a great rate of speed and can pull a heavy load behind it." A phonograph in the chest could "make some sort of an answer" to queries. Perew proposed sending his man "and its wagon" on a New York-to-San Francisco walking tour.

The *Gazette* noted that when Perew announced his motorcycle powered by an explosive, his fellow North Tonawanda residents thought him "gone in his upper story," but Perew reportedly imagined "he is sitting on piles of gold on a high throne, and holding the proud and coveted title of high official and mayor of the town of Tonawanda."

In 1918 *Motorcycling and Bicycling* noted that in September 1900 Herbert E. Fielding of New Haven, Connecticut, also had devised a gunpowder-fueled engine; the "powder fed into the cylinder in small doses and exploded there. . . . The novelty of the idea was its chief attraction, of course, as it never proved especially successful and had no appreciable advantages."

Pierce Cycle Company
Buffalo
1909–14
Trade Name: **Pierce**

Manufactured by men who had built some of the most respected bicycles and automobiles, benefiting from an innovative and successful motorcycle design, and operating at its inception in a successful bicycle factory, the Pierce motorcycle enterprise seemed destined for a long, profitable life. Yet, in spite of its assets, the Pierce company soon found itself in bankruptcy, struggling through reorganization, and within a few years gave up motorcycle construction altogether.

To be sure, the Pierce company bucked the automotive tide that swamped most producers of two-wheel motor vehicles in the 1910s. Because the Pierce machines were priced at the high end of the motorcycle spectrum, their market potential was probably even less than that of cheaper lines, which might have appealed to buyers without sufficient funds for a new car. Yet no matter their short production, Pierce motorcycles are remembered and, in the few cases where machines have survived, treasured for their unique design, high quality, and performance.

The George N. Pierce Company had begun to manufacture high-quality bicycles in the mid-1890s, at the height of the bicycle boom that swept the United States. In 1901, the factory commenced the manufacture of automobiles. From small, one-cylinder runabouts, the Pierce cars evolved quickly to large, luxurious machines. In mid-September 1906, the automobile and bicycle operations became two separate companies. The George N. Pierce Company, later the Pierce-Arrow Motor Car Company, was to survive as a manufacturer of high-quality automobiles for almost thirty more years.

Pierce Cycle Company factory building, now demolished, on Hanover Street in Buffalo. From the *Bicycling World and Motorcycle Review*, December 12, 1908.

The new Pierce Cycle Company was incorporated for the "manufacture and sale of bicycles, tricycles, motor cycles and everything appertaining thereto." Directors were George Pierce, his son Percy P. Pierce, Charles Clifton, William B. Colburn, and Moses Shire. Of the authorized $300,000 in capital stock, two hundred shares with a par value of one hundred dollars each were held by Clifton and the two Pierces. The company began business with $200,000 of capital. The attorneys for the incorporation were from the firm of Shire and Jellinek in Buffalo.

While George Pierce had an office at the bicycle factory, the president and general manager was Percy Pierce (1877 or 1878–1940). He had been involved with the development of the Pierce automobile in the early 1900s, and his name is prominent as the driver of the winning Pierce car in two Glidden reliability tours. Of Percy Pierce's building of bicycles exclusively, the *Bicycling World and Motorcycle Review* said Percy Pierce had turned his back on glamorous days as "champion automobile tourist of the country" to buckle down

George N. Pierce, Buffalo manufacturer. From the *Cycle Age and Trade Review*, April 25, 1901.

"to the business of making Pierce bicycles.... From the time he took up the bicycle business he has never driven an automobile, and it is doubtful that he has even sat in one." The secretary and treasurer of the Pierce Cycle Company was Colburn, a Pierce relative "by marriage." Shire, the corporate director, has been identified as "the Pierce attorney for twenty-five years."

The first four-cylinder Pierce, as announced in late 1908. From *Cycle and Automobile Trade Journal*, December 1908.

The cycle company operated in the former George N. Pierce Company building at 6-22 Hanover Street, and the automobile business moved to a new factory at 1695 Elmwood Avenue. Explaining why the bicycle and automobile endeavors were divided, George Pierce said that the growth of the latter was a critical factor, crowding the former "at every point. Our engines had hardly ceased running for a year, during which time we have worked a full force twenty-three hours a day." And then there was friction among the laborers. "The man working on a fifty dollar bicycle beside a man working on a five thousand dollar automobile were in conflict and their labors could not be made to harmonize."

As early as the fall of 1906, there was word that the Pierce Cycle Company was "preparing to put motorcycles on the market for 1907." The *Bicycling World* waxed philosophical about the news, saying,

> As a sign of the times, it is unusually significant.... For while the Pierce people had not resolutely set themselves against motorcycles they had steadfastly refused to "warm up" over the subject or to display any marked evidence of increasing interest. That they have now "taken up" the power drive bicycle is, therefore fraught with no little meaning.

The Pierce motor bicycle will employ the Thor [Aurora Automatic Machinery Company] engine and carburetor and other components and as the Buffalo manufacturers are sticklers for quality and for the most painstaking workmanship, that their machine will command quick attention goes without saying, as does the assumption that developments and "fine touches" on their own account are possible at all times.

Cycle and Automobile Trade Journal said, "The Pierce motorcycles were being developed in the fall of 1906 but the machines ... [were] ... not far enough advanced to be photographed," although the *Journal*'s "Buyer's Guide" published for January 1907 included the Pierce company as a source of motorcycles. A *Motorcycle Illustrated* list of motorcycle manufacturers printed for November 1906 also included the Pierce Cycle Company.

1909 Model Year

Pittsburgh riders were among the first to see a Pierce machine in the late summer of 1908. The motorcycle was being shipped to St. Louis, but the Pierce Cycle Company employee in charge stopped in Pittsburgh to show it to Banker Brothers, the local Pierce agents. *Motorcycle Illustrated* said the Pierce "was given a thorough trial on Heberton avenue, which is one of the steepest streets in the city," reaching the top 50 feet ahead of a "4½-h. machine of a famous make."

Soon the motorcycle press had details of the "First American Four-Cylinder." Several reports supplemented their descriptions of the new machine with mention of experimental machines. A *Bicycling World* reporter claimed those machines were "of various sorts ... each having been tried out thoroughly on the road" and long familiar to those "in the know." Another writer said that the experimental machines were "all of one type. They are being used in different parts of the country and although thousands of miles have been registered by them, it yet remains to have it reported that one has failed to operate at any time or anywhere. These machines delight in hill climbing. As for starting and running, all that is needed is gasoline and oil." The *World* thought the new Pierce "sensational in that it is the first American four-cylinder machine."

It appears that the FN (q.v.) served as a model for the Pierce, as the Pierce was to inspire other motorcycles. T. A. Hodgdon, in *Motorcycling's Golden Age of the Fours* (1973), notes a trip Percy Pierce made to Europe in 1908, where it was reported he was impressed by the FN four-cylinder, shaft-driven machine and returned with one to Buffalo. However, FN motorcycles had been imported and sold in the United States by the Golden Motor Company of New York City, beginning with the 1906 model year. In October 1905, the Harry Fosdick company of Boston also had "secured rights" to the FN four-cylinder machine. The first American reports of the FN had come a year earlier. Certainly, the Pierce company knew of the FN earlier than Percy Pierce's travels in 1908.

The "sensational" Pierce motorcycle used a T-head, air-cooled engine with a 6-to-7-horsepower rating. The individual cylinders measured 2.1875 by 2.75 inches. Gray iron pistons were fitted with three rings each. All bearings were phosphor bronze. A gear-driven oil pump provided lubrication, an innovation in an era of rider-operated hand pumps. Ignition came from a Bosch magneto with no provision for a battery. Drive to the rear wheel was through bevel gears and a shaft. A multiple disc clutch on the flywheel served to lessen the effect of an otherwise locked engine and transmission. This clutch, however, worked mostly as a shock absorber and could not be disengaged without loosening two bolts. In other words, the engine was always in gear unless two nuts were undone, in which case the engine was completely disengaged, and the machine could be wheeled or pedaled as desired.

The Pierce frame was unusual in that it incorporated the tanks for gasoline and oil within 3.5-inch-diameter tubing. There were precedents for such construction, such as the DeLong (q.v.) motorcycle earlier in the decade, but the Pierce was perhaps the most successful of motorcycles built in that style. The 18-gauge, interior copper-plated gasoline tank held seven quarts, reportedly good for 100 to 150 miles. The oil supply of five pints was sufficient for about 1,000 miles.

The front fork incorporated a combination coil spring and pneumatic shock absorber similar to that on Pierce bicycles, while the rear wheel was fixed to the frame with no suspension. Twenty-eight-inch, wire-spoke wheels were fitted with 2.5-inch-diameter pneumatic tires. The rear fender could be moved on a hinge to allow access to the wheel for tire changing. The rear-mounted stand similarly could be left undisturbed when one was tending to repairs on the wheel. The right twist grip served as compression release control (through sliding the camshaft and thereby raising the exhaust valves) and, with additional motion, as an ignition (retarding) control. The left grip operated the throttle. Both a coaster and a band brake were fitted to the rear wheel.

The Pierce motorcycle was shown at important motor-vehicle expositions during the winter of 1908–9. In New York City at Madison Square Garden, three machines, one all nickeled, were incorporated into the company exhibit. It was noted that "the Pierce company's intention was to give its dealers an option as to equipment. Any standard fittings will be furnished." On the show machines, G & J (Gormully & Jeffery), Morgan & Wright, and Empire tires were mounted, along with Mesinger, Troxel, and Persons saddles. The Pierce company also exhibited at the second big show, in Chicago. And at the Boston auto show in March 1909, W. A. Johnson, sales manager of the Pierce motorcycle department, told *Motorcycle Illustrated* the Pierce motor machine was "a happy venture," and he reportedly "does not have the slightest apprehension on the score that the low price automobile will be preferred to the high price motorcycle."

Pierce advertisements for the first year of the motorcycle emphasized the lack of vibration inherent in the four-cylinder engine. An early ad also noted a "Limited Output . . . offered to the trade for 1909" but sought "responsible contract agencies for both [motorcycle and bicycle] lines." A news story in the *Bicycling World* in late October 1908 quoted the Pierce company as claiming, "We already have allotted three-fourths of our entire motorcycle production for 1909."

Other advertisements tied the common root of the Pierce bicycles, automobiles, and motorcycles, claiming all were the "world's leaders." One ad stated that the Pierce motorcycle could only have been built "by men of skill and experience and only a firm having a wide reputation would dare to venture on the market with such a high class product . . . the same skill which has created PIERCE ARROW CARS and PIERCE BICY-

CLES has produced the PIERCE VIBRATIONLESS MOTORCYCLE. The firm which has built up its reputation on Pierce products now stakes that reputation on the Motorcycle."

1910 Model Year

With the announcement in the fall of 1909 of the 1910 Pierce line, the factory offered buyers a single-cylinder machine. The belt-driven motorcycle sold for one hundred dollars less than the four-cylinder; the *Cycle and Automobile Journal* said that the two models had been "designed and built [each] to supply a certain class of demand."

Although the wheelbase of the new motorcycle was six inches shorter than that of the four-cylinder, the same frame design, with large-diameter tubing forming tanks, prevailed. The fork on the single was identical to that on the larger Pierce. The ball-bearing-equipped ("which alone puts it in a distinctive class among single cylinder machines"), splash-lubricated, 3.5 inch bore by 4-inch stroke engine produced 5 horsepower and gave the single the same 60-miles-per-hour top speed rating as the four-cylinder. Transmission to the rear wheel was by flat leather belt adjusted by an idler controlled by a lever on the left side of the frame. The smaller Pierce was equipped with a single Corbin brake.

The four-cylinder Pierce received significant additions for the 1910 year, with a two-speed, sliding-gear transmission as well as a working multiple disc clutch, both controlled by a single lever. "Nickel steel gears, heat-treated and tempered," were used. Gear ratios were 4.125:1 in high and 7.125:1 in low. The English *Motor Cycle* was quoted in January 1910 by the American *Motorcycling* as claiming the Pierce two-speed gear "fool-proof, being in that respect like the gear on an English machine, the F.N."

According to *Cycle and Automobile Trade Journal*, the four-cylinder engine, "a replica in miniature of the engine used in the Pierce Great Arrow automobile," itself underwent enlargement, with cylinders now measuring 2.4375 by 2.375 inches. The flywheel increased 1.5 inches in diameter, bearings were fitted with "Parson's white brass" bushings, and a well in the crankcase fed the lubricating pump. Another change to the four was a wider rear stand. A Breeze carburetor, on both engines, was expected to produce "much better results . . . than was the case during 1909, when a few Pierce riders experienced carburetor troubles."

Of the motorcycles' builder, *Motorcycling*'s writer said there was "no more sensible conservative concern in the business" than the Pierce company. The four-cylinder motorcycle was a "fine, efficient auto-on-two-wheels," and the single "given recognition even before its actual marketing, through the reputation of its makers for making good. They say it runs very quietly and steadily."

On the West Coast, the Pierce Cycle Company in Oakland, California, established a branch managed by Fred L. Brown. The separate Pierce motorcycle and bicycle dealer in Oakland was the J. T. Chick Motor Company. And there was a Pierce Motorcycle Club in that city that, said *Motorcycling*, could "be found on the roads any pleasant Sunday or holiday, and take many long trips together." Among the riders were Brown, Chick, and "substantial business men, who have gone through the old bicycle game and are now enthusiastic motorcyclists."

In the spring of 1910, the Detroit motorcycle debuted in Detroit, Michigan. The one-cylinder machine was remarkable in its similarities to the smaller Pierce, with large-diameter frame tubes enclosing the gasoline and oil supplies. In the Detroit, designed by George W. Breed, the muffler, as well, was enclosed within the frame; positioned below the oil supply in the down tube, the muffler kept the oil "at the proper consistency" and emptied exhaust gas on the ground rather than "ruining the back tire." With a 4-horsepower engine, the Detroit listed at $210.

Unlike some other motorcycle manufacturers, the Pierce company did not participate in competitive events. Of course, individual Pierce riders did enter endurance runs. And the makers were pleased to acknowledge notable performances—for example, that of R. J. Connor (*sic*; probably L. W. Connor) of Oakland, who, with a perfect score and averaging 83 miles per gallon of gasoline on a single-cylinder Pierce, was one of nine riders to finish a 250-mile San Francisco endurance run in late 1910. Pierce sales manager Johnson said a four-cylinder Pierce was the first motor vehicle to climb Boston Hill near Buffalo, "a hill no other had been able to climb." Johnson told *Motorcycling* that the machine with standard gearing covered the 2.5 miles at a speed between 20 and 25 miles per hour, over "sand, soil and gravel and skull-like rocks." Johnson said he "knows the hill is there. He climbed it once with horse and buggy, or rather the horse climbed with the buggy, and the writer [Johnson] climbed by himself. He has vivid recollections of figuring the gradient of the hill at that time as being 199 per cent."

On March 23, 1910, George N. Pierce succumbed to heart disease at the age of sixty-four. He had severed his involvement (selling his stock) with the Pierce-Arrow Motor Car Company in 1908. For the next two years, according to one story, George Pierce retained a desk at the Pierce Cycle Company office but "occupied it only when he felt like it and gave himself up to travel." While George Pierce had remained a director of the Pierce Cycle Company, his son, Percy P. Pierce, said his father's death would not detract from the son's "devotion to it." In early August 1910, involuntary bankruptcy proceedings were brought against the Pierce Cycle Company in federal court after petitions were filed by creditors Donald S. McKay, Conrad J. Lang, and Gustav Benjamin, who together had claims amounting to one thousand dollars. To many, the receivership was a surprise, but explanations were quick to follow. *Motorcycling* said, "It has been known in trade circles for some time that the company was having hard sledding because of slowness in meeting its outstandings . . . the sales end of the company . . . until recently has produced more sales than the making end could take care of." The *Bicycling World* said that a "lack of sufficient ready cash capital to meet the conditions imposed by the production of four-cylinder and single cylinder motorcycles on a large scale is assigned the chief cause of the present embarrassment. Many deliveries were so late that agents refused to accept them." Johnson said the "receivership was made necessary by the tying up of our assets in stock taking the form of raw material, goods in process of construction, commercial parts, equipment, etc.," according to *Motorcycle Illustrated*.

It was those "very facts," Johnson continued, that would enable the Pierce company to prepare for the 1911 season earlier in the calendar year than had been the case previously. "The outlook is very bright," he said, "and because of the excellent showing which our machines have been making, we never felt quite so enthusiastic concerning the future possibilities for the sale of our motorcycles as we do at the present moment." Outside observers also were optimistic. A *Motorcycle Illustrated* writer thought the company "by no means in a hopelessly disordered condition, and it is generally believed that a re-organization will be possible." *Motorcycling* said that George Pierce's death had left "a considerable estate" and that in spite of Percy Pierce's reluctance to speak of the affair, "it has been taken for granted that the Pierce interests which control the business would personally float the ship as a matter of pride in the name." If for some reason the reorganization failed, the journal noted, Johnson, with a "deservedly high reputation both as a man and as a salesman . . . should be very valuable to any motorcycle maker."

William Colburn, secretary and treasurer of the Pierce company, spoke out, saying, "The reorganization will be accomplished as speedily as possible, probably inside of the year. We are thoroughly solvent. Our stock, machinery and accounts receivable will probably reach $500,000, and our liabilities do not come within a third of that amount. It is simply a case of not having the ready cash, due to delays in getting out the goods. Considerable delay occurred last winter in the shipment of castings and other parts for the 1910 single cylinder motorcycle, but the production is running smoothly now." The appointed receivers for the Pierce company were the lawyers Lawrence P. Hancock and Matthew W. Bennett. They indicated that the business would continue. At the end of August, an inventory was underway in preparation for an appraisal, but the word at that point was that the "company is perfectly solvent and that there is not the slightest danger of its not paying every creditor in full."

In April 1910, Percy Pierce represented his company at a Motorcycle Manufacturers' Association meeting at the Hotel Statler in Buffalo. But by the time of the October meeting of the MMA in Buffalo, Percy Pierce was gone from the Pierce Cycle Company, whose interests at the meeting were represented by Colburn. Percy Pierce's resignation as MMA treasurer was accepted.

1911 Model Year

Pierce motorcycles continued in the 1911 model year to impress riders and enthusiasts around the world. In January the first English agent, L. F. Jones, was announced, in Wold Newton, Hummanby, Yorkshire; he was going to handle both one- and four-cylinder machines. In September 1911, the first Japanese agency for Pierce machines was closed by Maruishi Shokai of Yokohama. *Motorcycling* reported the "Pierce people believe this is the start of a large amount of business which may be done in the Orient." In Argentina, at a commercial exhibition to celebrate the centennial of the republic, Pierce received the grand prize in the motorcycle exhibit. In all, Pierce motorcycles were sold in fourteen countries beyond the United States borders. While one might think that the closest large Canadian city to Buffalo would be a good market for Pierce motorcycles, a survey of machines at a Toronto gathering in the summer of 1911 showed only two Pierce motorcycles among ninety-six machines and twenty different American, Canadian, and European trade names.

Argentinean dealer Juan T. Billiet on his 1909 Pierce four-cylinder motorcycle. The *Bicycling World and Motorcycle Review* said that in Buenos Aires the Pierce was "in rivalry with European machines" (March 25, 1911).

Pierce factory representatives often traveled by motorcycle rather than train in many of the eastern and "Central-Western" states as well as the "Pacific Coast Territory." *Motorcycling* noted that all but one or two of the Pierce men were on motorcycles "soliciting bicycle and motorcycle business." Motorcycles reportedly were just as reliable as trains. And while commercial travelers on the railroad could make only two towns a day, the motorcyclists could cover as many as a dozen. Another advantage to a salesman on a motorcycle, of course, was that he "had his merchandise right with him." In all, the Pierce company claimed a "few hundred" American dealers. A list of thirty-one sellers within a Pierce advertisement named the agents in "the census of important cities." The inclusion of Scranton combined with the absence of Baltimore and Atlanta suggests a less than comprehensive distribution. On the West Coast in January 1911, the Pierce Cycle Company branch took over "the retail end of the business for Alameda County, Calif.," and announced it would sell from its distribution offices in Oakland. Fred Brown, who had been the Pierce branch manager, was to take charge of both wholesale and retail efforts, assisted by Connor, the "enthusiastic rider in that section."

The factory organization for 1911 was in the hands of Superintendent Henry J. Biggam, who had joined the Pierce firm in January 1910 after years of varied experience as machinist, salesman, electrician, model maker, bicycle dealer and builder, founder, soldier, and finally toolmaker in the Northway truck factory in Detroit. In the spring of 1911, L. J. Berger, editor of *Motorcycling*, visited the Pierce factory and noted that the "force was very busy when the writer was there last week and there was a big array of both the single and the 4-cylinder ready to ship, and Sales Manager Johnson expects a very good season." Earlier in the year, *Motorcycle Illustrated* noted that each Pierce motorcycle was road tested from 25 to 100 miles before shipment.

Four-cylinder 1911 Pierce with two-speed transmission. Note the long hand-shift lever. From the *Bicycling World and Motorcycle Review*, April 29, 1911.

The motorcycles Biggam and his colleagues built for the 1911 model year were refinements of the previous machines. A *Cycle and Automobile Trade Journal*

Belt-drive Pierce single for the 1911 season. From the *Bicycling World and Motorcycle Review*, April 29, 1911.

preview in August 1910 noted alterations to the single, with mention of a changed muffler, a modified piston, a different gear ratio, and provision for adjustment to compensate for the stretching of the drive belt. The four-cylinder was to receive a similar once-over, "nothing radical but rather small alterations and additional features" to halt waste of oil, stop loosening of gears on the drive shaft, and provide improvement in the "general efficiency." *Motorcycling* said there were "no radical changes" but "a great deal of detail refinement," with about one hundred changes to the two models, including, on the four-cylinder, larger piston rings, a "remodeled oiling system," a change in the clutch, mudguards, stand supports, and some different materials "in various parts of the machine."

In the summer of 1911, another motorcycle similar to the Pierce single was announced in Detroit. The Breed closely resembled the Detroit machine introduced a year previous, an understandable similarity since George W. Breed had been the designer of the latter and was president of the company building the newer machine. The Breed Manufacturing Company utilized a single-cylinder, overhead-valve Waverley engine, while the Detroit Motorcycle Company, organized in December 1910, installed a side-valve engine in their motorcycle. The Detroit equipped with magneto ignition cost $250, the same as the Pierce, but the Detroit's 60-inch wheelbase was 6 inches longer than the Pierce's. Both the Detroit and Breed machines utilized tanks within frame members, a design similarity that complemented the Pierce if it did not try to attract potential Pierce customers. Detroit and Breed motorcycles both had minimal sales and short life spans.

In July 1911, the Federation of American Motorcyclists (FAM) held their annual meeting in Buffalo. The Pierce company invited participants to visit their factory. In the FAM parade, seventy-one Pierce riders, many of them in shirts emblazoned with the Pierce name, represented almost a third of the estimated 250 riding members.

For the 1911 calendar year, the Pierce Cycle Company operated under the administration of the receivers Hancock and Bennett. The trade press in September noted that the business had turned a profit of $17,000 in the past year, "has been making headway, and apparently will, before long, be again in the hands of its stock holders." Hancock and Bennett, however, recommended that they be left in charge for another year "to clinch the improved business methods installed," among which were more Pierce agencies than ever before, the creation of a "repairs and parts" department, and the introduction of a "factory cost system." Everyday operation was in the hands of Colburn ("accounting") and Johnson ("sales"), "two competent department heads retained from the previous regime." Two months later, conditions were not quite so favorable, as Hancock and Bennett applied to the United States District Court for permission to borrow up to $60,000 to satisfy a need for "some ready cash." *Motorcycling* thought the authority to borrow would be granted on November 10. Both Pierce receivers, Hancock and Bennett, reportedly were motorcycle enthusiasts; Bennett rode a four-cylinder machine daily. Many factory employees rode also, making Hanover Street seem like the site of a "daily series of club runs."

1912 Model Year

The 1912 Pierce motorcycles, announced in October 1911, continued basically as the one- and four-cylinder offerings of the previous year. The most notable difference for 1912 was the arrangement of the one-cylinder line in three versions, known as 12A, 12B, and 12C. Visually, the most obvious change in appearance was a shortening of the frame head and spring housing, with a lowering of the handlebars.

The 12A, the price leader, was "practically the same as the 1911 single," according to *Motorcycling*. At $225, it was $25 cheaper than its predecessor. Improvements included reinforcement of the frame as well as minor modification (piston rings and timing gear mounting) of the engine, which was still rated at 5 horsepower. A band brake replaced the internal hub brake.

The 12B, at $250, had a longer stroke, larger valves, twin cams, and different cooling fins. While nominally rated at 5 horsepower, *Motorcycle Illustrated* noted the engine actually produced about 5.5 in test. Roller bearings were fitted to the connecting rod. A leather-faced wooden pulley replaced the steel type formerly used on the rear wheel.

The 12C, at $265, was similar to the 12B except for a Spartan-brand V-drive belt (contrasting with the flat belts on the other two singles) and a hand-lever-operated Eclipse clutch ("free-engine pulley"). A Pierce advertisement in October 1911 claimed that the "advance sale is very heavy on this model and 12B."

The four-cylinder Pierce for 1912 listed at $400. It benefited, as did the 12B and 12C, from the installation of an oil sight tube outside the crankcase, which allowed the rider to check on the level of oil within the engine. The three more expensive Pierce machines also had compound springs in the front fork instead of the single spring used on the price leader. All 1912 Pierce motorcycles had new, larger-diameter handlebars and easier operating twist controls. Another general Pierce offering was a $7.50 tubular luggage carrier to be fitted over the rear wheel. It was "made to bear an enormous load." Other options for Pierce motorcycles included $18 tandem equipment, $20 Stewart speedometer, $5 gas lamps (with or without generator), $10 Prestolite tank, and oil at $1.25 per gallon.

The four-cylinder had a new lubrication system with a rotary pump at the front of the crankcase, a new drive shaft with tapered gear seats to prevent stripping (such seats were also used on the fitting of the flywheel to the crankshaft), different mounting of the transmission gears, a shift lever moved from the left to the right to avoid cross-handed gear changes, and some other minor improvements. The aluminum engine case was to be polished, noted *Motorcycling*, "adding greatly to the appearance and cleanliness."

Pierce Vibrationless Motorcycles (1912), the Pierce Cycle Company catalog, said, "Just as Pierce bicycles for over twenty years have stood in advance of all competition, and Pierce-Arrow Motor Cars are everywhere recognized as the world's leading automobile, so Pierce motorcycles have earned ascendency over all other makes."

Motorcycle Illustrated, in describing the new Pierce motorcycles, wrote lavishly of Pierce engineering and production standards, in which

> costly experiments have been resorted to, and every part which seemed susceptible of improvement has received the attention of the designers. In the Pierce plant is found every facility known to modern shop practice and the company's staff embraces some of the ablest motorcycle mechanics in the East. The firm's policy has been one of true economy; there has been no sacrifice of quality in the attainment of low producing rates, and as a result the present prices are the lowest that can reasonably be expected.

Pierce machines for 1912 were subjected to rigorous testing. Engines were reportedly belt driven for six hours and then run four to six hours on their own power. Single-cylinder machines were scheduled for 75 miles of road testing, while fours were to be ridden 100 miles. The single was reported to reach 65 miles per hour on a stretch of road between Riverside Park in Buffalo and Tonawanda. Eight men employed as road testers were "kept constantly at this work." The *Bicycling World* reported that "present schedules call for 1,500 machines, of which 1,000 will be singles."

Pierce motorcycles for 1912 went to a variety of foreign countries, including South Africa, England, Uruguay, Ecuador, Brazil, Mexico, and Japan. An exporter in New York handled many of the Pierce overseas sales; the agent "pays cash for [the motorcycles] in New York, subject to a fee for his services as banker and forwarder," said *Motorcycling*.

As a result of the sale of eleven four-cylinder motorcycles to the government of the Philippine Islands in 1912, followed by "satisfactory work and service" by the machines, the Pierce company in January 1913 was able to place an agency with Winser and Company in Manila, which had ordered twenty-seven one- and four-cylinder models. *Motorcycling* credited Johnson's letter-writing skills with Pierce's success in distributing the motorcycles so widely: "far beyond where his personal presence is known, go his letters, which are cut from the same [wholesome] pattern as the man. From Bangor . . . to Buenos Ayres [sic], they get Johnson letters, if they do not meet Johnson himself; for Pierce motorcycles and bicycles are everywhere. Not quite thick as flies, but emphasized as to quality."

In the fall of 1911, there were claims that the 1912 Pierce motorcycle output was practically one-third sold, with dealers doubling or trebling their 1911 orders. "Indefinite contracts are replaced by early specified dates." At the beginning of June 1912, the Pierce Cycle Company claimed that its motorcycles were sold by 350 US dealers as well as forty-two agents in seventeen foreign countries.

An indication of the market percentage achieved by the Pierce company in the domestic market might be distilled from a survey of 385 riders who attended a FAM convention in Columbus, Ohio, in the summer of 1912. Of the motorcycles present, three were Pierces. FAM members did not necessarily mirror the motorcycle-buying preferences of the general riding public, and a more useful figure for understanding Pierce's success during 1912 would be absolute production figures for each manufacturer. Even then, with Pierce machines sold to riders who could afford more expensive motorcycles than other buyers, numbers would not necessarily point to success or failure. Production was up in 1912. In June, the *Automobile Trade Journal* (formerly the *Cycle and Automobile Trade Journal*) indicated that the factory was turning out ten single-cylinder and five four-cylinder motorcycles every day. For a six-day week, that would mean ninety machines, or roughly four hundred per month.

At the end of 1913, Massachusetts rider H. C. Wing wrote an article for *Motorcycle Illustrated* entitled "What It Cost Me to Ride 12,000 Miles." During the 1911 season, when he began his travels, and during 1913, when he finished his latest ride, he was on Indian motorcycles. During 1912, however, when he had a Pierce agency, he operated two different four-cylinder Pierce machines. The first of the fours he rode from January 27 until December 10, when it was destroyed by fire. Covering 5,162 miles on the two motorcycles, he averaged 70 miles to the gallon of gasoline and 100 miles to the quart of oil (74 gallons at $.20 each and 52 quarts also at $.20). Wing paid $320 for his first machine but does not specify whether it was new or used when he acquired it. Since he was a dealer, one is inclined to assume that the $320 figure was his dealer cost for a new motorcycle.

On the job at the Pierce plant for the beginning of the 1912 model run were Johnson as sales manager, Biggam as superintendent, Colburn as buyer, and (Charles G.?) Kaelin as mechanical engineer. Hancock and Bennett remained receivers. Total employment at one point during 1912 for the Pierce Cycle Company was 249 people. Of this number, nine were in the office force. There were 236 "men in shop" and four "children 14–16 in shop," according to the New York State Department of Labor's *First Annual Industrial Directory of New York State*. At the end of April, daily production was ten singles and five four-cylinder machines. Two hundred fifty men in fourteen departments, likely including bicycle builders, shared a weekly wage distribution of $3,500.

At the Pierce company, all machining was done at the factory. A "rigid inspection system, applied from raw material to finish [sic] motorcycle, is one of the things of which the organization is considerably proud." The only parts purchased from outside the company were such standard items as tires, belts, magnetos, and wheel hubs. It was noted that for "the motor brake test, before mounting in the frame, the propeller fan system is employed."

On June 3, Johnson wrote Greenfield, Massachusetts, dealer Wing that the Model 12A was available at $165, to be sold at $225, with the Eclipse clutch $10 extra. The four-cylinder model listing at $350, "net to you," was $280. There were "only a limited number of them left and we wish you to see your way clear to handle a few of them," he wrote.

Calendar year 1912 began with the Pierce Cycle Company still under the supervision of the receiver Lawrence P. Hancock; the coreceiver Bennett was no longer involved. In an early January meeting of Pierce creditors, Hancock was appointed as trustee for a period of ninety days. *Motorcycling* explained to its readers that a trustee had more authority than a receiver. The *Bicycling World* pointed out that the change was going to "impose considerable extra work for making reports and adjusting the affairs of the company so as to close the receivership." The change and extra work "deferred the payment of current accounts," which Hancock had proposed to begin paying on February 1. However, said *Motorcycling*, "The Pierce business is in good shape, and there is even a likelihood of some new capital being interested, and the concern being taken out of the court's jurisdiction entirely." The journal on February 1 reported that Hancock had made a "conclusive denial" that he was winding up the Pierce affairs. Subsequently, Hancock filed a petition to continue business for not more than sixty days from June 10. Creditors were duly notified.

With authority to operate the Pierce company expiring on September 9, a meeting of Pierce creditors was called for September 12 at the Federal Building in Buffalo before bankruptcy referee Barber S. Conable. At that gathering, on the motion of the creditors' and trustee's attorney Edward L. Jellinek, it was decided to settle company affairs by selling the plant on October 2.

The *Bicycling World* noted that the cost of "developing the motorcycle business was enormous, and during 1910 the company became financially involved, which precipitated a receivership on August 10, 1910." The *World* also reported a 50 percent increase in business and continued by stating that Pierce motorcycles, "little known in 1910, are now sold in all parts of the world and are everywhere famous for their design and construction." The *World* concluded by predicting that the plant would be sold "to an organization amply capitalized to continue the manufacture of both bicycles and motorcycles. It will probably be only a matter of three or four weeks before active production will be resumed. . . . The manufacturing and selling organizations are intact and will undoubtedly continue under the new control."

Motorcycling speculated about the Pierce company's bank, which would act to protect its interests, while Pierce stockholders lacked "harmonious feeling between them" and might not be inclined to acquire the business. In all, it seemed a fine chance for "an outside man" to acquire the Pierce concern at perhaps $50,000 to $75,000, free and clear.

In mid-September, the sale advertisement appeared, signed by Hancock as "Trustee in Bankruptcy." Included were to be the entire plant, stock in trade, and good will. Inventory to be auctioned included machinery and tools valued at $83,000 as well as bicycles, motorcycles, and raw materials valued at $180,000. And, as broadcast by the trade papers, the notice reported that business had improved 30 percent during the past year. Terms of the sale were given elsewhere as 5 percent down and the remainder within five days of sale consummation. All assets except accounts receivable were to be transferred. Included were the plant and the branch in Oakland, California. *Motorcycling*'s estimate of the value of the plant and machinery was $97,000; of the finished goods and raw materials, $125,000; and of the other assets, $10,000.

The sale to "New York Capitalists" (*Bicycling World*) or "Brokers" (*Motorcycling*) took place as scheduled; Joseph Frankel of New York City was the purchaser of record at $70,650. Frankel reportedly was in a partnership with William Wooster, Theodore Friedeberg, and R. J. Metzler. The *World*, saying, "It is a known fact that the new owners are willing to sell again," reported that they preferred to sell as a lot, so that the offers for the machinery were not being considered. "Prominent men in town are interested in a movement to maintain the plant as a producer, and the purchasers will talk the matter over with them before disposing of the property elsewhere."

In mid-October came news that the brokers had decided to operate the plant themselves. While the factory staff would remain, new officers would govern under new papers of incorporation, to be drawn up on October 29. New models for 1913 were to be ready by January 1, and a production run of five thousand motorcycles was expected. William Wooster, acting as general manager, noted, "There are tremendous possibilities in this, and we intend to develop them fully. I would not take a large sum of money for the Pierce name alone, with the prestige it carries. We have a big quantity of orders on hand right now, and as soon as we get everything working smoothly, as it will after we have handled it a little while, we will have a great business."

The new owners were reportedly negotiating with W. A. Johnson, the former sales manager, for a "higher position, as he is well thought of by Mr. Wooster." Other news included the announcement of a two-cylinder machine, the designer for which was on his way to Buffalo; the expansion of the bicycle business; the continued activities of Hancock, being assisted by "Mr. Seelbach, who was the western representative" in concluding work on bills receivable; and a visit from Edward H. Hinsman of the Pope Manufacturing Company in Westfield, Massachusetts, to give "some ideas on the [Pierce] company's plant."

In a *Motorcycling* story dated October 12, 1912, Johnson said that, as sales manager, he would endeavor to raise the "high standard of quality" while "increasing output." In the previous week Johnson had been out making contracts for "a large number of machines." With the startling news that Percy Pierce, "formerly head of the company, is to become connected with it again," the reorganization meeting was postponed until November 10.

The *Bicycling World and Motorcycle Review*, in a story dated Saturday, November 2, announced Pierce's purchase in New York City from Frankel and his associates of the "plant, machinery, stock fixtures and good will of the Pierce Cycle Co." under terms "not disclosed by the purchaser or the former proprietors." Pierce said from New York,

> I have just bought the plant, and am anxious to catch the 'Black Diamond' express [train], so as to reach home as quickly as possible. This much you can say: That plans are already made for the future development of the Pierce interests, and that the high standard of quality of the past will be rigidly maintained, and the goods will be produced in larger quantities than ever before. The company's corporate title will remain practically the same, and Mr. Johnson will be sales manager.

Both *Motorcycle Illustrated* and *Motorcycling* apparently used the same press release in their November 14 issues to report that Percy Pierce was forming a $250,000 company to take over the assets of the Pierce company. The *Automobile Trade Journal* joined other periodicals in reporting that the factory was operating at about half capacity. Supplies were being bought "constantly" so that production could proceed without any delays. Special price quotations were canceled as of November 7, so that motorcycle prices were again those in the 1912 sales contracts. Johnson was soon to leave on a trip to the West Coast; on his return he was to stop at all the important cities to arrange agencies for the 1913 models. Preparations for those new machines were underway, and their announcement was expected in about two weeks, at the end of

November. With a twin added to the line, Pierce would be the sole producer of one-, two-, and four-cylinder motorcycles. The *Bicycling World* reported the Pierce "people feel that they will be able to dominate the high-class motorcycle trade."

1913 Model Year

A significant departure for the Pierce company in the winter of 1913 was that of Johnson, who left for Akron, Ohio, and a position as assistant automobile tire manager with the B. F. Goodrich Company. Johnson had been a major figure in Pierce motorcycle operations. For eleven years, according to *Motorcycling*, Johnson had "enjoyed the most pleasant relations with the heads of the concern." In April, Fred Brown, manager of the Pierce company's West Coast branch in Oakland, arrived in Buffalo to take over Johnson's position as sales manager.

In January, reorganization plans for the Pierce company were reported complete, with Percy Pierce in full charge. "All departments in the Buffalo factory are being operated, and orders of 1913 motorcycles and bicycles are being shipped regularly. It is stated that orders now on hand will keep the factory busy until well along in May," said *Motorcycle Illustrated*. In March, the Pierce Cycle Company was reincorporated with Percy Pierce as president and general manager. Other officers were William H. Barr, vice president; M. W. Comstock, "a Buffalo attorney," secretary; and Theodore Friedeberg of New York, the fourth member of the board. Capitalization was $250,000. The *Bicycling World* reported the factory was "working fullforce, 60 hours a week, producing Pierce bicycles and motorcycles as heretofore." Friedeberg, it will be remembered, was part of the syndicate that bought the Pierce Cycle Company at auction in October 1912. He was probably now on the board to protect the syndicate's interest until Pierce could complete his purchase of the assets.

In February, *Motorcycling* reported additional information about the reorganization, showing that the Pierce Cycle Company was "gradually getting on its feet on a more independent basis than formerly." Percy Pierce, when he reportedly "joined the company recently on a partnership arrangement," had secured an option from Frankel and the other owners of the factory to buy them out by April 1, 1913. Pierce was now ready to consummate that deal. Of the $250,000 capitalization, it was noted that $100,000 was in preferred and $150,000 in common stock, the latter held by Percy Pierce. The former was "subscribed by local people and this will be used as the working capital with which to carry on 1913 production."

Between October 1, 1912, and September 30, 1913, the New York State Department of Labor surveyed the Pierce Cycle Company for the *Second Annual Directory of New York State*. The Pierce company, which gave its primary business as motorcycles, reported thirty-one men in the shop plus eight in the office force. Compared to the number of Pierce Cycle Company employees noted for the preparation of the first directory about a year earlier, the company, during or following the reorganization by Percy Pierce, operated with many fewer men. In contrast to the modest size of the Pierce Cycle Company staffing, the Pierce-Arrow Motor Car Company employed 3,333 people.

At the end of 1912, there was a major change in the Pierce distribution policy. In the past, the Pierce Cycle Company and its predecessor, George N. Pierce Company, had sold directly to dealers, "covering the entire country by salesmen" and maintaining the branch in Oakland. Now it was intended to work through distributors "at various strategical points in the country" while maintaining "salesmen in the field cooperating with the distributors." Johnson reportedly had traveled to "the important centers of the country" and made arrangements with several firms, "all of whom have arranged to carry stock parts and are empowered to give exclusive selling contracts to agents in behalf of the Pierce."

These nine distributors covered only a fraction of United States territory. The Pierce company claimed that under "the guidance of Percy P. Pierce, the old policy, which is so well known, will be maintained. We assure dealers and riders our hearty co-operation. We request dealers to write us for territory now. We are closing contracts every day, and now is the time for you to secure the Pierce Agency, before it is too late." Among the distributors was F. A. Baker and Company in New York City for "Greater New York," Long Island, and northern New Jersey. The Baker company, at least for a period in the winter and spring of 1913, competed for sales with the Pierce company as the former advertised single-cylinder Pierce motorcycles for $165. Called the "5-36" (5 horsepower and 36 cubic inches), these appear to have been the 1912 Model 12A motorcycles. A Baker advertisement offered a "limited number of these machines to dealers." This stock had been built during the summer and fall of 1912 and apparently kept from distribution during the period in which the factory was auctioned. Rather than dispose of the motorcycles, the Pierce company sold them to the Baker firm.

The Pierce company gave up its Oakland branch with the new distribution system, eliminating the need to replace Brown as West Coast manager. It seems likely that the number of Pierce salespeople also would have diminished. On the other hand, by installing a new layer of exchange between manufacturer and user, the factory reduced the potential profit on each motorcycle shipped.

In April, the Pierce factory replied to a *Motorcycling* inquiry about business conditions by reporting that their trade was 25 percent ahead of 1912. Orders were coming in "from all sides" for both one- and four-cylinder machines. Specifications for 350 machines in addition to those contracted for had just been received. Old agents were reportedly showing their loyalty to the reorganized Pierce Cycle Company under Percy P. Pierce. At the end of the month, the Pierce factory was working overtime. Carloads of motorcycles recently had been shipped to Boston and California. And a "number" of orders for four-cylinder machines had been received from Spain and Sweden.

By early-twenty-first-century standards, Pierce sales were tiny. Just in boasting in May 1913 that "repeat orders alone for 1913 Singles and Fours" caused the factory to order "raw material sufficient to produce 200 singles and 150 fours," the company claimed that "once again will the Pierce be a mighty factor in the Motorcycle industry." At the relatively small factory immediately following reorganization, "orders came in faster than we could handle them. But we have ample facilities and sufficient capital to meet all demands." *Motorcycling* reported the 350 additional machines had been specified "to take care of overflow orders outside of regular contracts."

The Pierce motorcycles were displayed for a week in January at the annual show held at the Grand Central Plaza. Johnson was on hand, with Percy Pierce expected toward the end of the week-long affair. Johnson, still sales manager at that point, signed an agreement at the show with John W. Wilson of Boston "to act as representative for the Pierce in the New England States, which includes both motorcycles and bicycles." Wilson's initial order was for 150 machines, both one- and four-cylinder types. The Pierce display consisted of one example each of the two motorcycle models plus "parts in the rough and finished states" as "an interesting feature of the exhibit." In describing the Pierce motorcycles at the Plaza, *Motorcycling*'s writer paid the frame a backhanded compliment, saying that when introduced the Pierce machines "were looked upon as largely in the nature of a freak," but now, after "several seasons of hard service . . . there is no longer any question of the stability of the frame."

The Pierce motorcycles for 1913 were among the last of the industry's new lines to be announced, the information reaching the trade press in early December 1912. The alterations to the one- and four-cylinder machines were minor, and the company subtitled its "Fifth Annual Announcement" with the "Tried and True" motto, which had long been used for Pierce bicycles. Perhaps the most significant addition to the motorcycles was a combined coil spring and pneumatic suspension system, similar to that in the fork, fitted under the saddle. The fenders on both machines were extended to the sides, front, and rear.

There were two versions of the single-cylinder Pierce for 1913. The model 13A had ball bearings in the engine, a stroke one-quarter of an inch less that the 4-inch specification for the Model 13B, and tires 2.5 inches in diameter instead of 2.75. The 13B was available with either flat or V-belt, effectively replacing Models 12B and 12C of the previous season. The 13B was fitted with improved roller bearings in the engine. The four-cylinder received a "very slight readjustment of the oiling system . . . just a trifle more oil will be fed to bearings and cylinder walls." A priming cup was installed on the four-cylinder, as were footrests in addition to pedals. Another change was a switch on the four-cylinder, and likely the (two) singles as well, to the Berling magneto made by the Ericsson Manufacturing Company of Buffalo.

1914 Model Year

As early as December 1912, *Motorcycling* had reported that the Pierce Cycle Company was going to market a two-cylinder motorcycle sometime around July 1913. In January 1913, the *Bicycling World* went so far as to describe the Pierce twin frame as a rigid (as opposed to rear-suspension) type. In May 1913, there was a *Motorcycling* story based on "reliable authority" that the Pierce Cycle Company had decided to replace their four-cylinder machine with a "big 10 h.p. twin, with a single-cylinder as the second string. The engines will be something like the DeLuxe, with Pierce ideas added." Certainly, there was incentive for Pierce to market a twin, given the increasing popularity of two-cylinder motorcycles across the industry. The Pierce dealer in Elmira, for example—who also sold Yale, Pope, and Monarch machines—said in the early spring of 1913 that he expected 50 percent of his trade to be "big twins" for the 1913 season.

Percy P. Pierce, manager of the Pierce Cycle Company (and George N. Pierce's son). From the *Bicycling World and Motorcycle Review*, June 23, 1914.

But in June 1913 the Pierce sales manager, Fred Brown, in speaking about the future of his motorcycle line, said that the four-cylinder machine was not going to be replaced by a twin. Both Pierce models in the 1913 season had sold better than in any previous year. *Motorcycling* reported that "as far as known now," the four-cylinder Pierce would continue as a 1914 model.

One each of the four- and single-cylinder machines were exhibited as 1914 Pierce models at the Chicago show in early November 1913. Fred Brown was there, assisted by C. W. Brewer and Jack Horner in demonstrating the new Pierce motorcycles. The one-cylinder was a single-speed machine, but a newly announced two-speed type, if it had been present, would have shown visitors a Thor-manufactured gear fitted to the rear hub.

The *Bicycling World* characterized the changes in the four-cylinder machine for 1914 as "few and far between and minor in character." These included improvements to the clutch (Raybestos-covered plates and a new bearing), a new arrangement for rear-wheel removal, and a new, U-shaped handlebar. On the single-cylinder Pierce, a plain bearing replacing a roller in the connecting-rod big end, several other minor engine changes, a drive chain instead of a belt, new handlebars, and "simplified controls" were the features on the 1914 version, both one- and two-speed variants. The four-cylinder machine was now fitted with a Siro carburetor.

The competitive motorcycle industry for 1914 saw a general decrease in selling prices. The effect on manufacturers was discouraging if not devastating. Whether a drop in the price of the Pierce four-cylinder to three hundred dollars and the single to two hundred dollars were critical to the company's eventual decision to suspend production is speculation here. Certainly, the profit margins were reduced drastically for Pierce, as for most other builders. The more popular makes, such as Indian, Excelsior, and Harley-Davidson, survived the mid-1910s. Others like Pierce, whose single equipped with a two-speed transmission listed for ten dollars *less* than the similar one-speed of the year before, were soon gone from the trade.

How many 1914 Pierce motorcycles ultimately were manufactured and the date on which production ended are not known here. The Pierce factory closed for inventory on August 5, 1914, reopening for production on August 12. It's unlikely that any motorcycles were made after that time. On the other hand, motorcycle production could have ended weeks or months earlier. The *Bicycling World and Motorcycle Review* at the end of April had omitted Pierce motorcycles in a compilation of specifications and photos of 1914 models. But Merkel and Spacher Inc., in the Rochester city directory appearing in July 1914, still advertised that they were agents for the "Pierce Motorcycle, Tried and True."

Undoubtedly, 1914 Pierce machines made their way to buyers, as evidenced by an advertisement in an August issue of *Motorcycle Illustrated* in which a party sought a buyer with three hundred dollars for a 1914 four-cylinder machine with the "latest improvements." By January 1915, single-cylinder Pierce motorcycles were being closed out by the longtime cycle jobber E. J. Willis Company (q.v.) in New York, which advertised $250 machines for $110 "new in original crates, while they last."

By the end of September 1914, the Pierce Cycle Company was done with the building of motorcycles. Brown told *Motorcycle Illustrated*, "We shall confine our efforts to the manufacture of bicycles for 1915 . . . and judging from present indications we will be kept busy." The Pierce Cycle Company, managed by Brown, continued to build bicycles in the Hanover Street factory until 1918. In the spring, $150,000 in debt, the Pierce company planned to reorganize. However, by the end of the year, the bicycle operations were acquired by a competitor, the Emblem Manufacturing Company (q.v.), a builder of bicycles and motorcycles, which moved Pierce bicycle manufacture to Angola. The Emblem company maintained a separate Pierce bicycle line until its own dissolution in 1940. A Pierce Manufacturing Company took over the assets of the Emblem company, but production of both Pierce and Emblem bicycles ended.

Henry Pokorney (?)
New York City (Manhattan?)
1904
Trade Name: **Pokorney**

The endpapers of Stephen Wright's *The American Motorcycle: 1869–1914* have an engraved image of an in-line, two-cylinder, overhead-valve engine. The label identifies the motor as the "1904 Pokorney, New York, New York." Whether the engine was a prototype or a production model and whether it was fitted to a motorcycle are unknown here.

"Pokorney" probably refers to Henry Pokorney, one of the organizers of the Thomas Cycle Company of New Jersey incorporated in 1902. Pokorney in that year also was superintendent of the E. R. Thomas Motor Company (q.v.) in Buffalo, maker of the Auto-Bi motorcycle. In 1910, George W. Sherman suggested that "Perarney [*sic*]" had designed the Auto-Bi.

Prospect Motor Manufacturing Company
1906–7
Prospect Motor Company
1907–9
Brooklyn (1906–7); Manhattan (1907–9)
Trade Names: **Simplex**; **Peugeot**; **Allright**

Simplex motorcycles sometimes combined French-built engines with locally fabricated parts. At other times, Simplex motorcycles were completely French-built Peugeot machines with the Simplex name attached.

An advertisement in the June 1906 issue of the *Cycle and Automobile Trade Journal* featured a cut of a V-twin engine. The text announced the Simplex motorcycle, powered by the French Sarolea engine, which "has no equal." The motorcycle builder using the imported engines was the Prospect Motor Manufacturing Company at 7 and 9 Park Place in Brooklyn.

William H. Wray on his two-cylinder Simplex Peugeot at Ormond Beach, Florida, in 1907. He made an official mile in 44²/₅ seconds (81 miles per hour) and an unofficial mile in 32²/₅ seconds (112 miles per hour). From the *Motorcycle Illustrated*, March 1907.

In October the *Journal* published an extensive description of two Simplex machines. The $275, 5-horsepower twin had cylinder dimensions of 70 by 80 millimeters. It weighed 145 pounds and was capable of reaching 50 miles per hour. A $200, 76-by-85-millimeter, 3-horsepower single was good for 40 miles per hour. The engines alone were available from Prospect at $125 and $90 complete.

The motorcycles used a low frame "so as to enable a person of average height to place both feet on the ground while resting in riding position on the saddle." The nickel-plated copper tank featured a hinged door for a central compartment housing the "imported double spark coil" and batteries. The 26-inch wheels were fitted with 2.25-inch tires. The band brake was cable-controlled, allowing "both pedals to be dropped into comfortable position without depriving the machine of its effective brake."

The Prospect Motor Company's 5-horsepower, two-cylinder Simplex with a two-gallon fuel tank. From *Cycle and Automobile Trade Journal*, March 1907.

Among the names prominently associated with the Simplex motorcycle is that of John J. McGuckin, often spokesman for the Prospect company. A partner was George Post, and the son of a Brooklyn real estate broker, William H. Wray Jr., was reported to be "interested in the manufacture of the Simplex motor bicycle." William Wray rode Simplex motorcycles competitively, winning a dirt-track race in Philadelphia in 1906 and setting a mile record at 44²/₅ seconds at Ormond Beach, Florida, in January 1907. In 1909, if not before, Howard K. Wray of Brooklyn also worked at the Prospect Motor Company.

In late 1906, Peugeot engines powered the Simplex motorcycles. McGuckin noted that the Prospect company had agreed with Peugeot Freres to use the latter's "motors and fittings, and we trust to have a line of machines and specialties unequalled by any other dealer in the country" (*Motorcycle Illustrated*, January 1907). McGuckin went on to report that his agent had returned from Paris with a "a number of interesting Motor Cycles."

An advertisement for Simplex motorcycles in this period shows two different two-cylinder machines. The first has a tall, European-style frame with a slab-sided fuel tank plainly marked "Simplex." The extreme rake of the front fork (fitted with a lamp) is set off by the handlebars sweeping back almost to the saddle. The other machine has a double-pointed tank mounted within the two top-frame tubes. The saddle is cantilevered over the rear wheel. The text for the advertisement mentions a one-cylinder machine, as well. The low frame and long wheelbase are emphasized.

The *Bicycling World* described the first of these machines, which appeared at the Grand Central Palace auto show in January 1907, as a roadster with

> a remarkable tank[,] . . . a big square receptacle occupying every inch of the space between the upper frame tube and the truss tube; it is divided into three parts—one holding two gallons of gasoline, another one quart of oil, while the third best may be described as a "pantry": it has compartments for tools and a spare inner tube and a little drawer for extra parts and what-not. The oil pump is located in the oil division of the tank and is operated in plain sight from the saddle.

A band brake was operated by backpedaling. The other show machine was a 110-pound racer. Both motorcycles had 26-inch wheels with 2.5-inch tires. Both used a V-belt drive from a 5-horsepower, two-cylinder engine in the loop of the frame. One ignition system was dry cell, while the other used a Simms-Bosch magneto.

A month later came word that the Prospect Motor Manufacturing Company, which "in a modest way had been producing the Simplex motor bicycle," had ceased production to concentrate on Peugeot motorcycles. "J. J. McGuchin [*sic*], the head of the company, made a quiet trip to France last month and obtained the Peugeot agency for the United States." The three single-cylinder (1.75-, 2.75-, and 3.5-horsepower) machines and two twins (3.5 and 5 horsepower) were to be imported in parts and sold under the Simplex-Peugeot name.

The *Bicycling World*, calling the Prospect company the "American agents for the Peugeot-Simplex," in September 1907 reported a move to a borough "in what very many consider the better half of New York City." The Prospect organization had leased a "glass-front establishment" in Manhattan at Broadway and Sixty-Third Street and "expect to cut a large figure in motorcycle affairs."

The relationship between the Prospect concern and Peugeot Freres apparently turned again in late 1907, when the National Sales Corporation at 296 Broadway in Manhattan became "United States representative for the Peugeot motorcycles, which are foreign made." Another source lists the address for the National Sales agency at 1900 Broadway, the same as the Prospect Motor Company. Advertisements by Peugeot Freres themselves in late 1908 and early 1909 listed the 296 Broadway address as the location from which they were distributing their *motors* and suggested that an ideal combination was a Peugeot engine in an American motorcycle.

National Sales was incorporated in September 1905 for the purpose of carrying on "a general manufacturing, merchandise and sales agency business." Emil Grossman, the largest shareholder, had been and continued to be involved in merchandizing of automobile supplies even after the demise of the National Sales Corporation. Whether National Sales was formed solely to serve as the United States distributor for Peugeot motorcycles or automobiles seems unlikely given the early incorporation.

In 1908 or 1909, both the National Sales Corporation and Peugeot Freres moved to 232 West Fifty-Eighth Street, which was also the location of the Emil Grossman Company. All three moved once more, to 250 West Fifty-Fourth Street. The National Sales Corporation was dissolved in March 1912 by its two stockholders, Grossman and Frank Lowe. At no time were Peugeot Freres or the National Sales Corporation

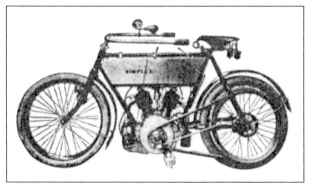

The 2-horsepower, 90-pound, $210 Simplex-Peugeot. From *Cycle and Automobile Trade Journal*, March 1907.

listed in the city directories as motorcycle manufacturers or distributors. Peugeot's line was variously given as "supplies," "motors" (which could have included motorcycles, automobiles, and engines), and "chains." The National Sales Corporation entries have no product identifier.

No longer marketing complete Peugeot motorcycles, the Prospect Motor Company (which likely dropped the "Manufacturing" element in its name in late 1907) returned to the fabrication of their own machines using Peugeot engines. In addition, in July 1908 came news of still another French motor, the Buchet, "favorably known abroad for their speed and reliability, and a favorite with racing men on account of smoothness of running and excellent wearing qualities." It was to be distributed to fill the demand for racing and pacing machines. The Buchet was characterized by overhead valves and available in 4-horsepower single and 8-horsepower double form. The bore was 3.375 inches, and the stroke 3.5. The single, at $100, was guaranteed to reach 60 miles per hour, while the two-cylinder cost $165. It's likely that the Buchet motors were sold only for installation on the purchasers' existing motorcycles; the *Motorcycle Illustrated* article noted that "Peugeot motors . . . will, as heretofore, be supplied on all their standard Simplex motorcycles."

In November 1908, the Prospect Motor Company, in advertising its Simplex motorcycles fitted with Peugeot engines ("a limited number of single and double cylinders in stock ready for immediate delivery"), used the Manhattan address at 1900 Broadway. In January 1909, the Prospect Motor Company announced that their Simplex motorcycles, together with the "latest Simplex accessories," would be at the Madison Square Garden show. It's likely that the Prospect company distributed rather than manufactured many of these items. The Simplex headlight, for example, was described as the "very best imported." At the show, the Prospect company also exhibited a Peugeot-powered motorcycle called the Allright, which *Motorcycle Illustrated* thought "reminds one very much of the [English] Vindec." The following June, a new catalog came from the firm at 1900 Broadway. A description in *Motorcycle Illustrated* lists new specialties, including a belt punch, a belt fastener, adjustable pulleys, and contact points. Mention was made of Peugeot motors and Bowden cables but not of Simplex motorcycles.

The final Prospect Motor Company Simplex with Peugeot engine. From *Cycle and Automobile Trade Journal*, March 1909.

The definitive end of the Prospect Motor Company and the Simplex motorcycle came in late 1909 "because of lack of capital," according to *Motorcycle Illustrated*. The two principals of the firm were noted as George Post, "who is reported to be living up in New Canaan, Conn.," and John McGerken (*sic*), "who is said to have obtained a position as a chauffeur." The demise of the Prospect Motor Company did not mean the end of the Peugeot in America. The 1910 models were "manufactured in this country" by C. F. Fulmer of Plainfield, New Jersey. A description of the machines suggests that again a combination of French engine and American components made the "American Peugeot." Two twins and a single-cylinder machine were offered at $250, $300, and $350 for 3-, 5-, and 7-horsepower engines, respectively.

By 1914, it appears that the Peugeot was gone from the American market; Amos Shirley, a former Peugeot agent in New York, reported to the *Bicycling World and Motorcycle Review* that he still had a "quantity" of parts to supply. Also in 1914, *Motorcycling* said that Louis Campana and Al Cocchi "used to manufacture the old Peugeot motorcycles, importing the motors and building the frames," apparently in Manhattan. In 1914, Cocchi was operating the Metropolitan Motorcycle Garage on Amsterdam Avenue. Campana was in the process of giving up his stepfather's surname, "Campana," for his original name, "Jeanroy."

In 1912, the Simplex Machine Works of Forty-Fifth Street and Sixth Avenue in Brooklyn introduced a line of motorcycle sidecars. Both passenger and van types were available. The underslung suspension of the commercial models was added to the passenger line for 1913. Whether there was any connection between Simplex motorcycles of the 1900s and the Simplex sidecars of the 1910s has not been determined here.

P. T. Motor Company
New York City (Manhattan)
1897?–1903?
Trade Name: **P. T.**

The "P" and "T" of the P. T. Motor Company were German immigrants Adolph Potdevin (1867–1964), a machinist resident in Brooklyn, and Michael E. Toepel (1870–?), an electrician living in Manhattan. The *Bicycling World* called P. T. designer Toepel "well informed, and with his one arm is far more expert in handling motor bicycles than are most men who have their full complement." *Motorcycle Magazine* thought Toepel "an expert" at induction coils and spark plugs and a "clever operator of the motor bicycle" even with "the second sleeve of his coat being filled with an artificial member."

Toepel in 1903 said he probably ranked with the earliest users of the motor bicycle,

> as I began riding one six years ago—one of my own make. It had [in] a frame of my own building a 1 horsepower motor, designed jointly by my partner and myself, the "P. T." motor, we called it. This lasted me about three years, when a young man who borrowed it smashed it against a tree. I sent another motor, one with 1½ horsepower, to a concern in New England to experiment with. They fitted it to a frame and put on a chain drive, and after a while sent it to me. I changed the chain for a belt, and used that until last May [1903], when I got an Indian.

The *Cycle and Automobile Trade Journal* for January 1900 reported that Toepel, at 230 Avenue B, had just "completed a small motor intended especially to be applied to bicycles and tricycles." This 1-horsepower motor would run on gasoline, kerosene, or acetylene and was "thoroughly tested and found to work eminently satisfactorily." The price was seventy-five dollars, less 20 percent to the trade. Castings in aluminum bronze were fifteen dollars, and in cast iron ten dollars "net." Toepel also had prepared "patterns" on which

the motor could be mounted behind the saddle. The engines and castings were to be available on January 15, 1900. Toepel was working on a 3-horsepower, two-cylinder engine, but in the meantime the one-cylinder version, he assured, was the "best motor on the market, and [he was] . . . preparing to supply a heavy demand." A surviving P. T. motor, apparently one of this early type, utilizes a make-and-break ignition system as well as a surface evaporator for the fuel. The machine's owner, Paul H. Walker Jr., reports that the evaporator "doesn't work too good."

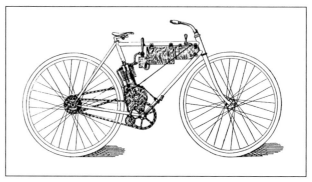

Chain-drive version of the P. T. with Type B engine, which introduced spark-plug ignition to the P. T. line. From the *American Automobile*, November 1900.

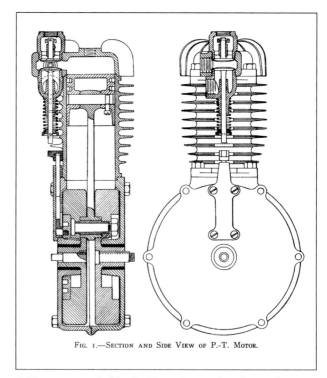

P. T. engine, probably the Type C introduced in early 1901. From the *Horseless Age*, June 12, 1901.

The *Journal* for April 1900 announced the 20-pound, 12-inch-high "P-T" bicycle motor, apparently the renamed Toepel engine, which could run on either gasoline or illuminating gas. Attached to a bicycle with a clamp, the engine powered the rear wheel "with a ball-bearing friction wheel through a sprocket chain connection that can be instantly detached if required." The seventy-five-dollar price excluded such accessories as a gasoline tank, muffler, and carburetor. A complete installation on a bicycle was displayed by Charles E. Miller (q.v.), a purveyor of cycle components on Reade Street in New York. The *American Automobile* for May 1900 reported seeing the "the first motor cycle to be made in New York . . . discovered by a reporter for the *Sun* in a loft on Reade Street. It has been ridden 1,100 miles and has been seen in motion." The *American Automobile* noted that "this machine is remarkable in several ways, [although] its crudities are obvious. The method of driving is as objectionable as might be conceived, but the construction and location of the engine would permit of a chain being run from it to a sprocket on the left-hand side of the rear wheel. The elevation of the motor above the saddle is another objectionable feature, as it would seriously interfere with the mount and dismount."

Within a month, Miller said he had given up the "United States sales agency for the P.-T. motor." And in yet another month, Frank B. Widmayer (q.v.), at 2312 Broadway, announced that he was "placing on the market" the "well-known P. & T. motor," which could be "applied to any bicycle with a monkey wrench and screw driver." The motor, said the *Journal*, offered "an excellent opportunity for the bicycle dealer and assembler to enter a new and profitable field." By September the P. T. Motor Company had been organized by Widmayer and "Torpel [*sic*]," who both were "well known in connection with motor cycles and their fittings," according to the *Journal*.

In August 1900, Toepel, Potdevin, and Widmayer applied for a patent on an "oil-engine." The patent, granted in September 1901, describes the P. T. engine, specifically dealing with "an improved bearing for the fly-wheel," which allowed a narrow case while making it possible "to dispense with the usual projecting shaft in one face of the crankcase." Another part of the invention was the arrangement of a groove on an exterior face of the two-part flywheel. In that slot, a "cam-disk" secured "a movement of the valve operating rod for each two whole revolutions of the crank without employing the reducing-gear which is ordinarily used in engines of this class."

Also in August 1900, the three men applied for a patent on a "motorcycle." This patent, granted in June 1901, describes the mounting of the engine "so that it shall form a section of the seat-post" in the interest of producing "compactness, a low center of gravity, ease of repair or inspection, and other advantages." The engine was to be removable for the installation of a section of tubing to convert the machine into an "ordinary bicycle to be propelled by foot pressure." The motor attached with screw fittings at the head and the bottom of the crankcase.

Beverly Rae Kimes and Henry Austin Clark Jr. say that less than a year after its introduction the rights to the P. T. engine were sold "to Crescent" (q.v.), but if so, that sale likely was only of the original design. For with the announcement of the P. T. Motor Company came the introduction of the Type B (P. T.) engine. New was a spark-plug ignition system. Of note, said the *Cycle and Automobile Trade Journal* for September 1900, was the continuing "ingenious valve cam, doing away with reduction gear usually used." The periodical also reported that the P. T. engines were built on the "interchangeable plan, so that any part of the same can be duplicated at short notice, and will be sure to fit." The engine could drive a bicycle either by a friction wheel on the rear tire or through a chain to the rear hub. Prices for a complete engine or for castings remained the same as for the original-style engine.

The *American Automobile* for November 1900 said the Type B, with "manganese aluminum crank chambers," weighed 20.5 pounds and measured 12.5 inches tall and 4 inches wide. The engine reportedly developed 1 horsepower, probably at 1,000 revolutions. With only twenty parts and large, self-lubricating bearings, the motor, as the P. T. company's other parts, had "proven entirely satisfactory in every respect." The other available products included a carburetor, muffler, and spark plug with iridium platinum points. The vaporizer also was offered, but the company "recommends the carburetor." The *Automobile* noted that an experimental P. T. motorcycle with the engine over the rear wheel had covered 1,500 miles on one set of tires, despite being driven by an "aluminum friction wheel."

It had subsequently been converted to chain drive at the rear hub.

The January 1901 issue of the *Cycle and Automobile Trade Journal* described the Type C engine. This was a 1.5-horsepower motor, 13.5 inches tall, weighing 24.5 pounds. Maximum power was developed at 1,100 rpm, with a useful range from 800 to 2,500 rpm. There was also a 2-horsepower, air-cooled engine and a variety of motorcycle accessories such as a waterproof battery, spark coils, carburetors, and mufflers. A "new complete motor bicycle" was to be available by the middle of May. The offices of the company remained at 2312 Broadway, with a factory at 404 West Twenty-Seventh Street. The June 14, 1901, issue of the *Horseless Age* described the 1.5-horsepower, 24.5-pound motor as having a manganese-aluminum crankcase, valves fitted to the cylinder head, and a pushrod controlling both the exhaust valve and the current flow for the ignition.

Chain-drive P. T., probably with a 1.5-horsepower Type C engine. From *Cycle Age and Trade Review*, June 27, 1901.

The *Horseless Age* also noted that the P. T. Motor Company was building a motorcycle equipped with one of their motors. Future engines were to have "a small generator" in place of battery ignition. Within two weeks, the P. T. Company, in the person of Frank B. Widmayer, "general selling agent" and "motor bicycle" inventor, reported that the dimensions of the cylinder had been increased from 2.125 by 2.625 inches, the "interior construction has been somewhat changed," and a positive make-and-break device had replaced a trembler.

In the late fall of 1901, the P. T. Motor Company incorporated with A. (Amuletta?) M. Hudson as president and Widmayer as secretary-treasurer. Offices were at 2312 Broadway, and the factory was on Seventh Avenue at Twenty-Eighth Street. By January 1902, the P. T. line consisted of the Model #6, a 2-horsepower, 23-pound bicycle engine; the #10 motor for pacing bicycles and tandems; and 4-, 6-, and 8-horsepower, air-cooled automobile engines. Kimes and Clark note the production of a 3-horsepower motorcycle, apparently using the #10 engine.

Paul Walker's P. T. Type A engine fitted to a Lovell bicycle in a 1998 view. Photo courtesy of Paul H. Walker Jr.

The life span of the P. T. company apparently was short. Kimes and Clark record its manufacturing years as 1901 and 1902, although the January 1903 *Cycle and Automobile Trade Journal*'s "Buyer's Guide" lists the P. T. Motor Company at 322-324 Seventh Avenue as a source of motorcycles. In addition to his complete early-style P. T. engine with an aluminum crankcase, Paul Walker reports the survival of an incomplete Type B engine with an iron crankcase.

R

Bill Reeves
Jamestown
ca. 1937

According to motorcycle historian Herbert Wagner, Bill Reeves built a 90-cubic-inch V-4 "on a Harley VL-like bottom around 1937 and which a Milwaukee firm reportedly inspected and rejected." There was a Bill Reeves Garage in Jamestown during the time referenced by Wagner.

Regas Vehicle Company
Rochester
1899–1903
Trade Name: **Regas**
J. Harry Sager
Rochester
1899–1912
Riggs-Spencer Company
Rochester
1901

James Harry (sometimes Henry) Sager's early inventions involved bicycle saddles, gearing, and frames; his first patent dates from 1890. In 1899 he founded the Regas Vehicle Company to sell automobiles, and in 1900 he competed in an event described as "among the first track races between automobiles in this country." In the same period, he produced a motorcycle, which the *Horseless Age* identified as having been built by the Regas ("Sager" in reverse spelling) Vehicle Company, makers of spring bicycle frames in Rochester. Powered by a 2.25-horsepower DeDion engine, the experimental machine had reached a speed of 25 miles per hour. Production motorcycles were going to have 1.25-horsepower engines and a weight of less than 75 pounds.

J. Harry Sager's prototype Regas motorcycle with a DeDion engine in Sager's innovative frame. From the *Bicycling World*, October 25, 1900.

The *American Automobile* in November 1900 said the Regas motorcycle was "a familiar sight to the people of Rochester, N.Y., during the past summer." The journal said the machine was "built for experimental purposes, to test the principle, and is somewhat heavier than is necessary." The *Automobile* observed that the short wheelbase and low weight made for steering "'steady as a clock' a point much appreciated by [bicycle racing] pace makers." The position of the engine behind the rider was seen as favorable, "so that all heat and fumes pass to the rear and not in the rider's face."

The *Bicycling World and Motorcycle Review* said the motorcycle had been in use for a year or more, although Sager had kept it under wraps from the trade press. The machine had "every earmark and appearance of being a sure winner"; the frame design was "far ahead of anything yet shown; the motor is stowed low down in the rear triangle, and is driven by chain and sprocket gearing." The front wheel could be replaced with an attachment to form a tricycle. In short, Sager had "struck it right." In 1918, *Motorcycling and Bicycling* recalled that when introduced, the Sager motorcycle "was expected to be a leader." And the "general design was commented on very favorably."

Sager's prime contribution to the motorcycle was, indeed, the frame. Basically, he extended its wheelbase behind the seat tube of the ordinary diamond construction. The down tube passed through the bottom bracket, looping to meet the chain stays. A second set of seat stays joined the seat tube at its midpoint. The engine was placed behind the seat tube with the cylinder parallel to the tube. A sprocket on the left side of the crankshaft turned the chain connected to the rear wheel. The normal pedal-crank arrangement remained to allow the rider to assist the engine or power the machine themselves, if necessary.

The *Bicycling World* noted the advantage of the low center of gravity. It also said that "any suitable motor can be used," suggesting that Sager was not interested in building engines. The emphasis was on the frame, with which "'any bicycle manufacturers,' say the Regas people, can immediately enter upon the manufacture of motorcycles at a very little expense." The Regas company was said to be ready to negotiate with manufacturers wishing to build "on royalty, or will furnish the trade the parts complete or any portion of them." The *Cycle Age and Trade Review* in this same period

The Regas motorcycle frame provided a low center of gravity, with the engine installed behind the seat tube. From *Cycle and Automobile Trade Journal*, August 1902.

suggested that Sager "does not intend to spend a lot of his good money building machines and experimenting for the benefit of other people. In other words he will endeavor to sell frames to manufacturers of motor bicycles so that they may apply any motor and equipment they please." The *Automobile*, on the contrary, in November 1900 indicated that the Regas company, in addition to dealing in parts and licensing manufacture of its motorcycle, also "propose[s] to deal . . . in the complete machines."

In January 1901, Sager and two of his motorcycles were at the important New York City cycle trade show. While the *Bicycling World* admired the carburetor exhibiting "a radical departure" in its simplicity, the *Cycling Gazette* noted the "specially built frame with the motor hung low down about the center." At the show, Sager said he could not "truthfully report any great business actually transacted, but I suppose we had our share." He also noted, "Men who believe it possible to convert ordinary stock bicycles into motor bicycles by merely attaching motors to the former are as bad as the freak inventors who would turn all horse drawn vehicles into automobiles. The horse drawn vehicles were never designed to withstand the strains and poundings of an engine, nor are the bicycles, as built for pedal propulsion. There must be as much thought given the design and strength of the bicycle proper as is given the motor itself."

In May the Regas Vehicle Company, capitalized at $25,000, was incorporated with J. Harry Sager, Cora B. Sager, and George D. Green as directors. The last was recipient of invention and design patents for the Regas frame, the patents assigned to "James H. Sager."

In June 1901, the *Cycle Age* reported that Sager, "designer of the Regas motor bicycle frame and organizer of the Regas Vehicle Co.," was having one hundred "motor bicycles built for him by the Riggs-Spencer Company of Rochester." The finished machines were "to be on the market in a few weeks." The Riggs-Spencer concern, according to information Frank C. Riggs imparted to a *Cycle Age* reporter, had been installed the previous winter "in the Sager building, on Otsego Street." Sager bicycle gears and Cinch coaster brakes were being built for Sager as well as "a number of other devices for other people." Riggs was so busy he had added a night shift. His partner was James B. Spencer. Both had been employed—Riggs as sales manager and Spencer as superintendent—by the E. C. Stearns Company in Syracuse before the American Bicycle

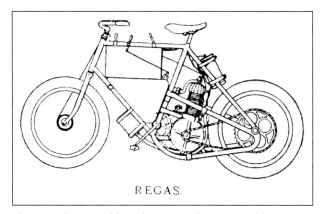

The *Bicycling World and Motorcycle Review* for January 10, 1910, looked back a decade at the pioneering Regas motorcycle.

Company (the Bicycle Trust) ended Stearns's use of the Sager gear. Incorporated in 1900, the Riggs-Spencer Company began operations with $25,000 paid in capital and with the expectation of building 25,000 Sager bicycle gear sets the first year, according to the *Bicycling World and the American Cyclist*.

James F. Bellamy has noted that the engines used by the Regas Vehicle Company were Flemings (q.v.). However, the *Cycling Gazette* in January 1901 notes that the "Patee motor is the same one that has been attracting so much attention on the Sager motor cycle. In fact, the motor used by Sager is the property of the Patee Bicycle Company, having been loaned by the latter for exhibition purposed for the New York show."

While the Patee engine had been designed by Joshua M. Morris (q.v.) in Rochester, the Morris operation had been acquired by Patee and moved to Indianapolis. The Sager Gear Company and Riggs-Spencer, in this period, were located at 25 Otsego Street; the Regas Vehicle Company was at 80 Main Street.

In late summer of 1901, three Regas motorcycles competed in the New York-to-Buffalo motor-vehicle endurance contest sponsored by the Automobile Club of America. Two Regas machines were 1.5-horsepower, 110-pound cycles, likely the standard production style, ridden by Sager and Warren L. Stoneburn. A 2.25-horsepower vehicle, weighing 160 pounds, was under the control of Green. None of the six motorcycles entered in the contest survived to Rochester, where the event terminated in the wake of the assassination of President William McKinley.

A year later, the *Bicycling World* reported that the Regas Vehicle Company had abandoned its idea of manufacturing complete motor bicycles. Instead, they were going to offer frames, with or without the internal springing for which Sager was known, "to all comers." The 26-inch-diameter wheels with wooden rims for 1.75-inch tires reportedly were lighter and stronger than the 28-inch types used on most motorcycles. An engraving of the motorcycle frame shows a design differing somewhat from the model announced in 1901. Missing in the new version were the supplemental seat stays. New was the optional incorporation of the "Regas spring frame attachment," which put coil springs into the surviving seat stays with the chain stays pivoted at the hanger. The "frame joint" was patented (714,402) together by Green and Sager in 1902. Other specifications, according to the *Dealer and Repairman*, include 22-inch height, 48-inch wheelbase, and 1.125-inch-diameter, 20-gauge Shelby tubing.

The unincorporated J. Harry Sager Company succeeded the dissolved Regas Vehicle Company in 1903, the new firm advertising Regas bicycle spring frames. The same year, the Regas Automobile Company at 45 South Avenue was incorporated, with J. Harry Sager as director, and a runabout was exhibited at the Chicago vehicle show. Before the dissolution of the Regas Vehicle Company, J. Harry Sager had separated himself from the Sager Gear Company, which also dissolved in 1903. According to Bellamy, the Regas Automobile Company endured until 1905.

In 1906 J. Harry Sager introduced the Sager Cushion fork for motorcycles; in 1911 he advertised that the fork was standard equipment on seven motorcycle brands, including Curtiss (q.v.), Marvel (s.v. "Motor Bicycle Equipment and Supply Company"), and Harley-Davidson. At the end of 1906, Sager said, "Motorcycles, I believe, will soon be as popular as bicycles were. They are getting cheaper everyday and now cost no more than bicycles used to a dozen years ago. They are being made with comparatively noiseless and non-grease-throwing engines, with easy riding cushion frames and non-slipping tire. . . . Manufacturers have ceased to advertise because they are unable to fill their orders fast enough."

In 1912 Sager patented a modified cushion frame, but in the 1910s and 1920s, the James H. Sager Company specialized in automobile bumpers. Sager assigned patents to his company as late as 1927, thirty-seven years from his earliest patented invention.

Reliance Motor Cycle Company
(briefly, in 1903, the **Empire Motor Cycle Company**)
Addison (1903–6); Elmira Heights (1906–7);
Owego (1908–11)
Ives Motorcycle Corporation
Owego (1911–15?)
Trade Names: **Reliance**; **Monarch**

Willis H. Ives (1861–1932) tied together the various enterprises that built the Reliance and Monarch motorcycles. Born in Connecticut, he manufactured bicycles in Oneonta before moving his Empire State Cycle Company to Addison in 1899. Four years later, Ives and fellow Empire director Charles D. Reynolds, as well as Buffalonians Victor E. Ripper and J. Frederick Doll, organized the Reliance Motor Cycle Company in Addison, capitalized at $15,000. Initially the motorcycle enterprise was the Empire Motor Cycle Company, but the name was changed quickly due to confusion with the Empire State Cycle Company.

1904 Model Year

The single-cylinder, four-stroke motorcycle, which the Empire Motor Cycle Company introduced in the fall of 1903, drove the rear wheel via a belt to a roller atop the tire. The rider operated a lever to engage the roller.

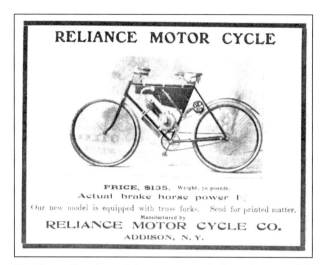

The first roller-drive Reliance. From *Cycle and Automobile Trade Journal*, February 1904.

The 1.75-horsepower engine and the transmission, reported the *Cycle and Automobile Trade Journal*, were the products of "two Frenchmen, who are engaged by the Empire Co., and have direct supervision of the manufacture." The 70-pound motorcycle was built of 1.125-inch, 18-gauge tubing, with an "especially heavy gauge forkside and quadruple plate crown with heavily reinforced stem." The gasoline tank, with enough fuel for 100 miles, was mounted inside the frame triangle. Pedals and roller chain allowed for conventional rider assist. A fender covered the rear wheel aft of the drive roller. The engine was also inside the triangle, its crankcase above the pedal bracket, and its cylinder parallel with the down tube. Announced at $125, in January 1904 the price was $135, "to put out a thoroughly first-class machine at a profit."

The *Automobile Review* deemed the 75-pound (*sic*) Reliance "one of the lightest" motorcycles "on the market." Commenting on the roller drive system, the journal said there "is not the least disagreeable thumping or jerking, a positive, steady drive is obtained and entire power developed by the motor is transferred to the rear wheel." The *Review* also approved of the lever that brought the roller into and out of contact with the wheel. The 1.75-horsepower engine was said to be of French design, with a French "spark advancer." The coil was enclosed in the gasoline tank, although reachable "through a sliding lid." The carburetor, reportedly the subject of a patent application, was said to "give a proper and uniform mixture at all times." Top speed was 32 miles per hour, although with higher gearing 40 miles per hour was attainable.

By spring of 1904 the Empire State Cycle Company had sold its factory to Reynolds, president of the Reliance Company, "as a permanent plant for the manufacture of the Reliance motorcycle." At the corner of Jones and Front Streets, a machine shop occupied the first floor of the 40-by-100-foot main building, while the second floor was set aside for "setting up & enameling."

1905 Model Year

The *Cycle and Automobile Trade Journal* noted an improvement in a V-shaped roller to provide a runway for water and mud on the periphery of the tire. New models using belt and chain drive determined that "in the matter of transmission the Reliance has literally formed a trust by itself." Reliance advertising claimed the new motorcycles were "greatly improved," with a more powerful engine, longer wheelbase, drop frame that lowered the engine for better balance, and a sight-feed oiler. The chain-drive model, with grip control and a "spring truss fork," was $150. The belt and roller drive models listed for $135.

1906 Model Year

For 1906, the $150 Reliance motorcycle's weight was up 15 pounds to 110, and the wheelbase extended to 55 inches. Handlebar-grip engine control was a feature. Chain drive remained an alternative to belt propulsion, but the roller was discontinued. The now vertically mounted, 2.75-inch bore by-3-inch stroke engine rated at 1.75 horsepower reportedly developed 2 or more.

Also available was a $175 2.5-horsepower machine with "G. & J. motor tires especially designed for touring. This model will weigh but 5 or 10 lbs. more than the standard machine, and will be well adapted to traveling men's use, being capable of carrying 25 to 75 lbs. of samples."

Ever the subject of discussions predicting relocation, in the fall of 1906 the Reliance Motor Cycle Company moved to Elmira Heights. While the initial announcement came early in the year, it was mid-autumn before the Reliance operation moved, and all 1906 model motorcycles were built in Addison. An important factor in the move may have been the involvement of Alexander P. Morrow, who had been associated with the Eclipse Machine Company in Elmira Heights. Morrow "invested considerable capital in the Reliance Motorcycle Company. . . . It is Mr. Morrow's intention to devote his personal attention to the Reliance interests." The new site was at the corner of Eighteenth Street and Oakwood Avenue, within yards of the Eclipse plant.

1907 Model Year

The Reliance motorcycle manufactured in Elmira Heights had a 3-inch bore by-3-inch stroke engine "in a loop in front of the crank hanger," a design "retained" from the previous model. The same report noted phosphor bronze bearings in the engine, a "slightly altered" rear frame, and a "new and heavier waterproof belt." *Motorcycle Illustrated* said of the 1907 Reliance, "Those that remember the Reliance as a machine with a frame little different from that of a common bicycle and with the transmission by means of a friction pulley applied to the tire of the rear wheel, would scarcely know the 1907 Reliance if the name were not on it. . . . The motor has 3 x 3 bore and stroke and develops three horse-power, the machine being capable of a speed of over 40 miles on the road gear. The price is $175."

1908 Model Year

In the fall of 1907, the Reliance Company had "heard the cry for lightweight motorcycles and [were] preparing to answer it." With a 52-inch wheelbase, the new model listed for $125. Its 15-cubic-inch (2.9375 by 2.875 inches) engine was rated at 2 horsepower and drove the rear wheel via a flat belt. The *Bicycling World and Motorcycle Review* called the Reliance Junior the "newest, and after a fashion, most radical motor bicycle" at the Boston automobile show. The other Reliance offering for the 1908 model year was a flat-belt-drive, 3-horsepower machine at $175, similar to the 1907 model except for a new, lower cushion frame and double-grip control.

A year after moving to Elmira Heights, the Reliance Motorcycle Company relocated to Owego. The Owego Business Men's Association coupled a "cash bonus" of $1,500 and an agreement to build a $3,000 factory. In return, the Reliance company "has given a bond to employ from 15 to 20 men for at least five years." Whatever arrangement Alexander Morrow had with the Reliance Company apparently ended with the move to Owego.

In the summer of 1908, it was announced that Ives, as president of the Reliance Motor Cycle Company in Owego, already expected to enlarge his East Main Street factory. The new concrete-block building was to cost $3,000. The company meanwhile planned to increase capital stock from $15,000 to $50,000, part of which was to be used for the construction of the factory enlargement. And Ives reported a deal for $12,000 worth of motors and frames with the Motor Cycle Equipment Company of Hammondsport. While the report does not specify whether the contract was for the sale or purchase of motors and frames to or from the Hammondsport firm, perhaps the explanation is the uncompleted state of the Reliance factory leading to the deal being struck to facilitate production of Reliance motorcycles until the enlarged Owego plant was operational.

1909 Model Year

In January 1909, a new one-story concrete building was ready on land purchased the previous fall. Still with laborers to be hired and machinery to be installed, the company reportedly had orders worth nearly $12,000 and anticipated "doing a business of about $75,000 during the coming year" based on five new motorcycle models.

The five Reliance models used two different frames, according to *Motorcycle Illustrated*; the machines appeared at the annual auto show in New York City in January. The smallest Reliance was the 2-horsepower, flat-belt-driven Model A, listing for $130 ($135?). Other Reliance models included a 3-horsepower Model B single with battery ignition on a 56-inch wheelbase at $175; a 3.5-horsepower Model C version of the single, with mechanical intake valve for $200; a 4-to-5-horsepower twin with automatic intake valves, like the larger singles on a 56-inch wheelbase, at $225; and a 7-horsepower twin for $250. Magneto ignition was an extra-cost option. Frames for the larger machines had double top tubes and torpedo-shaped tanks. The larger motorcycles used V-belt transmissions.

1910 Model Year

At the annual meeting of the Reliance Motorcycle Company at Owego on November 16, 1909, directors elected were Willis Ives; his wife, Alice M. Ives; Ward Decker; John P. Bell; and John G. Pemberton. The officers were Willis Ives, president; Decker, vice president; and Bell, secretary. James F. Bellamy has claimed that Decker, as majority shareholder in the Reliance Motorcycle Company, was responsible for the relocation of that firm from Elmira to Owego. Certainly, while Reliance operated at Owego, Decker was a pivotal figure. His having built some automobiles may explain the rumored Reliance automobile reportedly developed for the 1910 model year, as the factory was enlarged. There was, however, no Reliance automobile.

The largest 1910 Reliance was the 7-horsepower Model E twin, costing $250. A two-speed, planetary transmission was $30 more. From *Motorcycle Illustrated*, August 1, 1910.

At the Chicago automobile show in February 1910, the Reliance was deemed "a decided hit," with refinements such as double ignition system available for "only $5" on all but the Model C machines, and a new tank design—a trapezoid filling the space between the parallel top tubes. Also notable at Chicago were the spring truss fork, flexible conduits for gasoline and oil, "a most comfortable leather upholstered double seat stoutly yet simply attached to the rear axle," and a Reliance motorcycle with the planetary two-speed gear "in operation."

In brief, the Reliance offerings for 1910 included the Model C, which, as in 1909, was a 3.5-horsepower single for $200 with battery ignition; the Model F, a 4.5-horsepower, one-cylinder motorcycle at $210; and the Model E, a 7-horsepower twin at $250. The lighter singles of 1909, Models A and B, apparently had been discontinued. The two-speed gear was an extra $25 for the Model C and $30 more for the other two machines. Magneto ignition cost $25 for the one-cylinder Reliance motorcycles and $35 more on the twin. All the new Reliance motorcycles used V-belt drive.

The "probable output this year is 1,000 machines," claimed *Motorcycling* in late February. The report also mentioned the involvement of the Bandler family of Owego and New York City in the Reliance operation, they having taken "a large financial interest in the company."

1911 Model Year

In the fall of 1910, the Reliance company sent a letter to its creditors asking for cooperation in "continuing the business as a live, going concern." The company found itself "strapped for ready cash." A financial statement showed "assets and liabilities" in "a very fair condition" but "a lack of capital with which to convert present material into salable finished product."

In a news story, Ives was identified as "a well-liked and trustworthy man," who had controlled the Reliance stock. Now "some well-known New York people," not identified but obviously the Bandler family, had "taken stock and have assisted in keeping the ship afloat." They were offering to put up $10,000 "immediately and more as needed" for manufacture of motorcycles provided the creditors would take six-, eight-, and ten-month notes. In November 1910, the Reliance company reportedly had come to an agreement with its creditors. "Additional capital" had been secured, and by the end of 1910 the Reliance company had become Bandler property, they having secured Ives's stock, valued at $12,000. With Ives gone, George W. Favor became general manager, and George H. Greenlagh (his surname's spelling is unconfirmed here) plant superintendent. Decker, "experienced in motors and familiar with automobile construction," was to remain as vice president. J. M. De Lezene, "well known in the West as a Reliance missionary," was to be in charge of the "assembly department."

The Reliance company's annual meeting saw the election of a mix of old and new personnel. Directors included Decker of Owego as well as Henry W. Freeman, Arthur S. Bandler, Maurice E. Bandler, and David Bandler, all of New York City. New officers were Arthur Bandler, president; George W. Favor, vice president and general manager; H. Tatem Patton, secretary; and Robert Bandler, treasurer.

Brothers David (1870–1947), Arthur (1873–1932), and Maurice Bandler (1878–?) were former Owego residents. David was a lawyer, while Arthur and Maurice Bandler were associated with Bernard Bandler and Sons, importers of black diamonds for drill bits. The Bandlers allegedly "took hold enthusiastically," investing $50,000 in the Reliance factory on sand-blasting equipment, metal working machinery, and, in April 1911, a new foundry.

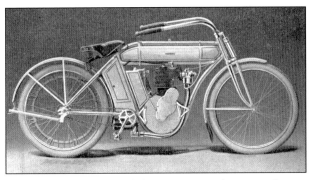

The expensive ($240 with battery ignition) G-11 Reliance. Its mechanical deficiencies led to Reliance Motorcycle Company bankruptcy. From the *Bicycling World and Motorcycle Review*, April 29, 1911.

The Reliance promised for 1911 was to be a 4.5-horsepower single with mechanically operated intake valve. A flat belt with idler provided the transmission; the two-speed gear was no longer available. French gray with black striping and red letters would "make an attractive color scheme." When it appeared, the G-11 Reliance was a much handsomer machine than its predecessors. No vise or file was allowed in motorcycle assembly, noted *Motorcycling*, because the "parts of the machine are so accurately made, they must assemble easily." The Reliance catalog said every nut on the Reliance motorcycle was castellated and secured by a cotter pin. Every engine was run six hours. And each motorcycle was road tested "up steep hills which abound near Owego, and over long stretches of smooth and level roads." After testing, the machines were cleaned and crated, "being protected from the weather by water-proof paper." Each motorcycle was guaranteed "for 1911." The G-11 was priced accordingly, the battery version at $240 and the magneto style at $275. The Reliance catalog said, "Incidentally it sells for more money than any other motorcycle. It costs us more to build; it costs you more to buy; and it is worth all it costs."

In the spring of 1911, when Reliance managers might have hoped to see a heavy shipment of motorcycles, the factory closed. David Bandler said,

> At the last moment, when things looked the rosiest in every respect, orders were coming in freely . . . two defects developed, one of which was due to a change made in the pattern of the cylinder, which the experts at the factory did not deem of any importance at the time, but which subsequently caused trouble. The engine showed a tendency to overheat as soon as warm weather came, and threw oil. It was therefore a question of selling a defective machine or ceasing to manufacture. . . . We may not be able to remedy them in time for the 1911 market, but we are now at work on our machine for 1912.

At a creditors' meeting in New York City, Arthur Bandler proposed that the Bandlers waive the $40,825 that they had invested to date in return for the creditors holding their claims until the 1912 model was produced. Meanwhile, the Bandler family would advance another "$10,000 or more"—that sum to be repaid first from 1912 model year proceeds, after which the income would be "distributed, pro rata, among the other creditors." Then the plant would be sold "for the best advantage of the creditors," unless the Bandlers decided to stay in the motorcycle business.

Within a few days, the Bandlers claimed they had acceptances from over half their creditors and the expectation that "an overwhelming proportion . . . will agree to the proposition, rather than to insist that the business be closed out at a forced sale." Meanwhile, a new engine design and a new oiling system were being tested for the proposed 1912 single-cylinder Reliance. Near the end of June, a bookkeeper was in charge of the near-dormant factory, with three draftsmen at work on the engine.

By mid-July, the Bandlers' plan was ruined. Clum and Atkinson—Rochester suppliers of solder and babbitt metal—acted on their claim of $789.46, which resulted in the Tioga County sheriff advertising the Reliance factory for sale. Assets of $54,652.84 included the plant on four acres valued at $13,000, "stock on hand, suitable for use" at $23,052.37, machinery and equipment at $17,719.96, office fixtures at $880.50, and insurance policies "on the property, $43,975."

Liabilities included a federal government fine of up to $1,000 for "failure to file its statement with the United States Internal Revenue Office" and wages due employees of $1,671.14. These two claims were "assigned to David Bandler of New York City." Secured creditors' claims totaled $6,610.57, including a first mortgage of $5,000 on the factory held by the Tioga National Bank in Owego. Unsecured claims amounted to $66,930.35, "mostly for small amounts."

1912 Model Year

On December 18, 1911, the Reliance assets after "spirited" bidding were sold for $17,500 to Willis H. Ives. His new partners were Elmirans Frank T. Carroll and Charles B. Swartwood, as well as Frank H. Baker and bankruptcy trustee H. Tatem Patton of Owego. The Reliance plant, closed since July 31, was on the verge of a new life at the first meeting of the Ives Motorcycle Corporation on January 6, 1912. Ives was elected president and general manager, Carroll vice president, and Patton secretary-treasurer. Organized with six hundred shares of capital stock at a par value of $100 each, the Ives corporation began work with a capitalization of $40,000, directors Ives, Patton, Carroll, and Swartwood each taking one hundred shares.

For their $17,500, Ives and his partners purchased 23,500 square feet in three buildings plus a separate aluminum foundry. Equipment, much of it new within the past two years, included "the latest cylinder-grinding machines, screw, milling, universal grinding and key seating machines, lathes, drill presses, sizing grinders, disc grinders, presses, power hack saws, a very complete nickeling outfit, sand blast, hardening furnaces, brazing outfit, pattern shop, large enameling department, etc."

"Monarch" was the name of the new Ives motorcycle appearing at the end of February. Explanation for the rapid development comes from the Monarch catalog for 1912, which claimed that Ives and plant superintendent G. W. Sayre had "spent a full year . . . in designing a motorcycle that will embody their joint ideas of a down-to-the-minute, practical, reliable, simple, and powerful machine."

Among new employees at the Ives Corporation were Herman J. Krackowizer and Lincoln Holland Jr., who were to travel on behalf of the Monarch, as well as C. Edward Clark, who was to be in charge of the Monarch "assembly room." By mid-March, fifty men were at work turning out the Big Five single. The factory fabricated both engines and frames. Only the iron engine castings were being purchased; the Ives aluminum foundry on-site provided all other cast parts. At a rate of eight to ten motorcycles per day, five hundred machines were foreseen as the season's production, with an output of twenty-five hundred to three thousand for 1913.

Figuring a hypothetical wage of ten dollars per employee per week and calculating half-year employment for a workforce of fifty, one arrives at a labor cost of $13,000. It's likely that the work year was longer and the payroll larger. Determining other production costs is guesswork without access to records. However, arbitrarily calculating material, subcontracting, taxes, and other expenses at $100 for each motorcycle, and supposing a wholesale price of $160 against a $200 list, net profit would have been $11,000 for the 1912 model year.

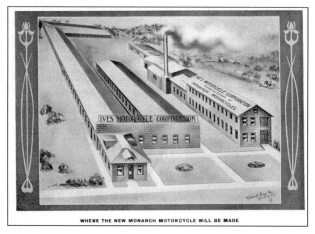

The former home of the Reliance Motorcycle Company, acquired by the Ives Motorcycle Corporation for manufacture of the Monarch in Owego. From *Motorcycling*, February 15, 1912.

Machine shop of the Ives Motorcycle Corporation turning out Monarch motorcycles. From the *Bicycling World and Motorcycle Review*, May 25, 1912.

The Monarch motorcycle that reached the market at this point was conservative but substantial. Its frame cradled the engine, with a loop that joined the down and seat tubes. The front fork was fitted with a coil-spring suspension. The engine displaced 33.55 cubic inches, with a bore of 3.375 inches and a stroke of 3.75. It had a pushrod and rocker-arm-actuated overhead inlet valve over a pushrod-operated exhaust valve. Transmission to the rear wheel was through an Eclipse clutch and a V-belt. Finished in brown with a gold stripe, the Big Five listed at two hundred dollars.

A twin scheduled to appear in March was to be an 8-horsepower "replica of the [single] in general construction." No twin arrived then, and in May came the announcement that the twin would not appear for the 1912 season, after all. "Heavy demand" for the single had "postponed" production. The single, according to a dealer—the Knight Mercantile Company—was "stay sold goods that allows the agent to keep his religion and sleep sound at nights."

1913 Model Year

Willis Ives predicted a production run of two thousand machines for the 1913 model year, including the chain-drive, 10-horsepower twin, which appeared in early October 1912. Practically, the two-cylinder machine was the same as the single, with a second cylinder added to the basic Monarch engine. The lower ends of the connecting rods on the twin were offset in the interest of reliability rather than sharing a bearing as on some other designs. While previously a belt-drive motorcycle, the Monarch single for 1913 came with either belt or chain drive.

One of each 1913 Monarch model was shown at the Grand Central Palace in New York. Of interest were the new "Feather Bed" saddle suspension, the enlarged bearing of the inlet valve rocker arm, greater tire clearance, and wider, deeper fenders. At the Chicago show, Lincoln Holland Jr., "the good-looking young Monarch traveler," was in charge of the exhibit of "the golden-brown beauty" from Owego. Also on hand were Ives; Carroll, identified as vice president; "Superintendent G. W. Sayre"; and "Salesman V. E. Yapp," elsewhere noted as "V. E. Rapp." One notes the similarity in name to that of Ives's partner from a decade earlier, Victor E. Ripper.

Both the Dreadnaught twin and the Big Five single for 1913 featured the new Monarch saddle-suspension design. From *Motorcycling*, February 6, 1913.

From a payroll of fifty in March 1912, the Ives company was down to thirteen men in the shop and an office force of two sometime before September 30, 1913. The 1913 season was a disappointment. The strong Ives presence at the trade shows and advertising campaign in the winter and spring failed to produce the great demand needed to succeed.

1914 Model Year

In 1914, most American motorcycle builders lowered prices. What effect this had on the activities of the Ives Motorcycle Corporation is difficult to determine. In fact, documenting any production of Monarch motorcycles for 1914 or 1915 is uncertain. That there were 1914 models, and even some 1915 Monarchs, is suggested by an advertisement for Mobiloils appearing in the spring of 1917. The Vacuum Oil Company listed oil requirements for both 1914 and 1915 Monarchs.

In the winter of 1913–14, there was a local, limited market for Monarch two-cylinder engines. In February 1914, the O-We-Go Car Company was organized in Owego. The makers of the lightweight automobile planned to manufacture their own engine but quickly adopted the Monarch motorcycle power plant. The O-We-Go Company was insolvent by November 1914 and bankrupt by January 1915. A successor endeavor was the Tribune Engineering Company, which in 1917 marketed the Tribune car, still with a "vee-twin Ives" engine.

1915 Model Year and Later

Monarch motorcycle production apparently had ended by late spring 1915, if not months before. A story in the Elmira *Star-Gazette* dated June 30, 1915, reported the "near-sale" of the Ives motorcycle factory. In August it was said that the Ives factory was the subject of negotiations by a new company, the Lackawanna Tube and Manufacturing Company. "Screw machinery, metal stampings, drawn steel tubes and similar products" were to be shipped. No motorcycles or parts were foreseen. "It is stated that W. H. Ives, head of the old Ives Motorcycle Corporation, will be a heavy stock holder in the new concern."

In 1920 Willis Ives identified his trade as "manufacturer" and his product as "auto goods." Ten years later, his Ives Manufacturing Company produced coat hangers.

A 1913 Monarch Big Five is housed in the collections of the Tioga County Historical Society in Owego. A Monarch twin and a Reliance survive in private hands.

Remington Arms Company
Ilion
1895

Beverly Rae Kimes and Henry Austin Clark Jr., as well as James F. Bellamy, note development in 1895 of a kerosene-fueled engine intended for use on bicycles and tricycles. The venture reportedly "remained ever at the experimental stage" (Kimes and Clark).

The Remington Automobile and Motor Company (not connected to the Remington Arms Company) was organized in 1900 at Ilion "to manufacture and sell motor vehicles of every description," according to the *Horseless Age*. However, automobiles apparently were the sole product of this and succeeding companies.

John F. Reynolds
Glens Falls
1909

In late summer or early fall of 1909, "J. F. Reynolds," a machinist, wrote to the *Cycle and Automobile Trade Journal* that he was building a three-cylinder, 2.25-inch bore by-2.5-inch stroke, two-stroke engine to power a "tandem motorcycle." He planned to cast the cylinders and then cut cooling flanges on his lathe. He proposed to copper-plate the cylinders to prevent rusting. Both intake and exhaust manifolds were to be separate castings attached with screws.

The *Journal*'s "H. D." suggested that Reynold's intended cylinder-casting thickness of 1.5 inches was excessive, the finished wall being best at three-sixteenths of an inch or less. And H. D. thought the idea of applying copper tubing on the heads as cooling projections was not a good thing since such "spines should always be integral with the cylinder walls because heat does not pass a joining of parts readily." Reynolds might best "make a single cylinder and try various kinds of cooling projections . . . before you build a 3-cylinder motor. . . . Or, if you do not want to find out for yourself, why not copy the work of others?" Further, H. D. said, "It is easy to waste a good deal of time building little gas engines to meet your own ideas. Look at other men's motors, and copy prevailing practice."

Carl C. Riotte
New York City (Manhattan)
1895
Trade Name: **Riotte**

The first issue of the *Horseless Age*, published in November 1895, announced the Riotte Kerosine Bicycle, invented by Carl C. Riotte of the Riotte and Hadden Manufacturing Company of 462 East 136th Street. The *Age* said Riotte had "been experimenting in gas and oil engines all his life, and has had a good deal to do with stationary and marine engines of all descriptions."

A photo shows a safety bicycle to which a single-cylinder engine was attached on the left side opposite the rear hub. A fuel tank was fastened to the upper side of the top tube. The text reports that operation was controlled by a "small handle at the oil tank." The engine itself consisted of "two small valves, a cylinder, piston and igniter." The last was supplied by a battery that reportedly "never polarizes or requires recharging." The Riotte engine was designed to be installed or removed "at a moment's notice."

The engine was geared directly to the rear wheel. Operation reportedly was "almost noiseless and without smell." A speed of 25 miles per hour had been attained on the level "and a pretty good speed maintained on grades of about four or five per cent." The tank held fuel for 75 miles. When empty, "a quart of kerosene or any kind of petroleum lamp oil can be bought at any country store or of any farmer."

Riotte was said to be building an automobile "with but one lever to start, stop reverse or go at any speed from 2 to 25 miles per hour. They expect to form a company to manufacture bicycle and carriage motors on a large scale." By 1896, the engine business had become C. C. Riotte and Company, with Eugene A. Riotte (Carl's brother) involved, and in the next few years it operated at several different New York addresses. In 1900, the Riottes' various ventures were consolidated into the Standard Motor Construction Company. They made various types of gasoline motors but specialized in marine engines. How many more, if any, motor bicycles or bicycle motors were built is unknown here.

Ritz Cycle Car Company
New York City (Brooklyn)
1913–15

The *Bicycling World and Motorcycle Review* for September 30, 1913, noted the incorporation of the Ritz Cyclecar (*sic*) Company "for the purpose of building cyclecars and motorcycles." The principal place of business was to be Brooklyn. The authorized capitalization was ten thousand dollars, but the Certificate of Incorporation filed with the New York secretary of state in Albany notes that the amount of capital with which the company began business was five hundred dollars. The certificate actually lists "automobiles" rather than cyclecars, as well as "motor cycles," as the objects that were contemplated for manufacture, sale, rent, and repair.

As it was founded at the time of cyclecar mania, production of motorcycles by the Ritz company is unlikely. For the 1914 and 1915 model years, there was a Ritz automobile. Beverly Rae Kimes and Henry Austin Clark Jr. note that the Ritz principals were Carl D. Ritzwoller; Solomon Satzauer; and A. Russell Smith, the designer (*Standard Catalog of American Cars*, 1996). Kimes and Clark report corporate headquarters at 246 West Sixty-Fifth Street in Manhattan and production of 215 cars under contract by the Driggs-Seabury Company in Sharon, Pennsylvania. The Ritz company was dissolved by proclamation pursuant to the state tax law in 1930.

Robinson Cyclenet Inc.
Himrod
1997–ca. 2004
Trade Names: **AR Streetracker**;
Robinson Streetracker

In 2000, David Robinson noted that his family had been in the motorcycle business for fifty years; Robinson Cycle Sales Inc. was organized in the 1960s. David Robinson reported that he once worked as a translator in Spain for the Yankee Motor Company (q.v.) of Schenectady. The Anderson-Robinson Streetracker motorcycle was created by the Robinson family ("brothers, sisters, spouses and sons") and a consultant, Mark Anderson, whom David Robinson credited with the "idea." The pattern for the Streetracker, especially the frame, came from a Yamaha dirt-track racing machine that David Robinson had raced in the early 1970s and restored in the 1990s. Anderson subsequently left Robinson to work on his own Streetracker-style prototype and created Norsman Motorcycles (q.v.).

Streetracker development and manufacture, funded by Robinson's mother, Ellen N. Robinson, and others, has produced about thirty-five machines. Early examples, dating from 1997, utilized a Yamaha frame in which was mounted a modified Yamaha 650-cubic-centimeter twin engine. Later machines, with Yamaha engines in three sizes, have used custom frames and other components from "around the world," according to Robinson. The motorcycles are styled to resemble dirt-track racing machines but are intended for use on public roads. Their buyers, says Robinson, are "middle-aged men who dream they are racing around [but] actually are going to the soda fountain."

The AR Streetracker, one of a series of Yamaha-engined road machines resembling dirt-track racing motorcycles. Photo courtesy of Robinson Streetracker.

In 2000, Robinson noted that he used a "chrome moly frame, billet-machined aluminum everywhere, our own wheels, seat and tank, our own exhaust system, electrical system and internal engine modifications done by us." A 2000 model retailed for ten thousand dollars.

Around 2001, Robinson Cyclenet initiated a new aspect of its operation by instituting a college program in Mankato, Minnesota. There, participants were able to spend two weeks building their own motorcycles from parts and instruction provided by the Robinson family's BuildaBikeInc.com division. BuildaBikeInc.com also offered instruction via a kit available on the internet, and a Dundee, New York, facility was to be retained for manufacturing motorcycles to order. Advertisements for a version of "BuildaBikeInc.com" appeared into 2004. In 2000, Robinson reported sales of about fifteen complete motorcycles per year, with most business coming from the sale of parts.

Royal Motor Works
(Emil F. Hafelfinger)
New York City (Manhattan)
1902–ca. 1906
Trade Name: **Royal**
Eclipse Machine Company
(engine manufacture on contract)
Elmira
1907–?

At the winter 1901 Madison Square Garden motor vehicle show, New Jerseyite musician Emil Hafelfinger exhibited a two-speed motorcycle, which "brought the people around as would a fire, and the inventor did not have opportunity to rest any day," according to the *Cycling Gazette*. The *American Automobile* said the machine "promises to eclipse anything in the motor-cycle field up to the present time. . . . Whenever the wheel was taken downstairs to show its work on the circle a large and enthusiastic crowd would follow, who showed a deep interest in every move made by the operator." A competitor reportedly said, "Hafefinger [*sic*] has us all beaten so far as design goes, but whether he has not sacrificed his construction for design is something only time can decide." Soon Hafelfinger was inundated with offers to buy, build, or distribute a production version of the prototype.

The Royal had its one-cylinder, F-head engine mounted as the bottom half of the seat post. Gear reduction came from spur gears mounted on the crankshaft and the pedal axle. A clutch allowed the pedals to be engaged or not according to the rider's desire. Final drive came through the single chain to the rear wheel. The Brown-Lipe two-speed gear with neutral position was incorporated into the rear hub. Hollow, open-ended cooling flanges were brazed to the engine cylinder. A one-gallon fuel tank was fitted behind the saddle. Speed control came not from a throttle but from adjustment of the timing.

The sensation of the vehicle show at Madison Square Garden in 1901, the Royal moved from a failed Massachusetts factory to Manhattan in 1902. From the *Bicycling World and Motocycle Review*, March 13, 1902.

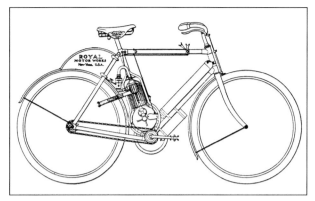

Designed by Emil Hafelfinger, the neat Royal, with its engine built into the seat tube, utilized chain drive to the rear wheel. From the *Dealer and Repairman*, July 1902.

In May 1901, the *Horseless Age* reported that the Royal Motor Works had been organized in Buffalo to build the "Heffelfinger [sic] motor bicycle" with a local bicycle manufacturer, the William Hengerer Company, working for Charles A. Persons of Worcester, Massachusetts. However, by September, the Royal Motor Cycle Company was planning to build motorcycles on its own in Chicopee Falls, Massachusetts.

Persons was a veteran of the cycle trade, having manufactured saddles in Worcester. According to a 1913 history of the American motorcycle in the *Bicycling World and Motorcycle Review*, Persons's "enthusiasm got the better of his judgement in this instance . . . and with insufficient resources . . . [he] was unable to swing the Royal to success." After the first few motorcycles were shipped in January 1902, the Royal Motor Cycle Company moved from Chicopee Falls to New York City; in March the Royal Motor Works at 29-33 West Forty-Second Street was advertising for agents. In September, the Royal Motor Works moved to 512-518 West Forty-First Street, where the motorcycle "will be assembled and the business of the concern conducted."

Although there is no entry for Royal among American motorcycle manufacturers listed in the January 1904 *Dealer and Repairman*, in April Emil Hafelfinger, and not the Royal Motor Works, advertised his "Perfect Motor Bicycle" from 243 West Forty-Fifth Street. His ad said that his latest version "shows great improvement." Apparently still preferring to have someone else manufacture, he said that "all patents are owned and controlled for license to build on royalty." There was no Royal (or Hafelfinger) at the 1905 Madison Square Garden automobile show and no Royal (or Hafelfinger) in the *Motorcycle Illustrated*'s list of manufacturers in November 1906.

Perhaps Royal production in New York had ended as early as 1904. At the close of 1906, at the latest, plans were laid to manufacture both an improved chain-drive model as well as a belt-drive "Model B" in Worcester, Massachusetts. The latter version appeared in July 1907, and production of belt-drive Royals continued into the 1910 model year. Engines for the revived Royal were manufactured on contract by the Eclipse Machine Company in Elmira; Ralph D. Webster, Eclipse secretary, wrote the Royal Motor Works Inc. at Worcester in July 1907, "Every Motor shipped you has been tested to 2¾ horsepower and better, and every one to be shipped you will have this rating."

Although the revived chain-drive version was stillborn, Hafelfinger's basic design—his engine surrounded by tubes joining bottom bracket and seat tube, battery, and coil in cases mounted on the down tube, even the fuel tank mounted over the rear mudguard—proved viable enough that it endured for a decade.

Frederick S. Ellett, from Elmira, held multiple patents for motorcycle clutches; the first was granted in 1908. Ellett granted the exclusive rights to use and license the clutch to the Eclipse Machine Company. Together they successfully fought to protect the patent in court with many motorcycle companies, including Indian and Harley-Davidson. Ellett had numerous patents for bicycle- and motorcycle-related improvements, including a two-speed gear device for motorcycles.

In addition to the motorcycle clutch, the Eclipse Machine Company manufactured automobile starters and other vehicle-related products. In 1929, Eclipse was part of a consolidation that formed the Bendix Aviation Corporation.

Hibbert B. Ruggles
ca. 1901–9
Rugmobile Company of America
1902–3?
New York City (Brooklyn)
Trade Name: **Rugmobile**

According to the *Dealer and Repairman* for June 1902, the Rugmobile had just been "placed on the market" by the Rugmobile Company of America at 54 Columbia Heights in Brooklyn. The innovative design eliminated many bicycle-derived components—diamond frame, saddle, cranks, and pedals—common on most motorcycles of the period. "If the rider's legs are not to perform the work of propulsion, there is no reason why the rider should not ride on a comfortable seat and in a comfortable position" (*Dealer and Repairman*).

A channel frame substituted for the tubular style, so that in case of damage a "blacksmith can make a repair in a few minutes, or it can be done by the rider himself with a piece of wood and wire." Two frame members, one above the other, curved from the head tube to the rear hub. The one-cylinder, air-cooled engine, placed between these two parts of the frame at a 45-degree angle from vertical, drove the rear wheel via a 1-inch flat belt. An idler, controlled by the right foot, allowed the machine to "stop with the motor running, thus avoiding the stopping of the motor when slowing up at a crossing or for traffic." The left foot operated a brake pedal.

The 3-inch bore by-3.75-inch stroke engine produced 3 horsepower. A hand crank started the motor. Sufficient fuel for a 100-mile range could be carried with "an extra tank . . . added if desired." The total weight of the Rugmobile was 154 pounds. As illustrated, the motorcycle had short-reach handlebars "for racing purposes," but longer reach bars could be fitted. The drop-style frame made the Rugmobile suitable for both men and women riders. The *Cycle and Automobile Trade Journal*'s January 1903 "Buyer's Guide" continued to list the Rugmobile Company at 54 Columbia Heights, but there are no city directory listings for the company, nor does the New York secretary of state have any records of incorporation. The identity of the Rugmobile designer would be unknown save for the similarity of its design and name to (1) the motorcycle design patented by Hibbert B. Ruggles in 1903 and (2) the motorcycle built by "H. B. Ruggles" of Brooklyn a few years later. The similarities in the "Rugmobile" and "Ruggles" names also suggest that the same party was responsible for all three designs.

Hibbert Ruggles (born in 1865 in Nova Scotia) was in the bicycle business at 13 Clinton Street in Brooklyn by the late 1890s. His patent application for "motor-cycle" improvements was filed on September 16, 1902, and the patent was granted on November 10, 1903. Along with similarities between the Rugmobile

The Rugmobile eliminated many bicycle-derived components. If the rider was not pedaling, there was no reason not to "ride on a comfortable seat and in a comfortable position." From the *Dealer and Repairman*, June 1902.

and the patented design, there are differences. While both utilize channel-stock curving from head tube to rear wheel, the patent design has the engine inclined from vertical to the rear, forming a post for the seat. The patent drawing shows a chair-style perch with a short backrest similar to that which was fabricated for the Rugmobile. Another design element described in the patent is a support for a second seat (behind the first) that pivots to form a stand for the motorcycle when not in use. This feature appeared on the second Ruggles motorcycle a few years later.

That second "H. B. Ruggles" machine received publicity in the motorcycle press from 1906 through 1909. The motorcycle depicted in the *Cycle and Automobile Trade Journal*, in the *Bicycling World and Motorcycle Review*, and in the *Motorcycle Illustrated* during the course of this period also used channel steel, now hot riveted for both frame and forks. Again, pedals were omitted but "can be attached if desired." Again, a hand crank was used to start the engine, which now was mounted with the cylinder vertical and, as in the patented design, served as a seat post. A clutch operated by the right foot and chain drive completed the transmission. The hand grips controlled the throttle and spark.

The 5-horsepower engine was fed by a three-gallon tank, "which is more than is usually carried, and is sufficient for a run of at least 150 miles" (*Horseless Age*, October 3, 1906), and could drive the motorcycle to 60 miles per hour. A second, padded seat over the rear wheel could be combined with the folding stand to form a platform "for carrying a large amount of baggage." The low center of gravity "lessens the tendency to skid" (the patent had for one of its objects "to lower the point of gravity"), and the cradling of the frame side members gave the engine and accessories protection from "injury through collision, etc."

In 1906, Ruggles was reported to have had "near five years . . . ideas of his own regarding motorcycles" and was "a step nearer to his idea of perfection." In May 1907, after completing the machine, design, and construction "without assistance," he was "negotiating with capitalists with a view of forming a company for its manufacture on a large scale." In the fall of 1908, Ruggles had "just placed on the market a new type of motorcycle, the design having been adopted with a view of increasing both the comfort and the safety of the operator." Two of the photographs accompanying the trade press stories about the Ruggles machine show a man and a woman passing the photographer on the motorcycle. One assumes the operator is Ruggles himself, whose address was given as 75 Hicks Street. In 1910, Daniel (*sic*) B. Ruggles was one of the incorporators of the American FN Company of Boston, Massachusetts, formed presumably to distribute the Belgian-made FN (q.v.) motorcycle.

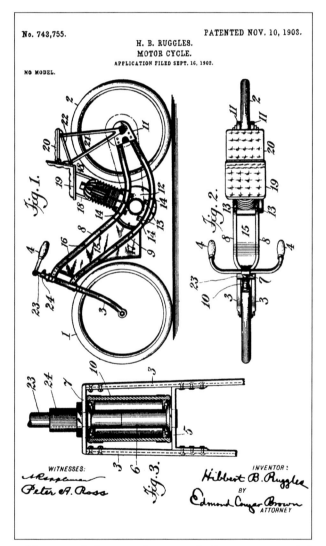

Hibbert Ruggles's patented motorcycle design was intended to "lower the point of gravity or depression of the frame to such an extent that riding is made safe and comfortable and tendency toward 'skidding' is reduced to the minimum."

The Ruggles 5-horsepower, 60-miles-per-hour motorcycle of 1906. The man in front is likely Hibbert Ruggles. From the *Motorcycle Illustrated*, May 1907.

S

Henri St. Yves
New York City (Manhattan)
1915

In December 1915, Henri St. Yves, a Frenchman living in New York City, received United States Patent 1,164,122 for a motorcycle. Although *Motorcycling and Bicycling* called the St. Yves idea a "hybrid" between a motorcycle and an automobile, his design basically remained a motorcycle. Whether any machine was built to St. Yves's specifications is unknown here.

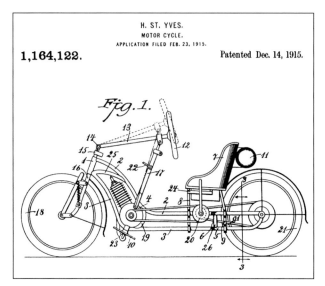

The patented (1915) Henri St. Yves motorcycle, utilizing some automotive elements, such as the geared-down wheel steering.

With two parallel down (front) tubes, St. Yves's motorcycle in side view resembled a drop-frame (woman's) safety bicycle. Cradled between these tubes was a one-cylinder, four-cycle engine. This frame design and engine location are similar to those used by Hibbert B. Ruggles (q.v.) in his Rugmobile motorcycle of 1901. Instead of a seat tube, St. Yves supplied four posts on which was mounted a bucket seat. St. Yves's four seat supports slid along frame tubes to provide adjustable leg room between the chair and footrests. St. Yves used an adjustable steering wheel geared down to provide "easy steering of the motorcycle." Otherwise, the St. Yves machine utilized standard motorcycle technology of the period, with chain drive to a clutch, mounted under the seat, and final drive (belt or chain is not specified) to the rear wheel.

In the early 1910s, St. Ives was a famous, world-class marathon runner and a well-known local professional motorcycle racer. He also worked in aviation, as a pilot and seller of airplanes. In 1913, he operated the St. Yves Aviation Company from an office in Manhattan's Park Row. In 1916, he went back to France to join the French army as a messenger during World War I. After returning, and as late as 1918, he repaired automobiles in the Bronx in partnership with Eugene F. Baessler, another veteran of the aviation trade and, perhaps, another expatriate Frenchman.

Salisbury Ball Bearing Corporation Inc.
Jamestown
ca. 1916

Motorcycle Illustrated in December 1915 reported the birth of the Salisbury Ball Bearing Corporation. The Salisbury certificate of incorporation mentions the manufacture of ball bearings, to be sure, but also of motorcycles, bicycles, automobiles, metal furniture, engines, and steel novelties. Clark W. Salisbury, John W. Eckman, and Thure Linderholm, all of Jamestown, as well as Theodore S. Abramson of St. Paul, Minnesota, and Edwin H. Sandin from Dunnell, Minnesota, were the first-year directors. The first four were subscribers of fifty shares each. The enterprise was capitalized at $300,000, although beginning capital was $5,000.

The Journal's Directory of Jamestown for 1913–14 lists the Salisbury Ball Bearing Company with Clark Salisbury as president in room 608 of the New Fenton Building at 2-6 East Second Street. Eckman, of Guantanamo, Cuba, was president of the Vinculo Realty Company at rooms 607 and 608 in the New Fenton. Thure E. Linderholm was secretary-treasurer of both the Elk Furniture Company and the Globe Cabinet Company.

Two years later, Eckman was president and manager of the Salisbury Ball Bearing Company Inc. The other officers were David Lincoln and M. J. Mead. Eckman was also involved with the Vinculo Realty Company and the Vinculo Sugar Cane Company. Linderholm remained secretary-treasurer of the Elk Furniture Company. Clark Salisbury was still associated with the ball bearing company, which had its factory at 1276-1290 East Second Street.

By 1920, Eckman and the Salisbury Ball Bearing Company were gone from directory lists. Clark Salisbury was running a "general repair shop," while Thure Linderholm remained with the Elk Furniture Company. At no time was the Salisbury company listed in the directories as a manufacturer of motorcycles.

Keinosuke "Keino" Sasaki
d/b/a **Keino Cycles**
New York City (Brooklyn)
2000–present

Keinosuke "Keino" Sasaki was born in Fukuoka, Japan. His father was a motorcycle enthusiast and an artisan. Sasaki got his first motorcycle at the age of eleven, a dirt bike that he shared with his brother. While attending college he apprenticed at a local custom motorcycle shop. In 1998, he decided to take his passion for motorcycles further and moved to the United States to attend the Motorcycle Mechanic Institute in Arizona.

In 2000, he moved to Brooklyn and found work at a small shop in the SoHo neighborhood of Manhattan. At this shop he met and worked with Indian Larry (Lawrence DeSmedt, q.v.). Sasaki has stated that it was Larry's "mentality and his approach of motorcycles and life that have influenced him." After Larry's passing in 2004, Sasaki and other members of the shop, including Paul Cox (q.v.), continued on, using the shop name Indian Larry's Legacy to honor him.

In 2008, Sasaki moved on to start his own shop, Keino Cycles. At the shop he follows his vision with a focus on "functionality and artistry on motorcycle." There he builds one-off custom motorcycles, offers metalworking classes, runs a service shop for engine rebuilds, and repairs custom build bikes requiring fabrication. Keino Cycles also has an online store for parts and gear. The company's website gives the following advice: "If you are in a rush, we are not the right shop for you." Sasaki's work has been featured in magazines, and he has won numerous awards.

Norbert H. Schickel
Ithaca and New York City (Manhattan)
1907–11
later, **Schickel Motor Company**
Stamford, Connecticut
1911–24
Trade Name: **Schickel**

Norbert H. Schickel (1886-1960), in Ithaca and Manhattan between 1907 and 1911, fabricated at least three experimental or prototype motorcycles. In New York City in 1910 and 1911, he purchased equipment, prepared tooling, and began making parts before production of motorcycles commenced at the Schickel Motor Company factory in Stamford, Connecticut.

Schickel was born in New York City, the son of Elizabeth and the architect William Schickel. At age fourteen, Norbert built his first internal combustion engine. During the summer of his initial year at Cornell University, he fabricated a motorcycle, which could not master the steep hills around Ithaca. A year later he built a two-stroke machine, "not a hill in or around Ithaca being steep enough to stall it." That encouraged him, according to *Motorcycle Illustrated*, to "plan to market a two-stroke motorcycle." In Ithaca, Schickel apparently did not have a workshop to use; a surviving receipt among the Schickel family papers at Cornell University shows that he paid Thomas and Grant in Ithaca $9.48 in June 1908 for work and a few parts for a motorcycle. The eighteen hours of labor suggest major repairs, modification, or development rather than maintenance or adjustment. During his Cornell years, Schickel also built an experimental V-4, two-stroke engine. During one summer break, he "devoted two months to a trip on which he visited all the large automobile plants in the country, studying the principles of automobile designing." Another summer, he worked at the Simplex Automobile Company factory in New York City "to apply himself to the problems of automobile engineering," and during his college years he "continued . . . to work on motorcycle power-plants at odd moments."

Having graduated from Cornell, Schickel went to work for a builder of automobiles, the H. H. Franklin Manufacturing Company in Syracuse. By 1910 he was back in New York City, where he created the prototype of the first production Schickel motorcycle. He was both "a serious young man who easily convinces you that he is a thorough motor student" and a man whose motorcycle features "point to extraordinary ingenuity in its designer, who disposes of the most serious problems confronting present-day designers by radical departures from accepted standards of construction," said *Motorcycle Illustrated* in 1911.

In New York he also apparently did not have a development facility of his own. Records of his expenditures in the late fall and early winter of 1910–11 indicate that much work on the motorcycle was undertaken by machinist Ferdinand L. Schmidt at Twenty-First Street and Eleventh Avenue in Man-

Norbert Schickel, depicted as about to board a train for the New York City cycle trade show in January 1915. From *Motorcycle Illustrated*, December 31, 1914.

hattan. In February 1911 alone, when Schickel took his prototype to the Chicago Motor Vehicle Show, he paid Schmidt over $512. Records of other expenses during the development period indicate purchases of generic parts such as levers, nipples, carburetor, belt idler, and fork sides, as well as orders for "machining blank pistons and making two piston rings" (Sier-Bath Company, September 1910, $12), "patterns for magneto case cover and handle bar center" (Schmidt, January 1911, $10.45[?]), "tank casting" (Queensborough Brass and Bronze Foundry, January 1911, $14.63), and "nickel plating and polishing" (Bayer-Gardner-Himes, January 1911, $22.98).

At the Chicago show, the two-stroke engine impressed visitors, since it was "the first of its kind to be staged at any American show"; every other Amer-

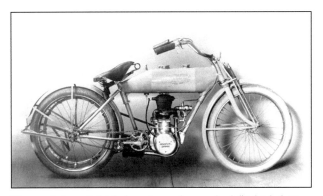

The prototype Schickel motorcycle, marked "Schickel New York." Photo courtesy of Norbert H. Schickel Museum, Private Collection of Patrick and Joan Anderson Cullen.

ican motorcycle engine at the time was a four-stroke design. Notable was the cast-aluminum fuel tank in place of the top tubes of the frame (patented by Schickel in 1915). Other innovations included the magneto, which was adjustable from the handlebars and enclosed in the crankcase; the spring fork; the integral crankshaft and flywheel ("insuring permanent alignment of . . . important parts"); and the clutch, or "free engine device," in the form of a belt tightener, according to the *Bicycling World and Motorcycle Review*. A grease cup at the end of the crankshaft served to provide lubrication and a seal, since the air-tight crankcase worked as a conduit for the fuel mixture en route to the combustion chamber. Several reports rated the Schickel engine at 4 horsepower (although the *Cycle and Automobile Trade Journal* claimed 5).

Schickel, according to the *Bicycling World*, having "looked after visitors and explained the various features, . . . occasionally making an inquirer get on the machine to test for himself the workings of the caster-actions spring fork," returned to New York optimistic about selling his motorcycle. In March 1911, the Schickel machine was included in the *Cycle and Automobile Trade Journal* "Eleventh Annual Motorcycle Review." The retail price given was $250. The address for the company was "5 E. 83rd. St. N.Y. City." Actually, 52 East Eighty-Third Street was the residence of Schickel's mother and probably his legal address. Schickel was reportedly "still using a machine which he built in 1907 and it's giving good service yet."

Whether Schickel built any motorcycles for sale during 1911 and, if so, where his factory was located are questions to which trade press stories suggest some answers. In 1916, *Motorcycle Illustrated* reported that Schickel, upon leaving Syracuse, had developed his new motorcycle "in his shop on the west side of the [New York] city." Perhaps Schmidt's establishment was meant, although, of course, some other facility could fit the description. The *Motorcycle Illustrated* writer continued by stating that "practically all of the year 1911 was devoted to gathering the necessary machinery and fitting out the factory" (in Connecticut).

Motorcycling in December 1911 reported that during the past year "the facilities for manufacturing were inadequate to manufacture in quantity." The journal continued by stating that "a large part of the tool making is being done in the old shop in New York, but all the manufacturing is now done in the Stamford plant." Unhappily, the extent of any production in New York is left unsaid, as is the location of the shop there. *Motorcycle Illustrated* at the end of November 1911 said that the motorcycle "was formerly made by Norbert H. Schickel, of New York City . . . but the facilities for manufacturing it were entirely inadequate to take care of the demand." *Motorcycling* in January 1912 wrote that "little was done in the way of putting this machine on the market during the past season." The *Bicycling World and Motorcycle Review* in December 1911 reported that the Schickel was "now making its real debut."

The state of Connecticut in September 1911 issued a certificate of organization for the Schickel Motor Company, capitalized at ten thousand dollars. The president of new firm was Norbert Schickel, who sold to the company a drawing board; table; "dies for making part No. 5 Drop Forgings"; "60 castings for part No. 120"; other dies; patterns for "cylinder," "crank case," "tank frame," and other parts; one thousand pieces of "Part No. 63 Stampings" and similar quantities of other parts; a Cincinnati 24-inch drill press; a Schuchard and Shutte No. 4 portable tachometer; a heating plant; enameling oven with connections; taps and dies; Jones and Lamsen flat turret lathe; and other equipment needed to outfit a factory. In addition, he sold to the company his "model [motorcycle], together with all designs and shop drawings," as well as the lease to the Stamford factory. In brief, it would appear that in preparation for the organization of the company and its settlement in Stamford, Schickel had purchased equipment and manufactured parts—one would be tempted to assume—by ordering them from shops in New York City. Since only one motorcycle is mentioned in the agreement (dated September 13, 1911), one also might be tempted to conclude that Schickel built no other motorcycles in New York after the prototype that was displayed in Chicago in February 1911. The model motorcycle and factory lease were acquired from Norbert Schickel for $7,000 in stock. For the tools and parts, he was paid $3,954.27. Norbert Schickel also became treasurer and general manager of the Schickel Motor Company, receiving a salary of $150 a month for the latter job only. His ninety-eight of one hundred shares gave him absolute control, which he maintained up to the Schickel Motor Company dissolution in 1924.

In April 1916, the Schickel Motor Company opened an export office at 47 Broadway in New York City, perhaps hoping that foreign markets would be more receptive to the two-stroke motorcycle than American riders had been.

In 1923, Norbert Schickel told *Motorcycling and Bicycling* his $150 Model "T" motorcycle was "the culmination of 15 years of work . . . which . . . is now a perfected product." He saw no "noticeable change in the next ten years" other than lowering prices due to increased production. However, the unaltered 1924 model was the final Schickel offered for sale. While the history of the Schickel motorcycle and the Schickel Motor Company in Connecticut lie beyond the scope of this volume, the writer suggests that the Schickel Motor Company records, which are part of the Schickel family papers at the Carl A. Kroch Library of Cornell University, offer researchers an opportunity for compiling a detailed, illuminating history.

One further point warrants attention here. Michael Gerald and Jim Lucas say that the Schickel was "last built in Ithaca, New York." Norbert Schickel, after a short sojourn in Detroit, in fact moved to Ithaca in the mid-1920s. On the other hand, the assets of the Schickel Motor Company were advertised by broadside to be sold at Stamford in 1924, specifically at an auction on August 7, "in piecemeal lots": lathe, grinders, drills, screw machines, paint-spraying equipment, "many new and used motorcycles," and a motorcycle business consisting of patterns, drawings, jigs, dies, and a "very large stock of finished and semi-finished parts," with "over 1,000 Schickel motorcycles now in operation."

A petition for the sale of the remaining assets of the bankrupt corporation notes that the sale of the real estate took place on August 28 and that "all tangible personal property" had been sold. The petitioner, the receiver for the Schickel Motor Company, asked for permission to sell the intangibles to Norbert Schickel for fifty dollars, which subsequently happened. Certainly, it is possible that Norbert Schickel purchased all of the Schickel Motor Company assets at the August 7, 1924, sale. In early 1925, Schickel received the trademark for the Schickel Motor Company. At least some patterns remained unsold, or at least unclaimed, apparently, since Schickel received a letter from the Myers Foundry Company in Waterbury in March 1925 asking him to remove the patterns that were "formerly the property of the Schickel Motor Company." In short, the succession of events in the denouement of the Schickel Motor Company might argue against the revival of the Schickel motorcycle in Ithaca but do not exclude it.

John Schnepf
New York City (Manhattan)
1898

The *Horseless Age* for June 21, 1899, reported a patent granted to Schnepf (half assigned to William C. Doscher of New York) for an "automobile." The vehicle plainly was a motorized bicycle.

Schnepf's engine was an electric motor, the armature of which was attached directly to a pulley that engaged the rear tire from above. The battery was carried in a case fitted into the diamond of the bicycle frame. A controller on the handlebars allowed the rider to adjust the current flow and, consequently, the speed of the motor and motorcycle. Schnepf said that

> because the pulley . . . and the wheel are relatively small and no great amount of power is required to revolve the armature, the same being determined by the relative sizes of the said pulley and wheels. As the motor has a capacity of very high speed, a sufficiently high speed may be transmitted to the driving-wheel. . . . The rider may readily employ the aforesaid driving means as the sole source of power, or, . . . as

the supplemental power, the pedals . . . being at all times available . . . for use. When the rider encounters a decline, the motor may be thrown into contact with the driving-wheel . . . and utilized as a dynamo to restore the battery. . . . It will be understood, of course, that the battery is usually charged from an outside source.

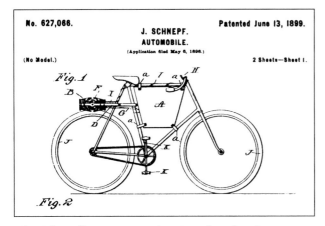

John Schnepf's 1899 patent drawing of an electric motorcycle. The battery housing is labeled "A," and the motor with a roller atop the rear tire is "B."

As a variation, Schnepf also designed a version of his bicycle motor using a worm gear to drive the pulley. And he provided for a lever system to raise or lower the motor from or to the tire. "It is obvious that without departing from the spirit of my invention that said means for elevating the motor may be readily modified or changed," he said. "This system of levers also permits of varying the degree of pressure between the friction and vehicle wheels."

Amos Shirley
New York City (Manhattan)
1907–8?
Trade Name: **Styria**

The Styria was an Austrian motorcycle manufactured by Puch and Company in Graz. In late 1907, Amos Shirley at 935 Eighth Avenue became a Styria agent, offering one- and two-cylinder versions with either belt or chain drive. A two-speed gear could be fitted inside the rear wheel. The *Bicycling World and Motorcycle Review* for April 25, 1908, listed Shirley among "motorcycle importers." According to the January 15, 1909, *Motorcycle Illustrated*, a strike at the Styria factory left delivery of the motorcycles to Shirly in doubt for the 1909 season.

Amos Shirley was selling bicycles in 1891 and added motorcycles by 1905. He dealt with numerous American and foreign brands and was active until at least 1925. He did not build motorcycles but had a repair shop.

William H. Slattery
New York City (Brooklyn)
ca. 1903

The January 1903 issue of the *Cycle and Automobile Trade Journal* "Buyer's Guide" lists William H. Slattery at 739 Manhattan Avenue as a source of motorcycles. Hugo Wilson's "unconfirmed marques" list includes "Slattery Brooklyn, NY c. 1903." *Upington's General Directory of Brooklyn* reports Slattery as in the bicycle business at the Manhattan Avenue address.

Morton W. Smith Company Inc.
New York City (Manhattan)
1920–21
Trade Name: **Skootamotor**
(variously, **A.B.C. Skootamotor**, **Scootamotor**, **Skootamota**, and **Skootermoto**)

Motorcycling and Bicycling in October 1921 noted the "invention of an Englishman" who was selling his Skootamotor (also spelled "Scootamotor" in the article) through the auspices of the Morton W. Smith Company, an automotive business at 10 West Forty-Fourth Street. A photo depicts a scooter-style machine with small-diameter wheels and a step-through frame. The engine is mounted over the rear wheel. The top speed reportedly was over 20 miles per hour, while fuel consumption was less than 50 miles per gallon. Operation was similar to that of an ordinary motorcycle, while the weight was so little that "it is possible for the average person to carry the cycle under his or her arm."

The original rights to the Skootamotor were held and most likely developed by the A.B.C. Motor Company of London. In 1919, Gilbert Campling Ltd of London and Coventry, England, purchased the sole rights and licenses to manufacture the machine, except in France. In 1920, Gilbert Campling came to America to promote the Skootamotor. The press referred to him as the inventor of the machine; however, that does not seem to be true. He appears to have traveled to vacation resorts touting the qualities of the machine. He carried a small, hand-sized silver model of the Skootamotor.

In August 1920, the *Berkshire Eagle* newspaper reported the following: "Miss Francis Plumb received [a] gift of a "skootamota" from Gilbert Campling, inventor and manufacturer. The machine, which is used on boardwalks and other runs, is popular at Newport and Palm Beach. There are about 90 of the machines in this country at present. They are made in England."

The Smith company was incorporated in March 1916 to buy and sell trucks. President Morton W. Smith, a resident of Southport, Connecticut, did business in 1921 at 19 West Forty-Fourth Street, according to city directories. In 1922, the Smith company changed its name to Isotta Motors Inc. to sell Isotta Fraschini vehicles. By 1925, Morton Smith was a paint manufacturer, president of the Elaterite Paint Company at an East Forty-First Street office.

Starin Company
North Tonawanda
ca. 1903

The "Buyer's Guide" in the January 1903 issue of the *Cycle and Automobile Trade Journal* lists the Starin Company as a source of motorcycles. A month previous, the Starin enterprise had advertised for sale a "new gasoline runabout" for $350, "LESS THAN COST to manufacture," since "we need the room for 1903 stock." Whether motorcycles were built is unknown here, although available advertising suggested that they dealt exclusively with automobiles. Beverly Rae Kimes and Henry Austin Clark Jr. note automobile production in 1903 and 1904.

E. C. Stearns and Company
Syracuse
1900–1902?

The *Cycling Gazette* and *Scientific American* in late 1901 ran photos of the "Stearns Motor Cycle for Pac-

ing" and the "Stearns Racer," respectively. The images show a modified diamond-frame machine with the saddle directly over the rear hub. The one-cylinder engine was mounted on the lowest part of a looping down tube. Chain drive from the end of the crankshaft was direct to the rear wheel. *Scientific American* noted the machine was a "1902 racing model" for pacing a bicycle rider. An 11-inch-wide hub was intended to shield the paced rider. The DeDion 3.75-horsepower engine, turning 600 to 2,000 rpm, allowed track speeds over 50 miles per hour.

Stearns pacing machine for bicycle racers, 1901. From *Scientific American*, December 21, 1901.

The manufacturer of the motorcycle remains unidentified in both journals, but, based on newspaper articles, it seems very likely that it was the Syracuse firm E. C. Stearns and Company, of which Edward C. Stearns was the principal. The company, with factories in both Syracuse and Toronto, had been prominent in the manufacture of bicycles in the 1890s. In 1899, according to the *Horseless Age*, the Canadian Stearns company became part of the National Cycle and Automobile Company of Toronto, with E. C. Stearns a director, while the Syracuse factory became part of the American Bicycle Company—the "Bicycle Trust." In 1900, Edward Stearns, according to the *Horseless Age*, "severed all connections with the American Bicycle Company" and became involved with the Anglo-American Rapid Vehicle Company. The organization of the (Anglo-American) subsidiary Stearns Automobile Company followed in 1900, according to the *Age*. Beverly Rae Kimes and Henry Austin Clark Jr. also note the Stearns Steam Carriage Company. By 1903, all firms except E. C. Stearns and Company were gone, the last continuing the hardware business begun in prebicycle days.

Where the manufacture of the Stearns pacing motorcycle fits into this chronology is unclear. Documentation exists for Stearns electric and steam automobiles in Syracuse as well as a "motor" tricycle. And in February 1903 the *Dealer and Repairman* said that the American Bicycle Company had bought out Stearns, while adding, "Last year a large number of Stearns machines [presumably bicycles] were placed on the market." Since nowhere in the notes about the Stearns pacer is the name of the manufacturer or the place of construction mentioned, it is conceivable, but not likely, that the Stearns pacing motorcycle was manufactured elsewhere, perhaps by F. B. Stearns and Company of Cleveland, Ohio, manufacturers of the Stearns automobile there from 1898.

Stellar Industries
also **United Stellar Industries Corporation**
also **Stellar Electronics and
Manufacturing Company**
Plainview
ca. 1962–ca. 1974
Trade Names: **Scoot-A-Long**; **Ran-Jet**;
Maxi Super; **Mark I**; **Mark II**

Stellar's product line was mini-bikes, the diminutive motorized vehicles often operated off-road by children. Stellar assembled its motorcycles in a plant at 131 Sunnyside Boulevard. Production began around 1962 with the "Stellar Scoot-A-Long" motor scooter. In 1962, the price was $99.50 for the scooter, which was 53 inches long and had a 2.5-horsepower engine, an auto clutch, and a recoil starter. Early advertisements were geared toward adults and economic "short-transportation," such as "less than [$0.]50 a day!" and "easy to the store, no parking problems." In 1965 the Scoot-A-Long cost "as low as $129.95," and advertising was still directed toward economic transportation. By 1970, the advertising was targeted to teens.

According to an interview with mini-bike collector Harry E. Hanson in 2000, by 1968 or 1969 fifteen different models were offered, ranging in price from $129.95 to $299.95. The former figure bought a 63-pound, 2.5-horsepower, suspensionless "Ran-Jet," while the latter price purchased a 93-pound, 5-horsepower, full-suspension "Maxi Super" with lights and fenders. Centrifugal clutches were used on all models. An undated instruction manual is marked "United Stellar Industries Corp."

By 1970, Stellar Industries had the Plainview plant; one in Joplin, Missouri; and one in Opa-Locka, Florida. The "Quasi Stellar" model was made in Plainview and the Model A and D Stellars were made at the other two plants, according to an article on mini-bikes in the February 1970 issue of *Popular Mechanics*. Stellar Industries also had added the "Fun Kart" go-cart to the line-up. It is not known here how long Stellar utilized the two additional manufacturing sites.

According to Hanson, around 1971, Mark I and Mark II models, which were more similar to full-scale motorcycles, were offered. He notes these were likely inspired by the more sophisticated Rupp mini-bikes that had reached the market. These Stellars used larger, 10-inch wheels on full-suspension frames. Four-horsepower engines worked through a "variable speed torque converter," belt-driven jack shaft, and a "heavy-duty #420 motorcycle chain." The Mark II added a front brake as well as a 12-volt lighting system. An undated instruction manual for the Mark I and Mark II is labeled "Stellar Electronics and Manufacturing Co."

In an undated announcement from around 1974–75, Stellar announced a new "ruggedly built, lightweight compact deluxe mini-bike" to lead a new effort to gain a major share of the mini-bike market. New models "for every purpose" were to be released within seven months. Featuring Tecumseh engines, they were to range in price from $159.95 to $299.95. The new models included chopper-style mini-bikes.

At the time of the 2000 interview, Hanson owned four Stellar mini-bikes. He noted that the Stellar mini-bikes "were sort of fragile so most did not hold up to the abuse they were subjected to by their 11-year-old owners." Of his Stellar Red Baron Jetspeed model, manufactured between approximately 1968 and 1973, Hanson says he purchased it from the original owner "who recalled it cost $140.00 new and came in a box to be assembled at home."

The Stellar operation may have had its origins in a machine shop founded as early as 1947. The New

York Department of State recorded the assumption of the Stellar Electronics and Manufacturing Corporation name in January 1970; the business previously was known as Trebarmish Inc. (organized in 1969). Stellar Electronics and Manufacturing merged into the Republic Corporation, incorporated in Delaware, in 1974.

United Stellar Industries Corporation was organized in 1971 and dissolved in 1981. In 2000, the Equine-Stellar Corporation, incorporated in 1978, operated at the Sunnyside Boulevard location, doing sheet-metal and machine-shop work. The company, according to several directories of manufacturers, was founded in 1947. The relationships among the various Stellar enterprises have not been determined here.

The Long Island–built Stellar Mark II mini-bike, ca. 1971. Image courtesy of Harry E. Hanson.

I. R. Stevens and Company
New York City (Manhattan)
ca. 1960
Trade Name: **JoyRide**

I. R. Stevens and Company, of 510 Madison Avenue, either manufactured or distributed the JoyRide folding scooter, or both. Keith T. King of Colchester, Illinois, invented this folding scooter, which was patented in 1952 (submitted in 1949). At least three different companies utilized the design with various trade names applied to their scooters: JoyRide, Argyle Scooter Cub, and Dinky-Cycle. It is not known here whether the scooters were made in one manufacturing site and given different names by distributors or each distributor shared the rights to produce and sell the folding scooter. Some sources state that there was a succession of builders who had the rights; other sources suggest that they coincided.

An article in the February 1960 issue of *Popular Science* highlights the JoyRide, including a set of photographs showing how the scooter folded up and a picture of a man riding one (see page 191 for images). According to the piece, the JoyRide had a 2.25-horsepower Power Products engine, the frame was cast aluminum, and the total weight was 51 pounds. Folding up the machine took about fifteen seconds. Further, the article states,

> The four-ply pneumatic tires measure 2.50 by 4. A pull cord operates the recoil starter. Transmission, through a V belt and pulleys, is automatic. The throttle can by rigged for foot or hand control; the single (rear) brake is pedal operated. One tiny tankful of gasoline—with oil mixed in—takes the scooter 40 miles. It goes 100 miles on a gallon.
>
> JoyRide is available at some department stores or direct from I.R. Stevens and Co., 510 Madison Ave., NYC. List Price is $174.50.

I. R. Stevens and Company appears in the Manhattan city directory at 510 Madison Avenue in 1960 but not 1959 or 1961. It is not clear how long the company existed and how many scooters they produced or distributed.

Stratton Motor Bicycle Company
New York City (Manhattan)
1901
Trade Name: **Stratton**

At the New York Cycle and Automobile Show in January 1901, the Stratton Motor Bicycle Company of New York City exhibited "for the first time" two of their motor bicycles. The *Bicycling World and Motocycle Review* said the Stratton was

Stratton Motor Bicycle Company | 191

a good looker, and also carries off the honors in the matter of price . . . at $150. The method of supporting the engine seems open to criticism on the ground of inadequate bearing and support, but it is claimed to have withstood exhaustive tests; the idea, however, of containing oil, coil and battery in one case [also praised by the *American Automobile*] is a step in the right direction. A Wall Street speculator is interested in the machine, the future of which is said to rest greatly in results obtained at this show.

The Stratton company also applied for exhibit space at the automobile show at the Chicago Coliseum held at the end of March. And the following June, a Stratton machine was shown in the Machinery and Transportation Building of the Pan-American Exposition in Buffalo.

In February 1901, the company, from an address at 7 Wall Street, published what the *Cycle Age and Trade Review* called a "neat," illustrated catalog for the motorcycle "now being marketed." A month later, the *American Automobile* noted that a "large factory" had been acquired on Thirty-Sixth Street, which was being "rapidly equipped with the most modern machinery." The *Automobile* also reported that "a well-known man in Wall St. is financiering the company, and the very fact of him taking hold of it practically insures a success in the start."

The Stratton company claimed, according to the *Cycling Gazette*, that its engine "can be kept under

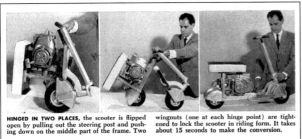

Images of the JoyRide scooter being tested out by *Popular Science* staff members, February 1960.

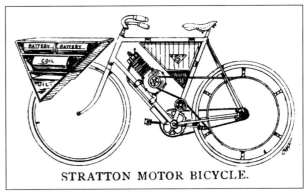

The enlarged image of the triangular case on the 1901 Stratton Motor Bicycle shows how the ignition components as well as the fuel and oil tanks all were enclosed in a single container. From the *Bicycling World and Motocycle Review*, January 17, 1901.

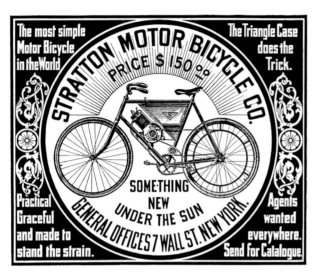

Stratton advertisement. The "Triangle Case" housed the fuel and oil tanks as well as the ignition components. From the *American Automobile*, March 1901.

absolute and perfect control and can be stopped within a short space either by turning off the current, or shutting off the mixture of air to the gasolene, or the gasolene itself." The batteries, coil, and oil supply were housed within a triangular box inside the frame triangle. A lever adjusting the spark could be used to control speed. The machine weighed 75 pounds and was "constructed of the best material obtainable." A new muffler design allowed "noise and vibration . . . [to be] brought to a minimum." Equipped with a coaster brake, the motor bicycle cost $150. A motor outfit for converting a bicycle sold for $115.

At about the same time that the catalog appeared, Edmond F. Gottschalk, who in this period changed his name to Edmond Francis Stratton, on February 18, 1901, filed a patent application for a "motor-cycle." Patent 686,284 was duly issued on November 12, 1901, the object of which invention was "to provide a motor equipment which may be attached to diamond-frame bicycles of ordinary construction without requiring any alterations." In addition, Stratton claimed that his device would make the equipment "as light and compact and simple as possible and to so mount it upon the bicycle that it will not interfere with the operation or control thereof or with the comfort or convenience of the rider; also, to provide a construction which may be readily attached to the various makes and sizes of bicycles."

Stratton said that any motor may be used, but that "I preferably use a gasolene-motor of the well-known de Dion [sic] type." Adjustable braces and clamps were used to mount the engine. A triangular case mounted above the motor but within the frame triangle was used to house the integral oil and gasoline tanks as well as the battery and coil. At the rear of the machine, an adjustable pulley was attached to the rim of the wheel (as opposed to the spokes in other designs). Stratton also noted that it "is an advantage of my invention that all parts of the power-generator are brought within the limits of the three main braces of the bicycle-frame and are so arranged and centered as not to seriously interfere with the balance or control of the machine."

In the March 1901 issues of *Cycle Age* and the *American Automobile*, display advertisements depicted the Stratton machine in profile. Except for a perhaps unusually tall diamond frame, the Stratton resembles some other motorcycles of the period, with the engine mounted on the down tube. In the case of the Stratton, the top of the engine lies close to the head tube, i.e., high in the frame. The text accompanying the advertisement claims that the product of the Stratton Motor Bicycle Company was "Something New under the Sun" as well as "the most simple Motor Bicycle in the World" and "Practical Graceful and made to stand the strain," adding, "The Triangle Case does the Trick" and "Agents wanted everywhere. Send for Catalogue." The price remained $150 then, but by June 1901 the price rose to $200, according to the *Bicycling World* and advertisements in *Cycle Age* and the *American Automobile*. The last noted "compactness in design and freedom from complicated parts." A 50-mile range at a cost of five to ten cents for gasoline was claimed, with speeds from 3 to 25 miles per hour. Indicated horsepower was 1.75. Shelby tubing of 16- and 18-gauge was used in the frame. Hartford 1.75-inch tires and a Morrow Coaster brake were fitted.

In September, Edmond F. Stratton was an entrant but nonstarter in the "motor bicycle" class of the New York-to-Buffalo endurance run organized by the Automobile Club of America. His machine was rated at 1.75 horsepower and weighed 78 pounds.

By October, the Stratton Motor Bicycle Company store at 23 Courtland Street closed "after a brief existence." The financial backer, Wall Street broker J. Overton Paine (1868 or 1869–1945), who had made a fortune in sugar equities, was reported to be "in a precarious financial dilemma" (*Cycle Age*) or a "peck of trouble" (*Bicycling World*). In December it was reported that a judgment against Stratton for $22,686 was found in favor of Paine "and another [person]" and that "it is believed to mark the end of the Stratton Motor Bicycle Co., of which Stratton was the active man and Paine the 'angel.'" Stratton was identified by the *Bicycling World* as the former Edmond Gottschalk, who invented the bicycle that had been "exhibited at the last New York show."

Even before the putative end of the Motor Bicycle Company, Stratton, "of 7 Wall street, New York, president of the Stratton Motor Cycle Company," was reported by the *Horseless Age* as organizing a company to build a "compact gasoline carriage to sell for $400. He intends to exhibit one of these vehicles at the Madison Square show." It was at the time of Stratton's announcement that the Manhattan Automobile Company, organized a year earlier by J. Overton Paine, Arthur B. Paine, and James A. Hands, went bankrupt, and its plant at 502 West Thirty-Eighth Street sold. The new owner was none other than Stratton. His partners in the Stratton Motor Company were David Wood of Manhattan and G. H. Murray Jr. of Hollis.

The cutaway patent drawing shows the storage of fuel, oil, and ignition components in one triangular case on the 1901 Stratton Motor Bicycle. From the *Horseless Age*, November 27, 1901.

The certificate of incorporation for the Stratton Motor Company was filed on December 12, 1901. The three directors of the firm were Stratton, Wood, and Murray, whose operation was "to build, construct, remodel, repair, sell, rent, lease, hire, keep on storage, care for &c. electric, gasoline and steam automobiles of every kind . . . also bicycles, tricycles and all other cycles." With capital stock authorized at $150,000, they began business with $500. Stratton, of 104 West Seventy-First Street, held three shares, while his partners owned one each.

The Stratton Motor Company, according to Beverly Rae Kimes and Henry Austin Clark Jr., reportedly built at least one car before the firm's demise, which occurred sometime after the beginning of April 1902, when they offered $50,000 worth of 5 percent first mortgage bonds.

Two Brooklyn riders thought highly enough of their Stratton motorcycles to enter them in a Boston–to–New York City endurance run on July 4 and 5, 1902. H. W. Wherett on a 2.5-horsepower machine and Charles A. Root Jr. on a 1.5-horsepower model "had trouble with their engine, and direct chain drive," according to the *Cycle and Automobile Trade Journal*, or both were involved with accident(s) "five miles from start," according to *Motor Age*, and neither made the first checkpoint at South Framingham. Of the motorcycles as a group, one observer—C. C. Bramwell in the *Horseless Age*—noted that the

> mufflers were inadequate in all cases. The exhaust could be heard for six or eight blocks. The finish on all was good.
>
> None of the machines entered exhibited any striking ideas in designing a "motor bicycle," but several showed considerable thought in combining an ordinary, heavy free wheeled bicycle, with a small motor attached more or less cleverly to the frame.

The durability of Stratton motor-bicycle construction is suggested by a compilation by the *Motorcycle Illustrated* of motorcycles registered in Rhode Island for 1907. One Stratton remained among the 402 machines.

Studebaker Corporation
Watertown
1913–14

In January 1914 the *Bicycling World and Motorcycle Review* reported, "Up in Watertown, N.Y., the local paper has heard that the abandoned plant of the New York Air Brake Co. has been acquired by the Studebaker interests which proposed using it for the manufacture of motorcycles. This rather sensational news, however, proves to be a 'mare's nest.' Vice-president Benson, of the Studebaker corporation, says there is not a word of truth in the rumor; that Studebaker has not acquired the plant and will not manufacture motorcycles."

Stylemaster Custom Motorcycles
Syracuse; Mississauga, Ontario
ca. 1996–ca. 2001

Stylemaster built air-cooled, V-twin-powered motorcycles in the popular Harley-Davidson-inspired idiom. The company advertised "custom motorcycle fabrication and assembly with a vision, a passion and a whole new attitude."

Al McIlvena was Stylemaster's "master engine builder," turning out motors with 106-to-140-cubic-inch displacements. An original frame design was called the "Fatman 230," designed to handle a 230-millimeter-diameter rear tire. Painting of Stylemaster motorcycles was "handled off-site by any one of Stylemaster's number of fine artists," and the finished parts were returned to the 938 Spencer Street shop in Syracuse for assembly. Stylemaster marketed their own line of custom parts in addition to sale of items manufactured elsewhere. In 2000, Stylemaster literature noted that they worked "with Dave Mackie Engineering [of Ventura, California] to provide dyno testing and product development feedback." (Mackie, a former motorcycle drag racer, specializes in modification of Harley-Davidson cylinders and heads for superior performance.)

McIlvena was principal of the Stylemaster operation. Stylemaster Custom Motorcycle Corporation registered as a foreign business corporation on May 15, 1998. The Syracuse facility opened by 2000 (if not sooner) and was an extension of a shop in Mississauga, Ontario, from where McIlvena moved to Syracuse. Stylemaster Custom Motorcycles Inc. of Mississauga was owned by David Fidani.

SuperMoto Italia Inc.
St. James
1985–present

Joe Tortora's Long Island dealership sells and services a number of Italian motorcycles. A branch of his operation both customizes extant motorcycles and fabricates custom motorcycles based on Ducati engines. Utilizing parts secured from many sources, Tortora ships his finished motorcycles to the world, a recent delivery having been made to Australia. In 2000, he estimated that during his fifteen years of operation, he had produced around twenty custom motorcycles. He also builds motorcycles for the American Motorcycle Association's "Super Twin" road-racing class. SuperMoto International Inc. is a wholesale, high-performance motorcycle-parts operation based in the same St. James facility.

T

Tarform Inc.
New York City (Brooklyn)
2017–present
Trade Names: **Luna**; **Scrambler**; **Racer**

Taras Kravtchouk built his first motorcycle in 2010. Its base was a 1982 Yamaha XS400. He continued to work on motorcycles, focusing on ones built in the 1960s and 1970s, learning from the process. Kravtchouk, a native of Sweden, explains how he came to the decision to build an electric motorcycle as follows:

During my day job I was helping startups actualize their ideas by providing plans that ranged from napkin sketches to complete technological solutions. As a counterbalance, I spent my nights and weekends at a shop restoring and building vintage motorcycles. I found something mystical in those machines: a combination of aesthetics and speed, a quest for innovation and pure thrill. One day, as I was working on my Triumph that was leaking oil, I was struck by how seriously these machines were due for an overhaul and that it was time to embrace new ways of approaching automotive sustainability. I wanted to think beyond electrification, to reconsider how the machines are actually made: what materials are being used during the fabrication and if it is possible to create contemporary vehicles that preserve the spirit of craftsmanship. That became the catalyst for Tarform.

The name Tarform means "taking shape" in Swedish. All of the parts for the Tarform were designed and engineered in-house at the company's Brooklyn headquarters. Once designed, they are manufactured by outside venders. According to a Tarform representative, "the motor is sourced from an external company specializing in electric motor technology (The details are proprietary)." Further, "multiple patents are being pursued related to design, sound generation and material science."

There are three models: the Luna, the Scrambler, and the Racer. The top speed is listed as 120 miles per hour, getting to 60 miles per hour in 3.8 seconds, with a range of 120 miles. The motorcycle offers three riding modes and charges up to 80 capacity in fifty minutes.

As of November 2021, after five years of development, four prototypes have been built. Orders are being taken, and delivery is slated for the summer of 2022; prices start at $24,000 for each model.

Tarform Luna electric motorcycle. Photograph by Ryan Handt, courtesy of Tarform.

Tedd Cycle Inc.
d/b/a **V-Twin Manufacturing**
Vails Gate
1968–present

Ted Doering organized Tedd Cycle in 1968 with his father, Jerry Doering, selling aftermarket parts for the remodeling of Harley-Davidson motorcycles into chopper-style machines. Since then, his business has grown to the point that he has published a 1,300-plus-page catalog. In 1977, he registered the V-Twin trademark. Through V-Twin Manufacturing, he distributes all the parts needed for the replication of many Harley-Davidson motorcycles. Complete, rolling chassis kits are among his offerings. Engines and wheels are assembled in Doering's Vails Gate facility. Frames are purchased from a Connecticut source. While Tedd Cycle does not offer complete, assembled motorcycles, Doering has on display a complete panhead-style machine built from his available components.

V-Twin Manufacturing's comprehensive line of Harley-Davidson replacement parts enables the company to offer all the pieces needed to reproduce a 1948 panhead-style motorcycle, such as this example assembled by V-Twin. Photo courtesy of V-Twin Manufacturing.

A 1946–47 replica "HM" knucklehead 30-degree rake frame made by V-Twin Manufacturing. Photo courtesy of V-Twin Manufacturing.

As of 2022, V-Twin manufactures thousands of parts, employs over one hundred personnel, and supplies parts to a network of over five thousand dealers worldwide.

E. R. Thomas Motor Company
1900–1901, 1902–5
Auto-Bi Company
1901, 1907–9
Buffalo Automobile and Auto-Bi Company
1902
Thomas Auto-Bi Company
1905–7
Greyhound Motor Works
1909–10
Greyhound Motor Company
1911–12
Buffalo
Trade Names: **Thomas Auto-Bi**; **Auto-Bi**;
Buffalo; **Greyhound**

The prototype Thomas "Design Number Two" motor bicycle announced in September 1900. From the *Bicycling World and Motorcycle Review*, January 10, 1910.

Perhaps the most significant of the first-generation motorcycle enterprises in New York, the E. R. Thomas Motor Company ranks among the pioneers of the American motorcycle industry. Unhappily for the makers of the Auto-Bi, fortune was fleeting, and within a decade the successor, Greyhound Motor Company, was a minor, failing endeavor.

At the end of the nineteenth century, Edwin Ross Thomas (1850–1936) claimed experience both in the manufacture of bicycles and in the construction of internal combustion engines. Born in Webster, Pennsylvania, by the 1890s he was associated with H. A. Lozier and Company, a prominent builder of bicycles in Cleveland, Ohio. In 1899 he was "managing partner" of H. A. Lozier and Company in Toronto, Ontario, manufacturing air-cooled engines. Interested in applying engines to road vehicles, Thomas traveled to "the fountainhead of the industry, France, and studied the actual conditions on their native heath," said the *Bicycling World*. In August 1899, H. A. Lozier and Company of Toronto Junction merged with three other Ontario bicycle makers, perhaps providing the impetus for Thomas to move to Buffalo in 1900, where "backing his faith with tireless energy and capital, [he] at once started making tools, jigs and other appurtenances to turn out motors in quantities," said *The Wheel*.

Looking back a few years from June 1903, Frank Lowell in the *Motorcycle Magazine* said "Edward [*sic*] R. Thomas" was the "father of the American motor bicycle," who had been motivated by the machine's "commercial possibilities" rather than altruism or enthusiasm for the motorcycle concept. Lowell claimed that while still in Canada, Thomas saw the superiority of the "single-track, two-wheeled machine," which could run on side paths, needed no special garage, and did not conflict with the automobile. Realizing the more fertile field for his enterprise lay in the United States, Thomas went to Buffalo. And, said Lowell, "it is right here that the motor bicycle owes to E. R. Thomas its greatest debt," for he took from his "capacious" fortune the money for a factory, for advertising, for travelers, and "so made the first real, sustained effort to make and market motor bicycles."

Thomas in 1903 said,

Lord! I wouldn't go through it again for this house full of money. Why it seemed as though a long lifetime of integrity and business prestige counted for nothing. Some of my best friends commenced to call me a 'fakir, confidence man' and what not. The odds were all against me. . . . But the public demand and our persistent hammering brought some of them [dealers] around, and to-day I have the satisfaction of knowing that those who protested the loudest are now among the strongest advocates of the motor bicycle.

In April 1900 came a report that Edwin Thomas and his brother, Orion F. Thomas, had purchased a quantity of machinery and leased space from the

Globe Cycle Company at Broadway and Elm Streets in Buffalo. They were to manufacture "motor tandems, tricycles, quadricycles, etc." The *American Automobile* confirmed that Orion Thomas was "interested in this enterprise." Capitalized at $150,000, the factory began work on April 16, and some products were to be ready for sale by July 1. Since Thomas motor tricycles and quadricycles had been shown at "the Toronto fair last September . . . there is no experimenting to be done." Edwin Thomas, according to the August 1900 *American Automobile*, remained a director of the Canadian Cycle and Motor Company.

In August 1900, the Thomas company announced a "complete jobbing department," which would provide "to the trade" all the parts needed for motorcycles, by which was meant engines for both tricycles and bicycles as well as "cylinders, carburetors, frames, gears, aluminum cases, sparking plugs, etc., almost all parts being of their own manufacture," reported the *Horseless Age*. Whether deliveries of complete vehicles took place during the summer of 1900 is not clear, but if there were such, they were likely motor tricycles rather than bicycles. In early August, the Thomas company informed the cycling press that the Autocrat name had been selected for the "line of motor cycles."

In September three Thomas motor-bicycle types were announced. One had the engine mounted on top of the down tube within the diamond of a bicycle-style frame. The *Bicycling World* said the engine drove the rear wheel via a belt to a roller on top of the tire, "an ingenious idea which permits the belt to be readily uncoupled and the machine to be driven by pedal power as usual." The other two motor bicycles were similar except for a curve in the down tube of one. On both, the engine was attached to the underside of the down tube by a "patented motor truss." With the truss, the engine was held forward of the pedal crank, giving a low center of gravity, "a feature for which many are striving." The engine drove the rear wheel on both versions via a belt and pulley.

A *Bicycling World* writer, who was "privileged to be the first outsider to catch a glimpse of the new motor bicycle[s]," was taken by the fork design; he thought the "most striking features of the whole machine," aside from the motor itself, "are the forks, joined at the head, thus making what is practically an unbreakable front." Within a short period of time, the diamond-frame design, with the engine suspended beneath a straight down tube, was abandoned, leaving "Design Number One," the version with the looping down tube, and "Design Number Two," the roller-drive machine, for the market.

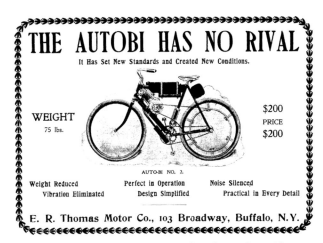

Among the first advertisements for the earliest Thomas Auto-Bi motorcycles to reach the market. Later spellings added the hyphen to the Auto-Bi name. From *Cycle Age and Trade Review*, January 18, 1901.

1901 Model Year

The *Cycling Gazette* noted that the Thomas designs had "overcome the serious disadvantages of top heaviness, heat, improper distribution of weight, strain and vibration while in steadiness, efficiency, simplicity and fine running qualities they are particularly noteworthy." The new machines were intended for sale to the cycle trade and subsequent resale to users for the 1901 season.

Emphasizing the jobbing of components, the Thomas company made individual parts available to other manufacturers and dealers, who would assemble motorcycles. Thomas Design Number One (also advertised as the Racer), combining the looping frame and engine, was to be "sold in quantities to bicycle manufacturers who are thus [by adding wheels, saddle, etc.] enabled to turn out motor bicycles to meet the immediate demands of their trade without the expense of motor experiments or investments in special machinery," reported the *Bicycling World*. The Thomas frame was a heavier gauge than the usual bicycle material. How many, if any, of Design Number One were built is unknown here; if it was produced, the number certainly was very small.

Design Number Two allowed the installation of an engine on an unmodified bicycle frame. A "bed plate of patented design" was mounted on the down tube, anchored at the head and seat tubes. The single-cylinder engine was fitted inside the triangle, with the cylinder head just below the top tube. A belt powered a roller on top of the rear wheel just below the saddle. "The motor and all attachments will be sold separately to bicycle manufacturers." The bed plate would fit any bicycle frame 22 inches or taller, according to the *Cycle Age and Trade Review*. A Morrow coaster brake on the Thomas motor bicycle allowed the rider to assist the engine, coast, or brake by backpedaling.

The engine itself was a four-stroke, air-cooled unit. The crankcase was aluminum, split vertically. Phosphor bronze bearings were used. A battery and coil ignition system incorporated a Thomas spark plug. Claims were made for parts "made to gauge, minutely adjusted," resulting in complete interchangeability and immediate duplication. The four-chamber muffler was constructed of aluminum. Several descriptions noted a carburetor large enough to carry a "sufficient quantity of gasoline for ordinary journeys without the use of a supply tank." High compression and power were noted in all three Thomas engines. These included the 20-pound, 1.5-horsepower type for bicycles; a 2.25-horsepower, 50-pound type; and a 3-horsepower, 56-pound version fitted to the Thomas Auto-Tri, the tricycle that had been shown in Toronto the previous year. With modification, the vehicle became an Auto-Quad.

The Thomas company in the early fall of 1900 reported "a rapidly increasing business, particularly in its air-cooled motors and motor frames for bicycle," according to the *Cycling Gazette*. Prices for complete motor bicycles, probably announced at the end of October, were $200 for a 1.5-horsepower, 175-pound model and $250 for a 110-pound racing machine with the 2.25-horsepower engine. At the turn of the year, the complete production $200 motorcycle, the Auto-Bi No. 2, also identified as the "Light Roadster," was ready for the winter bicycle shows. It was basically the Design Number Two with a belt drive to the rear wheel instead of a roller.

E. R. Thomas wrote an extensive essay for *Cycle Age* in 1900 explaining how the Auto-Bi met the requirements of a "commercially successful motor bicycle." First, the Auto-Bi would go "quietly, buoyantly and gracefully." While the Auto-Bi, Thomas continued, would not operate without attention, no engine or animal power would operate without care. The Thomas advantage, he claimed, was that the gasoline engine was so much easier to run for an amateur than steam power. "It is only necessary to learn not to choke the engine with too much fuel or too much or too little lubricating oil; each can be regulated by turning the lever on when starting, and off when stopping. All

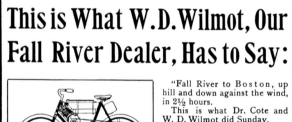

The thrill of pioneer motorcycling is explained in the text. "Scorchers" were fast bicycle riders. From *Cycle Age and Trade Review,* May 30, 1901.

other adjustment of levers is not necessary." Even "in case of forgetfulness a short experience will teach the most obtuse to regulate all troubles, none of which can be serious or expensive. As a last resort the belt can be detached and the bicycle pedaled home with but little, if any, discomfort."

Thomas said his motorcycle was light but strong. Heavier tubing and stronger reinforcements helped produce a measure of safety, while the engine being braced between the head and seat tube as well as by a felt-cushioned bed plate produced a vibrationless ride. As far as ease of operation was concerned, all the rider had to do was govern speed by the throttle and brake. If that proved too complicated, the brake alone would stop the machine with the power on. Thomas claimed his company was prepared to manufacture in large quantities. The capacity of his factory was six thousand machines a year, "which can be easily increased, as we have all the tools and fixtures completed for constructing interchangeable parts by the most accurate and economical means."

The Thomas motorcycle would glide "along with a sensation of quiet, ease, grace and comfort impossible to describe and only to be appreciated by those who have experienced it." *Cycle Age* should not be "afraid to boom the 'Auto-bi.' Boom it for yourself and boom it for the bicycle agents and riders interested . . . no new industry was ever started in so advanced a stage of perfection. It is the cheapest transportation known to mankind. It requires less power to propel than any other, and in many respects it is the most delightful and practical in results of all automobiles."

A description of the Thomas factory at 102 Broadway at the end of 1900 suggests a well-equipped, well-staffed operation, which had settled on its designs and prepared for major business. A reporter for the *Cycling Gazette* claimed that the facility would "astonish those whose faith in the permanency and stability of the motor bicycle industry has been so frequently and rudely shaken." With Thomas's years of experience in bicycle and motor matters combined with "thorough and exhaustive tests of the light motor bicycle and its enchanting possibilities," the company's prospects seemed bright as it "organized its new business on the lines of an old and thoroughly established industry," the bicycle industry. In spite of the inevitable delays in receiving materials, it appeared that one thousand No. 2 Auto-Bi's would be available for shipment by March 15. Further notes reported that each engine was tested at the factory and that Louis H. Bill, a bicycle industry veteran, had been hired to take charge of the sales department. Dealerships were being signed around the United States, and shipments were being made to foreign countries. Quoting phrases from a Thomas advertisement that appeared in his journal, the *Gazette* reporter said, "Enchanting in operation, charming in results and practical in every detail, entirely disinterested authorities predict that within a very short time all bicycles will be equipped with auxiliary motors, for with them 'all hills become plains and head winds cease to blow.'"

Cycle Age also was impressed with the Thomas factory, "the work now accomplished . . . [leaving] nothing to be desired." This, however, was followed by a period of discomfort while telegrams demanded motor bicycles and the Thomas company still needed time to perfect its tooling. E. R. Thomas's experience building bicycles was an advantage, but the construction of lightweight motors was a new endeavor. "And so it took months to complete the preparations. Now that they are completed the result is a set of tools and jigs which are veritable works of art." The factory in January 1901 was "crowded with work. It has a capacity of 150 complete machines a week."

One of five different motor bicycles at the New York Cycle and Automobile Show, the Auto-Bi was ridden by "everybody . . . racers, riders, amateurs" on the demonstration track within Madison Square Garden. One machine covered 1,208 miles after having traveled 2,000 miles before the show. Ernest L. Ferguson, former editor of *Motor Vehicle Review* and newly appointed assistant to E. R. Thomas, said to the *Gazette* that at the show

> our only trouble . . . was to hold back the agents. They want to give us a check and secure the agency at once. I had four men in the booth from one town and had a hard time, now I can tell you. They bid against each other. We are about the only people who have motor bicycles and have them where we can deliver them. People who have other motors will not be able to deliver for a year. It is one thing to have a sample and quite another to be ready to turn out the goods. Most of the bicycles on the floor of this class have been turned out by hand. We have not a motor bicycle so turned out. We are doing only machine work and won't start to assemble until February 1st. I could deliver fifty bicycles right here if we could supply them. I could take back with me $10,000 in advance checks. We do not know how far we are behind. It will take us a long time to catch up. We are going to hire another building about February 1st and will run this addition to the factory.

By midweek at the Madison Square Garden show, which ran from January 12 through January 19, Ferguson had sold eighty-eight motor bicycles. At week's end, the total was close to two hundred. A motor tandem bicycle arrived in Chicago for a later show. A reporter noted that the tandem "has a drop frame and entirely new in many features. It is arranged for the fair sex, which has hitherto been neglected." The E. R. Thomas Company also exhibited at the Pan-American Exposition in Buffalo, where *Cycle Age* noted that the company was "as energetic as its motor and the young man in charge is a splendid talker and never fails to interest those who wish to inspect the Thomas motor bicycle."

In spite of the careful preparations for the Auto-Bi No. 2, some improvements were announced in February. The described changes would seem to be shown in the advertising image used the previous month, so it may be that the improvements actually occurred before the January shows. In any case, these modifications included a strengthened frame and fork, a belt tightener working on the lower part of the belt, the elimination of a belt countershaft, automatic oiling, greater capacity for the tanks, simplified wiring, and improved carburetor.

At the end of February, Ferguson in New York explained the Thomas "invariable [dealer] terms," which were one-third with an order and the balance against the bill of lading. "Even these stiff terms do not seem to stagger people, however. They want motorcycles, must have them, in fact, and neither price nor terms prevent their getting them."

At the end of March, the Thomas Motor Company was reportedly shipping twenty Auto-Bi's a day. A *Cycling Gazette* reporter noted that the two-hundred-dollar price tag put a motor bicycle "quite within anybody's reach, whereas there are some people who cannot afford to indulge their desire for the more sumptuous motor vehicle," by which was meant an automobile. Thomas advertising emphasized the firm's ability to produce. Twenty machines a day was contrasted with "one or two a week in some back shop." The Thomas writer appealed to dealers, suggesting they not miss "the biggest chance in their life if they do not place their sample order at once." In addition to the complete Auto-Bi, the bicycle attachment, which listed at $140, was available to bicycle dealers and manufacturers at a discount. Charles S. Henshaw, a Thomas traveling agent, wrote the *Bicycling World* in late winter that "on the road not quite three weeks, I have placed eleven agencies between Buffalo and Glens Falls. . . . In Schenectady the other day the agent's store had from fifty to one hundred people all the evening . . . when the machine was running on a stand."

In May, in Omaha, H. E. Frederickson celebrated the opening of the 1901 bicycle season by handing out flowers and cigars. An orchestra of nine pieces played every evening for a week. "Mr. Frederickson had an attendant of his store constantly explaining the mechanism of the Thomas Auto-Bi, and two sales were the outcome." An early convert to Thomas motor bicycle sales was William McAllister, a Baltimore bicycle dealer. In the fall of 1900, he visited the Buffalo factory, where he tried out a Thomas on local streets. "I took one right out of the factory and . . . operated it . . . safely. . . . Between Buffalo and Niagara Falls. I traveled at . . . [a] two minute gait at times without use of the pedals," he reported to the *Cycle Age and Trade Review*.

By June 1901, the Thomas Motor Company was advertising that "hundreds" were using the Thomas Auto-Bi and more bicycle dealers were handling the Thomas than all other motor bicycle brands combined. The *Bicycling World and Motorcycle Review* in 1907 said "several hundred" Thomas motorcycles were "turned out" in the first year of production after a few motor tricycles. R. G. Betts, himself a motorcycle pioneer, in 1913 claimed that "nearly 1000 Thomas machines" were sold in the first production year. Yet a mistake had been made, he thought, in "utilizing bicycle frames and breakages that resulted created [sic] havoc. It speaks well of Thomas that he was able to weather the storm. His troubles in this respect, however, did not serve to increase the good repute of motor bicycles which, generally speaking, were viewed with doubt."

1902 Model Year

The volatility of American business life during the pioneer period of the motorcycle industry affected the E. R. Thomas Motor Company as it did other endeavors. Multiple rumors and reports of radical corporate changes were circulated even as the promise of the Auto-Bi forecast profit for all involved with its production and distribution. One story, in late March 1901, suggested that the "E. R. Thomas Motor Company of

Buffalo, N.Y., are said to be contemplating a removal to Middletown, Conn," site of the competing Keating Wheel and Automobile Company. This followed the January incorporation in New Jersey of the Thomas Cycle Company by Frank L. C. Martin of Newark, New Jersey and E. R. Thomas, Louis H. Bill, J. MacAdam, Louis Ohnhaus, and Henry Pokorney (q.v.), all of Buffalo. All the Buffalonians were associated with the E. R. Thomas Motor Company, with Pokorney acting as superintendent. In fact, George W. Sherman in 1910 said "Perkarney" was the engineer who designed the Auto-Bi.

In October 1901 came word that the motorcycle business of the E. R. Thomas Motor Company had been "disposed of to a new 'Auto-Bi Company.'" E. L. Ferguson was to be manager, assisted by Sherman and E. J. Edmond, all of whom came from the Thomas Motor Company. The new firm temporarily was to occupy quarters in the Thomas factory. The Thomas company announced it would restrict its activities to the production of engines for automobiles, motorcycles, and boats. One observer claimed that the Thomas move to building engines should encourage motor-bicycle builders who would otherwise worry about "motor troubles." An Auto-Bi advertisement picked up on the theme: "We Use E. R. Thomas Motors Only, They Are Most Efficient."

Sherman's tenure with the Auto-Bi Company was brief; in a month he moved on to a traveling position with the Hendee Manufacturing Company, builders of the new Indian motorcycle in Springfield, Massachusetts. Ferguson also left within a short time, returning to the trade press—specifically, the editorial staff of the *Bicycling World*, where he was to offer "a fund of practical and ripened experience with motors and motor bicycles alike in their manufacture, sale, operation and care."

The E. R. Thomas Company in the fall of 1901 began work on a new factory building on Niagara Street in Buffalo. Meanwhile, the Auto-Bi Company changed names and focus. In the late fall of 1901, two light automobiles were added to the product line of the new Buffalo Mobile (soon to be Automobile) and Auto-Bi Company. The $600 and $750 cars were to supplement two motorcycle models, one rated at 1.5 horsepower and the other at 2. A "number of new and original features . . . will add greatly to the comfort, appearance and efficiency, and will eliminate the objectionable features of motor bicycles."

In late February 1902, the Buffalo Automobile and Auto-Bi Company was incorporated, capitalized at $10,000 by Elmer Benton Olmstead, Frederic W. Armstrong, and Edwin L. Thomas, the son of Edwin R. Thomas. The incorporation of the E. R. Thomas Motor Company, which followed in May 1902, amounted to a transition from an unincorporated enterprise owned by E. R. Thomas to a corporation over which he maintained control and near-complete ownership.

A reporter for the *Dealer and Repairman* visited what he apparently viewed as a joint Buffalo Automobile and Thomas Motor Company factory in the spring of 1902, failing to distinguish between engine building and motorcycle construction. From mention of 150 mechanics turning out motors, he immediately stated that the company was building three distinct motorcycle models, the newest pattern being a "radical departure" from the early machines built by the Thomas company. The reporter concluded with a description of a ride on a motor tandem with C. S. Henshaw: "Mr Thomas sent the writer for a spin." Obviously, Thomas was involved with the Auto-Bi operation.

When the three Auto-Bi's for 1902 appeared in early February, they continued the numerical model designation begun the year before. The Model 3 was an "improved pattern of the 1901 machines." Twenty-five percent cheaper than the previous version, its $150 list was a "much talked of figure." The other two motorcycles, the belt-drive Model 4 and the chain-

Restored 1902 Thomas Auto-Bi, on display at the Motorcyclepedia Museum in Newburgh, New York. From the collection of Edward Doering on display at Motorcyclepedia.

drive Model 5, were variations of a completely new design, with their 2.5-horsepower engines mounted in place of the seat tube. The battery and coil were fitted to the down tube, and oil storage was inside the top tube. The gasoline tank was fitted on the stays behind the seat, with "all unsightly wires, levers, key switches, relief cocks, etc., . . . eliminated." The right-hand grip operated the spark advance, compression release, and ignition switch. Reportedly, the manufacturer recommended the rawhide belt model "as productive of the best results for general purposes, as chain transmission is noisy and inelastic."

Early in the 1902 model year, Olmstead showed a reporter an order for a "large number of machines for export and other orders, which showed that the Auto-Bi is being shipped to many foreign countries and, in fact, to all quarters of the globe." The Auto-Bi factory in April opened branch offices in New York and Boston. Edmond was in charge at 29-33 West Forty-Second Street in Manhattan, while Henshaw was at 243 Columbus Avenue in Boston. In all, there were probably more than five hundred Auto-Bi agents around the country. But in the spring of 1901 Indianapolis agent George Detch thought there were "few persons caring to put more than $150 in any kind of machine, or, if they do go above that, they generally spend their money with the automobile agent."

1903 Model Year

Any distinction between the E. R. Thomas Motor Company and the Buffalo Automobile and Auto-Bi Company ended on October 1, 1902, when the Buffalo company was absorbed by the Thomas company. By then, Darius Miller, a Chicago capitalist and first vice president of the Burlington Railroad, had acquired an interest in the Thomas firm. Paid-in capital now stood at $387,500, with plans for annual production of 1,500 automobiles and 1,000 motorcycles. *Cycle and Automobile Trade Journal* said that before the 1903 selling season, the Thomas company hoped to have built 750 and 500 of each, respectively, fabricating every part but tires and batteries. The *Dealer and Repairman* in April 1903 reported the Thomas capitalization at $500,000, with E. R. Thomas serving as president, secretary-treasurer, and general manager.

Staffing changes in the fall of 1902 brought a new "general superintendent," Herman J. Hass, to the Thomas company. The *Bicycling World* reported, "Few if any men have longer experience in fine mechanics than Mr. Hass; to him a large proportion of the credit is due in bringing the Cleveland bicycles to their high state of perfection." Hass's arrival reportedly allowed Albert B. Schultz, "gas engine expert," to concentrate on his specialty. In January 1903, S. F. Heath became sales manager of the Thomas company, arriving from a similar post with the Wisconsin Wheel Works.

In December 1902, the Thomas company announced the imposing Model 17, evidence of a move to more powerful and more expensive automobiles. Also announced was the single Thomas motorcycle for 1903, the Model 35, which delivered innovation in several areas; perhaps most striking was the full suspension frame. At the rear, the Auto-Bi utilized the enclosed coil spring "hygienic cushion frame" design found on some bicycles of the period. In this style, the rear wheel works against a spring with chain stays pivoting at their forward attachment. The Thomas spring was fitted between the seat post and the seat stays. At the front, another enclosed coil spring was fitted, this time in front of the head tube; the fork ends were slotted, allowing the wheel to rise and compress the spring by means of a rod. The patent for the "cushion-truss" was granted to Clarence E. Becker, a Canadian citizen employed by the Thomas company, to which the patent was assigned. Becker claimed that his design was intended to "produce a combined cushioning and trussing device . . . which is of simple and durable construction, which reduces the jar upon the cycle to a minimum, and which braces or trusses the steering-fork, so as to relieve the strain on the same and on the bearings in the steering head."

Another innovation was the transmission. Instead of the twin offerings of belt and chain drive of the 1902 seasons, the Model 35 combined the two, as a chain wrapped with two layers of leather ran over pulleys (rather than sprockets). The forward pulley was corrugated for better grip, while the idler was fitted with springs to compensate for the changes in distance between pulleys created by the movements of the rear wheel toward and away from the rear spring. The Thomas Company advertised that its new belt was "non-stretchable," would not slip or break, and was good for 10,000 miles. A patent for the design was issued on February 14, 1905, to Becker. Rights were assigned to Darius Miller and Edgar K. Ashby, the latter of whom in 1903 was "general manager" of the Thomas company. A report in the *Bicycling World* in April 1903 said that the belt chain was being manufactured by the Coventry Chain Company, apparently for general use with pulleys.

A story in the *Dealer and Repairman* suggested that for 1903 the lubricating oil was to be stored in the top frame tube, but whether any motorcycles were thus built is unclear. The gasoline tank was mounted on the down tube above another case for the three-cell battery. The coil was attached below the down tube. Also reported new for 1903 were a "larger" exhaust, a larger outlet for "refuse oil," "automatic spring idler," and an improved safety switch.

The motorcycle press greeted the new Auto-Bi enthusiastically. The *Bicycling World* was pleased that the rumors of "distinct departures in motor bicycles" were realized. They thought that the Model 35 "will bristle with new features, both great and small, all making for more comfort and reliability and much of it." And they were happy to pass on the Thomas news that the cushion frame was "so glorious as to surpass imagination." A month later, after viewing the Auto-Bi at the Madison Square Garden automobile show, the *Bicycling World* noted that it "bears out the picture and is an alluring machine" in spite of the belt, "about which information was lacking, [which] proves to be merely a bicycle chain covered with leather." The *Automobile Review* said the Auto-Bi was a "good specimen of a high-grade up-to-date motor cycle."

E. R. Thomas himself, quoted in the *Motorcycle Magazine*, said, "For the life of me, I can't see where or how we can improve the 1903 model much. The cushion frame and spring fork are, of course, a big improvement, and make for luxury in riding."

Thomas advertising for the two-hundred-dollar Model 35 stressed the spring frame, spring forks, and belt chain that solved "all the hitherto vexatious problems of entire strength and safety, transmission, hill-climbing, comfort and speed on country roads, vibration and general utility." A "New Art Catalogue" was available, and "Agents [were] Wanted Everywhere—To be at the top of the Motor Cycle Biz, get the Thomas Motor Bicycle Agency. WE ARE FILLING ORDERS ON RECEIPT." In September the *Bicycling World* said the Thomas Company had reported that the sales of their Auto-Bi's in August were "the largest in our history." But E. R. Thomas admitted that the motorcycle industry had yet to mature: "The quantity demand will come as soon as we, the motor bicycle manufacturers, are satisfied that our own conception of perfection is realized. Then will come the time for the price that attracts—when standardization and quantity production combine to reduce the past and present frightful cost of production."

1904 Model Year

The *Bicycling World*, in introducing the Model 36 Auto-Bi, noted that every year since its introduction—"and it was the first one made in marketable quantities"—the Thomas machine began the model year with "notable improvements." For 1904, those changes were less obvious to the casual observer, but the *Bicycling World* called them "more notable than of any previous year," and the *Cycle and Automobile Journal* called them "important refinements."

Perhaps most significant was a major increase in power, to 3 horsepower. The 2.75-inch bore by-3.25-inch stroke engine was fed by a new float-feed carburetor. Visually, the major change was a single case enclosing the 5-quart fuel and 1.5-pint oil supplies as well as the batteries. The oil drained into a sight-feed oiler that allowed the rider to inject a predetermined amount of oil into the cylinder without the risk of over oiling and fouling the spark plug. Improvements to the electrical system included enclosing the wires in rubber and fitting spring terminals. The right side of the handlebar was fitted with a throttle control, which the Thomas people noted "may be set at any desired speed and left there." The muffler for the 1904 machine was equipped with a cutout. Also on the right side was a control for partial compression, "designed to facilitate starting and riding through traffic."

Of the 1904 Auto-Bi, the *Automobile Review* said, "The little annoyances and troubles on previous motorcycles have been eliminated, with plenty of power to carry up any grade, without pedaling."

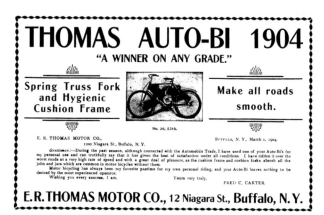

An advertisement for the dual-suspension Auto-Bi. From the *Bicycling World and Motocycle Review*, March 26, 1904.

The "days of experimental motor cycles is past. These machines . . . are destined to be the natural successors of the bicycle." The improvements in the Auto-Bi for 1904 had their cost. In January it was announced that the price of the Model 36 was to be $210.

In December 1904, the Thomas company advertised that its automobile trade was a million-dollar business, while its motorcycle income was less than a third of that. Still, the Thomas people were "proud" to have built the first practical motorcycle "in the world" and said that the coming 1905 model "promises to eclipse anything on wheels." Calculating an arbitrary figure of $175 as the wholesale price of an Auto-Bi and $300,000 for the Thomas motorcycle business in 1904 suggests a production of as many as 1,700 motorcycles. Of course, some of the motorcycle trade was in parts, so the actual number of complete motorcycles was less than 1,700.

1905 Model Year

The motorcycle and automobile pieces of the E. R. Thomas Motor Company split permanently in 1905. However, the naming of Edwin L. Thomas, E. R.'s oldest son, as vice president of the new Thomas Auto-Bi Company suggests continuing ties between the automobile and motorcycle builders. The Auto-Bi Company was incorporated in early March, with capital stock of $5,000, of which $2,100 was paid in. The president was Clarence Becker, who reportedly had charge of the "motor bicycle department of the E. R. Thomas Co. for the past four years." Joining Becker and Edwin L. Thomas as directors of the new company and serving as secretary-treasurer was William C. Chadeayne, "a newcomer in the trade, but . . . well known in Buffalo and vicinity as an enthusiastic motorcyclist." Operating at 1443 Niagara Street, the Thomas Auto-Bi Company announced it would put one thousand Auto-Bi's, designed by Becker, on the market in 1905.

The 1905 Model 37 Auto-Bi was very similar, if not identical, to its predecessor, although the Thomas Auto-Bi Company advertised "more practical improvements than any other motorcycle built." Among "special features," the Auto-Bi Company apparently was pleased with its truss spring forks, an oiler that "feeds in any kind of weather," and "handle bar control with both main grips tight when riding," the opposite approach of manufacturers who preferred twist grips. The Auto-Bi featured an "auxiliary grip on the handle bar . . . within easy reach of the rider's hand . . . to control the spark and exhaust lift." An advertisement in August 1905 depicts an Auto-Bi equipped with a tandem device that superimposed a portion of a second tubular diamond frame over the rear seat.

1906 Model Year

A redesigned, Model 44 Auto-Bi at two-thirds the price of the previous model was perhaps the revelation of the late summer of 1905. Announced as available for $135 without pedals, the standard price fully equipped was $145 throughout the model year, a figure that the *Bicycling World* thought was "likely to cause something of a stir." Missing from the previous year's equipment was the rear "hygienic" suspension. In its place was a spring seat post said to give the "same results as spring frame, and [do] away with extra parts."

The Model 44's new engine was in a new location, parallel to the down tube. A single casting served both cylinder and head. The crankcase was split horizontally. An exterior flywheel incorporated a belt pulley for the leather-covered Thomas chain. A forged crankshaft was used with a phosphor bronze connecting rod bearing. The 2.875-inch bore by-3.25-inch stroke engine was rated at 3 horsepower. Other innovations included a carburetor attached directly to the head, "thereby dispensing with piping to convey the mixture to the explosion chamber," tempered steel contacts replacing platinum in the ignition, and timing gears "plainly marked and . . . accessible merely by removing one nut."

Clarence Becker, in a letter to a potential agent in June 1906, said that the net cost of the $145 machine was $120. Terms were $25 cash with the order plus $95 cash on delivery or sight draft attached to the bill of lading.

Chadeayne, perhaps to promote the new Auto-Bi and perhaps to satisfy his thirst for adventure, in August 1905 announced a coast-to-coast ride, which he was willing to make a race. Apparently, there were no challengers, so he focused on beating George Wyman's record set in 1903 of 48.5 days. Starting from New York City, Chadeayne reached San Francisco just under 48 days later, on October 31. Described by the *Bicycling World* as a "clean cut, well built, agreeable young fellow of 29 years," he was also "the enduring type—short and compact and scarcely looking the 150 pounds at which he tips the scales. He is full of determination, and remarked modestly that he will 'get there' unless he is 'laid out stiff.' " His only baggage was the clothes he wore, a tool bag, and an extra inner tube.

During the New York automobile show in January 1906, Chadeayne's machine was on display in the city "and showed very little wear and tear from its trip of over 4,000 miles of continuous service over some of the worst roads in the country." A full-page advertisement in the *Bicycling World* immediately after Chadeayne's arrival in San Francisco was an extraordinary expenditure for the Thomas company, which generally used less-than-half-page displays. The text asked, "Get There? Did Chadeayne Get There? Of Course, He Did. The 1906 Thomas Auto-Bi . . . is built to 'get there' under any and all conditions. Agents wanted everywhere."

1907 Model Year

The little-changed Model 45 for 1907 listed at $175. The engine, while still rated at 3 horsepower, now had a 3.25-inch bore with its 3.25-inch stroke. The advertised weight had increased from 100 to 120 pounds.

Thomas advertising for 1907 continued to emphasize characteristic features such as the "Patent Truss Spring Forks," the chain-belt drive, and "Positive Grip Control," which allowed the throttle control to be set and left where desired. In addition, the lengthened stroke, dry-cell ignition ("batteries that you can buy anywhere"), an auxiliary exhaust port, an engine "that can be taken apart without removing from frame," and a choice of carburetors (float feed or "Regular Thomas Pattern") were talking points. The Thomas Auto-Bi Company guaranteed power to carry a 200-pound rider up a 20 percent grade. As usual, "live agents wanted everywhere." While production figures for the Thomas Auto-Bi are not available, a compilation printed in the *Motorcycle Illustrated* of motorcycles registered in Rhode Island in 1907 reveals that of the 402 machines, twenty were Auto-Bi's. The Thomas make ranked fifth, trailing Marsh-Metz, with ninety-four, and Indian, with fifty-one (both made in neighboring Massachusetts), as well as Merkel, at forty-eight, and Columbia, at twenty-two.

In February 1907, the Thomas Auto-Bi Company was reincorporated. As in the incorporation of 1905, the purpose of the company was described as involving vehicles of three wheels or less, "it being intended to exclude from the foregoing purposes motor vehicles running on four wheels, and known to the trade as automobiles or motor cars." This was perhaps an unusual distinction for an incorporation but understandable, as the two Thomas companies distinguished between themselves. For the Auto-Bi reincorporation, the capital stock was $30,000; the business was to begin its affairs with $10,000 paid in for shares valued at $100 each. Of the three directors, Becker and Chadeayne each subscribed ninety-nine shares. The third man, John W. Van Allen, with two shares, was a lawyer probably acting on behalf of the two principals in serving as the third director; Edwin L. Thomas had left the business.

Confusion about the Thomas Auto-Bi Company of 1905 and the Auto-Bi Company of 1907 resulted in more action by the New York Secretary of State; a certificate dated December 3, 1907, notes that the Auto-Bi Company (without the "Thomas" in its name) had merged with the Thomas Auto-Bi Company. The resulting corporation was known as the Auto-Bi Company.

1908 Model Year

The Auto-Bi Company in the fall of 1907 announced a removal one block from the old to a new, two-story,

49-by-220-foot brick-and-concrete structure at 1573–1575 Niagara Street. At the same time came word of the Auto-Bi models for 1908. The Model 47 Roadster for 1908 was distinguished by a double-coil spring saddle as well as 2.5-by-28-inch clincher tires fitted on hollow, nickeled steel rims and covered by steel mudguards. At $210, the cost of the better Auto-Bi matched the previous high figure for the Model 36 of 1904 and the 37 of 1905. The less costly Model 46 Semi-Racer listed for $185 with 2-inch single-tube tires fitted to wooden rims and without fenders. For the first time, magneto ignition was available at a premium of $40.

The last year for the Auto-Bi name was 1908. From *Motorcycle Illustrated*, August 1, 1908.

Auto-Bi advertising acknowledged only small changes, claiming "the main features of the Thomas Auto-Bi remain the same as when we first introduced this design." Noting that "the oldest motor bicycle on the American market . . . remains one of the most distinctive," the *Bicycling World* went on to say that the Auto-Bi was the only motorcycle that "adheres to the horizontally-inclined engine, which is built into and forms a part of the diagonal tube of the frame." Of the "few and relatively unimportant changes . . . advisable or necessary for 1908," the periodical noted a new float-feed carburetor "and a means [a fuel line] for priming or flushing the motor with gasolene." Other mechanical engine features continued from the previous year's model included the diagonally split crankcase, external flywheel, and auxiliary exhaust port.

The Auto-Bi Company in the late winter of 1907–8 announced a motorcycle component group called the Buffalo, reportedly "in response to the demand for a high grade, high powered motor set." This outfit consisted of a 3-horsepower engine ready to run, carburetor, belt, idler, "and handle bars ready to use. Other parts, less batteries and wheels, are furnished not machined." The goal was to "keep down the cost and let the purchaser do the fitting himself." A set of plans was to be furnished with each set, which was to be guaranteed by the company, said the *Cycle and Automobile Trade Journal*.

In the spring of 1908 came word of a two-cylinder Auto-Bi. In a motorcycle market populated by an increasing number of two-cylinder machines, the promised 5-horsepower Auto-Bi would have been a useful asset in a successful motorcycle line. The machine was to "be so unlike any of the 'twins' on the market that 'sitting up and taking notice' cannot well fail to be general," said the *Bicycling World*. The two-cylinder Auto-Bi never appeared, however, although in August the Auto-Bi "package delivery" was introduced. This had a 6-cubic-foot container mounted over the rear wheel. Its capacity was rated at 200 pounds. A folding stand under the side of the box allowed the carrier and motorcycle to be propped, "obviating the necessity of leaning it against the [c]urb or some convenient fence or wall."

In September 1908, representatives of a number of American motorcycle manufacturers met at the Hotel Statler in Buffalo. At the meeting, a trade group, the Motorcycle Manufacturers' Association, was created. Among the participants were Becker, Van Allen, and Julius Hengerer, representing the Auto-Bi Company. A second meeting in Detroit in October to adopt a constitution and bylaws was attended by Becker. He was also present at a special meeting in November in Buffalo to discuss trade matters, including arrangements with agents, trade shows, and freight rates.

1909 Model Year

A new name, Greyhound, for the 1909 model meant the end of the Auto-Bi designation. The Greyhound, however, was clearly akin to the Auto-Bi it replaced. Unique among American motorcycles, the engine still lay at a 45-degree angle from vertical and still powered the rear wheel by a leather-wrapped chain running over pulleys. The spring fork, reported *Motorcycle*

Illustrated, had been modified "to get a very wide range of frame movement with a narrow range of spring movement. Each inch of spring compression gives two inches of vertical frame movement to absorb vibration caused by rough roads, etc."

As "Greyhound" replaced the Auto-Bi name for 1909, a new spring-seat suspension was the major physical change. From the *Bicycling World and Motorcycle Review*, January 9, 1909.

A new spring-seat post was called by the Auto-Bi Company a "Shock Absorber [which] is the most efficient and satisfactory comfort device ever applied to a motorcycle . . . it completely robs rough going of its terrors." Completely disassociated from the hygienic cushion frame that formerly characterized Auto-Bi's, the new spring device reportedly gave "the use of the ordinary rigid frame construction, and without interfering in any way gives all the benefit of a spring frame without its disadvantages, such as loose frame parts, trouble in keeping spring frame in alignment, variable belt tension, additional strain on motor, etc." In practice, the seat suspension took the form of a supplementary, telescoping seat tube fitted on the inside with coil springs. The bottom of the auxiliary tube was fixed to a yoke, while the upper end pivoted from the top of the stationary post. The motorcycle was also available with a rigid saddle mount called the "racer seat attachment." Other changes to the Greyhound, née Auto-Bi, included a heavier-duty chain belt, guaranteed for 3,000 miles; a new timer; new handlebar design; folding stand attached to the rear fender; and silver-gray paint.

A new face was prominent at the Auto-Bi factory in 1909. William C. Overman came to Buffalo in late 1908 as a veteran of the bicycle trade. With his brothers, he had been associated with the Overman Wheel Company in Chicopee, Massachusetts, during the boom time for the bicycle industry in the 1890s. *Motorcycle Illustrated* said "his experience in the bicycle field will stand him in good stead in the motorcycle business." A year after Overman's arrival in Buffalo, *Motorcycling* thought that he, "one of the true gentlemen of this industry," had made it possible that the Greyhound "reflects the finish and stability of the famous Victor his brother used to make." As a vice president, Overman was to be in charge of the Auto-Bi sales department. Auto-Bi Company advertising for 1909 spoke of a reorganized sales department, "fully equipped with literature, detail information, etc. and inquiries will get immediate reply of no uncertain sound." According to another report, the sales staff had been enlarged, as had the advertising budget. In addition, the plant capacity had "increased largely." In the spring of 1909, C. B. Hull of Elyria, Ohio, was appointed general manager of the Auto-Bi Company, perhaps replacing Becker. Hull was described as a "motorcyclist of experience and an expert office and factory manager, and as such is expected to play an important part in the enlargement of Auto-Bi affairs which is in process." Overman's sales department, already "showing the results of his direction," was to remain "as at present." Still another official was Hengerer, who for about a year served as a vice president.

In the late summer of 1909, the Greyhound Motor Works advertised a "small stock of motorcycles of 1909 and [used] earlier models"; the company said it was "willing to make prices that will sell them." The unwritten message is clearly a lack of demand to meet production capability. One avenue for expanded business explored by the Auto-Bi Company was the motorcycle fire engine. A Greyhound was fitted with two Ever-Ready chemical fire extinguishers (one on either side of the rear wheel on spring brackets), a carbon tetrachloride extinguisher on the front fork, a headlight, a stand that folded automatically when the motorcycle was pushed off, and a bell mounted on the front fender. A photograph shows the gasoline tank labeled "B.F.D." for the Buffalo Fire Department. Chadeayne volunteered the machine and himself to serve at Chemical Number 5 on Cleveland Avenue in Buffalo for several weeks.

Auto-Bi Company advertising for the 1909 model emphasized the enduring qualities of the motorcycle in spite the name change; already in March 1909 it was the "Good Old Greyhound." Of course, the shock-absorbing seat mount was a major element in display ads, with the promise that "you can take cobblestone pavements at any speed without discomfort" and the "Greyhound shock absorber is the greatest comfort device ever applied to a motorcycle." The 1909 catalog said the Greyhound was "Next to Flying" and noted that each engine was brake tested and each motorcycle road and hill tested before shipment.

In the early fall, the Auto-Bi Company reorganized as the Greyhound Motor Works, and the Auto-Bi name went out of use. The certificate of incorporation reports that the company was to start its business with $50,000 paid in of the authorized $100,000 of capital stock. Of the 1,000 shares with a par value of $100, the seven directors each agreed to take one. These men were Overman, Chadeayne, Van Allen, Hengerer, Fred P. Fox, Burwell S. Cutler, and George McClure. The corporation for its purpose proposed to "manufacture, purchase, lease and sell self-propelling or horseless vehicles, motors, engines, motorcycles, motorcycle parts and bicycle motors, movable or stationary, aeroplanes . . ." In short, the Auto-Bi Company's corporate promise not to engage in the automobile business was gone.

1910 Model Year

The Greyhound for 1910 embodied the second major change in construction since the original Auto-Bi. From the engine being in the seat tube and then as part of the down tube, now the motor was mounted vertically inside the frame triangle in the standard fashion of the day. The engine itself was new, with a longer stroke than the old, producing 4.5 horsepower. An enclosed flywheel was different, and the chain belt was gone. In its place, buyers had a choice between V- and flat belts. A modified front-fork design replaced the previous style, although the patented shock absorber under the seat remained essentially unchanged.

The Greyhound Motor Works reported that the new model was "essentially a machine for service and while primarily everything else has been subordinated to good mechanical practice, we have still produced a model that is exceedingly trim, clean-cut and pleasing in appearance, and as simple as it is practical to make it, in view of the work to be done." Further, *Motorcycle Illustrated* reported, the motorcycle was the product of the "best intelligence we can command in interpreting the desires and requirements of the motorcyclist of today, and we are amply satisfied that the result as shown in this model fully justifies our endeavor."

The motorcycle press thought the new machine a good one. *Motorcycle Illustrated* declared it "a design of which the makers have given much intelligent thought." *Motorcycling* liked the long stroke engine as well as the large fuel tank, the shock absorber, "excellent position of the magneto, the engine position, ball-bearing front-fork rockers, exceedingly well-studied tool compartment, the lines and color—all these help in making a really splendid machine, designed and built by practical riders."

A handbill for "the splendid Greyhound for 1910" said the comfort provided by the shock-absorbing seat was "in a class of its own." The Greyhound people claimed in producing their new motorcycle that their designers "were not hampered by the first consideration of cost nor of factory precedent nor of any stock parts to be used—it is a new motorcycle from blueprint to crate . . . the most flexible thing you ever saw, almost answering your thought!" Perhaps it was a lack of caution in funding the development of the new machine that led to the financial difficulties that followed.

The new machine may well have been developed mostly under Overman's guidance. Becker had departed the Greyhound Motor Works, perhaps with Overman's arrival in 1909. And by the summer of 1910, it appears that Chadeayne, if still a stockholder, played little or no role in company matters. Overman, still only with the title of vice president, likely was in charge of Greyhound operations.

In anticipation of the motor vehicle show in Chicago, at which a "large and fat line of business" was expected, it was announced that Ira H. Whipple was to have exclusive distribution in Illinois, Wisconsin, and Indiana. "Of course the new arrangement involves the placing of a liberal stock order," *Motorcycle Illustrated* reported (February 1, 1910). Whipple, as "tri-state distributor," subsequently advertised that he wanted "agents in every county" of Illinois, Indiana, and Wisconsin for a "money maker" that "sells itself." On the other hand, he was to "sell at retail in Chicago and unoccupied territory." During the winter, it was announced that George E. Hengerer of Los Angeles had secured the "general agency" for Greyhound in California. What, if any, relationship George Hengerer had with Julius Hengerer has not been determined here.

In September 1910 came word of Greyhound's bankruptcy. A voluntary petition was filed by Overman on September 20. The *Bicycling World* reported that in developing the radically changed 1910 model "it got beyond financial depth, and because of capital necessary for its plans, has been . . . [at] what practically amounted to a standstill for some months." After settlement, it was not expected that the company would continue. Liabilities were estimated at $40,000, with assents at $33,000 "if $7,500 in patent rights be included." The inventory showed $20,237 in finished parts and $1,265 in motorcycles. Without knowledge of the factory markup over production costs, it's not possible to state definitively how many more machines this might be, but one would guess not more than ten. Other assets included machinery and equipment valued at $9,437.39 and accounts receivable at $2,083.84.

Motorcycle Illustrated reported that Overman had been appointed receiver. In analyzing the Greyhound's problems, the journal noted, "The company had made strenuous efforts to raise sufficient funds to carry on the business, but increased expenses and serious delays in placing 1910 Greyhounds on the market together with a very large indebtedness taken over with the good will of the old Auto-Bi Company, are announced as having prevented the successful consummation of the company's plans." A meeting of creditors on October 21 was to consider the sale of "all of the property, consisting of motorcycle parts and materials, machinery, tools, motorcycles, patents, and all other personal property, including the good will of the business."

1911 Model Year

The buyer of the assets of the Greyhound Motor Works was none other than John W. Van Allen, who received "several offers" for the Greyhound plant from firms wishing to pursue business other than motorcycle manufacture. He decided, however, that "such a sale would entail too heavy a sacrifice of good will, patent rights and business possibilities which attach to the property under the conditions of such a sale as now has been consummated," said *Motorcycle Illustrated*. Before the end of the year, Van Allen secured a buyer, none other than William Chadeayne. The value of the company at that point was said to be "about $29,000," reported *Motorcycling*.

The purchase on December 31, 1911, was followed within days by the incorporation of the Greyhound Motor Company. In effect, this was a reorganization of the Greyhound Motor Works, with the same corporate purposes and limitations. This time, the capitalization was $50,000, divided into 500 shares. Business was to begin with $25,000. Instead of seven directors, there were now to be three: Chadeayne, Frank G. Baker, and G. (Gertrude) A. Cotter. Of the directors, Cotter was to take one share of stock, Baker ten, and Chadeayne 250.

The 1911 and final form of the Greyhound, which evolved from the 1901 Thomas Auto-Bi. From *Motorcycle Illustrated*, July 13, 1911.

The Model 50 motorcycle the Greyhound Motor Company produced for 1911 differed little from the design of the previous year, not unexpectedly for a firm starting up with a stock of parts and partially completed machines. The ratchet for the belt idler was moved from the tank to the lower horizontal frame member. Mention has been made of an offset cylinder (to lessen wear) and an increased stroke, to 3.6875 inches, bringing displacement to 30.5 inches (although the Model 49 also was rated at 30.5 cubic inches).

In April, L. J. Berger, *Motorcycling*'s editor, visited the Greyhound factory. He noted a space of 12,000 square feet equipped with a comprehensive array of tools and machinery. He said he had not "seen a better equipped or neater plant of its size, while the 1911 machine is a worthy basis for a very large business. It is a fine looker, starts easily, runs steadily and is an excellent steady climber on big hills."

During the winter, spring, and summer, the Greyhound Motor Company advertised for agents, claiming as late as mid-July that the "1911 GREYHOUND is a live issue and in every town and locality we want a live agent." Success for the Greyhound's 1911 model was likely limited, however. Total sales probably were far fewer than one thousand.

1912 Model Year

In the fall of 1911, it was a rumored that Chadeayne was considering moving the Greyhound operation "lock, stock and barrel—to a point in Canada, there continuing to manufacture" (*Motorcycling*, November 11, 1911). If so, US sales would end, given a prohibitive tariff. But in Canada, the Greyhound would do well, given a "demand over there for machines of American type." Chadeayne responded by saying that nothing was definite regarding a move, and in any case Greyhounds would continue in production in the US and that "the statement of 1,000 machines as the present capacity of the Buffalo factory is an underestimate."

In January 1912, new speculation circulated about the Greyhound Motor Company. One story suggested that "the Russell people of Canada" (probably the Russell Motor Car Company Ltd. of Montreal) had sent a representative to Buffalo, "with the view to purchasing and removing the plant to Canada." Then there was rumor of a local Buffalo syndicate that "has tried to get an option on the plant . . . to use it in putting a new machine on the market." Chadeayne was "not saying anything for publication," but friends were quoted as saying he wished to retire from the motorcycle business "in order to take on the extensive real estate business now conducted by his father," said *Motorcycling*.

All of these stories notwithstanding, the 1912 Model 51 Greyhound motorcycle was built on Niagara Street in Buffalo. The machine was "without radical changes." Perhaps the most significant alteration was the price, at $175. Apparently, the V-belt and magneto options were dropped. The Breeze carburetor, which had been standard, was joined by the Heitger as regular equipment. A Greyhound handbill mentions a Parson's tool bag with tools and tire-repair outfit. The finish was "baked enamel, French grey, with blue striping" and nickeled trim.

In March, Chadeayne went to Ohio, stopping in Cleveland and "some of the other Ohio towns in search of business. He returned well satisfied." A few weeks later, however, the Greyhound Company in effect acknowledged its precarious state by selling the patent rights to its strongest design feature, the cushion seat. Again, a rumor circulated about the Greyhound Company's imminent move. This time it was the sale of its plant to the Triumph Manufacturing Company of Detroit, a new motorcycle enterprise. The reality was that Triumph had acquired the seat-post rights only and the "Greyhound is still doing business on its own hook, same as ever."

But *Motorcycling* suggested that the "old owners of the Becker patent haven't appeared to be in any position to assert their rights—what ever the value may be. The old Greyhound Co. had its financial limitations, and since it was reorganized W. C. Chadeayne has confined his energies to an output of a hundred or so machines per year. Maybe the uncertainties and expense of patent litigation to protect his rights didn't appeal to him." If in the end the Triumph Manufacturing Company benefited at all from the Greyhound transaction, it did so in its own use of the spring seat post (revised and renamed the "Nojolt") as well as from the services of Greyhound employee Frank Baker, who moved to Detroit to become factory superintendent. The Greyhound continued to use the Becker-designed seat post.

In Buffalo, Chadeayne announced a new product, a motorcycle sidecar. His effort certainly was not unique, as motorcycle builders sought to make their machines more like automobiles, which could carry several passengers in more comfort than the tandem seat on the two-wheeler afforded. The Greyhound's marketing device, which was unique in May 1912, consisted of a unit offer of reed sidecar, motorcycle, speedometer, horn, and light, all for $258. The idea was "for the rider to jump right on and dash away as soon as he gets the machine."

Motorcycle, headlight, speedometer, horn, and wicker sidecar, all for $258, were not enough to salvage the Greyhound; its maker dropped the motorcycle to concentrate on the sidecar alone. From *Motorcycling*, May 16, 1912.

After the 1912 Model Year

In October 1912, *Motorcycling* speculated about the 1913 Greyhound motorcycle. The writer predicted "no radical changes will be made in their machines." The engine would remain as unaltered, but the frame would be simplified, with "straight tubes being used throughout." Sidecars were to be "an important portion of the output," while accessories would also receive attention. The *Automobile Trade Journal* also noted plans for 1913 Greyhound motorcycles, saying there would be "very few changes . . . for the coming season."

Although the Greyhound Motor Company continued to manufacture sidecars, there were few or no Greyhound motorcycles for 1913. *Motorcycling* in January 1913 reported that the Greyhound company had "to a great degree, discontinued production of the motorcycle." Perhaps the Greyhound Motor Company marketed a few machines, either left from the previous season or made up from parts on hand. Sidecars now were the only Greyhound product, and at one point during 1913, according to the state labor department's *Second Annual Directory of New York State*, the Greyhound company had thirty-four men in the factory, now at 1050 Main Street, building sidecars. It was a great increase from two years earlier, when fewer than ten men represented the Greyhound workforce. In 1915, Chadeayne sold his sidecar-manufacturing equipment to the new Cleveland Sidecar Company,

which acquired "stock machinery and good-will." At the same time, he "turned over his entire motorcycle plant to [and went to work for] the Curtiss Aeroplane Company," according to Glenn Curtiss biographer Clara Studer. Curtiss (q.v.) himself was a pioneering producer of motorcycles, who had dropped the construction of the two-wheelers in favor of aircraft.

In the fall of 1912, the Auto-Bi name appeared in the press once more. Joseph P. Ness of Detroit was identified as designer of a new motorcycle with the old name. A Canadian company was to build it with capital supplied by investors in Keeton Motors Ltd. and the Harvester and Steel Products Company in Canada.

It appears that Auto-Bi production in any one year never exceeded much more than one thousand machines. Greyhound numbers may have dipped below one hundred, based on *Motorcycling*'s analysis in 1912. Using an average of 750 for twelve years of Auto-Bi and Greyhound production would suggest a total of nine thousand machines. Several Auto-Bi and Greyhound motorcycles have survived. Among public institutions, the Henry Ford Museum in Dearborn, Michigan, has a Greyhound.

Frederick Thourot
New York City (Manhattan)
1902

On August 9, 1902, the New York Motor Cycle Club staged a fuel-efficiency contest for motorcycles on the Manhattan Beach race track. Among the contestants was Frederick Thourot of New York, who had built his own 2.75-horsepower "special machine." Unfortunately for Thourot, after 8 miles his motorcycle was brought to a stop because, said the *Cycle and Automobile Trade Journal*, a "tire crept and cut valve stem." The winner was E. J. Edmond on an Auto-Bi, which consumed 4 pints and 5 ounces of gasoline over 50 miles.

One assumes that Thourot's motorcycle at Manhattan Beach incorporated the clutch for which he was granted a patent in November 1902. On the race entry list published in Brooklyn's *Daily Standard Union* on August 7, 1902, Thourot's machine has the name "Clutch." It is possible that he named it to bring attention to his clutch design. The application for that patent was filed on August 22, 1902, shortly after the contest. The patented device was to be

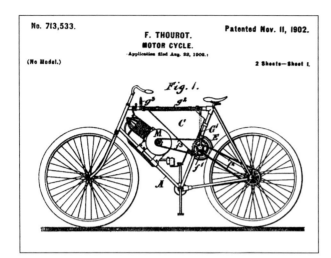

Patent drawing (713,533, November 11, 1902) of Frederick Thourot's motorcycle, with its disc clutch mounted on the seat tube. With his invention, "the starting and stopping of the motor-bicycle by the starting and stopping of the motor is dispensed with."

a hand-lever-operated disc type mounted on the seat tube. Roller chains would connect the clutch both with the engine, mounted in the fashion of the day, on the down tube, and with the rear wheel. Both sprockets were to be fitted on the left side of the machine. This arrangement would allow for the pedal crank chain on the right side to control a coaster brake.

With his clutch installed on a motorcycle, Thourot claimed that

> the starting and stopping of the motor-bicycle by the starting and stopping of the motor is dispensed with and in place thereof the motion of the cycle is controlled by the operation of the clutch mechanism—that is to say, by the meshing or unmeshing of the clutch members. In this manner a better control of the bicycle is obtained and the starting and stopping of the same greatly facilitated without the use of the pedals and without frequent annoying stopping and starting of the motor. (Patent application, November 11, 1902)

Thourot was a member of the New York Motor Cycle Club. In addition to his clutch patent, he also held one for a "cooling attachment for internal combustible motors," granted in 1902. There were at least three Frederick Thourots living in the New York City area at this time. It is hard to say for sure which one was the inventor. The only one with a Manhattan address was a waiter and butler.

Harvey E. Toms
Dansville
1908

In the spring of 1908, Harvey Toms had designed what the *Cycle and Automobile Trade Journal* called a "unique but neat motorcycle with an opposed motor and V transmission." The frame height was 21 inches, and the wheelbase 56 inches. Toms was said to be interested in receiving catalogs from motorcycle-parts suppliers as well as desiring "to interest capital for the purpose of getting his machine on the market."

At the end of 1906, the *Journal* had reported that H. E. Jones (q.v.) of Dansville, an agent for Thomas and Indian motorcycles, had submitted a drawing of a motorcycle with opposed cylinders running parallel to the long axis of the frame. Local newspaper ads and articles demonstrate that "Jones" was actually Harvey E. Toms. Toms was the owner and operator of a sporting goods store in Dansville. In addition to selling sporting goods, he had a machine shop where he repaired bicycles and automobiles. He was the agent for Thomas and Indian motorcycles and numerous automobile brands. Furthermore, he also built a boat and automobile in his shop. Toms also served as foreman for the short-lived Klink Motor Car Company (1907–10).

Vanguard Moto Inc.
New York City (Brooklyn)
2013?–2018?
Trade Name: **Vanguard Roadster**
VanguardSpark
New York City (Brooklyn)
2018–19
FUELL Inc.
New York City (Manhattan)
2019–present
Trade Names: **Flluid** (e-bike); **Fllow** (e-motorcycle)

François-Xavier Terny is the person who ties the Vanguard and FUELL enterprises together. Serving the business side, Terny joined together with motorcycle designer Edward Jacobs around 2013 to start Vanguard Moto Inc. The small start-up utilized digital engineering and three-dimensional printing to design their prototype, the "Vanguard Roadster." The roadster made its debut at the 2016 New York Motorcycle Show. The Roadster utilized a V-Twin engine that also served as part of the motorcycle frame and used a drive shaft to power the rear tire. Production was slated to begin in 2018, with a sale price of thirty thousand dollars. It appears that production was never started and the company decided to go in a new direction.

In 2018, Terny joined up with motorcycle racing designer Erik Buell and Frédéric Vasseur of Spark Racing Technology, which built Formula E (electric) race cars. The new name would be VanguardSpark, and they would focus on electric-powered two-wheeled vehicles for urban environments. It is not clear here whether plans were still in place for the Vanguard Roadster when the new venture started. It does seem clear that the Roadster was never produced in big numbers, if at all, after the prototype. VanguardSpark was planning to start with two models, one called the "SpeedBike" and the other the "Commuter." Before plans to produce the models in the Brooklyn Navy Yard could come to fruition, in 2019 another transition was made, and VanguardSpark became FUELL Inc.

Still an e-mobility company, FUELL moved its headquarters out of the Brooklyn Navy Yard to Manhattan. The name of the company stands for "Freedom Urban Electric Love Life." The target audience remains those looking to ride in an urban environment. According to their webpage, "the components for the Flluid are sourced from US, Japan, Europe, China and Taiwan. Manufacturing and final assembly is done in Taiwan." Furthermore, they state that Fllow electric motorcycles will charge in thirty minutes and have a range of 150 miles, and the motor is in the rear wheel. First deliveries of the Fllow e-moto are slated to take place in 2022 at a cost of $10,995.

Erik Buell, the founder of the Buell Motorcycle Company, stayed on as the main engineer. Well-known as an innovator of motorcycle-racing technology, Buell is a member of the AMA Motorcycle Hall of Fame. Buell's influence is certainly reflected in the performance of the e-motorcycle. According to a September 3, 2019, *Ultimate Motorcycling* article, the Fllow has the acceleration of a superbike and weighs only 400 pounds. The motorcycle includes forward, reverse, and walk-assist modes. The article further describes the motorcycle: "The connected dashboard receives regular updates and evolutions. The system is designed to assure access to the latest technology. . . . The Flow [sic] includes ABS brakes with integrated regeneration at the rear brake. One of the striking innovations that goes along with the rear wheel motor lies in the intelligent ABS braking system's linkage that use the rear wheel motor for progressive braking instead of having a separate rear brake" (Gary Ilminen, "Exclusive: Erik Buell's FUELL Flow and Fluid EVs—Exposed").

The Fllow, designed for urban use, has a top speed of 85 miles per hour, but it is not designed to maintain that speed for cruising. The recommended speed to keep within the projected range of battery power is 55 or below.

Stefano Venier
d/b/a **Venier Customs Inc.**
New York City (Brooklyn)
2012–present

Stefano Venier takes old "donor bikes" and rebuilds them to look and function like a modern one. Venier favors Italian-made motorcycles and uses a mix of original parts and equipment, with aftermarket parts and components fabricated in-house at Venier Customs Inc. Using this approach, Venier and his team produce a limited number of production motorcycles and one-off customs.

The description on the company website is as follows: "Venier has honed his focus on a profound exploration of modern design and traditional aesthetics, the expression of which can be found in a limited offering of custom motorcycles built from vintage and new motorcycles already existing in the market. Only high quality materials, mainly aluminum and carbon fiber, are used in redesigning the aesthetics, components and chassis. The finalization of each motorcycle gives each customer a custom collectible motorcycle numbered and with a certificate of authenticity."

Venier Customs, according to the objectives outlined on their website as of April 2022, is planning to do the same type of work but with brand-new motorcycles serving as the donor bikes. The company also sells handmade Italian apparel.

W

Julius W. Walters
New York City (Manhattan)
1898–99

Julius William Walters, a mechanical engineer at 254 Columbus Avenue, patented (in 1899, nos. 624,414 and 635,620) motor wheels suitable for two-, three-, and four-wheel vehicles. Applied to a bicycle, his device would have replaced the front wheel. Whether vehicles of any type were constructed using his ideas is unknown here, although motor wheels for bicycles were offered by several manufacturers in the 1910s.

The earlier Walters design used a "gas or gasolene" engine fitted inside a disc wheel. The engine was stationary, driving the wheel via a gear train culminating in a rack attached to the interior of the wheel itself. The "bevel gear-wheel . . . is arranged to be thrown in and out of mesh with the other gear-wheel . . . and for this purpose an arm . . . is connected by a link . . . with a lever, . . . journaled on the fork of a bicycle, and a link connects with a hand lever . . . under the control of the operator" (letter for Patent 635,620, October 24, 1899). Another lever would have operated a brake on the rim of the driving wheel, "after the driving mechanism between the engine and the wheel is thrown out of gear."

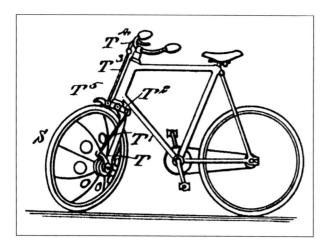

Julius Walters's patent drawing (1899) of his disc motor wheel. The stationary engine within the disc was to drive the wheel via a rack and pinion.

The later patent was intended to "simplify the construction of the propelling mechanism" and to provide a reversing mechanism; the latter goal, of course, was not applicable to motor bicycles.

Walters was a former sea captain and held numerous patents. He spent his last years around the Glens Falls area. He continued to invent in his retirement and was involved in the Mechanical Devices Company, of Albany, incorporated in 1909.

Walton Motor Company Inc.
Lynbrook
1908–9
Trade Name: **Midget Bi-Car** or **Bicar**

English inventor and manufacturer John T. Brown, whose company was J. T. Brown and Sons, introduced his Midget Bi-Car in London in 1904. The Walton company four years later began the manufacture of Brown's creation for the North American market. Perhaps the outstanding feature of the Bi-Car was its channel steel frame covered with sheet metal, which enclosed all but the engine. Advantages to the covering reportedly were the elimination of the "niches and corners in which dust accumulates so rapidly" and the protection for the rider, who was "fully protected from the mud." Imported components included the spring forks and the engines; a 3.5-horsepower, one-cylinder Fafnir and 5-horsepower Peugeot and Sarolea twins were offered for the 1909 season. Other Bi-Car parts were American—either fabricated by the Walton company (e.g., the frame) or purchased from US vendors (e.g., saddles and tires).

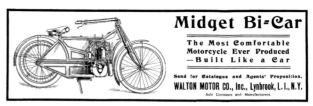

From the *Bicycling World and Motorcycle Review*, October 17, 1908.

The frame, which was reinforced "at all joints and angles," incorporated compartments for the batteries, coil, and tools as well as gasoline and oil. A V-belt inside the covering drove the rear wheel. The width of an optional five-dollar Brown drive pulley was adjustable for eight different gear ratios vis-à-vis the driven pulley; the belt had to be removed before the pulley was adjusted, so the gearing could not be changed underway. Footboards were fitted instead of rotary pedals. A stand allowed either the front or rear wheel to be held clear of the ground. The engines—at "the small cost of $7.50," said the Bi-Car catalog—could be arranged so "that by merely undoing the gasoline union and one nut" they could be swung "out clear of the frame" for repairs. The foot-actuated brake operated on the driven pulley. The price for the 135-pound, one-cylinder model was $275, or $350 with the two-speed transmission. The 170-pound, two-cylinder model was $310, according to a Midget Bi-Car catalog. (Another source says $325.) Other options included magneto ignition, storage battery (instead of dry cells), and spring fork.

The Walton Motor Company was incorporated in May 1908 to manufacture, repair, and deal in transportation vehicles, as well as other machinery; to trade in phonographs, foodstuffs, and tobacco, among other substances; and even to sell lunch to the traveling public. Capital stock amounted to ten thousand dollars in hundred-dollar shares. Directors and subscribers were the president, Julian N. Walton of Lynbrook, who took forty shares; the secretary-treasurer, Eldridge N. Smith of Brooklyn, who took fifty shares; and George F. Hickey of New York, possibly a lawyer, who took ten shares. In October 1908, half the stock had been paid in, when the capital stock authorization was increased to twenty thousand dollars.

As early as October, the Walton company advertised, as "Sole Licensees and Manufacturers," that they had the "most comfortable Motorcycle produced. Built like a car." Later they suggested, "Agents better hear our proposition before closing contracts." The Walton company exhibited at the New York motorcycle show at Madison Square Garden in January 1909, showing two 3.5-horsepower singles, one with a two-speed transmission and a "self-starting motor" and the other a 5-horsepower twin. *Motorcycle Illustrated* thought one of the "most clever innovations" was the swinging motor, which facilitated "grinding in valves or general 'tuning up.'" Space was secured at the Chicago show, as well. And at the Boston Auto Show in March, Walton secretary and treasurer Smith, as well as sales representative Franz Engels, "discoursed to the interested on the merits of the Midget Bi-Car." The Walton product also appeared at an auto show in Keene, New Hampshire.

McKay Brothers Rubber Company of Los Angeles became "Coast agents" for the Walton company in February 1909, when the McKay firm was to "have in stock a full line of the Midget Bicars." The Walton organization reportedly, at that point, had at Broadway and Merrick Road a "fine factory . . . and are now ready to appoint agents throughout the entire United States."

In spite of early-season optimism, the Midget Bi-Car apparently lasted only one year on the US market, with advertisements appearing as late as September 1909. Other manufacturers subsequently utilized the "Bi-Car" name, notably the Detroit Bi-Car Company, which in the fall of 1911 introduced its pressed-steel-framed machine. In 1910, the former Walton factory, a one-story, 50-by-20-inch building divided into two sections, housed an auto repair shop on one side and a machine shop and auto parts store on the other—both operations likely continuations of the Walton Motor Company's several business activities. The Walton Corporation was dissolved by proclamation of the New York secretary of state in 1926.

Frank B. Widmayer
New York City (Manhattan)
1900–1901 (1907?)

Frank Widmayer, a bicycle dealer at 2312 Broadway in Manhattan, applied for a "motor bicycle" patent in June 1900; a patent certificate followed on February 12, 1901. His straightforward design had a single-cylinder, four-cycle engine mounted horizontally above the rear wheel. The end of the crankshaft was connected directly to the wheel hub by a chain, although Widmayer provided in his design for a possible intermediate shaft for alternate gearing. With no clutch available, a "relieve cock" was to be opened to cut power to the engine. Alternatively, the ignition could be interrupted, the compression allowing the engine to be "then operated as a brake, which is useful in going down steep inclines." An illustration of the Widmayer design shows a battery ignition system attached to the seat tube and a fuel tank strapped to the head and top tubes of a diamond-frame safety bicycle.

Widmayer in his patent application carefully delineated three modes of operation for his machine. In one, the engine propelled the bicycle, often with the assistance of the rider, who worked ordinary cranks, driving the rear wheel via sprockets and a second chain. In the second mode, the compression of the nonfiring engine provided braking. And in the third, with compression relieved by means of the valve, the rider drove his machine alone, the motor effecting "no influence except by the almost inappreciable friction of the well-lubricated parts and of the air."

Widmayer described longitudinal ribs on the cylinder of his engine to provide for cooling as the machine moved forward through the air. Widmayer claimed as inventions in his patent the arrangement of the controls, including the ignition switch used to cut power from the motor, and the arrangement of the drive train, encompassing an adjustable chain tightener that was a pulley or chain wheel on a clamp moving along the seat stay. It seems likely that a machine built to Widmayer's specifications, with an engine always in engagement, would have been extremely tiring to ride as an unassisted bicycle in spite of the designer's claims about modest friction and air movements.

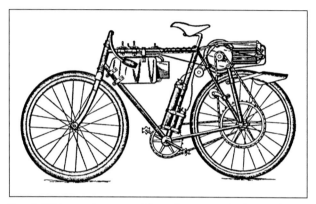

Frank Widmayer's patented (1901) motorcycle that in theory could also be pedaled, since, with the engine compression relieved, there was no drag from the motor other than "the almost inappreciable friction of the well-lubricated parts and of the air."

Whether any motorcycles were built to Widmayer's specifications is unknown here, but he was a principal in the P. T. Motor Company (q.v.), which produced several different engines and perhaps complete motor bicycles in the 1900–1903 period. Patents for an engine and for a motorcycle were granted to Widmayer, Adolph Potdevin, and Michael E. Toepel (the latter two the "P" and the "T" in the P. T. enterprise) in 1901. In that year, Toepel was reported to be the designer of the P. T. engines, and Widmayer was identified by the *Horseless Age* as "general selling agent." In the fall of 1901, when the P. T. Motor Company was incorporated, Widmayer served as secretary-treasurer.

The bicycle motor marketed by Frank Widmayer. From *Cycle Age and Trade Review*, April 11, 1901.

Widmayer in April 1901 was described by *Cycle Age* as one "of the several energetic motor makers which are making a specialty of providing . . . material for the motor bicycle builder." The periodical said Widmayer was "not a spring chicken at the motor and motor cycle business and in designing his motor has worked with reference to data gathered through actual experience." He was able to provide rough engine castings, partially or completely finished parts, or a "complete outfit ready for application to the bicycle." A positive characteristic of the engine was its narrow construction, which reportedly did not sacrifice "crank shaft bearing . . . for width." A photo of the "Widmayer Motor" depicts the P. T. engine. The *Cycle Age* article strangely never mentions Widmayer's association with P. T.

Hugo Wilson's list of "unconfirmed marques"

includes "Widmayer New York, NY c. 1907." Widmayer was an active inventor with numerous patents. He owned a motorcycle dealership at 2312 Broadway and later 2304 Broadway in Manhattan. In 1909 he was an agent for Indian, Thor, Royal, and RS, and in 1914 he also sold Henderson motorcycles.

J. Newton Williams
New York City
1910–15

The Williams motorcycle design is remarkable for the location of the revolving engine within the rear wheel. Four Williams motorcycles were fabricated, one of them surviving as of 2000.

John Newton Williams (1840–1929) came to his motorcycle design from a long career as inventor and manufacturer. Williams, according to *Typewriter Topics* in 1923, secured a typewriter patent as early as 1875. The peripatetic Williams was in St. Paul in 1884, patenting a check-punching machine; in Stapleton, Staten Island, in 1885, producing a journal bearing as well as a stop and lock for a pawl and ratchet mechanism; in New York City in 1886, for a combined pocket match safe and cigar cutter; and in 1888, two more check-punching machines. In Brooklyn in 1890 and 1893; in Newark, New Jersey, in 1894; and twice in Derby, Connecticut, in 1897, Williams received typewriter patents. The Williams typewriter, with two fonts of type striking the top of the platen, was manufactured in Derby. In 1897, Williams received the John Scott Legacy Premium and Medal from the Franklin Institute in Philadelphia for his "improvement in typewriting machines," but in 1909 the Williams Typewriter Company was bankrupt, and shortly thereafter the factory was taken over by the Secor Typewriter Company.

Williams now was working in another field, that of helicopter flight. Aligned with the Aerial Experiment Association, he was in Hammondsport in the summer of 1908. Cecil Roseberry said, "Especially intriguing" to his fellow experimenters was the helicopter he "nursed along." He "kept it tied down with ropes, but its rotors lifted it a foot or two off ground" (Roseberry, *Glenn Curtiss: Pioneer of Flight*). Williams's design, with counter-rotating propellers on concentric shafts, was rewarded with patents in 1912 and 1913.

The most important of Williams's fellow AEA members was Glenn Curtiss (q.v.), who achieved success with his aircraft engines and fixed-wing aircraft. Curtiss had already made a reputation and a living as a manufacturer of motorcycles in Hammondsport.

J. Newton Williams posing with the first of his rotating engines fitted to the rear wheel of a motorcycle. From *Motorcycling*, June 29, 1911.

The idea for a wheel-mounted engine was not original to Williams in the 1910s. As early as 1900, the *Horseless Age* noted a patent granted in the United States to Edwin Perks of Coventry, England, for a "motor wheel." Perks's design described by *Cycle Age and Trade Review*, however, had the one-cylinder engine stationary inside the wheel, while *Motorcycling*, the Chicago journal, reporting on the invention

J. Newton Williams seated on his first motorcycle, ca. 1911, in front of the Adams Company factory in Dubuque, Iowa. It's likley that Williams had his engine built here, where the Adams-Farwell car was manufacturered with a rotary engine. Photo courtesy of Laurie Williams and Gordon Williams.

of "Prof. Williams" of Derby, Connecticut, in 1911, described a three-cylinder engine revolving on the axle of the rear wheel. Williams's motor had 2.75-inch bore and 3-inch stroke. With a gear reduction, it weighed 34 pounds and produced a remarkable 9 horsepower. Williams at that point was in St. Paul, where a frame was being built for the engine. "The machine, when completed, is expected to develop great speed."

Williams's son, N. Halsted Williams (1893–1976), on July 17, 1921, documented in longhand four Williams motorcycles as well as several tri-cars built in 1917 and later with their engines in the driving wheels. Of his father's first motorcycle, Halsted said it was built in 1910 and 1911 in Dubuque, Iowa. The black-painted machine used "soft bearings, etc. flanges [cooling fins on the cylinders?], single speed." Fitted with a clutch, the engine was geared 4:1. Automatic intake valves worked with overhead exhaust valves. Halsted recorded 500 miles for the "Model A" engine.

J. Newton Williams's engine in the wheel was patented in May 1915 (no. 1,139,616) following an application filed in 1912 and renewed in 1913. On the same 1915 day, he was granted a patent for a fuel induction system for a multiple-cylinder engine (no. 1,139,617). Later that year, *Motorcycle Illustrated* printed a photograph of a Williams motorcycle, which was built

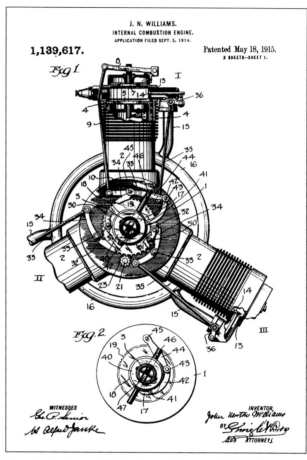

Patent drawing (1915) for J. Newton Williams's rotary motorcycle engine.

as described in the patent. The accompanying article delineated the Williams features. These included the cylinders revolving concentric with the wheel but at a speed four times as great; the induction system, which used the fixed, hollow crankshaft and intake valves in the pistons; and an exhaust valve at the top of each cylinder (the gas passing into the atmosphere through small holes in the cylinder head).

The weight of the motor was reported as 31 pounds, and the complete motorcycle weighed a third less than the lightest twin on the market. Great smoothness and a lack of vibration were due to the perfect balance of the three revolving cylinders. Greater torque, efficient cooling, the elimination of drive chains, and the possible future opening of the frame for riders in skirts were other reported advantages of the Williams design. Of the earlier Williams motorcycle, the journal said,

"The first model was given a very long and thorough tryout by the inventor before being even publicly demonstrated."

Halsted noted for the second gray Williams motorcycle, with the "Model B" engine of 1913, that it was built in New York City. It was similar to the first machine except for the "indian front fork. Hardened bearings, etc." It had magneto ignition instead of a battery. It used gravity oil feed. He also noted "flanges" and "variable comp." The Model B covered 2,500 miles.

The first of four Williams experimental motorcycles with revolving engines in the rear wheels. From *Motorcycle Illustrated*, November 18, 1915.

A little over a year later, Williams had produced two new motorcycles featuring engines enclosed within the rear wheels. Williams, according to *Motorcycling and Bicycling*, was now working at 1931 Broadway in New York City (the *Bicycling World and Motorcycle Review* said the Miller Building at Broadway and Sixty-Fifth Street). *Motorcycling* in January 1917 printed photographs of the two different machines. One was built around a diamond frame. The other utilized a series of straight tubular members in varying diameters to form a drop frame for a "Lady's Wheel." It was noted that the latter style could also lend itself to a "real side-by-side double seat." The horizontal, cylindrical fuel tank for the drop frame was mounted behind the head and under the handlebars. This latter machine is the one that survives, although with a single seat and not the side-by-side shown in some period photos.

The engine in these final Williams motorcycles remained the focus of interest. The four-cycle motor had a fixed crankshaft, which served as the axle for the rear wheel, while the cylinder revolved. Fuel was taken into the crankcase through the hollow crank. Valves in the pistons were closed without springs by centrifugal force. A two-speed spur-gear transmission was fitted. Specifications for the engine were bore and stroke of 2.81 by 3.25 inches, weight of 30 pounds, and 10 horsepower. *Motorcycling* noted that one of the machines had been ridden over 5,000 miles in four states "on all sorts of roads." It had averaged 70 miles per gallon.

Halsted Williams in 1921 documented the two final, "Model C" engine motorcycles, dating from 1915. Built in New York City by "J.N.W. Pearson's assist.," they were "countershaft and dog," two-speed machines geared 2.5:1 and 5:1. They were equipped with a geared old pump, magneto, and "no flanges." A "whistle spring fork" was fitted. One "white motorcycle" had traveled 6,000 miles, while the other, "Drop Frame" machine had covered 11,000 miles.

A 1997 story by J. Ridge in the *Antique Motorcycle* describes operation by Brad Wilmarth of the surviving Williams motorcycle, with serial number four, owned by Jim Dennie. The starting mechanism involves the footrests, which spin the rear wheel via roller chains. About riding the Williams, Wilmarth said, "After only a few blocks I can appreciate why it was never a commercial success. It is quite cumbersome."

Williams's motorcycles were ingenious, well crafted, and potentially practical. *Motorcycle Illustrated* in November 1915 thought that "one of the Eastern motorcycle makers has taken an uncommon interest in the Williams machine, and it may so happen that among 1917's motorcycle offerings, there will . . . be . . . a 'triplet.'" But in January 1917, "no serious attempts at manufacture ha[d] yet been made." Williams, working in a period in which the motorcycle had reached a near-standard form built by a thinning number of established manufacturers, concentrated on developing the tri-car concept.

Ernest J. Willis
New York City (Manhattan)
ca. 1903

Hugo Wilson's list of "unconfirmed marques" includes "Willis New York, NY c. 1903." Lists of motorcycle suppliers appearing in the *Dealer and Repairman* and the *Cycle and Automobile Trade Journal* in 1903 and

1904 show the firm of E. J. Willis at 8 Park Place in Manhattan. While many of the other names on those lists clearly represent manufacturers, such as the E. R. Thomas Motor Company of Buffalo (q.v.) and the G. H. Curtiss Manufacturing Company of Hammondsport (q.v.), the Willis operation was likely restricted to jobbing.

By 1902, the Willis Park Row Bicycle Company, founded in 1891 and the "largest exclusive bicycle jobbing house in the country," had seen a "brilliant future of the motor bicycle" and ordered five hundred Marsh (Massachusetts-made) and one hundred Merkel (Wisconsin-made) machines. Late in the year, Willis turned to automobiles, moving to a six-story building at 8 Park Place. The *Bicycling World and Motocycle Review* said Willis "will not lose sight of his bicycle business, however, and will devote more attention than ever to motocycles, having just added the agency for the entire Orient [Massachusetts] line." In 1903, Willis incorporated the Ernest J. Willis Company with $75,000 capital to take over the Park Place jobbing house "devoted to the motor cycle and motor vehicle business."

The *Dealer and Repairman* called Willis "the most progressive motor cycle agent in America." In 1902, when he was president of the New York Motor Cycle Club, he was identified by the *Bicycling World* as "agent for a number of motor cycles" rather than as a manufacturer. In 1903, at the Madison Square Garden show, Willis showed Merkel and Orient machines rather than any motorcycle identified as a "Willis." In 1907, the E. J. Willis company was bankrupt. The *Bicycling World* said creditors agreed to a 30 percent settlement, a third of which was in cash and the remainder in notes. None of the creditors listed in a news story were motorcycle manufacturers. A few months later, the Willis company had been reorganized and "centralized" at 8 Park Place. Bicycles and motorcycles were to be "handled" anew.

Joseph Wroblewski
Grand Island
1974–94

Joseph Wroblewski notes that he "built [custom] motorcycles for a living for eighteen years." Employed by various western New York enterprises, Wroblewski worked as a welder-fabricator. Notable are his collaborations with James DiTullio (q.v.) and Paul Gast (q.v.), known for their drag-racing motorcycles. Wroblewski reports that, except for a few choppers, he worked mostly on such racing machines. Frames were fabricated to fit the riders by bending and welding straight tubing. Determination of the wheelbase and placement of the engine were the most important steps in the construction process, says Wroblewski.

During the winter of 1974–75, Wroblewski constructed a motorcycle for his own use. Starting with a purchased frame and a four-cylinder Kawasaki engine, Wroblewski built himself a custom motorcycle with the extremely long, raked fork in the chopper style fashionable at that time. The parts for his project came from Gary Larsen's Biker's Bedlam. And it was

Joseph Wroblewski's motorcycle as restored in the early 1990s. Photo courtesy of Joseph Wroblewski.

Joseph Wroblewski on his self-built motorcycle, on tour in California in 1976. Photo courtesy of Joseph Wroblewski.

at Larsen's Grand Island shop that Wroblewski built his machine. That motorcycle was crashed in 1978 and abandoned until the early 1990s, when Wroblewski repaired it.

Y

Yankee Motor Company
1966–75
Ossa Sales Corporation
1975–78?
Schenectady
Trade Names: **Yankee**; **DMR**; **Ossa**

John A. Taylor, a Schenectady machine tools salesman, turned his motorcycle-trails-riding interest into a business. In 1962 he became the eastern United States distributor for the Spanish Bultaco motorcycles, and by 1968 *Cycle* magazine reported he had made "a dollar or two" as chief executive officer and a shareholder of the Cemoto East Importing Company. Nevertheless, by then he had abandoned Bultaco to become United States distributor for the Spanish Ossa motorcycles and formed the Yankee Motor Company to manufacture a line of motorcycles under the Yankee name. The Yankee plant was at 2910 Campbell Avenue in Schenectady in an early-twentieth-century factory building at the Rotterdam town line.

Frank Conner, who worked with Taylor, wrote in 1973 that it was Bultaco's reluctance to build the engine Taylor wanted for his motorcycle that resulted in his Ossa arrangement (*Cycle Guide*). In return for his distributing the Spanish motorcycles in the United States, Taylor was assured of the 500-cubic-centimeter (cc) engine he desired. By September 1966, the Yankee Motor Company, a stock company, had been organized. Engine drawings were completed in January 1967, and the first engine was tested in Spain in December.

The first Yankee motorcycle design, the Boss, intended for off-road scrambles racing, was a composite of fabricated and purchased components. The major in-house contribution was the frame designed by racing veteran Dick Mann. The engine and transmission unit, on the other hand, were Spanish. Essentially, the engine was an Ossa unit—in fact, a single-cylinder

Yankee 500 Z production, ca. 1972, depicted in the owner's manual. Photo by Frank Conner, courtesy of Bob Fornwalt.

Ossa design transformed into a simultaneous-firing, two-stroke twin. Of the engine, *Cycle* said that Ossa chief engineer Eduardo Giro did "the actual design layout" with a "lot of whizzing back and forth between Barcelona and Schenectady for consultations, and everything was finalized at a 5-day conference at the Yankee plant . . . with Giro, Taylor, Jim Corpe and Dick Mann attending." The finished engine design was owned by Yankee and to be used by them "on an exclusive basis." That the Yankee company was hesitant to comment on the relationship of their engine to Ossa designs created for *Cycle* "a complete mystery. . . . Considering Ossa's competition record, one must conclude that Yankee could hardly hope to do better than using multiplied Ossa pieces. It is a means and perhaps the only means, of obtaining guaranteed reliability and a high power output."

The Mann frame was fabricated from thin-walled, 4130 chromium-molybdenum brazed steel with a 2.5-inch diameter backbone and 1.5-inch tubes surrounding the engine. The 22-pound frame was designed to hold an oil supply in the backbone. The fork was a Spanish Telesco unit, as were the rear shocks. The body parts were of American fabrication, with flexible fiberglass forming the front fender as well as the integral tank, seat support, and rear fender.

The first engine was mated with a chassis in Spain just before the Boss made its American debut in March 1968, according to *Motorcycle Sport Book* by Bob Greene (3rd annual ed., Petersen Publishing, 1968). In April, *Cycle* said there was still only a "pre-production prototype." But there were plans at that point to make the Boss available also as an enduro machine with muffler and lights. By July 1968, there were to be twenty-five motorcycles manufactured for the International Six Days' Trials, with some of the "'replicas' . . . offered for sale." And for 1969 there was to be a "road-racer" as well as a "street/scrambler." A road-racing prototype was photographed in early 1968, and such a motorcycle reportedly survives, owned by a collector. The enduro was to be the Yankee company's most successful motorcycle.

Staffing at the Yankee company at this point included Mann, manager of research and development; Jim Corpe, project manager; and Don Butler, service manager. *Motorcycle Sport Book* said all three were race veterans who "knew what they wanted" from an engine. The selection of Ossa avoided adding "years to the project," not to mention a large capital expenditure. (Ivan Wagar in *Cycle World* estimated $750,000.) The in-house development and manufacture of the frame, however, exploited Mann's experience.

In 1969 the Yankee Motor Company was acquired by the Bangor Punta Corporation, controlled by Nicholas Salgo, whose early financial dealings had been in Cuban sugar plantations. According to Conner, Bangor Punta "wanted a motorcycle company." AMF had purchased Harley-Davidson, so Bangor Punta turned to Yankee, adding it to the Smith and Wesson firearms, Piper Aircraft, and Alouette snowmobile operations. (In other manufacturing operations, Bangor Punta

The Ossa ST 1 dirt-track racing motorcycle, assembled in Schenectady by the Ossa Sales Corporation in 1977 and 1978. Photo courtesy of Alex Snoop and Ron Edlin.

produced boats, internal combustion engines, and motor homes.) Yankee was operated as a subsidiary of Bangor Punta Operations Inc., itself a subsidiary of the holding company known as Bangor Punta Corporation. Bangor Punta headquarters moved at about the time of the Yankee acquisition from Manhattan to Greenwich, Connecticut. In 1984 Bangor Punta was purchased by Lear Siegler Inc., which by 1995 was known as Lear Siegler Diversified Holdings Corporation of Livingston, New Jersey.

In 1970 a Yankee Boss arrived. But unlike the off-road prototype announced two years previously, this Boss was an Italian-made mini-bike distributed but not built by the Yankee company. A rather sophisticated,

No stranger to working internationally, Yankee imported the Yankee Boss "mini-cycle" with eyes toward American teenagers. The Boss was larger and more powerful than a mini-bike but smaller than a full-sized dirt bike. It had full-sized accessories, and advertising claimed that it handled like a true dirt bike. NYSM H-2022.18.1.

$345 machine on the larger end of the mini-bike scale, the Boss had a Morini fan-cooled, 55-cc, 6-horsepower engine mated to a four-speed transmission. The tubular frame was fitted with suspension components at both ends. Distribution was handled by the Yankee Motor Company's Gardena, California, branch.

Next appeared the Yankee Motor Company's DMR of 1970–71, according to Paul Dean in *Cycle Guide* for November 1978. This was a racing machine built in Schenectady for Class C (250-cc) American Motorcyclist Association short (dirt) track events. "DMR"

Advertisement for the Yankee Boss showing two versions available in 1972, the "'Boss' Super T.T." with 12-inch wheels and "Maxi 'Boss'" with 14-inch wheels. The museum's Boss (*pictured on page 222*) has 12-inch wheels but does not have the "T.T." or "Maxi" logos. From *Snowsports Dealer News*, March 1972. NYSM H-2022.18.2.

denotes "Dick Mann Replica," a name acknowledging Mann's design ideas realized in the frame. *Cycle* magazine claimed that the Yankee frame was "very similar to ones built by Dick for his BSA singles and twins." Chromium-molybdenum 4130 tube components of the production Yankee were "almost an exact copy of the original." Double down tubes ran beneath the engine. A swing arm suspended the rear wheel. Yankee produced the steel hubs for wire spoke wheels (fitted with Akront alloy rims). The fork as well as the 244-cc engine and four-speed transmission came from the Ossa Stiletto motorcycle. In fact, *Cycle* called the motorcycle a "Yankee/Ossa." Kent DeBie, associated with the Yankee factory racing effort, has claimed that he was the only rider to win a flat-track race on a Yankee machine. He also reports a victory on ice.

The motorcycles were heavy, but, he added, so was he. Steve Ritzko, a veteran of the motorcycle business near Schenectady, has estimated that 175 complete DMR motorcycles were built, along with about fifty extra frames.

The $1,495 Yankee 500-cc Z enduro motorcycle, based on the 1968 prototype, finally appeared in 1972. Frank Conner, who had worked for Yankee, in his 1987 memoir, "Yankee Ingenuity" (*Cycle World* magazine), said the prototypes had been lent to

> motorcycle magazines, who were so impressed with the potential of the machine that they wrote about it fulsomely. Then disaster struck. There was an unaccountably long delay of several years in the shipment of production engines. And numerous vendors of chassis components either were unable to produce acceptable goods, or failed to deliver on time. Consequently, John [Taylor] discovered. . . . If you tantalize 'em with the prototype but don't deliver the product right away, public interest dies dead, never to be revived.

Delay aside, Yankee publicity in a sales brochure claimed their Model Z carried the first new American motorcycle trade name in thirty years and was the "culmination of years of dirt riding experience by many people at Yankee Motor Company." Taylor said the inspiration for the machine was the "need for a second, American made motorcycle—particularly, a large displacement I.S.D.T. type dirt bike." Among the stated goals for the Yankee design were dirt-handling agility equal to a 250-cc enduro machine as well as "good road manners." Sprockets of fifteen and forty-six teeth working with a wide-ratio, six-speed transmission would allow speeds so slow that the operator could "walk along beside the Yankee" yet also give a 70-miles-per-hour cruising speed and an 88-miles-per-hour top.

The Yankee simultaneous-firing twin engine was oversquare with a 72-millimeter (mm) bore and 60-mm stroke. Twin magnetos operated without points. Twin 27-mm carburetors provided fuel mixture. Again, the Dick Mann large cross-section, thin-tube wall frame provided the skeleton for the motorcycle. Forged aluminum fork clamps came from the Smith and Wesson plant. The rear swing arm was made of 1.375-inch tubing. Among other mechanical features of the 325-pound Z were a hydraulic disc brake in the rear, an under-engine flat muffler, and a skid plate.

Cycle World said of the Z in April 1972, "Massive, beautifully constructed and rugged enough to withstand a parachute drop are terms that best describe the frame and swinging arm," which were "the design work of Dick Mann." In all, the motorcycle was "truly a work of art. Some features that the experienced, as well as the relatively inexperienced, rider will appreciate are the flexible plastic fenders that can be bent practically double before breaking" as well the comfortable seat which could be removed with one thumb screw for access to components underneath. "One thing that riders of smaller stature won't appreciate very much is the sheer largeness and hefty weight of the motorcycle. . . . Add to that the width of the machine and you'll find some disappointed short riders.

> Lifting the Yankee out of a mudhole or dragging it around a hillside can tire one out pretty quickly. . . . [Yet] the entire package is so well thought out and constructed that it's fairly hard to get into difficult situations. . . . The engine is powerful and tractable enough to make it up almost any hill with decent traction, and the superlative suspension system is ideal for riders weighing 165 lbs. and up.
>
> The Yankee is disappointingly late in its arrival, but the finished package is worth the wait for the enthusiast.

Motorcyclist stated that Taylor had realized the "Great American Dream of many an enthusiast to once again field a running partner to Harley-Davidson, a motorcycle born of Yankee ingenuity and bearing the brand: Made in U.S.A." Ten years after his "entry into the motorcycle game," Taylor supposedly had "realized that dream." For the journal, the Yankee remained "as fresh and strong as the dedicated man who conceived it."

Motorcyclist's test rider liked the Yankee, a "winner at a round $1500, with dumbfounding torque and what I'd take to be a bulletproof engine and frame." The motor was being built in Spain, but "future plans are for it to be manufactured here in America." *Motorcycle World* thought the Z was heavy, perhaps its "only basic fault," but the motorcycle's power was adequate to deal with the weight.

Trail Bike for spring 1973 also commented on the Yankee's 350 pounds versus the 200-pound ideal of most motorcross manufacturers. The Yankee's attraction, thought the journal, was that its rider didn't need to manhandle his machine; "you just sit down in the thing, crank on as much power as your reflexes can cope with, and let it do the work for you." The "frame, hubs, brakes, fork crowns, tank and seat are made here [in the United States] and assembled at Yankee's . . . factory with a Spanish engine and suspension and Italian wheel rims."

A *Dirt Rider* story in April 1973 echoed comments in other reports that pointed to an unacceptable noise level in the Z. The journal also thought the front brake inadequate. The chassis was "superb," but "for serious off-roading the super 'Z' is a little overdone for our tastes." *Modern Cycle* in April 1973 was mostly pessimistic about the 500 Z: "exceptionally well thought out, exceptionally well executed, and it is exceptionally heavy and unfortunately exceptionally late." Other builders had made "great strides in an advancing state of the art in just the last several years." On the other hand, the prospect of a street version held out some hope for the Yankee company.

In 1972 Yankee produced a motocross prototype called the Yankee X, which *Cycle Guide* thought was going to be produced in numbers beginning in September 1973. The looping, tubular frame resembled those on other Yankee motorcycles. The one-cylinder, two-stroke, 456-cubic-centimeter engine reportedly was built by Moto Sacoche (an "aircraft firm," according to *Cycle World*) in Switzerland. The motorcycle was raced at several venues in 1972, undergoing continuous modification. In March 1973, *Cycle Guide* said the "basic feeling one gets about the Yankee 'X' is a very positive one. . . . Next year in its first full season of competition, Yankee's single-cylinder mount may send a few other motocross marques back to school for a refresher course."

Motorcyclist in 1972 reported the expected arrival in 1973 of a "sports-touring" version of the Yankee that would be introduced with a 120-mile top speed and a "fail-safe" oil-injection system. A photo of the prototype 500 SS, according to Yankee collector Robert Fornwalt, was distributed to Yankee dealers in late 1972 or early 1973. The "street scrambler" shown is fitted with wire wheels, front disc brake, upswept dual-exhaust pipes, dual saddle, bright metal fenders, and turn signals, among other lighting equipment. The finish was dark red or maroon with white stripes.

Apparently, the sports-touring machine did not get beyond the prototype stage. At the beginning of 1974, *Big Bike* reported on a custom road machine assembled by Taylor's son Trent for his own use. Starting with a Yankee Z frame, he and his Yankee colleagues produced a 400-pound, 58-horsepower bike, thanks to some modifications of the basic Yankee twin.

Cycle Sport's "Stars of '73" described encountering a four-cylinder, 1,000-cc racing prototype at the Schenectady factory. The engine, basically two Yankee Z powerplants "mated through the crankshafts," was mounted in an entirely unsuitable Yankee Z frame. The Yankee company reportedly viewed the machine a "work in progress" and suggested that the engine would be useful to drag-racing competitors. *Motorcyclist* in 1994 suggested several such four-cylinder engines were assembled in Schenectady, inspired by an example assembled by a "wealthy Spanish road race privateer," according to Taylor.

Although *Supercycle*'s 1974 "Buyer's Guide" lists the Yankee 500 at $1,550, production of the Yankee Z apparently ended in 1973. *Cycle World*'s David Edwards in late 1997 observed that the machine "was tardy getting to market and plagued by lack of development." Edwards claims a total of 750 Z machines.

Conner summarized the 500 Z by noting,

At first glance, the 335 pound Yankee seemed a formidable machine to take into the wilderness. But you didn't have to muscle the Yankee; you could steer it with the throttle. It had such good throttle response and so much torque that you could just let the engine do the work. And with all its power, it could climb hills that most 250s wouldn't get halfway up.

But by the time John [Taylor] had the bike, he no longer had the market . . . the off-road standard had become the Matador inspired enduro bike: a 250cc two-stroke Single that weighed around 250 pounds. But John was offering the riders a 335-pound 500 Twin. Their reaction was, "God, what an elephant . . ." Quickly and quietly, then, the Yankee faded into obscurity. As an idea, it had been way ahead of its time; but when the idea became reality, it was too far behind the times.

Clement Salvadori in *Rider* (1994) said the Yankee Z was a "great bike, a lot of fun bounding over hill and dale, quite competent on the twisty asphalt. It may have been too good a bike for the American market; most buyers didn't need all that ability. . . . It took a particular type of Yankee to want a Z, and there weren't all that many."

In June 1974, John Taylor's eighteen-year-old son Trent was killed in a motorcycle accident. According to the late Denis Petrie, a witness to the accident, Trent was test riding a Yankee machine without a helmet and crashed. The trauma caused by the accident led John Taylor to take some of the Yankee machining equipment to the local landfill. Petrie insisted that the death of Trent was the main reason for the end of Yankee motorcycle. One newspaper account of the accident states that the motorcycle was being tested in preparation for an upcoming race.

An unidentified motorcycle periodical clipping dated October 8, 1975, reports that John Taylor purchased the Yankee Motor Company from Bangor Punta on September 9 of that year. The Yankee operation was then "divided into three companies." The Ossa Sales Corporation with Taylor as president was to import Ossa motorcycles to be distributed by six "well qualified motorcycle distributors." The Ossa Parts & Service Corporation was to operate in Schenectady. The Yankee Accessory Corporation was to supply Full Bore accessories "direct to Full Bore dealers from Schenectady."

Taylor maintained his relationship with the Ossa Sales Corporation at least to the end of 1978, according to *Cycle Guide*. A product of the Ossa partnership was the Ossa ST 1, the model designation of which suggests its function as a short-track racing machine. Alex Snoop, owner of an ST 1, estimates thirty-five to fifty were assembled in Schenectady in 1977 and 1978. A Red Line Manufacturing Company double down-tube frame and Ceriani fork were used with a 244-cc, two-stroke Ossa engine and five-speed transmission. A mechanical disc brake was fitted to the rear wheel. No similar Ossa motorcycles were built in Spain.

But the Ossa company itself, as John Carroll notes in *The Motorcycle: A Definitive History* (1997), utilized the Yankee twin engine on a street motorcycle called the "500 Yankee." The Spanish journal *Solo Moto* for November 26, 1976, published an article about the new machine, the prototype of which already had covered 25,000 kilometers. With the 488-cc twin rated at 58 horsepower, the Ossa Yankee fitted with alloy wheels and disc brakes achieved a 115-miles-per-hour top speed. Fornwalt says the 500 was announced in 1977 and one "was even tested in the U.S." And Clement Salvadori in *Rider* (1994) noted the "Yankee 500 was still for sale in Spain in 1979, with down-swept pipes and OSSA written large on the gas tank."

Motorcyclist for July 1977 reported on its test of one of two prototype "Ossa Yankee 500" in the United States. The $2650 motorcycle "Thankfully" utilized the Dick Mann double-cradle frame, although with mild steel replacing the 4130 alloy. The engine had oil injection. Disc brakes were on both cast aluminum wheels. The journal noted that "noise and emission controls" were likely to snuff out the Ossa Yankee's chances in the United States. And "the scheduled production run of 200 [were] too few . . . it is a real shame the Yankee 500 didn't get into production ten years ago when it was supposed to."

The Yankee Motor Company entity survived until 1981, according to Snoop. In the early 1990s, John Taylor retained the Yankee logo (characteristic lettering combined with a flag) for use by his Yankee Audio Corporation in Fallbrook, California. A number of Yankee 500 Z, DMR, and Ossa ST 1 motorcycles, including, reportedly, the prototype Yankee Boss, survive in private hands. The New York State Museum has a Yankee Boss mini-cycle in its collection.

John E. Yost
Troy (1975); Averill Park (1989–90)

John Yost (born 1948) was a student when, in 1969, he acquired a former police motorcycle—a 1957 Harley-Davidson missing its engine—at auction in Rochester. That same year in a Bath junkyard, he purchased a 1963 FLH Harley engine and transmission from a fire-damaged motorcycle. During the next two years, as Yost bought and sold parts, he acquired pieces of three other machines. These enabled him to build his own motorcycle while living in Troy in 1975. The finished machine was done in the chopper style, with raked front end, sissy bar, and unsprung saddle. The fuel tank came from a Harley-Davidson Hummer.

Yost's motorcycle remained in storage until 1989, when he rebuilt to be "less 1970s, more comfortable," in his words. The saddle now incorporates springs, easing the ride on a machine that has no rear suspension. Some of the trim was replated. The color changed from green to black.

Yost notes that his motorcycle utilizes much original Harley-Davidson technology, such as the wire spoke wheels, brakes, and 6-volt electrical system. Since the Rochester police motorcycle was used with a sidecar, the raked front fork arrangement is also original. In 2000, Yost reported that he rode the motorcycle "occasionally."

John Yost's motorcycle as rebuilt in 1989–90. Photo courtesy of John E. Yost.

Maker Unknown

Maker Unknown
Buffalo or Fulton (?)
ca. 1903–6

Clarence V. Armstrong, a machinist residing in Fulton, wrote to the *Motorcycle Illustrated* in the spring of 1908 to tell about the tandem motorcycle that he had been riding with his wife for two years. According to Armstrong, "the designer of our tandem built two, and the first one—his own—built in the winter of 1902–3, is still running in the beautiful city of Buffalo, N.Y." That machine supposedly had covered "nearer twenty thousand miles" in the hands of its builder-rider.

Armstrong claimed that the two motorcycles were the only two similar machines "in this part of the country" combining a diamond front frame section and a drop frame for a woman rider in a skirt in the rear. The motorcycling alternative, according to Armstrong, was a single machine with a tandem attachment, i.e., a seat mounted on the rear fender. The disadvantages to the latter system were numerous, he thought:

> It throws too much weight on the rear wheel for one thing, and makes harder steering for another. It is also practically out of the question for ladies to ride with ordinary dress. Then, too, the rear rider cannot help start the machine [by pedaling]. This last fault is alone enough to sicken one of carrying a companion on the tandem attachment. All these troubles are due to the fact that the single motorcycle cannot be built to carry two as well as one.
>
> But our tandem, or any other properly designed, does away with all of the aforementioned faults.

Armstrong said that his motorcycle was "'home built' but from standard Thor parts throughout," by which he meant that the builder utilized a Thor engine and other running gear manufactured by the Aurora Automatic Machinery Company of Aurora, Illinois. Unfortunately, Armstrong in his article does not identify the builder of his tandem. One possibility might be Charles Haberer (q.v.) of Buffalo, who in 1915 said that between 1903 and 1908 he used Thor parts in assembling "six to 25 machines a year, calling them under their own name of 'The Yankee.'" Another possibility is Ira C. Palmer (q.v.) who lived in the same town as Armstrong (Fulton) when the tandem was built and then moved to Buffalo around 1906–7. Palmer also had a tandem and as early as 1904 was taking trips with his wife on "their motorcycle."

In appearance, Armstrong's tandem resembles the standard mixed-frame tandem bicycle of the 1890s and 1900s, except that the drop-frame section is in the rear rather than in the more common front position. Armstrong argued,

> If you are whirling along at a 20 or 30-mile gate [sic] with some friend or loved one trusting your skill you feel as though you wanted pretty near full control of the machine, and the only place to get this is "up in front." Another thing, I would feel like a coward or hypocrite, or something, to ask a lady to face the dangers incident to motorcycling and me take the back seat. This was all right on the old pump tandem, but that was child's play. Motorcycling is a life of continual excitement and good quality of excitement, too, and this is what we modern Americans demand.

Clarence and Inez Armstrong with their tandem motorcycle. From *Motorcycle Illustrated*, April 1908.

Armstrong noted that his machine utilized a frame with a 72-inch wheelbase and ran on 2-inch tires. The rear handlebars were fixed. The rear crank hanger was three inches higher than the front. The 1.75-horsepower engine drove the rear wheel through a 7 ⅓:1 reduction. The gasoline tank held enough fuel for a 115-mile range. Armstrong said his "record speed against time, 28¼ miles per hour, was with a girl weighing 130 pounds."

His longest trip was 112 miles in a day over the local roads "where hills, stone, sand, ruts, etc. abound in unbridled profusion. Yet over these roads we have enjoyed it immensely. It a sport of which we never tired." His average Sunday ride ran 50 to 75 miles, and he and his wife had visited "one hundred towns," coming back "every night, too." Sometimes, he said, the two would spend an hour "talking over the scenes and incidents of the trip when we get home. My wife can always tell me lots of things that I failed to see. She has a chance to look around most of the time, and I catch only fleeting glances." The coming season he intended to carry a camera so they would have "a collection of views that will be of lasting interest." The tandem, he said, "has given us more pleasure than anything else we could have purchased for many times the money it cost."

Maker Unknown
Rochester
ca. 1950
Trade Name: **Bearcat**

Under an "unconfirmed marques" listing in his *Encyclopedia of the Motorcycle*, Hugo Wilson notes the Bearcat as a Rochester product at mid-twentieth century. Rochester city directories of the period 1949–51 have no "Bearcat" listings.

Maker Unknown
New York City
ca. 1900
Trade name: **Boulevard**

The endpapers of Stephen Wright's *The American Motorcycle: 1869–1914* have an engraved image, probably from a trade journal, labeled "1900 Boulevard, New York, New York." This motor bicycle has an engine mounted behind the seat of a diamond frame. A chain drives the roller working against the rear tire between the down tube and the seat stays. No further information about the Boulevard is given in the book.

The Automobile: Its Construction and Management, by Gerard Lavergne, first published in Paris, France, in 1900, describes a motor bicycle called the Boulevard. The description matches up with the image from Wright's book. Lavergne notes that the motor was mounted behind the seat. Further, he writes that "the motor is fixed to a double fork which holds the rear wheel axle, and a chain-driven counter-shaft has a concave friction wheel which imparts motion to the tyre of the wheel." However, no builder or location is mentioned by Lavergne. It is not clear whether the Boulevard was in fact made in New York or who made it.

1900 Boulevard, New York, New York

From Stephen Wright's *The American Motorcycle: 1869–1914*.

Maker Unknown
Rochester
1905

The *Bicycling World and Motocycle Review* in January 1905 said a Rochester newspaper was reporting that Eloise Breese, "one of the best known society young women of New York," was having a motorcycle built for her by a Rochester company. The newspaper was said to throw "this fog light on the construction of Miss Breese's machine: 'It will have the piston rod and other mechanism so placed that she can sit beside that part of the framework much as one would in a chair, with her feet resting on a pair of pedals controlling gearing and brakes.'"

Eloise Breese possibly was Eloise Laurene Breese Norris (1855–1921). At the time of her death, she lived in Tuxedo Park, although earlier, the Breese family had been included among the *Prominent Families of New York* (Lyman H. Weeks, editor, 1898).

Among motorcycle manufacturers exhibiting at the January 1905 Madison Square Garden automobile show, according to the *Bicycling World and Motocycle Review*, was the Breeze Motor Company of Newark, New Jersey, which displayed three Breeze motorcycles.

Maker Unknown
New York City (Manhattan)
1901
Trade Name: **Canda**

A handbill published in 1999 by the Excelsior-Henderson Motorcycle Manufacturing Company of Belle Plaine, Minnesota, listed the "Canda" as a motorcycle built in New York City in 1901.

City directories of the 1900 period include Charles J. Canda, Lee Canda, F. Mora Canda, and Ferdinand E. Canda, with professions noted as president, president, treasurer, and civil engineer, respectively, at several lower Manhattan addresses (Charles and Ferdinand always together). Whether any of these men were associated with a motorcycle enterprise has not been determined here.

Maker Unknown
New York City (Manhattan)
1961
Trade Name: **Centaur**

Michael Gerald and Jim Lucas, in their "Complete Roster of Two-Wheeled Motorized Vehicles Made in the U.S.A. 1869–1979," note the Centaur as being manufactured in New York, New York, in 1961. Hugo Wilson, in his *Encyclopedia of the Motorcycle* (1995), perhaps using Gerald and Lucas as a reference, has the same data.

Maker Unknown
Trade Name: **Jewel**

In 1908, the McGrane Company at 875 Main Street in Buffalo told *Motorcycle Illustrated* that they "used to handle the Jewel, but they deal only in second-hand machines now." The McGrane Company (James L. McGrane and Stephen B. DeWitt), according to city directories, were in the "stoves and bicycle sundries" business. The name of the manufacturer as well as the place and dates of manufacture for the Jewel motorcycle unfortunately have not been determined here.

Maker Unknown
New York City (Brooklyn)
ca. 1901
Trade Name: **Lewis**

Hugo Wilson's "unconfirmed marques" list in his *Encyclopedia of the Motorcycle* (1995) notes "Lewis Brooklyn, NY c. 1901."

Maker Unknown
Buffalo
1916–20
Trade Name: **MB**

Michael Gerald and Jim Lucas in their "Complete Roster of Two-Wheeled Motorized Vehicles Made in the U.S.A. 1869–1979" list the MB as a motorcycle built in Buffalo between 1916 and 1920. Erwin Tragatsch in his *Illustrated Encyclopedia of the Motorcycle* (1991) notes that the MB motorcycles were "modern machines with 746cc parallel-twin engines and shaft drive to the rear wheel. The . . . design was never fully developed." Buffalo city directories show no "MB" listings under the "motorcycles" heading.

Maker Unknown
Taberg?
1905?
Trade Name: **Pansy**

Three recent compilations list the Pansy motorcycle. While Hugo Wilson's *Encyclopedia of the Motorcy-*

cle (1995) confines the name to his "unconfirmed marques" list with a "c. 1905" date attached, Michael Gerald and Jim Lucas ("Complete Roster of Two-Wheeled Motorized Vehicles," 1979) note the place of manufacture as Taberg and the date as 1905. Tod Rafferty's *Complete Encyclopedia of American Motorcycles* (1999) omits a place of fabrication but says the Pansy dates from 1905. A Pansy motorcycle survives, although its whereabouts are undisclosed. The motor is marked "PANSY." It is possible that this motor was built by the Pansy Motor and Cycle Works in Denver, Colorado.

Maker Unknown
Rochester
1903–4
Trade Name: **R & H**

The Antique Motorcycle Subject Index (1982) has two listings for information about the "R & H" motorcycle, purportedly manufactured in Rochester in 1903 and 1904. See volume 14, number 2 (1975) for a photograph, as well as volume 20, number 4 (1981). Tod Rafferty's *Complete Illustrated Encyclopedia of American Motorcycles* (1999) says the R & H was manufactured in Brockton, Massachusetts, in 1905.

Index

Note: The photo insert images are indexed as *p1, p2, p3,* etc.

A. P., *9*, 9–10
Abell, Rollin, 7
Abramson, Theodore S., 183
acetylene-fueled motorcycle, 57–58, *58*, 145
Acme bicycle engine, 24, *24*
Adams, Oliver W., 41, 45
Afanador, Angel, 82, 83
airships, 28–29, 32, 33, 146
Allright motorcycles, 161, 163
Allyn, Ed, 7–8
American Bicycle Company, 8, 141
American Chopper, 142–143, 145–146
American Cycle Manufacturing Company, 8
American Ever-Ready Company, 11, 12–14
American Hoffmann Corporation, 8
American Machine Company, 67, 69, 72
American Militaire Cycle Company. *See* Militaire Autocycle Company of America Inc.
American Motor Company, 8–9
The American Motorcycle (Wright), 4, 29, 121, 160, 228, *228*
American Motorcycle Parts, 9, *9*, *p2*
Anderson, Douglas G., 38, 39, 42, 44, 46
Anderson, Mark, 137, 177–178
Apex Wheel Company, 10
AR Streetracker, 177–178, *178*
Armstrong, Clarence and Inez, *227*, 227–228
Armstrong, Frederic W., 201
Asarisi, John, 54

Ashby, Edgar K., 203
Ashely, George A., 106
Assmann, Frederick P., 132, 136
Aurora Automatic Machinery Company. *See* Thor engines
Auto-Bi Company and motorcycles. *See* E. R. Thomas Motor Company
Autocyclette Manufacturing and Sales Corporation, *10*, 10–11, *p8*
automobile
 etymology, 1, 5
 hybrid motorcycle, 102–103, *103*
 motorcycle popularity compared with, 2
Automobile-Aviation Industries Corporation, 11
Autoped Company of America Inc. (and Autoped scooter), 2, 11–14, *12*, *13*, 108, 109

Baessler, Eugene F., 183
Baisden, E. J., 14, *14*
Baker, Edwin B., 51
Baker, Erwin G. ("Cannonball"), 134
Baker, F. A. (and Company), 158
Baker, Frank G., 209
Baker, Frank H., 174
Baldwin, Thomas Scott, 28, 33, 34
Ballou, E. I., 14–15
Bandler brothers (David, Arthur, and Maurice), 173–174
Bangor Punta Corporation, 222, 225
Barber, William (and Barber Special), 15
Barney Bike, 140–141, *141*

Bates, Ralph E., 139, 140
Battelle, Seavey, 89
batteries. *See* e-bikes and motorcycles
Battey, Sumter B., 15–16, *16*
Bearcat (unknown maker), 228
Becker, Clarence E., 202–203, 204, 205, 206, 207, 208, 210
Belgium, 55, 80, 84, 104
Bell, Alexander Graham, 32, 33
Bell, John P., 172–173
Bellamy, James F., 3, 10, 53, 102, 168–169, 172, 176
Bendix, Vincent H., *16*, 16–17, 27
Bendix Aviation Corporation, 17, 180
Benjamin, Gustav, 151
Bennett, Arthur E. and Edmund W., 128–129
Bennett, J. A., 116
Bennett, Joseph D., 17
Bennett, Matthew W., 151, 153, 155
Bensen, Gordon, 102
Berliner, Joseph "Joe" (and company), 17, 97
Berserker, 26
Betts, Ritchie G., 95, 200, *p1*
Betts, Susan, *p1*
Biagi, Dave, 38
Bi-Car (Detroit), 131
Bi-Car (Fauber), 80–81
Bicar (Walton Motor Company Inc.), *214*, 214–215
bicycle motors/motor bicycles. *See* motor bicycles
Biggam, Henry J., 152, 155
Biker Build-Off, 54, 146
Bill, Louis H., 199, 201

231

Billiet, Juan T., 152, *152*
Boisselot Automobile Company (and Special Gasoline Motor Company), 17–18
Boller Brothers, 18
Bordman, John J., 18, *18*
Boulevard (unknown maker), 228, *228*
Bowman Automobile Company, 19
Braam, John F., 39, 46
Bradley, L. M., 116
Brady, Charles P., 60
Brainard, Jay, 19, *19*
brakes, 229
    Abell back-pedaling, 7
    Autocyclette, 11
    Autoped, 13
    Clark, E., and Brewster, William H., designs for, 24–25
    Cyclemotor, 43
    Dragner design for, 59
    E. R. Thomas Motor Company, 198–199, 208
    Emblem, 64, 78
    Fllow, 213
    Gibson Mon-Auto, 85
    Heitchen, 91
    Hercules, 27
    Indian Larry design for, *p5*
    Jehle, 98
    Kiefler motorcycle, 99, 100
    Militaire, 114
    Motor Bicycle Equipment and Supply Company, 122, 125
    Ner-A-Car, 134, 135, 136
    Pierce, 149, 150, 154, 155
    Prospect Motor Company, 161, 162
    Regas Vehicle Company, 168
    Rugmobile, 180
    Stellar, 189, 190
    Stratton Motor Bicycle Company, 192
    Walters design for, 214
    Widmayer, 215
    Yankee Motor Company, 224, 225, 226
Bramwell, C. C., 193
Brandenburg Brothers, 19–20
Brecher, E. A., 20
Breed, George W., 150, 153
Breese, Eloise, 228–229

Bretz, John C., 20, 20n2
Bretz Cycle Manufacturing Company, 20
Brewster, William H., *24*, 24–25
Brewster, William J., 82
Briggs, Patrick "Pat" (and companies), 20
British market and motorcycles
    Autoped and, 13
    Emblem and, 76
    Harlvin and, 7–8
    Herschmann and, 93
    Midget Bi-Car and, 214
    Ner-A-Car and, 4, 132, 136
    N.S.U. and, 138
    Skootamotor and, 187–188
Broadway Choppers, 20–21
Brown, Fred L., 150, 152, 157, 158, 159–160
Brown, John T., 214–215
Brown, Llewellyn H., 30, 35
Bruce, George H., 86
BSA, 8, 223
Buck, Harry, 97–98
Buell, Erik, 213
Buffalo Automobile and Auto-Bi Company. *See* E. R. Thomas Motor Company
Buffalo Motorcycle Works Corporation, *21*, 21–22
BuildaBikeInc.com, 178
Bullard, E. P., 116
Bullen, Dana R., 132
Bulley, Sam, 43
Bullis, William R., 22, *22*
Burwell, George W., 104
Butler, Don, 222

Campana, Louis, 163
Campbell, Homer, 46
Campling, Gilbert, 187–188
Canda (unknown maker), 229
Carroll, Frank T., 174, 175
Carroll, John, 226
Cars Made in Upstate New York (Bellamy), 3, 102
Centaur (unknown maker), 229
Chadeayne, William C., 204, 205, 207–208, 209, 210, 211
Chain Bike Corporation, 22–23
Chamberlain, Herbert W., 46, 47, 49

Chaos Custom Motorcycle Corporation (Chaos Cycle), 23, *23*, *p2*
Chapin, John J., 131
Cheeftah, 103
Chick, J. T., 150
choppers
    American Chopper television show on, 142–143, 145–146
    Broadway Choppers, 20–21
    Chaos Cycle custom, 23, *23*, *p2*
    Copper Mike, *p4*
    County Line Choppers, 20
    Indian Larry custom, 53, 53–54, *p5*
    Long Island Choppers, 104
    Musto, T., 130, *p4*
    Nigro, *p2*
    NYC Chopper style, 26, 53
    OCC, 142–143, *143*, *p6*
    Paul Cox Industries, 26
    popularity of custom, 2, 142–143
    Stellar Industries mini, 189
    V-Twin Manufacturing, 195
    Wroblewski, Joseph, *220*, 220–221
    Yost, 226, *226*
Christensen, Tyvald, *23*, 23–24
Christianson, Ron, 3
Clark, C. Edward, 126, 128, 174
Clark, Edward P., *24*, 24–25
Clark, George W. and George E., 106
Clark, Henry Austin, Jr., 3, 18, 26, 53, 62, 81, 165, 166, 176
Clement Motor Equipment Company, 25, *25*
Cleveland, Chauncey, 138
Clifton, Charles, 147
Clinton Engine Corporation, 103
Clum, Frederick H., 120
clutch
    Abell steam motorcycle one-way, 7
    Christensen disc, 24
    early advancements, 1, 2
    Eclipse, 65, 66, 68, 71, 73, 154, 155, 175, 180
    Ellett, 180
    Emblem, 65, *66*, 68, 71
    Ruggles, H. B., mechanism for, 181
    Schickel innovation for, 185
    Spangler. J., *54*, 55
    Stellar, 189
    Thourot, 211–212, *212*

Widmayer "relieve cock" in place of, 215
Coalition Company, 85–86
Cocchi, Al, 163
Colburn, William B., 147, 151, 153, 155
Cole, Michael (Copper Mike), 25, 25–26, *p4*
Coleman, Charles, Sr., *p3*
Coleman, Charles Clifford, Jr., *p3, p8*
The Complete Illustrated Encyclopedia of American Motorcycles (Rafferty), 4, 19, 230
"The Complete Roster of Two-Wheeled Motorized Vehicles Made in the U.S.A., 1869–1979," (Gerald and Lucas), 3, 86–87, 229–230
Compton, Lewis R., 86
Connelly, Cody, 143, 146
Conner, Frank, 221, 222, 223, 225
Cook, Albert, 31, 33, 102
Cook, Donald C., 63, 74
Copper Mike (Michael Cole), 25, 25–26, *p4*
Corkhill, Thomas, 119–120
Corpe, Jim, 221, 222
corporate names and iterations, organization of, 5
Cotter, G. A., 209
County Line Choppers, 20
Cowie, Alexander H., 132, 136
Cox, Paul, 25–26, 53, 54, 183
Crescent Auto Manufacturing Company, 26, 165
Croft, H. W., 48
Crouse, Huntington B. (and Crouse-Hinds Company), 132, 135, 136
CT Newman Engineering, 136–137, *137, p5*
Curtiss, Glenn H. (and "Curtiss" motorcycles and companies), 1, 169
  1903 Model Year, 27–29, *28*
  1904 and 1905 Model Years, 29–30, *30*
  1906 Model Year, 30–31, *31*
  1907 Model Year, 31–32
  1908 Model Year, 32–33
  1909 Model Year, 33–35
  1910 Model Year, 35–36

1911 Model Year, *36*, 36–37
1912 and 1913 Model Years, 37–38
aviation competition fame, 34–36
aviation designs and awards, 28–29, 32, 33, 34–35, 37, 217
background, 26
Bendix, V., venture with, 16–17
Curtiss Exhibition Company of, 36, 38
Curtiss Motor Company incorporation and directors, 37
Curtiss Motorcycle Company unincorporated branch of, 34, *36*, 36–38, 127
E. R. Thomas Motor Company and, 26–27, 211
early investors in, 27
factory, 29, 30, 32–33, 34, *34*, 36, 37
G. H. Curtiss Company investors and incorporation, 30
Hercules engine development by, 16, 26–38, 51, 101
Herring-Curtiss Company partnership and bankruptcy for, 26, 34–37, 38, 124–126, 127
Marvel Motorcycle Company and, 34, 36, 37, 124–127, *127*
museum collections and, 38
racing of, 16, 26, 27, 28, 30, 31, 32
sidecar options, 30–31, 32
speed record of, 32, 38
Wehman frame design for, 33, 35, 36, 37, 125
Curtiss, Lena, 30
Curtiss Aeroplane Company, 36, 38, 97, 126, 128, 211
custom-built motorcycles. *See also* Harley-Davidson-based custom motorcycles
  American Motorcycle Parts, 9, *9*
  Ballou, 14–15
  Brainard, 19, *19*
  Briggs, 20
  Chaos Cycle, 23, *23, p2*
  Fabbro Industries, *130*, 130–131
  Harlvin, 7–8, *8*
  Indian Larry, 23, 26, 53–54, 183, *p5*
  Musto, T., 129–131, *130, p4*
  OCC, 142–143, *143, p6*

popularity of, 1
Robinson Cyclenet Inc. kits for, 178
Stylemaster, 194
SuperMoto Italia Inc., 194
Venier, 213
Wroblewski, *220*, 220–221
Cutler, Burwell S., 208
Cycle Creations, 38
Cyclemotor Corporation. *See also* Evans Power Cycle
  Cyclemotor attachment market decline for, 44–45
  Cyclemotor debut and development of, 38–43, *39*
  dealers in 1918 for, 44
  engine design and evolution, 39, 40, 48, *48*, 49
  engine testing process at, 41–42
  General Railway Signal production for, 38–40, *39, 40*, 42, 43–44, 46–47
  G.R.S. Products Inc. absorption of, 47–49
  international interest in, 40, 43, 46
  Merkel and, 44, 45, 46, 47, 112
  payment scheme for, 44
  World War I and, 42, 43, 44

Davies, John E., 138
Day Manufacturing Company, 49, 62
De Lezene, J. M., 172
DeBie, Kent, 223
Decker, Ward, 172–173
DeDion-Bouton Motorette Company
  motor tricycles, 49–50, 61
  motors used in other motorcycles, 50, 61, *61*, 90–91, 98, 105, 118, *167*
DeLong, G. Erwin (company and motorcycle), 27, 50, *50*–52
Deninger, Andrew J. (Deninger Cycle Company), 52
DeSchaum, William A., 53
DeSchaum-Hornell Motor Company, 52–53
DeSmedt, Lawrence (Indian Larry), 23, 26, 53–54, 183, *p5*
Detroit Bi-Car Company, 131
DeWald, George, *54*, 54–57
Dickerson, Edward N., Jr., 57–58, *58*

DiMartino, Vinnie, 143, 146
dirigibles, 28–29, 32, 33, 146
dirt-track racing, 2, 137, 161, 178, *178*, 222, *222*
Discovery Channel. *See* television shows
DiTullio, James R., 58, 220
DMR, *221*, 221–226, *222*, *223*
documentation, 3–4
Dodge, Lyman E., 39
Doering, Ted and Jerry, 195
Doll, J. Frederick, 169
Dolson, W. L., 101
drag racing, 2, 58, 84, *84*, 220, 225
Dragner, James J., 59, *59*
Ducati, 17, 194
Dunham, George W., 115, 116
Dunn, R. L., *59*, 59–60
Duryea, Charles E., 92

E. A. Brecher and Company, 20
E. C. Stearns and Company, *188*, 188–189
E. & F., 81–84
E. J. Edmond and Co., 61–62
E. R. Thomas Motor Company (and variations), 87, 160, 196–211
  1901 Model Year, *197*, 197–200, *198*
  1902 Model Year, 200–202, *201*
  1903 and 1904 Model Years, 202–204, *204*
  1905 to 1908 Model Years, 204–206, *206*
  1909 Model Year, 206–208, *207*
  1910 and 1911 Model Years, 208–210, *209*
  1912 Model Year and after, 210–211, *211*
  Auto-Bi Company and motorcycles, 5, 61–62, 91, *201*, 201–202, 211
  Buffalo Automobile and Auto-Bi Company formed from, 196, 201–202
  corporate reorganizations and name changes, 5, 196
  Curtiss, G., and, 26–27, 211
  dominance, 1, 196
  Edmond, E. J. of, 61–62, 201, 202, 211
  factories, 199, 200, 201, 202, 210, 211
  founding, 196–197
  Greyhound Motor Company as successor to, 5, 196, *209*, 209–211, *211*
  museum collection including Auto-Bi of, *201*
  racing motorcycles, 205, 211
  tandem seating, 200, 204
  Thomas Auto-Bi Company and motorcycles of, 196, 197, *197*, 200–202, *201*, *204*, 204–205, *p7*
Eastern Truckford Company Inc., 60
Eastern Wheel Works, 60–61
e-bikes and motorcycles
  Baisden, 14, *14*
  Flluid and Fllow, 212–213
  Musto, T. and, 130
  PJD designed, 146
  Tarform Inc., 194–195, *195*, *p7*
Eckman, John W., 183
Eckman, Joseph, 33
Eclipse Machine Company, 42, 109–110, 171
  clutch, 65, 66, 68, 71, 73, 154, 155, 175, 180
  Royal Motor Works and, 178–180
Edmond, E. J. (of E. R. Thomas Motor Company), 61–62, 201, 202, 211
Edmond, E. J. (of Edmond motorcycle), 61, *61*
Edwards, David, 225
Eisenhuth (John W.) Horseless Vehicle Company, 62, *62*
Elder, Clara A., 95
electric bikes and motorcycles. *See* e-bikes and motorcycles
Ellett, Frederick S., 180
Elliott, J., 25
Ellis, Charles A., 101
Ellis, Seele H., 83
Ellis & Fleming Manufacturing Company, 81, 83–84
Emblem Manufacturing Company (and Emblem motorcycles), 49
  1907 and 1908 Model Years, 63–64, *64*
  1909 Model Year, 64–65, *65*
  1910 Model Year, 65–67, *66*
  1911 Model Year, 52, 67, 67–68
  1912 Model Year, 68–70, *69*
  1913 Model Year, *70*, 70–72
  1914 Model Year, *72*, 72–73, *73*
  1915 Model Year, *73*, 73–75, *74*
  1916 Model Year, *75*, 75–76, *76*
  1917 Model Year, 76–77
  1918 to 1920 Model Years, 78–79
  1921 to 1924 Model Years, 78–80
  1925 Model Year and final production for, 80
  bicycles, 43, 52, 63, 64, 69, 71, 74, 76, 78
  dealers/distributors, 65, 66, 68, 69, 70, 75, 78
  endurance runs, 65, 66, 71–72
  factory and production rate, 63, 66, 67, 68–69, 70–71, 74, 78–79, *79*, 80
  founding, 62–63
  international market, 72, 74–75, 78, 80
  Pierce bicycle operations acquisition by, 160
  side-by-side seating design, 68, 72, *72*, *p8*
  sidecar options, 70, 73, 75, 78, *p3*
  women riders and, *67*, 68, 69, 72, *p3*
Emiliussen, John F., 134
Empire Motor Cycle Company. *See* Reliance Motor Cycle Company
The Encyclopedia of the Motorcycle (Wilson, H.), 3, 15, 19, 228, 229–230
endurance runs
  Curtiss, G., performance on, 30
  Emblem performance on, 65, 66, 71–72
  Kiefler motorcycle and, 100
  Neracar, 134
  Pierce motorcycles in, 150–151
  Regas motorcycle, 169
  Stratton Motor Bicycle Company, 192, 193
  Yankee Boss and, 222
Engels, Franz, 215
engines. *See also* Thor engines; *specific makers*
  A. P. innovation for, 9–10
  acetylene-fueled, 57–58, *58*, 145
  Acme bicycle, 24, *24*
  Bendix, V., self-starter drive, 17

Bordman gas turbine, 18, *18*
Bullis gasoline, 22, *22*
"Curtiss," in museum collections, 38
Cyclemotor, 39, 40, 41–42, 48, *48*, 49
DeDion, 50, 61, *61*, 90–91, 98, 105, 118, *167*
early ideas and evolution, 1–2
Hercules, development by Curtiss, G., 16, 26–38, 51, 101
Kelecom, 49, 84
P. T. Motor Company, 9, 17, 26, 117, *164*, 164–166, *166*, 216
pedal-to-start, 15
Pierce Cycle first four-cylinder, shaft-driven, 1–2, 148, *148*, *p6*
in rear wheels, 59, 59–60
rotary bicycle, 10, 15–16, *16*
run-to-start, 59
steam-powered, 1, 7, *7*, 57, 129, *129*, 198
water-cooled, 17, 113
Engle, Frank, 136
Erie motorcycle, 34
Evans, Fred, 89, *89*
Evans, Leigh R., 38–39, 42, 43, 46
Evans Power Cycle
1917 Model Year, 41–43, *42*
1918 Model Year, 43–44
1919 and 1920 Model Years, 44–45
1921 and 1922 Model Years, 45–46
1923 and 1924 Model Years, 46, 46–47
1925 Model Year, 47–48, *48*
1926 Model Year and beyond, 48–49
Cyclemotor attachment market decline relative to, 44–45
Cyclemotor development and predecessor for, 38–43, *39*
General Railway Signal/G.R.S. Products Inc., production of, 38–40, *39*, *40*, 46–47
German production of version of, 48
international interest in, 43
Morley Machinery Corporation acquisition of, 49
in museum collections, 49
price decrease in 1925, 47–48

sales success, 45
Sport Model, 46, *46*, 48
Everwine, T. J., 74, 75, 111

Fabbro Industries, LLC, 129–131, *130*
Fabrique Nationale d'Armes de Guerre (FN motorcycles), 55, 80, 149, 181
Fairbanks, Lewis B., 94, 95
FAM. *See* Federation of American Motorcyclists
Fanciulli, Jerome, 35, 36, 37
Fast by Gast, 84
Fauber, William H. (and Fauber Bi-Car), 80–81
Favor, George W., 172, 173
Federation of American Motorcyclists (FAM), 30, 65, 68, 69, 72, 77, 100, 153, 155
Ferguson, Ernest L., 61, 199, 200
Fielding, Herbert E., 146
Finck, August, Jr., 51
Finck, George, 51
Fisher, Daniel R., 81, *81*
Fisher, G. Kenneth, 139–140
Fleming, Peter G., 82, 83
Fleming Manufacturing Company (and Fleming motor), 81–84, *82*, *83*
Fleming Motor Vehicle Company, 81, 82–83
Fllow, 212–213
Flluid, 212–213
FN motorcycles, 55, 80, 149, 181
Ford Motor Company, 2
Fornwalt, Robert, 225, 226
Fowler, L. E., 134
Fowler-Manson-Sherman Cycle Manufacturing Company, 106
Fox, Fred P., 208
Frankel, Joseph, 156, 157
Freeman, Henry W., 173
French market and motorcycles, 118
Clement Motor Equipment Company origins and, 25, *25*
E. R. Thomas Motor Company and, 196
Hedstrom and, 90
Ner-A-Car and, 134
Prospect Motor Company production, 161–163
Reliance and, 170

Frick, Morton, 134
Friedeberg, Theodore, 156, 157
FUELL Inc., 212–213
Funke, Albert H., 16, 84

G. H. Curtiss Manufacturing Company. *See* Curtiss, Glenn H.
Gainsford, E. A., 56
Gale, Maurice (and family), *67*, 68, 71–72, *72*, *73*
Gallaway, John A., 95
gas lights, 98, 154
Gasoline Alley, 26, 54
Gast, Paul, 58, 84, *84*, 220
Gearless Motor Cycle Company (and Gearless motorcycle), 84–85, *85*
Geer, Harry R., 29
Geffon, Abraham, 96, *96*
General Railway Signal/G.R.S. Products Inc. (G.R.S.), 38–49
Cyclemotor Corporation absorption of, 47–49
Evans Power Cycle production by, 38–40, *39*, *40*, 46–47
Genung, Harry, 38
George V. Lyons Motor Company, 104
Gerald, Michael, 3, 11, 17, 30, 86–87, 186, 229–230
Gerini, Fred, 142
German market and motorcycles, 8
Autoped in, 13
Evans Power Cycle version production and, 48
International Motorcycle Company and, 97
JeBe and, 17
Jehle and, 98
N.S.U. motorcycles and, 138
Oldfield and, 140
PJD e-bike production and, 146
Stinsman, G., motorcycle and, 23, *23*
Gibson, Hugo C.
Autoped Company of America and, 12
Mon-Auto Company, 85–86
Gibson Mon-Auto Company, 12, 85–86, *86*
Gillette, King C., 132
Giro, Eduardo, 221

Glas, John C., 49, 63, 65, 71, 77, *77*, 78
Gliesman, August E., 87
Gliesman, Harry A., 86–87
Globe Cycle Company, 87, 88, 196–197
Glouster Cycle Company, 88
Goddard, H. A., 116–117
Goforth, W. Frank, 113
Gold, Egbert H., 132, 136
Goldman, Annette, 89–90
Goldman, Meyer, 89–90
Gordon, Edwin K., 132, *133*, 134, 136
Gottschalk, Edmond F. *See* Stratton, Edmond F.
Grant, Gideon, 113
Gravesend Cycles Inc., *25*, 25–26, 130, *p4*
Green, George D., 168, 169
Green, Lincoln, 60
Greene, E. A., 86
Greenlagh, George H., 172
Gressier, Romaine, 87
Greyhound Motor Works/Company. *See also* E. R. Thomas Motor Company
 evolution and motorcycles of, 5, 196, *209*, 209–211, *211*
 museum collections with motorcycles from, 211
 sidecars, 210, 211, *211*
Gridley, Francis W., 142
G.R.S. *See* General Railway Signal/ G.R.S. Products Inc.

Haberer, Charles, 87–88, 227
Haberle, William H., 51
Hafelfinger, Emil, 99, 178–180
Hall, G. Ray, 30, 36, 127
Hancock, Lawrence P., 151, 153, 155–156
Hands, James A., 193
Hansford, VanBuren N., 49
Hanson, Harry E., 189
Harley-Davidson, 91, 91n4, 169
 popularity of, 1
 production rate, 74
 V-Twin Manufacturing parts for, 195, *195*
Harley-Davidson-based custom motorcycles
 Brainard, 19, *19*

Broadway Choppers, 20–21
Chaos Cycle, 23, *23*, *p2*
Copper Mike, *25*, 25–26, *p4*
CT Newman Engineering, 136–137, *137*, *p5*
Cycle Creations, 38
Harlvin, 7–8, *8*
Iacona, 97
Indian Larry, *53*
Klingerman, 102
Musto, T., *p4*
Nigro, 9, *9*, *p2*
prevalence of, 2
Yost, 226, *226*
Harlvin, 7–8, *8*
Harper, David, 88
Harper, Roy E., 86
Harper Engineering Company, 88, *88*
Harper Motor Company, 88
Hartshorne, Edward C., 89
Hartshorne and Battelle, 89
Hass, Herman J., 202
Hatfield, Jerry H., 106, 123
Haverford Cycle Company/Haverford Cycle Company of Buffalo Inc., 89–90
Hedstrom, Oscar (and Hedstrom motorcycle), 87, *90*, 90–91
Heil, George A., 63
Heil, William J., Jr., 63, 78
Heitchen, John O., 91, *91*, 91n3
Hendee, George M., 90
Hendee Manufacturing Company, 74, 110, 112, 201
Henderson, William G., 91–92, *92*
Hengerer, George E., 209
Hengerer, Julius, 206, 208
Henshaw, Charles S., 87, *90*, 90–91, 200, 201–202
Hercules, 16, 26, 51, 101
 1903 Model Year, 27–29, *28*
 1904 and 1905 Model Years, 29–30, *30*
 in museum collection, 38
Herkert, Ambrose L., 47, 49
Hermance, Pulver G., 27, 51
Herring, Augustus M., 34, 35
Herring-Curtiss Company, 26, 34–37, 38, 124–126, 127
Herschmann, Arthur, 92–93, *93*
Hickey, George F., 215

Hilaman, 93
Hiscox, Gardner Dexter, 105
Hitchcock (Caleb B.) Manufacturing Company, *93*, 93–95, *94*
Hodgdon, Ted A., 74, 149
Hoffinger, Martin, 103
Hoffmann, 8
Hogle (Edwin E.) Motor Sales Corporation, 95–96
Holland, Lincoln, Jr., 174, 175
Hollett, J. M., 116
Holley, George M. (and Holley Motor Co.), 117, *141*, 141–142
Holliday, Bob, 92
Holtzman, John, 96, *96*
Hoover, Percy, 74
Hopkins, Harvey J., 53
Hopkins, Nelson S., 96–97, *97*
Hoppe, Robert A., 109, 110, 112
Horschel Brothers Precision, 19
Howard, Frederick C., 89–90
Howard, Samuel B., 116
Hubbs, J. Seymour, 27
Hubert, Conrad, 13
Hurlburt, William B. (and Hurlburt Motor Truck Company), 12
hybrid motorcycle-automobile, 102–103, *103*

I. R. Stevens and Company, 190, *191*
Iacona, Steve (Iacona Custom Cycles), 97
Illustrated Encyclopedia of the Motorcycle (Tragatsch), 3, 13, 123, 229
Indian Larry (Lawrence DeSmedt), 23, 26, 53–54, 183, *p5*
Industrial Machine Company, 27, 50–52, *51*
Inside American Motorcycling and the American Motorcycle Association, 1900-1990 (Sucher, H.), 4
International Motorcycle Company, 17, 97
International Sport Motors Ltd., 97
Ives, Willis H. (and Ives Motorcycle Corporation), 128, 169, 172, 174, 176. *See also* Reliance Motor Cycle Company

J. B. Special, 17

Jacobs, Edward, 213
James, Jesse, 23, 142
Japan, 43, 111, 135, 152, 153, 154, 183
JayBrake Enterprises, 19
J-Be or JeBe, 17
Jehle, Herman, 97–98, 97n5, *p1*
Jencick Motor Corporation, 98
Jensen, Charles, 87
Jewel (unknown maker), 229
Johnson, W. A., 149, 150–151, 154–159
Johnston, David James, 114
Jones, Charles O., 33
Jones, H. E., 98–99, *99*, 212
Jones, L. F., 151–152
Jordan, John, 104
journals, trade, 3–4
JoyRide (folding scooter), 190, *191*

Karolevitz, Bob, 15, 93
Kawasaki, 23, 38, 84, 220
Kay, Samuel, 120
Keating, R. M., 62
Keating Wheel and Automobile Company, 62, *62*, 201
Keef, John H., 111, 112
Keeler, George H., 27
Keim, John R., 99
Keino Cycles, 183
Kelecom (motors and motorcycles), 16, 49, 84
Kiefler, Charles J., 99–100, 101
Kiefler, Henry, 99–100, 101
Kiefler Motor Works (and Kiefler motorcycle), 99–101, *100*
Kimes, Beverly Rae, 3, 18, 26, 53, 62, 81, 165, 166, 176
King, Keith T., 190
King, Percy N., 56
Kircherer, Eugene C., 138
Kirkham, Charles B.
 Hercules and "Curtiss" motorcycles development role of, 16, 27, 29, 36, 101
 Kirkham Motor Manufacturing Company of, 30, 101–102
Kirkham, Clarence and Percy, 27, 101
Kirkham Aeroplane and Motor Company, 102
Kleckler, Henry, 124, *124*

Kleitsch, Donald, 112
Klingerman, Kenneth, 102
Klink Motor Car Company, 99, 212
Krackowizer, Herman J., 174
Kravtchouk, Taras, 194–195, *195*
Krupp, 13
Kulture, 52
Kurtz, Samuel B., 102–103, *103*

Lane, Chauncey L., 132, 134
Lang, Conrad J., 151
Lavergne, Gerard, 228
Layman, H. Bernard, 138
Lehning, Allan D., 80
Lehr, Ari, 21–22
Leitner, David C., 11
Leitze, Edward P., 11
Lewis (unknown maker), 229
lights, gas, 98, 154
Lincoln, Hart H., 53
Lincoln, N. S., 116
Lomart Engine Products/Lomart Perfected Devices Inc., 103
Long Island Choppers, 104
Longwell, Harry E., 126, 127, 128
Louis C. M. Reed Company, 13–14
Low, M., 3
Lozier Motor Company, 104
Lucas, Jim, 3, 11, 17, 86–87, 186, 229–230
Ludwig, Frederick W., 89
Luna (e-motorcycle), 194–195, *195*, *p7*
Lyons, George V., 104

MacAdam, J., 201
Mackie, Dave, 194
Madden, Burt L., 40, 46
makers, unknown, 227–230
Maltby, Frank D. (Maltby Automobile and Manufacturing Company), 104–105
Mann, Dick, 221, 222, 223–224, 226
Manson, George W.
 Manson Bicycle Company of, 105–106
 motorcycles, 52, 105–106, *106*
manufacturer resources, 4
Mark I and II, 189–190, *190*
Martin, Frank L. C., 201

Marushi Shokai Company, 43, 152
Marvel Motorcycle Company, 120–128, 169
 1910 to 1913 Model Years, *124*, 124–128, *127*
 Curtiss, G., and, 34, 36, 37, 124–127, *127*
 Motorcycle Equipment and Supply Company reorganization as, 123–124
 Reliance Motor Cycle Company relation to, 121, 123, 128
 Waters management of, 34, 121, 123, 124–125, 126, 127–128
Masson, Linn D., 34
Masson, Victor and Jules, 27
Maxi Super, 189–190
MB (unknown maker), 229
McClure, George, 208
McColgan, Patrick, *p2*
McGrane Company, 229
McGuckin, John J., 161–162, 163
McGuire, F. G., 116
McIlvena, Al, 194
McKay, Donald S., 151
McLaughlin, John F., 106, 138
McLaughlin & Ashley Motor Company, 104, 106, 138
McLean, A. N., 113
McLean, R. T., 113
Mead, M. J., 183
Meadowbrook Cycle Company (and Meadowbrook motorcycle), 106–107, *107*
Mears (John W.) Cycle Machine Works/Company, 107
Meehan, Frank P., 96
Merkel, Joseph F. (and Merkel Motor Wheel Company Inc.)
 Autoped scooter design of, 12, 13, *13*, 108
 Cyclemotor Corporation and, 44, 45, 46, 47, 112
 distributors for, 111
 financial problems, 111–112
 international market for, 110–111
 Motor Wheel design and evolution, 107–110, *108*, *110*
Mertz, Louis C., 98
Mesco motorcycle, 120–121
Metz, Charles H., 99, 129

238 | Index

Miami Cycle and Manufacturing Company, 12, 67, 108
Mike, Copper, 130
Militaire Autocycle Company of America Inc. (and company variations), 112–117
  company name change, 115
  factory, 114, *114*, 115, *115*
  founding, investors, and officers, 112–114
  Militaire Autocycle development and evolution, 103, *113*, 113–114, *114*
  post-bankruptcy reorganization of, 115–116
  sidecars, 116
Militor Corporation (formerly Militaire) and Militor motorcycle factory, 115, 116
  investors and officers of, 115–116
  Militaire post-bankruptcy reorganization as, 115–116
  reorganization in 1920 as Sinclair Motors Corporation, 116
Miller, C. W., 85
Miller, Charles E., *117*, 117–118
Miller, Darius, 202, 203
Miller, George C., 113, 114
Miller, Henry, 27
Miller, W. F., 114
Mills, Edwin, 113, 114, 115
Miner, George L., 110, 111
Minerva motorcycle, 104, 123
Minor, C. G., 116
MMA. See Motorcycle Manufacturers' Association
Monarch motorcycles. See Reliance Motor Cycle Company
Mon-Auto (Gibson), 12, 85–86, *86*
Moody, Herman L., 118, *118*
Moore, William G., 112–113
Moreau, Margelia, *67*
Morgan, George D., 46, 48
Morgan, R. E., 46
Morgan, Ralph L. and Charles H., 119
Morgan, William A., 113
Morgan Motor Company, 118–119, *119*
Morley Machinery Corporation, 38, 49

Morris, Joshua M. (and Morris and Corkhill Motor Cycle Company), 119–120, *120*, 169
Morrow, Alexander P., 171
Morton W. Smith Company Inc. (and Skootamotor), 187–188
Moto Guzzi, 17
Motor Bicycle (Motorcycle) Equipment and Supply Company, 120–128
  Erie motorcycle of, 34, *121*, 121–123, 128
  founding, 120–121
  mail-order business after Marvel end, 128
  Mesco motorcycle of, 120–121
  reorganization as Marvel Motorcycle Company, 123–124
motor bicycles and bicycle motors. See also Cyclemotor Corporation; Evans Power Cycle
  A. P., 9, 9–10
  Abell steam-powered, 7, *7*
  attachable wheel motor for, 96, *96*
  Baisden, 14, *14*
  Battey, 15–16, *16*
  beginning of, 1, 5
  Boisselot, 17–18
  Boller Brothers, 18
  Bretz Cycle Manufacturing Company, 20
  Bullis, 22, *22*
  Christensen invention for, *23*, 23–24
  Clark, E., and Brewster, William H., *24*, 24–25
  Clement Motor Equipment Company conversion kit for, 25, *25*
  DeDion engine for, 61, *61*
  DeLong design for, *50*, 50–52
  Dickerson design for, 57–58, *58*
  E. A. Brecher and Company, 20
  E. C. Stearns and Company racing, *188*, 188–189
  E. R. Thomas Motor Company, 197
  Evans, F., invention for, 89, *89*
  Fleming Manufacturing Company, 81–84, *82*, *83*
  Herschmann, 92–93, *93*
  Hopkins, N., 96–97, *97*

  introduction of, 1
  Keating Wheel and Automobile Company, 62, *62*
  Keim, 99
  Kelecom, 84
  Merkel, 107–110, *108*, *110*
  Miller, Charles, motor for, *117*, 117–118
  Morgan Motor Company, 118–119, *119*
  Okay Motor Manufacturing Company Inc., 138–140, *139*, *140*
  Olive Wheel Company, *141*, 141–142
  P. T. engine for, 9, 17, 26, 117, *164*, 164–166, *166*, 216
  Raders compressed air design for, 57, *57*
  Remington Arms Company, 176
  Schnepf electric, 186–187, *187*
  Stratton Motor Bicycle Company, 190–193, *191*, *192*, *193*
  tandem seating for racing, 90
  Walters, 214, *214*
motor tricycles, 5, 189
  Boisselot, 18
  Bullis, 22
  decline of, 1
  DeDion-Bouton Motorette Company, 49–50, 61
  E. R. Thomas Motor Company, 197, 198, 200
  Edmond, E. J. (of Edmond motorcycle), 61, *61*
  Lozier Motor Company, 104
  Miller, Charles, motor for, 117
  Morgan Motor Company, 119
  P. T. engine for, 164, *164*
  Remington Arms Company motor for, 176
  Sager attachment for, 167
  Stearns, 189
motorcycle. See also specific companies and topics
  definition and etymology, 1, 5
  early automobile popularity compared with, 2
Motorcycle Car Corporation, 128–129
Motorcycle Mania, 54, 129, 142

Motorcycle Manufacturers'
    Association (MMA), 66, 70, 80,
    125, 138, 151, 206
Motorcyclepedia Museum, *53, 201*
motors. *See* engines; motor bicycles
    and bicycle motors; Thor engines
Motosacoche motorcycle, 104
Mulcock, E. R., 116
Murphy, Charles and William, 130, *130*
Murray, G. H., Jr., 193
museum collections
    Auto-Bi in, *201*
    Autoped in, 14
    Curtiss, G., engines at, 38
    Evans Power Cycle and Cyclemotor
        in, 49
    Greyhound in, 211
    Indian Larry motorcycle in, 53, *53*
    Jehle's Spiral in, *p1*
    Monarch and Reliance motorcycles
        in, 176
    Neracar in, 136
    Yankee Boss in, *223*, 226
Musto, Alexis, 130
Musto, Terence "T," 129–131, *130*, *p4*
Myers, Jacob C., 110

Napora, Dennis, 91
Ner-A-Car Corporation (Neracar)
    factory, 133–134, *134*
    international market, 4, 132, 135
    investors and directors of, 132–133
    motorcycle development and
        evolution, 2, 4, *131*, 131–136,
        132, 133, 135, p8
Neracher, Carl A., 131–133, *132*, 136
Ness, Joseph P., 211
New York Motor Cycle Club, 16, 27,
    28, 98, 211, 212, 220, *p1*
New York Motor Cycle Company
    Inc., 86–87
Newman, Christian, 136–137, *137, p5*
Nicol, George, 116
Nigro, William, 9, *9, p2*
Nioga Cycle Works, 137
Niveson, William O., 95
Norris, Eloise Laurene Breese. *See*
    Breese, Eloise
Norsman Motorcycles, 137, 178
North American Motor Corporation,
    138

Norton, 8, 17
Notman, R. L., 115, 116
N.S.U. Motor Company, 138
NYC Chopper style, 26, 53

OCC. *See* Orange County Choppers
Ohnhaus, Louis, 201
Okay Motor Manufacturing Company
    Inc., 138–140, *139, 140*
Oldfield, Andrew H. (and Oldfield
    motorcycle), 140–141, *141*
Olive Wheel Company, *141*, 141–142
Olmstead, Elmer Benton, 201, 202
online resources, 4
Orange County Choppers (OCC),
    142–143, *143, p6*
Osborn, Alden E., 143–144, *144*
Osborne, John A., 38
Ossa Sales Corporation (and Ossa
    motorcycles), *221*, 221–226, *222,
    223*
Ostrowski, Gregory, 61
Oswald, Edward, 51
Overman, William C., 207, 208, 209
Ovington, Earle L., 80
Ovington Motor Company, 55, 80
Owen, William, 63, 78
Owens, Florence, *12*

P. T. Motor Company
    engine, 9, 17, 26, 117, *164*,
        164–166, *166*, 216
    Widmayer leadership in, 216
Page, J. Robert, 113
Page, Victor W., 10, 11, 90
Paine, Arthur B., 193
Paine, J. Overton, 192–193
Palmer, Ira C., 145, *145*, 227
Pam Autocyclettes, 10–11
Pansy (unknown maker), 229–230
Parisi, Mike, 20–21
Parkhurst, Gabriel H., 126
Parsons, W. H., 38, 46, 79, 133–134
Patee, Fred, 119–120, *120*, 168–169
Patton, H. Tatem, 174
Paul, William C., 53
Paul Cox Industries, 25–26
Paul Jr. Designs (PJD), 145–146
Paulson, W. G., 78–79
Peerless S. D. motorcycle, 54, *55*,
    56–57

Pemberton, John G., 172
Pennington, Edward J., *93*, 93–94, *94*
Pennsylvania Motor Car Company,
    146
Perew, Philip, 146
periodicals, 3–4
Perks, Edwin, 217
Perrin, Earl R., 40, 44, 111, 112
Persons, Charles A., 179
Petrie, Denis, 225
Peugeot motorcycles, *161*, 161–164,
    162
Pierce, George N., *147*, 147–148, 151
Pierce, Percy P., 147–148, 151,
    157–159, *159*
Pierce Cycle Company, 80, 146–160
    1909 Model Year, 148–150
    1910 Model Year, 150–151, *p6*
    1911 Model Year, 151–153, *152,
        153*
    1912 Model Year, 153–157
    1913 Model Year, 157–159
    1914 Model Year, 159–160
    bankruptcy, reorganizations, and
        acquisitions, 78, 79, 156–158,
        160
    bicycle production, 146–148, 154,
        156, 160
    factory, 147, *147*, 148, 152
    first machine from, 1–2, 148, *148*
    founding and directors of, 146–
        148
    international market, 151–152,
        154–155
    Merkel Motor Wheel and, 110
    Osborn, A., slide-valve system and,
        144, *144*
    Schack 1918 acquisition of, 78, 79
    West Coast distribution, 150, 152
PJD. *See* Paul Jr. Designs
Plough, M. C., 27
Pokorney, Henry, 160, 201
Pomeroy, Robert W., 113
Pope Manufacturing Company, 8
Potdevin, Adolph, 164, 165, 216
Powell, Harry, 132
Pratt, Aaron G., 30
Prospect Motor (Manufacturing)
    Company, *161*, 161–164, *162*
Psycho Cycles, 26, 53
Puliafico, Joe, 146

Quant, Cornelia Heitchen, 91, 91n4

R & H (unknown maker), 230
Race Visions, 58
Racer, 194–195
racing and racing motorcycles
    Auto-Bi performance as, 205, 211
    Ballou, 15
    Curtiss, G., and, 16, 26, 27, 28, 30, 31, 32
    dirt-track, 2, 137, 161, 178, *178*, 222, *222*
    DiTullio, 58, 220
    drag, 2, 58, 84, *84*, 220, 225
    E. R. Thomas Motor Company, 205, 211
    Emblem success in, 66–67, *72*
    Gast, 58, 84, *84*, 220
    Hercules performance as, 16, 27
    Kirkham, C. B., 101–102
    Simplex Peugeot, 161, *161*
    Stinsman, G., 23
    tandem, 90
    Wyman record for, 205
    Yankee Motor Company and Ossa, 221, *222*, 222–223, 225
Raders, Joseph F., *57*, 57–58
Rafferty, Tod, 4, 19, 230
Ramsdell, Harry T., 113
Ran-Jet, 189–190
Reed, Charles L., 120
Reeves, Bill, 166
Regas Vehicle Company, 119, *167*, 167–169
Reilly, George V., 116
Reliance Motor Cycle Company (and Monarch motorcycles), 29
    1904 to 1906 Model Years, 169–171, *170*
    1907 to 1910 Model Years, 171–172, *172*
    1911 Model Year, 172–174, *173*
    1912 to 1914 Model Years, 174–176, *175*
    1915 Model Year and later, 176
    factory, 171, 174, *174*, *175*
    founding and directors, 169, 172
    Marvel Motorcycles and, 121, 123, 128
Remington Arms Company, 176
Renshaw, Alfred H., 47, 48–49

resources, 3–4
Reynolds, Charles D., 29, 169, 170
Reynolds, John F., 176
Rice, Augustus "Gus" C., 42, 43, 44, 45–46, 62
riders athleticism, 2
Riggs, Frank C., 168
Riggs-Spencer Company. *See* Regas Vehicle Company
Riotte, Carl C., 177
Ripper, Victor E., 169, 175
Ritz Cycle Car Company, 177
Ritzko, Steve, 223
Ritzwoller, Carl D., 177
Robinson, David, 137, 177–178
Robinson Cyclenet Inc. (and Robinson Streetracker), 177–178, *178*
Rogers, G. N., 105
Root, Charles A., Jr., 193
Roseberry, C. R., 27, 30, 35, 38, 124, 217
Ross bicycles, 22
Royal Motor Works, 99, 178–180, *179*
Rubin, J. Robert, 138
Rudd, Clarence, 124, *124*, 126, 128
Ruggles, Daniel B., 80, 181
Ruggles, Hibbert B., 180–182, *182*
Rugmobile Company of America, *180*, 180–182, *181*, *182*
Russell Motor Car Company, 38, 46, 210

S. D. Manufacturing Company (and S. D. and S.D.M. motorcycles), *54*, 54–57, *55*
Sager, J. Harry (and Regas motorcycles), 119, *167*, 167–169
St. Yves, Henri, *182*, 182–183
Salgo, Nicholas, 222
Salisbury, Clark W., 183
Salisbury Ball Bearing Corporation Inc., 183
Salmon, W., 39, 48
Salvadori, Clement, 225, 226
Sandin, Edwin H., 183
Sandruck, F. W., 56
Sanford, Homer F., 11
Santee, Ellis M., 95
Sasaki, Keinosuke "Keino," 54, 183
Satzauer, Solomon, 177

Sayre, G. W., 174, 175
Schack, William G., 62–79, *69*
Schaefer, C. T., 114
Schickel, Norbert H. (and Schickel Motor Company), 183–186, *184*, *185*
Schmidt, Ferdinand L., 184, 185
Schnepf, John, 186–187, *187*
Schultz, Theodore E., 86
Scoot-A-Long, 189–190, *190*
scooters
    Autoped, 2, 11–14, *12*, *13*, 108
    Chain Bike Corporation, 22–23
    JoyRide folding, 190, *191*
    Scoot-A-Long, 189–190, *190*
Scott, Campbell, 115
Scrambler, 194–195
Seamark, Harry F., 63, 78
seating, side-by-side, 68, 72, 219, *p8*
seating, tandem. *See* tandem seating
Seeger, Bobby and Elisa, 54
Shannon, Mathew E., 101
Sheldon, Burton K., 47
Shepker, Albert W., 63, 78
Sherman, George W., 201
Shire, Moses, 147, 148
Shirley, Amos, 187
shocks and suspension systems
    Allyn, 8
    Cyclemotor, 45, 48
    DeWald, 54, 55, 56
    E. R. Thomas Motor Company, 202, 204, *204*, 207, *207*, 208
    Emblem, 63, 71, 72
    Fisher, D., rear, 81, *81*
    Heitchen, 91
    Militaire, 116
    Monarch, 175, *175*
    Musto, T., 130, *130*, *p4*
    Pierce Cycle Company, 149, 159
    S. D. Manufacturing Company, 55, 56
    Stellar options for, 189
    Yankee Motor Company, 222, 224
Shoemaker, William W., *108*, 109, 110, 111, 112
Shone, James W., 10
Shone-Hanna Company, 10
sidecars, 2
    "Curtiss" motorcycles options for, 30–31, 32, 36, 37

Emblem options for, 70, 73, 75, 78, *p3*
Gearless Motor Cycle Company, 85
Greyhound, 210, 211, *211*
Militaire options for, 116
Simplex Machine Works production of, 163–164
Sikes, Lee, 20–21
Simplex Machine Works (sidecars), 163–164
Simplex motorcycles, *161*, 161–164, *162*
Sinclair, Neil R., 113, 114, 115, 116
Sinclair Motors Corporation (formerly Militor), 116–117
Skinner, Kenneth B., 50
Skootamotor, 187–188
Sladkin, Max M., 89–90
Slattery, William H., 187
Smith, A. Russell, 177
Smith, Albert R., 53
Smith, Carlton M., 113
Smith, Don B., 141, 142
Smith, Eldridge N., 215
Smith, Frances, *12*
Smith, J. Allan, 132, 133–134, 135, *135*, 136
Smith, J. Allan, Jr., 134
Smith, Morton W. (and Company), 187–188
Snoop, Alex, 225, 226
Snyder, Ray, *72*
Snyder, W. H., 69
Solvay, Albert, 118
Spangler, Harry, 56, 57
Spangler, Jacob R., *54*, 55, 56, 57
Spicer, Frederick E., 136
Spiral motorcycle, 97–98, *p1*
Splitdorf Electrical Company, 110
Standard Catalog of American Cars (Kimes and Clark, H.), 3, 18, 26
Stanton, A. W., 27
Starin Company, 188
steam-powered engines, 1, 7, *7*, 57, 129, *129*, 198
Stearns (E. C.) and Company, *188*, 188–189
Stellar Industries (and variations), 189–190, *190*
Stevens, J. Hubert, 95–96
Stewart, David L., 101

Stinsman, Devin, 23
Stinsman, George T., 23, *23*, *p2*
Strange, Douglas J., 4
Stratton, Edmond F., 192–193
Stratton Motor Bicycle Company, 190–193, *191*, *192*, *193*
Streeter, Edward W., 113
Studebaker Corporation, 193–194
stunt riding, 23, 54
Stylemaster Custom Motorcycles, 194
Styria, 187
Sucher, Harry V., 4, 80
Sullivan, E. Dunbar, 60
Sullivan, John H., 60
Sullivan, T. J., 45–46, 110
SuperMoto Italia Inc., 194
SuperTrapp Industries, 19
suspension. *See* shocks and suspension systems
Swartwood, Charles B., 174
Swetland, Ira, *67*
Sydney B. Bowman Automobile Company, 19
Sykes, John, 63, 78

tandem seating, 61
Auto-Bi, 200, 204
"Curtiss" motorcycles, 27, 28, 36
E. R. Thomas Motor Company, 200, 204
Emblem, 68, 78
Hedstrom, 87, *90*, 90–91
Kulture, 52
motor bicycle racing, 90
Palmer, 145, *145*
Pennington, 93–94, 95
Reynolds, J., motorcycle, 176
unknown maker, *227*, 227–228
women riders and, 145, *145*, *227*, 227–228
Tarform Inc., 194–195, *195*, *p7*
Taylor, John A., 221, 223, 224–226
Taylor, L. S., 66–67, 69
Taylor, Trent, 225
Taylor Instrument Company, 40
Tedd Cycle Inc., 195, *195*
television shows
American Chopper, 142–143, 145–146
Biker Build-Off, 54, 146
Motorcycle Mania, 54, 129, 142

Terny, François-Xavier, 212–213
Teutul, Paul, Jr.
at OCC, 142–143, *p6*
Paul Jr. Designs of, 145–146
Teutul, Paul, Sr., 142–143, 145
Thomas, Brenden, 146
Thomas, Edwin L., 201, 204, 205
Thomas, Edwin Ross, 196–197, 198–199, 201, 203. *See also* E. R. Thomas Motor Company
Thomas, Orion F., 196–197
Thomas Company (and Thomas Auto-Bi). *See* E. R. Thomas Motor Company
Thompson, Clyde S., 116
Thor engines, 227
Brandenburg Brothers use of, 20
Emblem motorcycle in 1907 using, 63–64, *64*
Manson use of, 106
Pierce use of, 148, 160
Yankee Motor Company use of, 87–88
Thorn, L. M., 134
Thourot, Frederick, 211–212, *212*
Thurn und Taxis, Gloria von (princess), 23
Tiger Cycle (and various companies), 31, 86–87
Tiger Special, 86–87
Toepel, Michael E., 164–165, 216
Toms, Harvey E., 98–99, *99*, 212
Tortora, Joe, 194
trade journals, 3–4
trade names, organization of, 5
Tragatsch, Erwin, 3, 13, 14, 17, 92, 123, 229
transmissions, early evolution of, 1–2
Trenton motorcycle, 60–61
trick riding, 14, 54
tricycles. *See* motor tricycles
Triumph, 8, 142, 194, 210
Tunley, Joseph H., 110

United Stellar Industries Corporation (and variations), 189–190, *190*
unknown makers, *227*, 227–230

Valiant, Frank Libbey, 67, 68, 69
Van Allen, John W., 205, 206, 208, 209

Van Dam, Eduard, 18
Van Deventer, H. R., 110
Van Doren, J. I., 51
Van Patten, L. A., 116
Vanderpoel, W. Chester, 47
Vanguard Moto Inc. (Vanguard Roadster and VanguardSpark), 212–213
Vasseur, Frédéric, 213
Venier, Stefano (Venier Customs Inc.), 213
Victor Page Motors, 10
Vincent motorcycle, 7–8
V-Twin Manufacturing, 195, *195*

Wacker Motopede, 13
Wagner motorcycle, 104
Waibel, Otto, 63
Walker, Paul, 166
Wallace, Priscilla, 138
Walters, Julius W., 214, *214*
Walton, Julian N., 215
Walton Motor Company Inc., 214, 214–215
Warwick, John M., 63, 78
Washburn, Lloyd D., 140–141
Waters, C. Leonard
    as Curtiss Manufacturing Company director, 34, 37
    Marvel Motorcycle Company and, 34, 121, 123, 124–125, 126, 127–128
Webster, Ralph D., 179
Wehman, Harry
    Curtiss Motor Company factory position of, 37, 127
    as Curtiss Motorcycle Company distributor, 31, 34
    frame design, 33, 35, *36*, 37, 125
Werner, Frederick W., 107
Wesley, George W., 86
Wheeler, Monroe, 30, 34, 36
Wherett, H. W., 193
Whipple, Ira H., 208–209
Whipple Cycle Company, 31
Wickwire, Ward A., 113
Widmayer, Frank B.
    motorcycle designs and company of, 215–217, *216*
    at P. T. Motor Company, 165–166, 216
Wilcox, Henry H., 80
Willbe motorcycle, *59*, 59–60
Williams, J. Newton, 60, *217*, 217–219, *218*, *219*
Williams, N. Halsted, 218, 219
Willis, E. J. (and Company), 160, 219–220
Williston, G. A., 88
Wilmarth, Brad, 219
Wilson, Hugo, 3, 13, 15, 19, 187, 216–217, 219, 228, 229–230
Wilson, John W., 159
Wolke, Eric, 38
women riders, 30, *p1*, *p8*
    Armstrong, C., tandem seating and, *227*, 227–228
    Autopeds and, 12, *12*
    Breese motorcycle and, 228–229
    Emblem and, *67*, 68, *69*, 72, *p3*
    Palmer tandem seating and, 145, *145*
    Rugmobile and, 180
Wood, David, 193
Woodruff, Lee S., 139–140
Wooster, William, 156
World War I, 42, 43, 44, 72, 183
World War II, 98, 140
The World's Motorcycles, 1894–1963 (Tragatsch), 3, 92
Wray, Howard, 25, 161
Wray, William H., Jr., 81–82, 161, *161*
Wright, Stephen, 4, 29, 121, 160, 228, *228*
Wroblewski, Joseph, 84, *220*, 220–221
Wyman, George, 205
Wyse, Abram, 86

XRTT 1750, *9*

Yankee Motor Company, 221–226
    founders son accident and end of, 225
    founding and staff at, 221–222
    international market, 222, 226
    museum collections of, *223*, 226
    racing motorcycles, 221, *222*, 222–223, 225
Yankee motorcycle (Haberer), 87–88, 227
Yost, John E., 226, *226*